MANAGERIAL CONTROL THROUGH COMMUNICATION

Managerial Control through Communication

Systems for Organizational Diagnosis and Design

GEORGE T. VARDAMAN

Professor of Administration
College of Business Administration
University of Denver

CARROLL C. HALTERMAN

Director, Executive Programs
College of Business Administration
University of Denver

JOHN WILEY & SONS, INC., New York · London · Sydney

Library of Congress Catalog Card Number: 68-21184
Printed in the United States of America

PREFACE

PURPOSE AND APPROACH

Stated directly, the purpose of this book is to provide the means by which managers can improve personal and organizational operations. We do so by setting forth a new model of managerial activity, one built directly on three elements: communication, the manager, and the control dimension. These elements are integrated into practical systems and procedures that can be used by any industrious and intelligent manager to get results.

But there are a few reasons for caution. In a book of this kind it is necessary to bring out both theory and practice. We include the necessary useful theories but we relate them to practical managerial activities. This means that we are not writing primarily for scholars; nor are we presenting a series of mere unrelated techniques and devices that presume to guarantee managerial success. Many other treatises have been directed toward scholars, and managerial success is admittedly impossible to guarantee. Moreover, we assume that the reader can make specific applications to his own managerial situation. Certainly no one can do this for him. In other words, we consider it our task to present operationally useful theories, concepts, and principles, which the manager can then translate into action on the job.

TARGET GROUPS

To whom is the book addressed? In general, its contents are applicable to any and all levels and types of manager, but the ideas have *special utility* to two vital types: *middle managers* and *trouble-shooting management analysts*. Middle managers ultimately are the people who can make or break an administered organization—simply because they determine whether the unit's objectives and purposes are properly carried out. Top management sets broad policies and guidelines; workers and first-line

v

supervisors carry out specific tasks; but it is the middle, or operating, manager who links up the two echelons, who hooks executive policies and guidelines into the grubby, grimy details of day-to-day operations. Clearly no organization is any better than the quality of its middle managers. This book presents principles, systems, and procedures that can directly help to improve their organizations and themselves.

Trouble-shooting management analysts are also the key to organizational growth and development. Within the last decade certain staff and line people have become administrative and organizational specialists charged with keeping tabs on operations by determining answers to these questions: What are the organization's existing deficiencies? What are the sources of potential problems? Where are changes needed? What kinds of change should be made? How should changes be carried out? How will it be known whether the changes made are for the better? It is easy to see that trouble-shooting analysts answer a real need in modern administered firms.

The job of diagnosis and design of organizations has become an involved and complex specialty, one requiring knowledge and skill significantly beyond that of the typical line or staff manager. This job requires the kind of background and approach suggested in this book.

SPECIFIC CONTRIBUTIONS

In what specific ways is the book valuable to the middle manager and the management analyst? First, it presents *background for understanding how organizations work.* This is done by presenting pertinent theories and concepts so that the manager or analyst can know the people and parts of the firm and how they fit together, an understanding essential to any worthwhile professional approach to management. Second, the book presents *analytical and diagnostic patterns through which the manager can determine what is right and wrong in his organization.* The preceding theories and concepts are translated into workable methods and procedures so that the manager can make useful appraisals of his firm. Third, the book presents *ways for the manager or analyst to design his organization's improvement,* a phase growing directly out of the first and second steps. Once he knows what is right and wrong, the manager can then set up means to capitalize on the strengths and overcome the weaknesses in his organization. Practical procedures are given to make this possible.

In a word, the book blends the *theoretical and practical into a useful form*—a form that permits general application by the manager or analyst to any or all of his operations.

PRESENTATION

Our presentation differs somewhat from the traditional pattern because we have deliberately combined our own views alongside other outlooks.

Our views are given in the seven chapters of text material. In this part we have attempted to set forth, in as simple a manner as possible, the most important principles and methods for analysis and improvement of managerial communication and control.

In Chapters 1 through 3 we give *necessary theoretical and conceptual background*. We have selected—out of the enormous available mass— only those ideas possible for *general* managerial application. In order to do this economically, it has been necessary to cast most of the old concepts into new molds and to put them together by using different blueprints. In all cases we have held onto the "old" when useful and have added the "new" when gaps exist.

In Chapters 4 through 6 we present *sound analytical and diagnostic approaches*. Thus we move directly from the conceptual foundation to practical systems and procedures for assessment of managerial and organizational operations. The materials are discussed in a logical sequence and then put into useful analytical schemes so that specific algorithms can be applied by the manager to accomplish his objectives.

In Chapter 7 we map out *useful patterns for improvement*. Here, after a brief summary of the preceding material, we describe systems and procedures for designing and redesigning organizations. In so doing we integrate all components of communication, management, and control into a coherent pattern, which, in fact, becomes *an integrated theory of managerial activity*. This model, which forms a genuine professional basis for management, is, in our judgment, a major contribution of the book.

Other outlooks are presented in the section Related Readings. Divided into four parts, this section contains twenty-eight articles, ranging from the fairly pragmatic to the highly theoretical. We have included this range to satisfy differing managerial demands and needs. Students of relatively high sophistication can focus on articles of greater difficulty; readers with less background can start with the basic materials and progress to more difficult ones as understanding is built.

In the bibliographies at the end of each chapter we list, along with other sources, germane Related Reading selections. This permits the manager to compare and contrast our ideas against those of other writers. Out of this mix he can then judge the concepts that are most useful to him.

SOURCES

The manager should know the sources of our ideas. They came from our studies, from our own experiences as managers and analysts, and from our observations of and work with many action-oriented managers. Needless to say, we have found the last our most valuable validating means, for having tried out these ideas in many organizations—small and large, private and public, product-oriented and service-oriented—we were able to profit from the direct criticism and experience of a large group of these perceptive managers. The final product is represented in this book.

George T. Vardaman
Carroll C. Halterman

College of Business Administration
University of Denver
May, 1968

CONTENTS

MANAGERIAL CONTROL THROUGH COMMUNICATION

1

THE TEXT

1

COMMUNICATION AND CONTROL

This is a book about the relationships between managers, communication, and control within the administered organization. It attempts to do what has not been done before: to put into a systematic and operational form the many existing disparate, discrete thoughts about these three concepts.

Today's reader is literally deluged with an outpouring of fragmented and unrelated ideas about management, communication, and control. Although this mass of information is not without merit, it needs to be put into a useful working model for the manager. It should be understood that we are not offering any sure-fire formulas for managerial success. The intelligent reader knows that there are no such things. However, we believe that we can provide a general approach, which, used judiciously, can be of real value to those who want to improve managerial and organizational operations. We start by defining our basic terms.

DEFINITION OF TERMS

[The term *manager* refers to a person who has authority to allocate or allot resources to problems or situations. The definition is straightforward and simple, but it must be understood clearly. First, the manager is a human being, not a process or thing. Second, he has the prerogative of assigning people, money, and equipment to tasks, endeavors, and conditions. And, third, he judges the what, why, and how of allocation.] Obviously, not all those commonly identified with "management" come under this definition. Supervisors of routines, or those who have little or no judgmental latitude, are not managers in the sense that we are using the term.

[By *communication* we mean the flow of material, information, perceptions, and understandings between the various parts and members of an organization. This definition looks simple, but it takes in a vast array: all the

3

methods, means, and media of communication (communication technology), all the channels, networks, and systems of communication (organizational structure), all the person-to-person interchange (interpersonal communication), and all the data and information necessary to carry out organizational tasks (job-relevant communication). This is a much broader concept of communication than that normally taken. It includes all aspects of communication: up, down, lateral; speaking, writing, listening, reading; methods, media, modes; channels, networks, flow; interpersonnel, intraorganizational, interorganizational. And when seen in this light, it is apparent that communication is central to managerial control and to organizational survival.

By *control* we refer to the planning, the adjustment, and the correction of the parts in a situation in order to achieve some end or objective. In other words, the manager knows what he is after, sets up the means to achieve it, checks to determine how he is doing, revises or changes as necessary, until he gets what he wants. By definition the manager is the one who controls. And it is obvious that proper control can be maintained only by proper communication.

VIEWPOINT OF THIS BOOK

In other words, our view is that there is a sensitive relationship between (*a*) the manager's perception of a situation, (*b*) his plans and procedures to handle it, and (*c*) the communication necessary for him to understand and direct ongoing activities. We take the position that it is the manager who makes things happen. We assume also that "good" results are tied to good managerial control. And we assert that "good" control depends on proper capability to communicate decisions and information. If the manager's communication does not function properly, his perceptions will be distorted, his inferences will be inaccurate, and subsequent decisions will be faulty.

The nature of modern management activity is very different from that of earlier times. Many managers of twenty-five years ago could rely on, say, capital or technical expertise or even driving ambition to successfully accomplish their jobs. But today's managers are confronted with a much more complex array of variables, obstacles, and situations requiring the most discerning perception, wise conception, and careful handling for predictable success. Several implications flow from this.

First, the modern manager is no longer a "provincial" specialist. He must know more than his specific job of the moment. He must be conversant with and able to apply relevant theories and concepts from all areas of human study: the social sciences, the natural and biological sciences, the humanistic disciplines, as well as the newer field of communication and information systems.

The second point grows out of the first: the modern manager must be capable of using effectively both today's and tomorrow's technology. Exponential rates of change in the accumulating knowledge concerning important components affecting organizational operations—climate and culture, commitments of personnel, work team dynamics, systems analysis and design—require commensurate adjustments by the manager. It is clear that the modern manager is confronted with a situation where current practices can rapidly become obsolescent.

A third point is directly related to the first two. The modern manager's practices grow out of the best available theories and concepts. No longer can the split between "theory" and "practice" be rationally defended. No longer can the manager be concerned with a kit bag of techniques, devices, or activities to manipulate any situation that arises.

In sum, this means that today's manager must be thoroughly familiar with those theories and concepts giving rise to today's operations. And this is why we are presenting a concise rundown of the most important underlying philosophies of modern managerial activities.

For some managers, this presentation may be rather elementary. If so, they may wish to go on to succeeding chapters. To others, however, this summary may be good review, a chance for a refresher. In this case, a rather rapid scanning may be sufficient. But for others, the ideas may be relatively new. In this event, the materials should be read more thoroughly.

OVERVIEW OF CURRENT THOUGHT

Problem Theory and Practice

The manager's sole reason for being is to handle problems within his surveillance. All managerial competence and communication capability contribute to this end. Problems must be sensed, defined, and, in some way, resolved. Good managers are those who have a systematic means of handling their problems.

There is an abundance of varying views regarding problems and problem resolution falling into four basic categories: (*a*) generalized faculty; (*b*) prescribed patterns; (*c*) mathematical models; and (*d*) machine systems.

Generalized Faculty. Implicit in this outlook is a "thinking center" in the human mind. Therefore, if this putative center is developed properly it is capable of thinking through any problem. Those holding to this theory assume that if a person is exposed to a given type of background or experience, he learns to think. And having learned to think, he is consequently equipped to resolve problems, specific or general, in whatever area he works. Examples of managerial use of generalized faculty include staff planning, setting policies and procedures, setting organizational goals and objectives, and research and development activities.

That people possess the capacity to think is true. And that this capacity can be developed and refined into general and specific problem-solving abilities is also true. However, that such a generalized faculty is sufficient for handling any and all situations is quite another proposition. To the extent that the manager can think better he is a better manager. Yet, the ability to think is a requisite but not sufficient in itself. Certainly it is not enough for the modern manager.

Prescribed Patterns. By this we refer to routines and procedures for dealing with situations. In this approach it is assumed that there are "right" ways to handle problems. All that need be done is to determine all possible situations then set up the right procedures to control each. As a problem of a given type arises, the manager hooks in the appropriate procedure to resolve it. Examples of prescribed patterns commonly employed by managers include quality and production control standards, standard operating procedures, hiring and firing procedures, standard organizational forms, and ongoing departmental practices.

Without doubt, the prescribed pattern is of great importance to managers. Indeed, most organizational problems are processed in this way. One of the most important of the manager's functions is to routinize situations as much as possible. By routinizing as far as possible, the manager can efficiently control a great multitude of recurring problems. It is here that the prescribed pattern plays a vital role.

However, since the manager's basic job is to deal with the important nonroutine, the prescribed pattern has severe limitations. Therefore the manager must have something more if he is to carry out his mission.

Mathematical Models. This may also be called operations research, management science, and decision making. This approach to organizational problem processing has emerged since World War II. It has been very successfully used in certain types of situations. Managers frequently employ mathematical models in linear programming, inventory control systems, queuing systems, sales forecasting models, and decision-making models.

The term mathematical models generally refers to the application of scientific method to problems expressible by quantitative means. It involves the construction of models that allow comparison of alternatives, with the objective of determining the best. This pattern has great utility for analysis of problems where all important variables can be known and where these can be expressed quantitatively. Often, however, the manager is confronted by a host of problem conditions where the technique is inapplicable.

Machine Systems. This covers the hardware systems most commonly associated with computers. Computers are really "thinking machines" which can be used for a great number of problem calculations. Common managerial applications of machine systems include central address and mailing systems, personnel data systems, on-line budgetary systems, and customer information systems. Once programmed, computers can perform computations at rates far beyond those possible by human minds. The programming, however, is a human function. Furthermore, the interpretation and use of computer output is only as good as the managerial judgment brought to bear on it. In sum, then, machine systems serve the manager but certainly do not replace him. The manager needs to know where machine systems articulate with the other problem processing means.

Situation Today. Each of the four preceding concepts has a bearing on understanding the manager's handling of his problems. However, they must be understood and used judiciously, and each must be properly related to all others. Each potentially fits uniquely into a managerial problem-solving framework. It is our job to point out how this can be done.

Communication Theory and Practice

It can be argued cogently that communication is man's highest attribute. Some maintain that communication potential is the *one* factor that differentiates man from other beings, the quality that permits him to bind time and space.

Since his earliest appearance on Earth it is evident that man has recognized and used his powers of communication to manage and control situations. Today's organizational manager is the heir to a large body of knowledge evolving out of millenia of thought about and practice of communication. However, almost all of this great volume and mass falls into four groupings: (*a*) personal communication; (*b*) communication media; (*c*) organizational communication; and (*d*) communication systems.

Personal Communication. This covers the study and practice of all the oral and written, auditory and visual forms of *personal* symbolic interchange. Included are person-to-group communication (e.g., public speeches, written directives to specific people), person-to-person communication (e.g., face-to-face discussions, correspondence between specific people), and intragroup communication (e.g., conferences, meetings, seminars). The essential characteristic of personal communication is that it involves *specific people* communicating with each other.

Obviously, personal communication is a very important facet of managerial communication. Much of the manager's time is spent in just this kind of activity. And most existing literature is directed at this subject. Books on speaking, writing, conference leadership, reporting, and the like, pour from the presses. But there is a great need to put personal communication into a practical managerial context.

Communication Media. The study and practice of the *impersonal means* of symbolic interchange are covered by communication media. Included are books, newspapers, magazines, radio, television, remote consoles, displays, mass reports, and other presentational *vehicles*. Communication media, then, are nonpersonal *carriers* of data and information.

There is little doubt that communication media are significant in organizational operations. House organs, company periodicals, advertising, and large-scale promotional campaigns cost organizations billions of dollars annually. And the use of media seems to increase at an exponential rate. Indeed, this increase has contributed mightily to the "data inundation" which most managers are now experiencing to greater and greater degrees.

There is a large body of literature on communication media. Unfortunately, however, in most writings each medium is considered separately from the other media. So, again, we find the manager facing the task of trying to tie them together in some practical way. Further, communication media are seldom related by writers to the other components of communication capability, leaving the manager the almost impossible job of trying to determine where they fit within the whole. The result is that the writings are of little use to the operating manager because he cannot find anything that will be of help on the job.

Organizational Communication. This covers the study of the dynamics of intragroup and intergroup symbolic interchange in organizational units. As differentiated from personal communication, organizational communication is concerned more with impersonal *theorization* about group structure and behavior. The fields of social psychology, sociology, and anthropology have made heavy contributions to this area. Objects of organizational communication study include interactions among cultural sets within a firm, the dynamics of unit-to-unit functioning, the power groups of small and large administrative units, relationships between formal and informal structures in organizations, and systems and networks analysis and design.

A great and still growing volume of literature is emerging about organizational communication, ranging all the way from studies of small groups to studies of whole societies. Without doubt, there is much of potential value to the manager in all this mélange. But, as in the case of personal communication and communication media, it has not been sufficiently put into the managerial context. Therefore the potential has not been realized.

Communication Systems. There is a vast spectrum of communication systems, ranging from relatively simple mechanistic electronic systems to highly complex human systems. Within the past decade communication systems have had a revolutionary impact on managerial operations, and no doubt an even greater thrust will be seen in the future.

Four broad categories can be identified under communication systems: (*a*) information theory; (*b*) cybernetics; (*c*) automatic data processing systems; and (*d*) general systems theory.

Information theory is, in essence, a technical means of handling a sequence of electronic signals. It is not concerned with human meaning or impact. One of the most popular presentations of information theory is that given by Shannon and Weaver.[1] *Cybernetics* is concerned with communication control, whether in purely technological or in animate form, whether with individuals or with organizations. The person most commonly identified with cybernetics is Norbert Wiener.[2] Cybernetic systems range from the mechanical and simple to the interpersonal and complex. Mechanically, a thermostat in a heating system acts as a cybernetic control; intrapersonally, hunger pangs signal the need for food in the human being; interpersonally, symptoms of anger on the part of one employee toward some remark by another indicate hostility—the perception of this hostility by any person is a cybernetic function; intraorganizationally, the rejection of certain production output by quality assurance inspectors constitutes a form of cybernetic control. *Automatic data processing systems* encompass all the "software" and "hardware" components related to computers and other data processing technology. Included are all of the elements of programming, processing, and output control. The explosion in this area has had more obvious impact on managerial operations than any other in communication systems. *General systems theory* is concerned with theoretical model-building; this theory falls between pure mathematics and the specific theories of specialized areas of knowledge. It is concerned with the *general* relationships of the real world. General systems theory has recently been brought into play to study communication and organizations. In the future, no doubt, it will be of increasing importance to managers. At present speculation is proceeding along the lines of analogies between functioning of the human organism and social organizations, analogies between economic models and biological models, relationships between animal societies and human societies, and relationships between mechanical systems and human systems. Kenneth E. Boulding [3] has been an influential spokesman, and his article included in the readings is considered a classic.

Situation Today. In spite of the tremendous body of communication knowledge, today's manager has little to work with to help him do his job. He is confronted with a great number of differing, disparate communication principles and practices, many apparently unrelated—if not contradictory or inconsistent. There is, in a word, no coherent, useful model to which the operating manager can turn. What is needed is a practical and useful method of analysis of communication capability in the context of the manager and his problems.

Managerial Theory and Practice

With all the current ferment about the importance of proper management of organizations, it may be surprising that there is no common agreement about what a manager is or how he is to act. Differences in view are many, broadly grouped into four outlooks: (*a*) the administrative activities orientation; (*b*) the task orientation; (*c*) the human relations orientation; and (*d*) the organizational orientation.

Administrative Activities Orientation. Evolving out of the thoughts of people such as a German, Max Weber, [4] and a Frenchman, Henri Fayol, [5] the administrative activities orientation assumes a hierarchical view of an organization. The manager's purpose is to direct his organization through knowing and practicing some presumed universal managerial activities, generally classed as (*a*) planning, (*b*) organizing, (*c*) directing, (*d*) staffing, and (*e*) controlling. It is held that these functions obtain for the manager in any organization, at any level, and in carrying out any task.

The administrative activities theory has had much influence on current managerial thought. In fact, it is probably the most commonly held view of most of today's practicing managers. Undeniably there is in it a useful strand. However, even cursory observation of the modern manager in action will reveal his job as far more complex than is assumed by this school.

Task Orientation. Growing out of the emphasis on specialization and technology, the task orientation emphasizes a production-performance view of doing the job. The manager is manager of given tasks or specialized functions. Generally the manager is a specialist first and a manager second: managers of engineering functions are first of all engineers; managers of accounting units are first of all accountants. Many professional groups formalize this view by setting up requirements that the administrator must evidence his task expertise by having a certain educational background, a specified kind of experience, or membership in certain groups.

Two of the better known early exponents of task orientation are Frederick W. Taylor [6] and Frank Gilbreth.[7] Their studies of better ways to do manual jobs gave rise to modern industrial management, especially to that segment dealing with motion and time study.

The task orientation school has had great influence among managers in industrial production and jobs lending themselves to routinization. It has had less impact in other areas of managerial concern. There is a real need for managers to draw on worthwhile principles from this area and to put them in proper relationship to those from the other schools.

Human Relations Orientation. Emphasizing people as the managerial focus, the human relations orientation assumes that organizational administration and task management can be no better than the handling of the personnel element. Clearly this school draws heavily from the fields of psychology, social psychology, and, to a certain extent, sociology. Elton Mayo and F. J. Roethlisberger of the Harvard Business School were among early exponents. Their studies at the Hawthorne plant of the Western Electric Company, started in 1927, brought about a new view of the worker. The conclusions of the study were that a worker's attitudes are far more important in his performance than the physical conditions, that his informal social organization is far more important than the formal hierarchy of an administered firm. In addition to Mayo and Roethlisberger, many other persons are identified with the human relations orientation. Among them are Chris Argyris,[8] Norman R. F. Maier,[9] and Carl R. Rogers.[10]

The human relations orientation school has made many valuable contributions to better managerial theory and practice. However, realistically, managers must be able to put the many, many theories, concepts, ideas, and suggestions from this area into some workable, useful form. And in so doing, managers must also draw relevant and useful ideas from the administrative activities orientation, from task orientation, and from the school discussed next, the organizational orientation.

Organizational Orientation. The newest of the schools, this one has grown out of the recent increasing number of theoretical and empirical studies of organization theory. Closely related to the "systems" approach, it views an organization as a set of interdependent variables. Changes in one segment of an organization produce changes in other parts. From this perspective, the manager is only one factor among many. His actions produce effects in other parts of the organization; however, what is done in any other part of the organization also affects him.

The so-called behavioral sciences—psychology, sociology, anthropology—are the basic cognitive sources of the organizational orientation. Among those identified with it are Chester I. Barnard,[11] who views the organization as a communication system, Herbert A. Simon,[12] who views the organization as a communication-decision system, and Victor A. Thompson,[13] who views the organization as a general system and set of subsystems. These are merely three among the many.[14]

As the newest approach, the organizational orientation is at this stage less clearly defined than the preceding three. But it is undoubtedly a future source of much value to the manager. There are already some studies that have real practical value,[15] but even the experts admit that there is a great need to make the organizational orientation more meaningful to the operating manager.

THE PROCESS OF MANAGERIAL CONTROL

The preceding review is sufficient to demonstrate the need for bringing together the essential elements of communication and managerial control as a problem-solving process. We must remember that the basic purpose of managerial control is problem solving. The schematic drawing in Figure 1.1 gives the total managerial control, or problem-solving, process. We see that there are three different stages in the process: (*a*) a situational input; (*b*) a managerial throughput; and (*c*) a situational output.

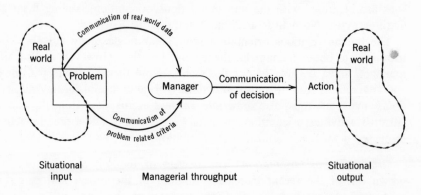

Figure 1.1. The managerial control process.

Situational Input. The situational input is the real world of events possible for the manager to view. It is this event-level the manager must perceive and put into some useful order (called the problem). He must see the crucial symptoms and he must see them in meaningful relationships (syndromes) to know what his real problem is.

Managerial Throughput. By what means does the manager process or "throughput" the problems he conceives? Basic to successful processing is his communication capability. Communication capability consists of cueing facilities, carrying out facilities, and critique facilities.

The *communication cueing facility* is a generating function. It calls forth data as needed. If the data are adequate, that is, sufficiently informative, the manager makes a decision. If the data are inadequate, he calls for more data. He may also reexamine the problem, depending on economics.

The *communication carrying out facility* is a message sending or receiving function. Once the need for communication is established, the manager assesses the situation, then plans and executes the necessary transmission and reception of messages to handle the situation adequately.

The *communication critique facility* is a monitoring and corrective function. It works in conjunction with the cueing and carrying out facilities to determine when and where adjustments are needed, where new problems are arising, where new decisions are needed. Further, it points to necessary corrective steps.

The paradigm in Figure 1.2 will help to illustrate communication capability in managerial control.

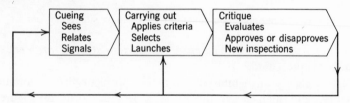

Figure 1.2. Communication capability in managerial control.

Situational Output. The old situation, symptomatized by the problem, is what existed before managerial throughput. Together with all changes, including those instituted by the manager, and any environmental shifts, this metamorphoses into a *new* or current situation. This must be judged for adequacy by the manager. If the new situation is adequate, attention is directed to other situations. If it is still failing when measured against the preset criteria, the total process is repeated: new cueing, new carrying out, and a new critique. Figure 1.3 illustrates this process.

SUMMARY

This book is about *managers, communication,* and *control.* These three factors are critical to organizational success; in fact, there is a crucial interdependence among them. Understanding managers depends upon an understanding of current *managerial theory* and *practice;* therefore a review of this area is presented. Understanding communication depends upon a clear concept of contemporary *communication theory* and *practice;* therefore a synopsis of this area is presented. Understanding control depends upon a clear concept of the parts in action—which is directly related to the

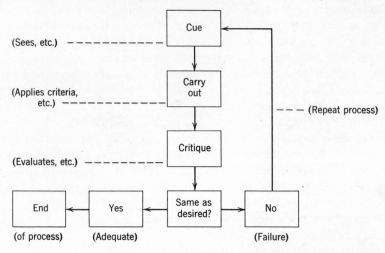

Figure 1.3. Communication capability in assessing situational output.

problem under surveillance. Therefore the current state of *problem theory* and *practice* is presented.

To further clarify this summary, we review problem theory, communication theory, and managerial theory in schematic form in Figures 1.4 through 1.6.

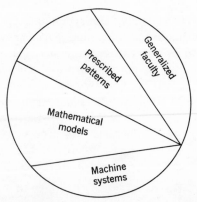

Figure 1.4. Problem theory and practice. The field of problem theory and practice is shown to be composed of four areas: generalized faculty; prescribed patterns; mathematical models; and machine systems.

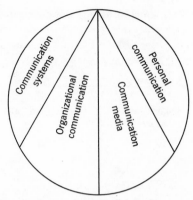

Figure 1.5. Communication theory and practice. The field of communication theory and practice is shown to be composed of four areas: personal communication; communication media; organizational communication; and communication systems.

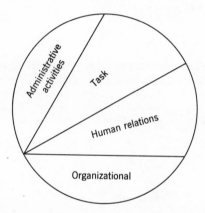

Figure 1.6. Managerial theory and practice. The field of managerial theory and practice is shown to be composed of four areas: administrative activities orientation; task orientation; human relations orientation; and organizational orientation.

SIGNIFICANCE

We have already discussed several important deficiencies in current approaches to the study of management in administered organizations. We now look at some of the gaps, using the following fixes: the traditional approach, the human relations approach, and the systems approach. These are shown in Figures 1.7 to 1.9.

The preceding approaches are at best limited in their perspectives of managerial control. The need is to put all the dimensions of these three conceptual areas into relationship to one another. The schematic shown in Figure 1.10 is an attempt to do this.

Figure 1.7. A traditional approach to studying managerial control. The traditional, or classic, approach treats these areas discretely and assumes that if the prospective manager reads and understands something about the three separate conceptual areas, he will somehow be able to understand organizations and thereby be able to wield adequate control. No attempt is made in this literature, however, to show more than "tangency" of the areas of interest, and in some cases even that relationship is ignored.

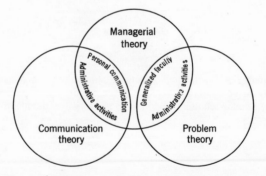

Figure 1.8. The human relations approach. In literature dealing with the human relations approach, much is made of the relationship between the manager and how he communicates in terms of human problems. In other words, concern centers on personal relationships (communication theory) and on generalized faculty (problem theory), both of which are handled by administrative activities (managerial theory), but most else is ignored.

The basic idea of this chapter, as illustrated in Figure 1.10, is that a managerial problem has more than one face. Managerial theory, as we

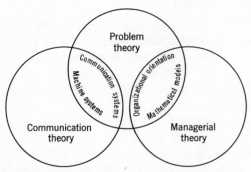

Figure 1.9. The systems approach. Most of the literature dealing with the systems approach is concerned with the relationship between communication systems (communication theory) and machine systems (problem theory), together with the use of mathematical models (problem theory), in an organizational orientation (managerial theory). The manager as a person is implicitly recognized as involved in problems, but since he is difficult to deal with as a system entity, his presence is not specifically treated.

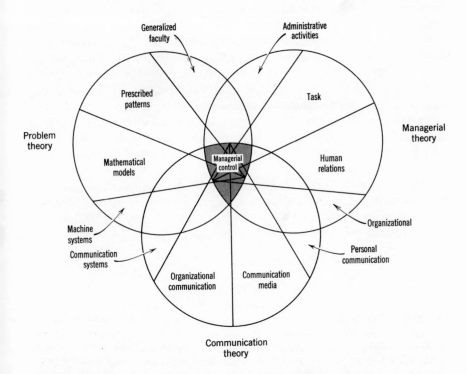

Figure 1.10. An integrated approach to managerial control. This approach takes the view that all the dimensions of the three conceptual areas are interrelated. By understanding this relationship, better organizational functioning and a higher level of managerial control is possible.

17

have defined it, focuses on the place of people, including the manager himself, in administered organizations. Communication theory, according to our view, centers on the organizational setting within which people and other components operate. Problem theory, as we see it, is concerned with the level of technology or culture from which the entire managerial problem or situation springs.

Clearly, then, of managerial theory, communication theory, and problem theory, no one is sufficient by itself. All are required, each in its proper proportion, if the modern manager or analyst is to know what he is about. In other words, the manager must consider all if he is to be: (a) making the best use of his people in the context, that is, the culture and climate, of the organization; (b) allocating optimally the resources available to him, taking into account both human and cultural limitations; and (c) solving the full range of managerial problems that every organization experiences.

In ordinary terminology, the manager, using the complete conceptual background sketched here, will be able to examine better whether or not problems are really connected to his organization's purposes, objectives, and goals. He will not overlook the key aspects of the organizational climate and culture, which are actually a composite of all the preceding variables. He will be able to identify and judge the significance of personal actions and interactions in order to manage best both human and physical resources. Using the foregoing basic triad, the manager will be able to discern areas of possible conflict—between people, between personal and organizational goals, and between the organization and its environment. With this perspective, the manager is in a position to deal with conflict wisely, thus keeping the organization's activities moving toward progressive—not destructive—ends.

Our thesis, then, is this: It is the manager who controls. Therefore it is he who must understand and use a broad range of dimensions in order to gain and maintain the level of control necessary to carry out his job. It is the purpose of this book to show how this can be done.

NOTES

[1] Shannon, Claude and Warren Weaver. *The Mathematical Theory of Communication.* Urbana, Ill.: University of Illinois Press, 1949.
[2] Wiener, Norbert. *Cybernetics: The Human Use of Human Beings,* 2d ed. New York: M.I.T. Press and John Wiley and Sons, 1961. See also Beer, Stafford. *Cybernetics and Management.* New York: John Wiley and Sons, 1961; Wisdom, J. O. "The Hypothesis of Cybernetics," *General Systems,* I (1956).
[3] Boulding, Kenneth E. "General Systems Theory—The Skeleton of Science," *Management Science,* 197–208 (April 1956); see also L. Von Bertalanffy, "General

Systems Theory: A New Approach to Unity of Science," *Human Biology,* 303–361 (December 1951).

4 See Gerth, H. H. and C. Wright Mills. *From Max Weber: Essays in Sociology.* Fairlawn, N.J.: Oxford University Press, 1958, esp. Chapter VIII. See also Thompson, Victor A. *Modern Organization.* New York: Alfred A. Knopf, 1961, esp. Chapter 2.

5 Fayol, Henri. *General and Industrial Management,* translated by Constance Storrs. London: Sir Isaac Pitman and Sons, 1949.

6 See Taylor, Frederick Winslow. "The Principles of Scientific Management," *Scientific Management.* New York: Harper and Brothers, 1947.

7 See Spriegel, William R. and Clark E. Myers, Eds. *The Writings of the Gilbreths.* Homewood, Ill.: Richard D. Irwin, 1953.

8 Argyris, Chris. *Personality and Organization.* New York: Harper and Brothers, 1957.

9 Maier, Norman R. F. *Principles of Human Relations.* New York: John Wiley and Sons, 1952.

10 Rogers, Carl R. and F. J. Roethlisberger. "Barriers and Gateways to Communication," *Harvard Business Review,* 46–52 (July–August 1952).

11 Barnard, Chester I. *The Functions of the Executive.* Cambridge, Mass.: Harvard University Press, 1938.

12 Simon, Herbert A. *Administrative Behavior.* New York: The Macmillan Company, 1957.

13 Thompson, Victor A. *Modern Organization.* New York: Alfred A. Knopf, 1961.

14 For a variety of views and outlooks, see Rubenstein, Albert H. and Chadwick J. Haberstroh. *Some Theories of Organization.* Homewood, Ill.: The Dorsey Press, 1960.

15 For example, see Blake, R. R., J. S. Mouton, L. B. Barnes, and L. E. Greiner. "Breakthrough in Organization Development," *Harvard Business Review,* 133–155 (November–December 1964); see also Stogdill, Ralph M. "Basic Concepts for a Theory of Organization," Reading 28 in the "Related Readings" section of this Book.

BIBLIOGRAPHY

PROBLEM THEORY AND PRACTICE

Ackoff, Russell L. *A Manager's Guide to Operations Research.* New York: John Wiley and Sons, 1963.

Boulding, Kenneth E. and W. Allen Spivey. *Linear Programming and the Theory of the Firm.* New York: The Macmillan Company, 1960.

Bross, Irwin D. J. *Design for Decision.* New York: The Macmillan Company, 1953.

Bruner, J. S., J. J. Goodnow, and G. A. Austin. *A Study of Thinking.* New York: John Wiley and Sons, 1956.

Case, Keith E. and George T. Vardaman. *Mature Reading and Thinking.* Denver, Colo.: Communication Foundation, Inc., 1964.

Dewey, John. *How We Think.* Boston: D. C. Heath, 1933.

Duckworth, Eric. *A Guide to Operational Research.* New York: Dover Publications, 1962.

Larrabee, Harold. *Reliable Knowledge.* Boston, Mass.: Houghton Mifflin, 1945.

Luce, R. D. and H. Raiffa. *Games and Decisions: Introduction and Critical Survey.* New York: John Wiley and Sons, 1958.

Maier, Norman R. F. *Problem Solving, Discussions and Conferences: Leadership Methods and Skills.* New York: McGraw-Hill Book Company, 1963.

Mander, A. E. *Logic for the Millions.* New York: Philosophical Library, 1947.

Osborn, A. F. *Applied Imagination: Principles and Procedures of Creative Thinking.* New York: Charles Scribner's Sons, 1953.

Simon, Herbert A. *The New Science of Management Decision.* New York: Harper and Row, 1960.

COMMUNICATION THEORY AND PRACTICE

Beer, Stafford. *Cybernetics and Management.* New York: John Wiley and Sons, 1961.

Boulding, Kenneth E. "General Systems Theory—The Skeleton of Science," *Management Science,* 197–208 (April 1956).

Case, Keith E. and George T. Vardaman. *Mature Reading and Thinking.* Denver, Colo.: Communication Foundation, Inc., 1964.

Cherry, Colin. *On Human Communication.* New York: M.I.T. Press and John Wiley and Sons, 1957.

Greenberger, Martin. *Management and the Computer of the Future.* New York: M.I.T. Press and John Wiley and Sons, 1962.

Haney, William V. *Communication Patterns and Incidents.* Homewood, Ill.: Richard D. Irwin, 1960.

Homans, George. *The Human Group.* New York: Harcourt, Brace, 1950.

Kozmetsky, George and Paul Kircher. *Electronic Computers and Management Control.* New York: McGraw-Hill Book Company, 1963.

Leavitt, Harold J. *Managerial Psychology.* Chicago, Ill.: University of Chicago Press, 1958.

Lee, Irving. *How to Talk with People.* New York: Harper and Brothers, 1952.

Metcalf, Henry C. and Lyndall Urwick, Eds. *Dynamic Administration: The Collected Papers of Mary Parker Follett.* New York: Harper and Brothers, 1941.

Minnick, Wayne C. *The Art of Persuasion.* Cambridge, Mass.: Riverside Press, 1957.

Pigors, Paul. *Effective Communication in Industry.* New York: National Association of Manufacturers, 1949.

Redding, W. Charles and George A. Sanborn. *Business and Industrial Communication: A Source Book.* New York: Harper and Row, 1964.

Redfield, Charles E. *Communication in Management.* Chicago, Ill.: University of Chicago Press, 1958.

Schramm, Wilbur. *The Process and Effects of Mass Communications.* Urbana, Ill.: University of Illinois Press, 1954.

Shannon, Claude E. and Warren Weaver. *The Mathematical Theory of Communication.* Urbana, Ill.: University of Illinois Press, 1949.

Snygg, Donald and Arthur W. Combs. *Individual Behavior.* New York: Harper and Brothers, 1949.

Steinberg, C. S. *The Mass Communicators.* New York: Harper and Brothers, 1959.

Thayer, Lee O. *Administrative Communication.* Homewood, Ill.: Richard D. Irwin, 1961.

Whyte, William H. and the Editors of *Fortune. Is Anybody Listening?* New York: Simon and Schuster, 1952.

Wiener, Norbert. *Cybernetics: The Human Use of Human Beings,* 2d ed. New York: M.I.T. Press and John Wiley and Sons, 1961.

Witty, P. A. *How to Become a Better Reader.* Chicago, Ill.: Science Research Associates, 1958.

MANAGERIAL THEORY AND PRACTICE

Argyris, Chris. *Personality and Organization.* New York: Harper and Brothers, 1957.

Barnard, Chester I. *The Functions of the Executive.* Cambridge, Mass.: Harvard University Press, 1938.

Blake, R. R., J. S. Mouton, L. B. Barnes and L. E. Greiner. "Breakthrough in Organization Development," *Harvard Business Review,* 133–155 (November–December 1964).

Brady, Robert A. *Organization, Automation and Society.* Berkeley, Calif.: University of California Press, 1963.

Dale, Ernest. *Management Theory and Practice.* New York: McGraw-Hill Book Company, 1965.

Fayol, Henri. *General and Industrial Management,* translated by Constance Storrs. London: Si. Isaac Pitman and Sons, 1949.

Koontz, Harold. *Toward a Unified Theory of Management.* New York: McGraw-Hill Book Company, 1964.

Mayo, Elton. *The Social Problems of an Industrial Civilization.* Boston, Mass.: Graduate School of Business Administration, Harvard University, 1945.

Roethlisberger, F. J. and William J. Dickson. *Management and the Worker.* Cambridge, Mass.: Harvard University Press, 1939.

Rubenstein, Albert H. and Chadwick J. Haberstroh, Eds. *Some Theories of Organization.* Homewood, Ill.: The Dorsey Press, 1960.

Simon, Herbert A. *Administrative Behavior.* New York: The Macmillan Company, 1957.

Stogdill, Ralph M. "Basic Concepts for a Theory of Organization," *Management Science,* Series B, B-666–B-676 (June 1967).

Taylor, Frederick Winslow. "The Principles of Scientific Management," *Scientific Management.* New York: Harper and Brothers, 1947.

Thompson, Victor A. *Modern Organization.* New York: Alfred A. Knopf, 1961.

Urwick, Lyndall F. *The Pattern of Management.* Minneapolis, Minn.: University of Minnesota Press, 1956.

2

MANAGERS AND CONTROL

In Chapter 1 we saw the need to pull together the components of problem theory and practice, communication theory and practice, and managerial theory and practice. Our purpose was to show their interrelationships so that managers could gain and maintain control. This chapter is devoted to describing how the manager can tell whether he has a "problem," that is, whether he has a situation that is "out of control." Such a determination is very important in today's organizations for several reasons.

First, a great deal of harm can be done to an organization by a manager's changing things merely for the sake of change. Such activity—solving problems *where problems do not exist*—obviously destroys a great many favorable aspects of the ongoing organizational climate and culture and promotes undue apprehension among the other members. We call such "managerial" activity *dysfunctional.*

Second, if a problem *does* exist, it should not be overlooked and allowed to fester. When situations are indeed discrepant, and are not repaired by the appropriate manager, the organization begins to function in a very inefficient way. As a result it fails to reward the participants at all levels for their membership. In such a case the manager concerned is soon perceived as not meeting organizational demands, and his ability to work with others is weakened. We call such "managerial" activity *nonfunctional.*

Finally, when a manager, by using a hit-or-miss approach to his analysis, attacks problems without determining the proper priority for their solutions, he allocates the organization's resources in a suboptimal manner. This results in a noncompetitive posture, so far as his organization is concerned, because of his significantly poor level of managerial control. Such activity, which is both *nonfunctional* and *dysfunctional,* is probably the most common kind. It is a sort of combination of the two preceding activities.

How can a manager know that he has adequate control? The answer lies in knowing the interrelationships of three crucial variables: problem definition; communication capability; and managerial competence. Note that we are leading toward an awareness of the need for *interrelating* the three variables. First, however, we are going to examine each in turn, then we shall point out the rationale of each and how each ties into the previously introduced concepts of problem theory, communication theory, and managerial theory. Finally, we shall then arrange them as a group into a managerial control index whereby a manager or analyst can safely and correctly answer the question: "Is there a problem?"

PROBLEM DEFINITION

Problem definition is one basic facet of managerial control. In fact, the reader should probably be cautioned at this point, since many older approaches to management represent it as a total theory. It is admittedly a cornerstone of the structure we are erecting, but it takes its proper place only in context with the others. With this warning in mind, we proceed.

Drawing from our discussion of problem theory and practice, the conceptual areas of generalized faculty, prescribed patterns, mathematical models, and machine systems suggest a rough hierarchy or sequence of the types of events necessary for problem definition to be carried to completion. To illustrate: the manager must first be able to perceive the symptoms of trouble in his situation (generalized faculty); next he must be able to grasp them cognitively and give them meaning in the total constellation of events (prescribed patterns); then he must be able to organize the key variables into a routinized, quantified model which admits of solution (mathematical models and machine systems).

Stated another way, the sequence amounts to the manager's perceiving "symptoms," putting these symptoms into "syndromes," then determining the problem that underlies them. Obviously, unless the manager has properly identified his real problem, he cannot know his real communication need, which in turn means that he cannot improve his situation.

A manager's problem will vary according to his place in the organization. Remember that there are many managers in an organization. Each one, whether carrying the title of "manager" or not, is simply an individual who somehow has gained the authority and the wherewithal to allocate resources to "improve" his situation. In order to understand this and the following material, the reader should not read the phrase "the manager" as though it refers only to some chief executive officer—or to some department head—or even to some other "middle" or "lower" manager who is recognized by virtue of his formal title. A *manager* is any *man who man-*

ages. He is a man in a situation, able to allocate resources to what he perceives as a "real problem."

It must be borne in mind that this "real problem" is a concept, that is, a picture in the head of the manager. It is a representation of reality, not reality itself. Put another way, the problem is a managerial inference or mental construct. The implication is clear: a problem may be right or wrong, well-defined or ill-defined, according to the communication capability and managerial competence brought to bear. Figure 2.1 illustrates the sequence of problem definition.

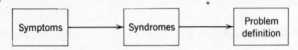

Figure 2.1. Sequence of problem definition.

COMMUNICATION CAPABILITY

As we stated, problem definition is but one of the three important variables necessary to managerial control. Interacting with it is communication capability. Some of the frequently observed down-to-earth (but very restricted) approaches to improving this variable in organizational settings are workshops in "paperwork flow improvement," "interaction analysis," "how to interview," and "effective listening." These are cited only to give the reader the assurance that they are part of the variable discussed; but each is only a very small aspect of the area as we see it.

Drawing from our discussion of communication theory and practice, the conceptual areas of communication systems, organizational communication, personal communication, and communication media suggest a rough hierarchy or sequence of type of events for communication capability to be carried to completion. To illustrate: There must be in existence a certain technology (communication systems); there must be certain organizational structure (organizational communication); there must be interpersonal interaction (personal communication); and there must be means for channeling data to and from the problem site (communication media).

All the foregoing affect the way in which communication functions in any managerial situation. Stated another way, the technology, the structure, the face-to-face interchanges, and job-related data are joint variables whose relationships must be optimized for ideal managerial control. These variables will be treated in depth later in this book.

At this time, we want to review the sequence of activities of communication capability in managerial control mentioned in Chapter 1. First, the manager solicits or draws data from a source (cues); second, he uses those data to energize or direct within a situation (carries out); and third, he arranges for, elicits, and *insists upon* feedback from performances, comparing those data with criteria (critiques). Or, paraphrasing our discussion in Chapter 1, the *cueing facility* refers to the way in which a communication need is signaled or made known. The *carrying-out facility* refers to the manager's execution or "launch" of communication; this includes all possible means: written or oral, hardware or software, symbol or sign. The *critique facility* refers to the monitoring and correction of both the cueing and carrying-out facilities. It acts to rectify, or properly adjust, total communication capability, and, of course, problem definition. These interrelationships are shown in an elementary way in Figure 2.2.

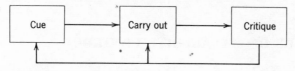

Figure 2.2. Interrelationships of dimensions of communication capability.

MANAGERIAL COMPETENCE

Our discussion of managerial theory and practice indicates that the conceptual areas of human relations, task, administrative activities, and organizational orientation form a rough hierarchy of the types of events necessary for complete managerial competence. For example, the manager must be an intelligent listener and observer in order to be sensitive to people and product interactions in the event-world around him (human relations); his education, experience, and training affect his fitness for the managerial job (task); his skills in planning, organizing, and directing affect his carrying out of managerial functions (administrative activities); and how well he responds to the firm's total demands depends upon how well he is able to recognize those that exist (organizational orientation). For our immediate purpose, this can be reduced to the manager's intelligence, his education and experience, and his orientation. Stated in different terms, the basic factors of a manager's competence are his perceptual capacity, his conceptual capacity, and his managerial style.

By *perceptual capacity* we mean the ability to discern crucial factors in a given situation. By *conceptual capacity* we mean the ability to put the crucial dimensions into proper relationship. By *managerial style* we mean the way the manager deals with people, the tools he employs, and the ways that he meets organizational requirements. It is important that meeting organizational requirements be viewed from the perspectives of: (*a*) people and products; (*b*) superiors, peers, and subordinates; and (*c*) both internal and external organizational demands. Managerial competence functions as shown in Figure 2.3.

Figure 2.3. Managerial competence.

TWO VIEWS OF MANAGERIAL CONTROL

Problem definition, communication capability, and managerial competence have been identified as key variables for the analysis and evaluation of managerial control. Each variable has been examined separately; we now look at them in relation to one another. We shall present two approaches: a *managerial control cube* and a *managerial control index.*

The Managerial Control Cube. This is a three-dimensional pattern, or cube, which allows visualization of the variables in relationship to one another. The *optimum situation* is an idealized case where all three factors are at the desired level. In mathematical terms each can be represented by units, or the number "1.0" as we depict it in Figure 2.4.

The Managerial Control Index. This is a quantitative means of looking at managerial control; it is very useful in making comparisons between organizations or among organizational parts.

In this approach the variables are considered *joint values.* Using the *expected situation* example in Figure 2.5, the total level, or index, can be shown to be (0.5) (0.3) (1.0) or 0.15. Obviously, few managers would judge this an adequate level of risk.

Despite the 1.0 level of communication capability, it is clear that only a very small percentage of managerial success is shown. In other words, we experience a very low level, or *index* value, of managerial control.

The managerial control index can help the manager in several significant ways. First, as a conceptual scheme, it permits him to view his situation in a systematic way. Second, it gives the manager a practical way to assess his control, both totally and in terms of each of the separate factors. Third, it provides a means for the manager to pinpoint broad areas of weakness, thus making possible the correction of control deficiencies. The following material, including the case at the end of this chapter, gives the manager a feel for how the method is employed in actual practice.

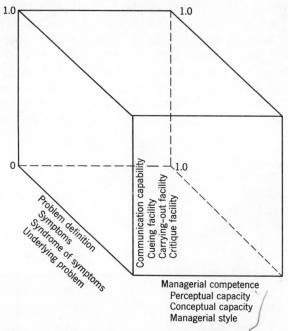

Figure 2.4. The optimum situation in managerial control.

A PROCEDURE TO DETERMINE THE MANAGERIAL CONTROL INDEX VALUE

The foregoing concepts are especially valuable because they can be made *operational* to the manager in his job. The authors have on many occasions successfully used the following procedure in determining index values for real-life managerial situations. Actually, the method is relatively simple. Moreover, any intelligent manager of an analytical bent who is willing to put forth the time and effort can use it to get surprisingly accurate estimates.

The four sequential operations in determining the managerial control index are: (*a*) listing the complaints; (*b*) collecting related complaints into syndromes and patterns; (*c*) allocating the syndromes to the *index* areas; and (*d*) quantifying the severity of the weaknesses as established.

Listing Complaints and Discrepancies. An exhaustive list of all "complaints," however vague they may appear, must be made. The manager should go to all sources; he must be patient, because only after a systematic approach is made can the manager know the full scope of the situation. A few specific admonitions: Be *descriptive* in your annotation. Write down the complaint verbatim. Record the complaint at the time offered; do not trust memory. Identify the source. Connect each item with its full range of impact (department, process, policy, level, etc.). A few possible methods which may be employed to gather these data include: (*a*) review of established reports; (*b*) interviews; (*c*) casual conversations; (*d*) special reports; (*e*) conferences and meetings; and (*f*) systematic professional assessments, where outsiders may assist in gathering the data.

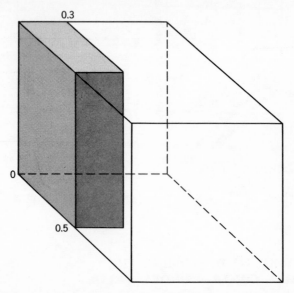

Figure 2.5. An expected situation in managerial control. An *expected situation* obtains when one or more of these variables is at less than a value of 1.0. For example, Figure 2.5 shows an 0.5 level of problem definition, an 0.3 level of managerial competence, and a 1.0 level of communication capability.

Collecting the Complaints into Related Groups. Once gathered, the complaints can be examined to detect clusters, interrelationships, patterns. These clusters and patterns are symptomatic of underlying causes. Since this is a process of managerial inference, extreme care must be exercised to determine the real causal connections.

Allocating the Groups to Index Areas. Each group or cause should be linked to that index area where it points to a flaw or weakness. The manager should note that a cause may point to more than one area. For example, a cause such as "inadequate performance" may indicate a lack of problem definition, a lack of communication capability, or both.

Establishing the Severity of Weaknesses. Once the flaws or weaknesses have been tied to the index areas, their adverse effects on those areas must be estimated. The initial values established are *minus* values; they are the manager's best estimate of how they detract from the optimum or idealized value of 1.0. Making these estimates is a task of managerial judgment and although it is not easy, the judgment can be improved by the following procedures:

1. Obtain several estimates from managers or analysts working separately.
2. Compare estimates.
3. In committee, clarify any variances among the estimators about the material.
4. Reach a consensus of estimates in this new climate.
5. Compute the index.

The procedure is exemplified in highlighted form, in Figure 2.6.

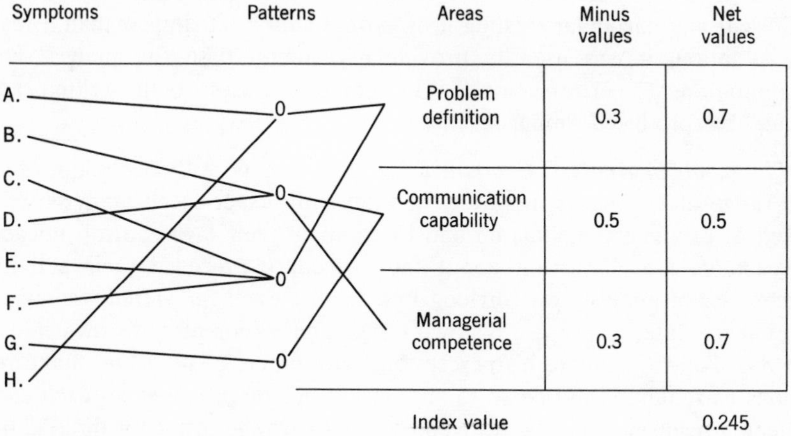

Symptoms	Patterns	Areas	Minus values	Net values
A. B.	0	Problem definition	0.3	0.7
C. D. E.	0	Communication capability	0.5	0.5
F. G. H.	0 0	Managerial competence	0.3	0.7
		Index value		0.245

Figure 2.6. Procedure for determining managerial control index value. Index value is joint product of net value.

A CASE ANALYSIS

(How Managers and Analysts Approached an Actual Situation)

"Is this approach possible for people at a lower managerial echelon to use?" "Is it as useful to people in the field as it is to scholars?" "Has it been tested—and proved?" These are but a few of the questions one can expect to be raised about the foregoing procedure. The authors have in fact used the technique time after time, and quite successfully; they have tested whether others can employ it, and have found that even when a wide range of different kinds of analysts attack the same situation, the results are quite reliable—that is, the indexes different groups compute are similar to each other. The following record of an actual experience demonstrates how tests of reliability and applicability were made.

The Type of Situation Examined. In order to present a number of different kinds of analysts with the same "problem," a written description of a situation was employed. This, called *The Wheatridge Company,* was compiled by the authors from some incidents excerpted from other sources and included several additional situational aspects repeatedly perceived in real practice. The case itself is fictitious and is not intended to represent any particular existing firm. Admittedly a bit simpler than a real-life situation, it was used to provide a common base for analysis and computation. Experience with more complex cases, both written and "real," has produced similar results.

The Kinds of Analysts Examined. In order to expose the techniques to a full range of evaluators, a variety of differently experienced analysts were asked to examine the situation and to compute their own control indexes. In each case a discussion about the procedure preceded their activity. Each class of analysts was divided into teams. Each *individual* was asked to read the case, to prepare his own notes, and to compute his own index. He was then to compare his perceptions with others of his team, make revisions as required, and come to any necessary compromises. In each case a "team" result was arrived at. Reported here are the results of three kinds of performers:

Group I: Seventeen middle managers attending a university-level executive development course. (Six teams were formed.)

Group II: Twenty-five graduate students in a fully accredited college of business, many of whom held managerial positions at the time the study was made. (Four teams were formed.)

Group III: Thirty-six undergraduate students in a fully accredited college of business. (Six teams were formed.)

Results. All groups came up with a decision that "there was a problem." In quantitative terms the indexes computed were as follows:

Group	Median Value	Range	Result (Is there a problem?)
I (Practicing middle-managers)	0.052	0.105(0.015–0.120)	Yes
II (Graduate students in management theory)	0.110	0.180(0.040–0.210)	Yes
III (Undergraduate business students)	0.112	0.114(0.080–0.294)	Yes

There was unanimity in the answers to the question: Is there a problem? The indexes show that the practicing middle-managers were more demanding in their expectations—which is what one would expect. Further, they were more consistent among themselves, as the narrower range indicates. One expects such performance among analysts with more experience. What is remarkable, however, is that *even in the hands of relatively naive analysts* the approach *produced very nearly equivalent results.* It can be said to be reliable in this sense. As a matter of interest, an experienced consultant was asked to compute the index, using the same information. His index was computed as 0.120, a result very similar to those cited above.

Extracts from the Case Solution. In order to give a feel for the flavor of this activity, the case itself is now presented, followed by a number of extracted examples of the way it was approached.

A CASE

THE WHEATRIDGE COMPANY

(*A Fictitious Situation*)

The Wheatridge Company was a small, rapidly growing distributing company using its own brand name throughout several adjoining states. It had grown by both merger and expansion and had demonstrated more than usual skill in negotiations with suppliers and others. It was dedicated to intensive promotional activity, and has shown increasing profits over the years. Profits had not matched the scale of operations, however.

Employee turnover was low, and wages were in line with competition. Many of Wheatridge's managers and other workers had, however, been attracted from similar companies nearby, due to a high status associated with working for the company. There was no high-handedness with even marginal employees; nevertheless, it was recognized that "everyone saw to it that their work was OK."

The home-office group was an example of enthusiasm and energy. In fact those now in top management positions were the original founders, who had even infected some of their own customers' managements (according to a number of the Wheatridge division chiefs) with their boundless drive. This group was still the only policy-making agency and retained financial management responsibility. All supplies were negotiated through them, as were any contracts with important customers. They did give a little weight to subordinate managers' views on policy, and they delegated a great amount of operating authority to these subordinates.

Sam Beck had received a lot of attention from the home office during the year he had been with the company as the manager of the Rocky Mountain District. He had attended numerous seminars and pep-talks and, in addition, enjoyed visits from one or the other top official almost every week. The subject of these visits was usually the need to "keep costs down," and the urgency of such pleas increased. Beck did not respond positively and unburdened himself to both his superiors and his staff, saying that Wheatridge "was getting as bad as his former employer."

The Rocky Mountain District offices had been leased in one of the plush office buildings in the city's heart, near its shopping, finance, and cultural centers. Rental was about $60,000 yearly, and renewal of the lease (which was nearing expiration) would raise that amount to about $75,000. In addition to this expenditure the company had a large overhead in the warehouse area that it had to maintain. The warehouse area was located in a combined railroad and trucking transportation terminal area and was one of a number of such facilities rather closely clustered together.

Beck was solid in his opposition to what was now the firm suggestion by the home office that he move his offices to a newly renovated frame structure in the terminal area. The structure had in fact once housed the district office, but after the move to the city it remained vacant.

Although top management did not *demand* the move take place, in deference to its policy of respecting the judgment of district managers, it pressed the point. The company's president, on a recent visit, had expressed himself with what Beck perceived as "strong feeling" on the subject, so the move was agreed on. Accordingly, the building was soundproofed, painted, upgraded, and generally renovated. Within a few months time Beck and his 42 employees were operating in their new location.

A new atmosphere was noticed in this new location. By the end of only a few weeks time, Beck was seriously concerned with the unrest of the office employees. He felt the lack of enthusiasm, the interpersonal strain, the depressed activity that existed and that was totally at odds with the atmosphere of the previous year. Joking, repartee, and bantering completely disappeared, and even his right-hand assistants were stiff and formal in their relations with him. He characterized the whole group's performance as lethargic and dull. For example, the inventory supervisor began complaining about being submerged in work and being behind. Clerks and customer relations workers began to be concerned with highly piled in-baskets, and they cut their lunch periods short voluntarily to return to the office. In general the work force was well below the level of crisp performance that they had met in the past.

Beck mulled over the many problems he now had at some length. Members were complaining about the time wasted in driving to work. They griped about the dirt and noise in the area, and about the quality of food. They did not like to remain around the area during the lunch period, to eat at the nearby lunchrooms and counters. They were used to eating at better restaurants uptown, they said, where they did not have to rub shoulders constantly with factory hands, truck drivers, and production workers. So far no one had actually quit, but there were a number of requests for better wages, and some talked about finding better jobs.

There had not been any change in staff, nor in the organization itself. Procedures and operations were the same, even to individual jobs. Beck even noted that some activity had actually been simplified. Office force members could now discuss problem areas directly with warehouse personnel, whereas previously they had to spend time on lengthy and cumbersome telephone calls and visits. Sam was confident that the new quarters were much quieter than the old ones. The work force now had free parking (which did not exist before) and, to avoid the traffic rush, the office opened and closed thirty minutes earlier than the rest of the warehouse area. This gave the people additional shopping time. Beck usually lunched at "Henry's"—with the rest of his staff—where the food was well prepared and nicely served, though the rattle of dishes and the general noise level was a far cry from downtown restaurants.

The morale of the organization continued to decline. Pressures for wage and salary increases kept up. Beck fought against these demands, since he knew that the company paid well for the area, and even better than most companies. Furthermore, he was concerned with savings and was trying to avoid increased cost. Finally, however, he came to the conclusion that there was no alternative but to increase salaries and wages. Since he could not justify a selective increase, he proposed an increase for the entire district, to which, after some discussion and delay, the company agreed.

Now that salaries had improved, the work force devoted more time to complaining about the company in general, and in picking on "working conditions." Shortly thereafter, when the degree of organizational degeneration had become serious, Beck felt that some kind of strong, immediate action would have to be taken. Unrest was spreading to the rest of the plant, through the warehouses, where there had previously existed a patient, loyal, hard-working group. This was passed to Sam by the warehouse superintendent, who said that though the men voiced no specific complaints, they talked about the firm going "down the drain."

This surprised Sam. Although he was inclined to share their feelings about the company losing its spirit and about the loss of competitive aggressiveness, he knew that the previous year was one of the highest in terms of sales and profitability. His own pay was the largest of his career. The home office's penurious attitude was disturbing to him, however, and one of his best marketing men had said, "Well, Sam, we're on the way down—not going ahead any more." Beck was not able to understand it. He knew that the company would not stand another wage hike with the last one still so recent. He could not move back to the old midcity location. In any case he really did not believe that wages were the crux of the problem. But something had to be done if the situation were to be salvaged. What was the problem?

Complaints and/or Discrepancies. The analysts first listed the complaints (or discrepancies) as they were found. They then keyed them to one or more areas of concern (problem definition, communication capability, or managerial competence), as shown in the example below.

COMPLAINTS

Item	Complaint Record	Key [a]
A	Profits not in line with expansion	PD, MC
B	Casual approach to inept employees	MC
C	Top officials make weekly "inspections and supervisory visits"	MC, CC
D	Lease is about to expire (see E)	MC
E	Top officials retain all "important" negotiations	CC, MC
.	.	
.	.	
.	.	
X	(Note that not all are shown)	

[a] Legend: PD = problem definition; CC = communication capability; MC = managerial competence.

The complaints were then tied together into groups, using an alphabetical cross-reference system. This resulted in the list of syndromes or patterns in the following table.

GROUPS AND PATTERNS OF COMPLAINTS (SYNDROMES)

Item	Groups of Symptoms	Key
I	A,B,C,D,F Top management in routine areas (fire-fighting, etc.)	PD, MC
II	E,G,N,T,X Middle manager not "in contact" with upper echelons and subordinates.	CC, MC
III	L,P Transportation failures	
.	.	
.	.	
.	.	
X	(Note that not all are shown)	CC

The syndromes were then related to the areas of concern in a manner described in the text.

This demonstrates the validity of the approach described before, which is:

1. Obtain several estimates from managers or analysts working separately.

2. Compare estimates.

3. In committee, clarify any variances among the estimators about the material.

4. Compute the index.

An experiment containing three classes of investigators, each class of which had several replications, demonstrated that there is a consistency among the results obtained.

SUMMARY

There are three dimensions of managerial control: problem definition, communication capability, and managerial competence.

Problem definition refers to the process by which the manager perceives symptoms, conceives their relationship, and infers the underlying problem. *Communication capability* refers to the cueing, carrying out, and critique facilities, all of which are essential in the manager's communication system.

Managerial competence refers to the manager's perceptual capacity, conceptual capacity, and operating style.

By using these variables it is possible to derive a *managerial control index*. This is useful for finding where emphasis must be placed to bring the level of managerial control up to the point where success is probable. A quantitative index value can be computed by using the procedures set forth in this chapter. Using a case analysis, we have illustrated how the procedures have been used by analysts.

BIBLIOGRAPHY

Anshen, Melvin and G. L. Bach. *Management and Corporations: 1985.* New York: McGraw-Hill Book Company, 1960.

Daniel, D. Ronald. "Management Information Crisis," *Harvard Business Review,* 111–121 (September–October 1961). [15] *

Dearden, John. "Myth of Real-Time Management Information," *Harvard Business Review,* 123–132 (May–June 1966). [10]

Drucker, Peter F. *The Practice of Management.* New York: Harper and Brothers, 1954.

Haberstroh, Chadwick J. "Control as an Organizational Process," *Management Science,* 165–171 (January 1960). [8]

Kaufman, Felix. "Data Systems That Cross Company Boundaries," *Harvard Business Review,* 141–155 (January–February 1966). [9]

Kozmetsky, George and Irving J. Lieberman. "A Mathematical Model for Integrated Business Systems," *Organizing for Effective Systems Planning and Control, Special Report No. 12.* New York: American Management Association, 1956. [24]

McNiece, E. H. *Production Forecasting, Planning and Control,* 3rd ed., New York: John Wiley and Sons, 1961.

Melitz, P. W. "Impact of Electronic Data Processing on Managers," *Advanced Management,* 4–6 (April 1961).

Savitt, Morris A. "Limitations of Managerial Control," *Advanced Management,* 20–23 (April 1962). [7]

Scholz, W. "Communication for Control," *Advanced Management,* 13–15 (November 1959).

Schwitter, Joseph P. "Computer Effect Upon Managerial Jobs," *Journal of Academy of Management,* 232–236 (September 1965). [11]

Urwick, Lyndall F. "The Manager's Span of Control," *Harvard Business Review,* 39–47 (May–June 1956).

* Number in brackets refers to reading number in "Related Readings" section of this book.

3

ORGANIZATIONS AND CONTROL

Chapters 1 and 2, respectively, were concerned with theories of communication in relation to managerial control and with a model for determining the level of managerial control. This is necessary background for the manager to know his control *status*: with this information, the manager can know the *what* of his situation. But it will not tell him *why*. And it is only by knowing the why (reasons, causes, contributing factors) that the manager can do anything to resolve his problems. In other words, once a manager has determined where his strengths and weaknesses lie (determine control status), he must then make an analysis of the conditions (determine why they exist) in order to redesign his department or firm for improvement (determine how to gain and maintain optimal control).

In other words, the previous material provided some feel for the scope of the disciplines a manager must draw from (in Chapter 1) and also provided him with a way of answering the questions: "Is the situation in control?" or "Is there a problem?" (in Chapter 2). Now we must prepare him to *solve* his problem—if he finds one to exist—and for that he needs a basic analytical scheme. He needs a practical, theoretically sound model which will guide him in his further analysis and repair. What does an organization consist of? How do the people and parts fit together? How have these people, or these parts, or both, somehow broken down in their relationships so that the perceived problem has occurred? To answer such meaningful questions requires a conceptual scheme—a model of organizations—equal to the job.

Let us be clear: the analysis of organizations is not an easy task. Further, there are few models sufficiently descriptive to permit meaningful examination. Most existing models are "mixed"; that is to say, they consider the organization to be composed of parts that are neither mutually exclusive nor collectively exhaustive. These models do not consider all the critical parts and relationships, nor do they define those parts and relationships in a way that separates one from the other. A few examples of existing inadequate models are line and staff, upper/middle/lower management, and formal/informal systems. Even so, these inadequate models provide many insights, and the model proposed here is a logical development from such earlier ones. For just that reason it is useful to review how organizations are traditionally portrayed.

We propose here a new and improved organizational model, one that permits the manager to view intelligently his unit so that he can then determine where and how needed action should be undertaken. The model developed is primarily to enable the investigation, analysis, and redesign of administered organizations, which Thompson defines as

Collectivities which exhibit sustained activity; are part of a larger system; have specialized purposes; and are dependent upon interchange with the larger system.[1]

However, the scheme is adequate to employ with any size unit. The reader should not hasten to infer (for example, from noting occasional references to business terminology) that the approach is specific *only* to profit-making, or "business," firms. Undoubtedly, there is a predominance of such activities in our Western culture; the theory, nevertheless, is a general one and can be equally applied to government agencies, churches, educational institutions, research units, aerospace firms, and/or job-shops. Essentially our model looks at the organization as (*a*) a collection of *personnel networks;* or (*b*) a constellation of *output systems;* or (*c*) a composite of *both*. This chapter will focus on the first two; in a later chapter we shall deal with the third, a more sophisticated scheme.

TRADITIONAL ORGANIZATIONAL ANALYSIS

Most people who deal with formally prescribed organizations are accustomed to seeing them represented as an "organization chart." This is an orderly arrangement of boxes and lines arranged in some hierarchy, wherein even the size of a box may indicate the importance of the person whose name appears therein. Generally speaking, in such a chart one has some control or influence over those shown beneath him, and if he is directly connected to such subordinate individuals by a solid line, he is their supervisor. Although the charts may vary widely, the simple illustration shown as Figure 3.1 represents this approach. The idea is so familiar that it requires no further elaboration.

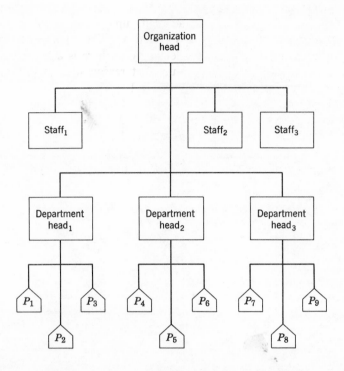

Figure 3.1. Traditional design in organization: personnel assignment. This chart shows, in a simplified way, relationships between *people* in the "formal" organization. It is a "line-and-staff" model and shows "who reports to whom" (and, implicitly, who bosses whom) and little else. Names could be added with no real increase in informative value. "P_n" stands for *person*.

Depicting Additional Interpersonal Relationships

By drawing a few additional lines on the traditional organizational *personnel* chart, additional relationships can be shown. Chartists have become expert in adding dotted lines (to depict occasional relationships, something like the flowing of intermittent streams), and in encasing clusters to outline departments, geographical locations, or nonformalized activity patterns. We are interested primarily in nonformalized patterns. Figures 3.2, 3.3, and 3.4 give an indication of how such specialized relationships are usually shown.

A Social Grouping. Figure 3.2 shows a cluster that may be a bowling team. Although the full set of relationships among the team members (as team members) is not fully depicted and, further, is somewhat over-

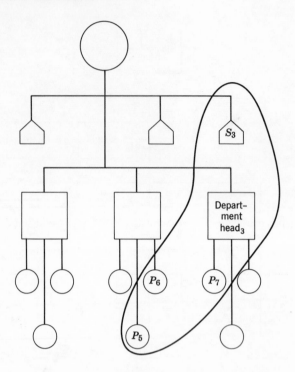

Figure 3.2. An informal, or social, grouping. This chart indicates an "informal" grouping (for example, a bowling team). Note that the statuses shown are those of the "formal" unit, a drawback to this approach.

shadowed by the chart's conventional status symbols, it is nevertheless apparent who the participants are.

Specialist Groupings. Figure 3.3 has a number of specialists grouped together, probably in an attempt to differentiate a batch of members with some common professional concern or skill. It is implied but not stated here that the staff member (S_1) is senior in the group. Still, the membership is relatively clear.

An Ad Hoc (Problem-Solving) Group. Figure 3.4 suggests that a group of members is sorted out to accomplish some job which excludes Department 3 and Staff 3. This could easily imply that a problem common to these others has necessitated a temporary gathering among them—with some subsequent activity possibly at variance to normal administrative rules. Here, too, the administrative status may be confused with the group members' problem-solving statuses, but membership is clear.

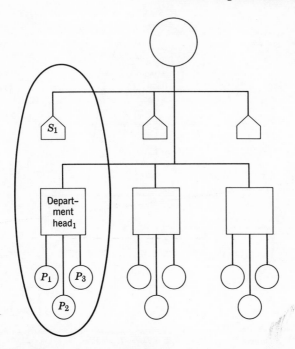

Figure 3.3. A semiformal, specialist, or "functional" grouping.

Total Formal Grouping (Administrative Network). The standard chart over which the social, specialist, and ad hoc groups are drawn represents the formalized, or institutionalized, pattern of relationships among the members. It could be thought of as the "bureaucracy" of the organization. However, since the word "bureaucracy" is so heavily loaded with different meanings for different people, it is dangerous to employ. A better term is "administrative network" since the lines show channels through which directions and responses flow in the course of administering the organization.

Insights Gained from Traditional Personnel Charts. By looking at the traditional personnel chart, one can infer the formal hierarchy (which we called *administrative relationships*). Clusters of individuals relating in ways not spelled out by the formal chart can be depicted by encircling those concerned. Some of the clusters which can be shown overlying the traditional chart are social, specialist, and special (or ad hoc) groupings. Admittedly, insight can be gained from painting these pictures; a drawback is the bias introduced by the basic chart "showing through."

Thus a certain level of sophistication in analysis can be attained through the examination and elaboration of standard personnel charts. Al-

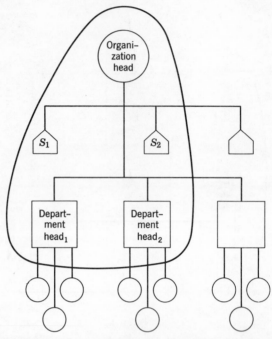

Figure 3.4. An ad hoc "special topic" grouping. Note that only those members concerned with the problem are indicated (for example, Staff member 3, and Department head 3 are not included).

ternatively, one can seek information about an organization by examining a chart of its task structure, as we shall note.

Depicting Specific Task Relationships

An organizational chart is often confounded by adding names to duties or tasks, or by adding tasks to the names thereon. To avoid this, it is common to generate some corollary or subsidiary documents wherein individuals are re-sorted on the basis of "what system(s) they are a part of" or on the basis of "what kinds of activities certain people do." A useful variant of a traditional organizational chart relates one activity to another in a sort of hierarchy of "tasks" or jobs. Figure 3.5 is such a chart in highly simplified form. By drawing some additional lines on this chart it is possible to depict "subsystems" which lie within the total unit. Some of these follow.

A Performance System (A Total Job). Figure 3.6 shows how several different activities, A_7, A_8, A_9 are combined into performance 3. This

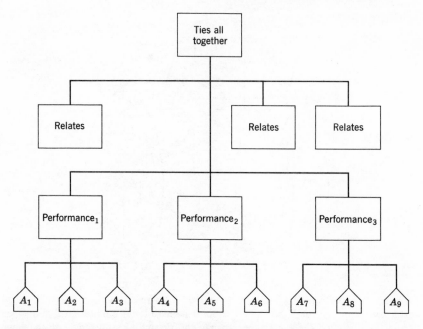

Figure 3.5. Traditional design in organization: task assignment. This chart shows, in a simplified way, the relationships between *tasks* in the "formal" organization. It is a sort of top management/middle management/worker model showing a hierarchy of activities. Names could be added here with little informative value. "A_n" stands for *activity*.

could be something like "assembling a wheel" (where one man performed all three activities), or it could be something like "driving a rivet" (where one man holds, one man guides, and the other man strikes it). Whatever the description it implies, the idea of several different activities *combining* to produce some larger whole act or output is basic.

An Integrating or Balancing System. Figure 3.7 suggests that the "ties all together" process somehow relates the separate performances 1, 2, and 3 in such a way that an awareness of total organizational performance is reached.

A Relating, or Transacting, System. Figure 3.8 indicates that the process of relating outside demands (through relate 1, 2, and 3) to total organizational output can be considered a process in itself.

Insights Gained from Traditional Task Charts. By inspecting the traditional task or job chart one can infer the approximate sequencing of activities to produce (*a*) performances, (*b*) item production or task integration, and (*c*) internal-external transactions. Once again the method em-

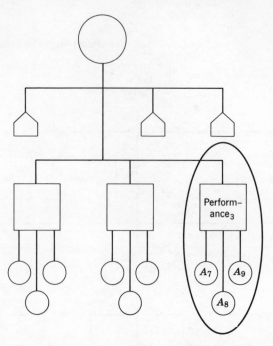

Figure 3.6. A performance, or task, grouping. Activities 7, 8, and 9 contribute to performance (or "accomplishment") 3. Note that there is no implication that a single person does activity 7, for example, or that one person does not do more than one activity.

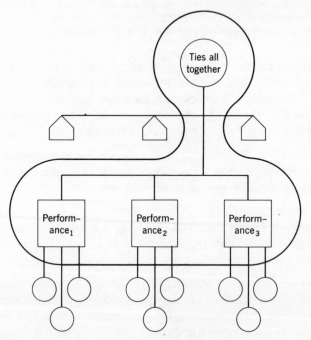

Figure 3.7. An internal balance, or form maintenance, grouping. Performances are kept related, and in context, to insure a predetermined internal whole.

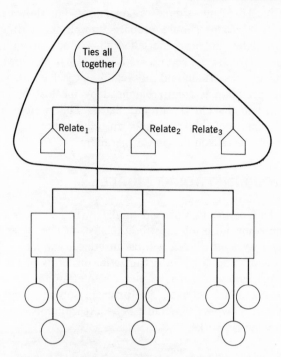

Figure 3.8. An internal-external, or transactional, grouping. The top job, "ties all together," compares internal total activity with broader demands or changing requirements. Relate 1, 2, 3, connect to other organizations (environment) such as the market, professional organizations, publics.

ployed is to encircle or "box in" such subsystems, making such denotations over a standard chart. As with personnel charts, much insight is gained, but here too understanding is somewhat confounded by having to contend with the limitations of the underlying traditional symbols and relationships. In short, it has been demonstrated that even by means of ordinary, traditional, charting procedures we can attain a moderate degree of cross-classification or analysis. Our next step will be to improve on this accomplishment.

A NEW MODEL FOR ANALYSIS

From the preceding discussion, it appears logical that the idea of "who is involved" and "what is happening" forms a dichotomy to be refined as a method of analysis. The model proposed next also looks at the organization as a collection of *personnel networks* or a constellation of *output systems,* as well as a *composite of both.* To move from the reasonable but inadequate traditionalist approaches already described, it will first be necessary to introduce the same simple organization—but shown in a slightly altered design. The reader should prepare himself for a different set of (circular) coordinates and arm himself with a modicum of imagination. The organization will now be represented on a radial plan instead of with horizontal-vertical axes. It should be readily perceived that any initial problem in interpretation is counterbalanced by the loss of psychological loading contained in the old traditional charts. This prejudice practically obviates the possibility of thinking about an organizational member in any terms except where he falls in the power hierarchy.

THE PERSONNEL NETWORKS MODEL

This is one-half of the two-phased model, which extends on, and improves, the foregoing ideas of the traditionalists. (The other half of the model, the *output systems model,* will be introduced later.)

Personnel networks describe an organization in terms of the patterns of *interpersonal interactions* which take place. Centering around social activities, skills, organizational statuses, and problem solving, they are named, respectively, social networks, specialist networks, administrative networks, and problem solving networks.

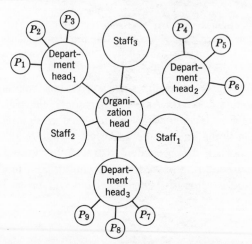

Figure 3.9. A modified organizational design: personnel assignment. This chart shows, in a simplified way, the "official" relationships of people in an organization. It shows all members as they relate to each other so long as they act in their prescribed roles. This is, in fact, an *administrative net* (a network restricted to administratively prescribed interactions).

Social Networks. Social networks contain people who engage in face-to-face activities, largely in order to satisfy their members' gregarious needs.[2] Participants act in small group situations and develop systems of expectancies, relationships, and norms. Collectively, the norms of social networks are compatible but not necessarily congruent with those of the larger organization in which they are found.[3]

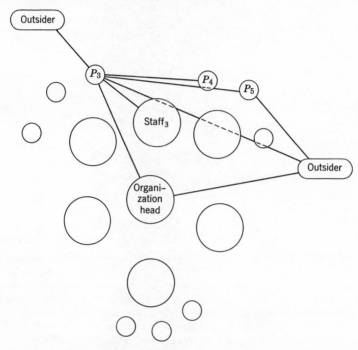

Figure 3.10. A social network. This shows the interaction pattern between members in, say, a bowling team. Although most of the members are members of the larger organization, there are two "outsiders" involved. In this social network, it is apparent that P_3 is the leader, even though the team contains individuals with social statuses incongruent with their administrative roles.

In large administered organizations the daily interfacing and interaction of people produce dozens (perhaps even hundreds) of different social networks. These contribute to the organization in several ways; among them are satisfying human interaction needs, absorbing activity surpluses, and providing better anchorages for people throughout the larger organization by reducing ambiguity and apprehension. Incidentally, the added communication channels provided by social networks contribute to the clarification of personal objectives, as well as organizational goals.

Specialist Networks. Specialist networks contain people among whom communication is facilitated by some commonality, such as an inherent characteristic or acquired capacity. In businesses, the commonalities are

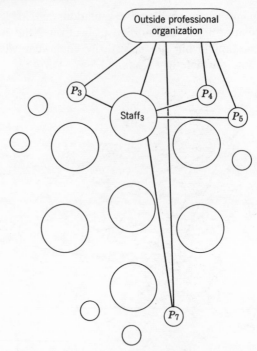

Figure 3.11. A specialist network. Here is shown the interaction pattern between members who are, say, clinical psychologists in the larger organization. Note that within the organization Staff₃ appears to be the leader. However, the common contact with the outside professional organization (and members thereof) implies a greater allegiance. This connection also provides for added transaction between the parent administered organization and others.

usually the result of *professional training* or *skills.* They may develop as a result of assignment to a functional area or department. Whatever the situation, the primary reason for the members' interaction is to exploit, or take advantage of, an area of mutual characteristics, jointly held competences, or common concerns. As a result, the norms and values arising out of and governing members' activities are *specialty-oriented,* not socially oriented. Some kinds of specialists to be found in organizations are accountants, females, mathematicians, Negroes, males, laborers, white-collar workers, and engineers. There are many other types.

It must be noted that the norms and values of specialist networks are never entirely compatible nor entirely congruent with the total larger organization within which the specialists work. Yet for any specific, enduring arrangement they are largely so. And this is not strange. The benefit the specialist brings to the larger organization is his uniqueness, or "professional personality." Should he lose this quality through complete socialization into the "bureaucratic institution," his value and identity *as a specialist* are lost. Therefore he is committed to be what has been called a myopic "local" [4] *within* the organization (e.g., concerned about only one department or operation), and he is probably contemptuous of the institution's broad objectives. To this extent specialist networks and parent organizations are never entirely compatible. And, by definition, specialist network norms are never entirely congruent with those of the organizations of which they are part. Since their members' commonality usually stems from expertise, they remain allegiant to the larger body of their co-professionals, members of which are scattered throughout society in organization after organization. To this extent, they are "cosmopolitans" in Gouldner's sense,[5] and they must always be primarily responsive to the standards of their profession or speciality.[6]

Administrative Networks. People in administered organizations hold positions and offices whose specifications are generally well prescribed. Figure 3.9 is such a net. Certain relationships are demanded and certain activities are well outlined; most are specified even to form and content. Allowable, expected, and forbidden patterns and routines are established for organizational members who occupy such institutionalized jobs. These people, when acting as office-holders, are playing *roles* formally established solely for the purpose of *perpetuating* the set of *official relationships* within the organization, with the primary consideration perpetuation of what is perceived as an *ideal system state.* That state, at the time its ideal nature was determined, was deemed most compatible and congruent with the total organization's goals and purposes.

By definition, then, we can deduce the degree of compatibility and congruence of the administrative network's norms and those of the organization. They are, by *design,* entirely compatible and congruent. Stability, structural maintenance, and impersonality are the network's attributes. The features of stability and impersonality are shared with specialist networks. The administrative network's impersonality characteristic suggests why it generates a need that only social networks can serve. And the built-in rigidity of administrative networks points to the need for another arrangement, the problem-solving network (see Figure 3.12).

Problem-Solving Networks. A manager (problem solver) is an allocator. That is, he is one who restations either problems or resources in order to capitalize, or optimize, in an existing situation.[7] When a problem solver restations or reallocates resources we often say that he is budgeting, reorganizing, or controlling. Therefore the problem-solving network is a manager's arena of action.

A problem can be thought of as a discrepant situation, that is, as a situation where the actual and the ideal are not congruent. Individuals have personal problems; the problems a manager deals with are organizational

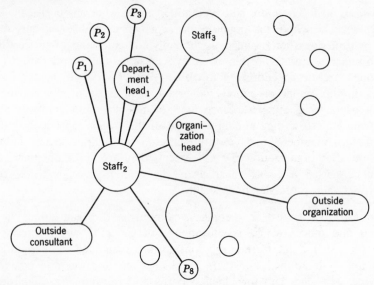

Figure 3.12. A problem-solving network. Here is an interaction pattern between a problem-solver and others who have a contribution to the problem's solution. It is apparent that Staff₂ is the leader, or problem-solver, and that he is soliciting from and directing others, including some outside contacts and the administered organization's administrative head.

problems. To a business organization they are cases where the structure of the firm, its capabilities, and/or its outlook are not in tune with the environment.

Problem solvers exist at any and all levels of organization, and their authority to act is an implicit admission of unmet needs by other networks. A problem solver's flexibility often comes from some special competence (perhaps as a specialist), or from some special attraction as a person (charisma), or from a lack of confidence and capability on the part of the bureaucracy to establish absolute limitations on his role. Further, when perceived as a leader, he is partially exempt from usual constraints. In *periods of crisis* the leader scouts the "twilight areas of sin, crime, and quasi-ethics," searching for solutions that are forbidden to other members of the network.[8]

Thus the problem-solving network is alien to other networks. To elaborate: a manager may perceive a problem and feel the need to solve it; he will then *seek and solicit information to that end*. To the extent that he must intrude into social networks, that he must make unethical demands of specialist network members, and that he must ignore the established chains and hierarchical relationships of the administrative networks, he is incompatible. And to the extent that the demands of problem solving require adjustments of any of the goals of other networks, there is incongruence.

Yet this network is the organization's real problem handling means, and since its criterion-set by definition is "organizational survival and betterment," the problem-solving network is the only one possible to be maximally compatible and congruent with total organizational goals. This is a basic paradox, little recognized in the literature of organizational and management theory today.

PERSONNEL NETWORK CONTRIBUTIONS TO THE ORGANIZATION

Each network is peopled by different "kinds" of members who interact due to compelling reasons of their own. Yet it can be shown that the nets as entities contribute differentially to the organization; in fact they provide for the four basic organizational necessities: *action, stability, environmental intelligence,* and *adaptation.*

Contributions of Social Networks. These make it possible for numbers of people to endure working together in organizations. Their emergent behaviors, acting as buffers between individual needs and the organization's almost impersonal demands, make tolerable the continued total activity at the level required. In a dynamic situation, they provide for a great amount of extra communication.

Contributions of Specialist Networks. These networks provide two things often overlooked. First, they act as assurors of professional competence and quality. Also, the members, by their cosmopolitan nature, provide continuing interorganizational contacts.

Contributions of Administrative Networks. These provide the greatest possible routinization of recurring activities. And, although they admittedly reject creativity, they do provide effective barriers to dysfunctional innovation.[9] Further, the administrative structure makes possible the existence of all other nets. For example, the administrative network maintains the arena wherein social activities take place; it provides the specialist with a sphere wherein he can excel; it frees managers from housekeeping tasks, allowing them to direct their attentions to critical problems.

Contributions of Problem Solving Networks. These provide the adaptive mechanisms through which the total organization survives. Comprised of managers, their resource contacts, and their problems, the problem-solving networks make it possible for the organization to change, to create, to innovate.

In a word, it can be seen that no one network can live long without the other three. Examples of each, together with interactions among all networks, can be identified in any living organization. Figure 3.13 shows in an abstract way how different types of networks fit together.

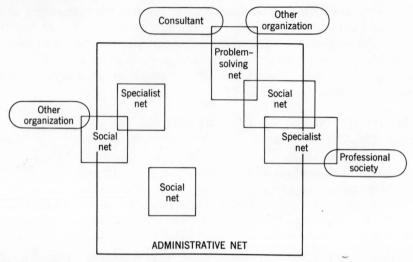

Figure 3.13. Relationships between networks. The administrative net is the backdrop against which network analysis is made. Members of the administrative network are also members of social nets, specialist nets, and problem-solving nets. In the process of their interactions as network members, they come in contact with others outside the organization. Importantly, networks are not mutually exclusive. A single individual may belong to several simultaneously. In this respect, networks differ from systems.

THE OUTPUT SYSTEMS MODEL

This is the other half of our two-phased model. If attention is directed to human activity, an organization can be explained by the four personnel networks we have discussed. However, additional insight can be gained if concern is shifted to structural arrangements whereby an organization may be thought of as a complex of facilitating systems.[10] We refer to these as *output systems* because the focus is on "what is done," or what is facilitated.

In Figure 3.14 a simple organization is shown as an arrangement of output systems. Although naive, the diagram has significant heuristic value. Each system is pictured as a "black box" in the paradigm, since at this point the essential ideal is the sequential or *integrative* nature of the arrangement. Each system has inputs and outputs; all are related; each can be seen to contribute to and depend upon others.[11]

Each type of output system serves a different purpose. Four basic organizational needs and their respective systems can be identified:

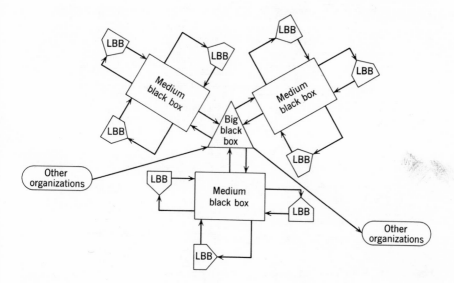

Figure 3.14. A modified organizational design: system activity. This shows an organization as a series of interrelated systems. Each system is shown as a black box for simplicity. Little black boxes serve as inputs to (and are controlled by) medium black boxes. Each medium black box feeds into the big black box and is controlled by it in turn. The big black box receives inputs from, and makes outputs to, other organizations. Although in complex organizations each of the systems—black boxes—contains humans among its parts, there is no implication in this model that a person is connected to a particular system, or is not connected to many.

1. Individual tasks must be accomplished. The greatest number of output systems in an organizaton serve this purpose. To achieve this goal, there are *performance systems*.

2. Internal balance must be maintained among task-activities, which means assuring a proper set of subsystem relationships within the unit. To accomplish this, there are *informative systems*.

3. The organization must keep in touch with its environment. To do this, there are *transactional systems*.

4. There must be provision for necessary adaptation and change. To serve this end, there are *innovative systems*.

Performance Systems. This system, shown in Figure 3.15 provides for the starting, control, and completion of a particular task. A task may be simple (such as tightening a screw) or complex (such as interviewing an employee), depending on the level of perspective. Performance systems, obviously, are like building blocks to the organization. But there must be

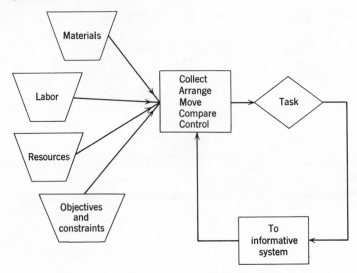

Figure 3.15. A performance system. This could be analogized as the little black box. As inputs, the performance system has one or many of such things as materials, labor, resources. These inputs are converted into some task (something being accomplished). This output is fed into the informative system where it is collated and compared with other performance systems' outputs. A certain amount of adjustment of each performance system can be made by the informative system.

an organizational means for collation, coordination, and tying them together. This function is provided by the informative system.

Informative Systems. This system brings the individual performance systems into context. It is shown in Figure 3.16. Each task makes its own contribution, which theoretically can be neither ignored nor exceeded if the larger organization is to keep in balance. To keep this internal balance among the separate performance systems, the informative system assures (*a*) that each individual task system state is kept within limits and (*b*) that the collective system state is maintained within a range of acceptable relationships.[12] It must be remembered that the informative system works solely *within* the organization. "External" relationships are facilitated by the transactional system.

Transactional Systems. Transactional systems, shown in Figure 3.17, arrange for inputs and outputs between the organization and the outside world. Through these exchanges the organization relates to external demands and pressures and becomes aware of environmental changes. Just as the organization becomes dynamic and responsive to internal activities through its informative system, so it becomes a sensitive part of life *around* itself through its transactional system.

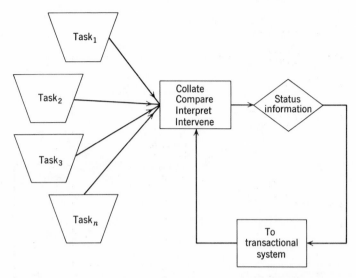

Figure 3.16. An informative system. Imagine this to be the medium black box of Figure 3.14. Tasks from individual performance systems provide inputs to the informative system. These inputs are converted into internal organizational balance (or awareness of the lack of it). Internal status information is fed into the transactional system, where it, along with extra-organizational inputs, is processed.

Innovative systems. Innovative systems provide mechanisms for orderly search for and design of new optimal system structures. To an extent, those data communicated through the transactional systems into the informative systems do affect activity at the performance systems' levels. But it follows that it is possible to attain only that flexibility originally built into the three systems. Whenever systems limits are either reached or exceeded, or when there is a danger that either is probable, provision must be made for a restructuring of existing routines. This need is met by the innovative system (see Figure 3.18).

The output of innovative systems includes new structures, new systems, new relationships among the parts of the organization, or between the organization and its environment. These changes may be ephemeral or lasting, trivial or substantial, conservative or radical. Some important possible changes which may occur are in the goals, criteria, or objectives of the unit.

The most common type of innovation is problem solving. Since a problem can be defined as a discrepant situation (i.e., evidence that existing routines have been inappropriate), some new set of relationships must be imagined, perceived, conceived, and constructed in the process of analysis and accommodation. Since problem solving depends upon an ability to re-

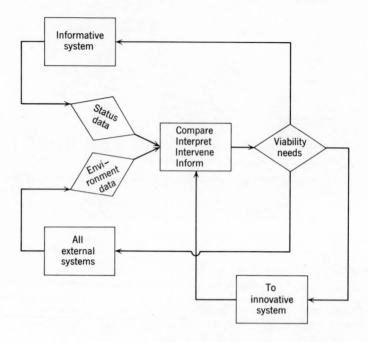

Figure 3.17. A transactional system. Refer to the big black box of Figure 3.14. Inputs from the informative system (about internal activity levels) are combined with data from other organizations (the environment). These inputs are processed to develop as outputs "awarenesses of needed change." These "viability needs" may trigger demands of the informative system, or of external systems, or both. If these systems, when solicited, are incapable of adequate response, then the innovative system is set into motion.

source and to apply a wide repertoire of conceptual schemes, it can be no better than the capability of system members.[13] In administered organizations the ones most concerned are managers. Thus it can be seen that the innovative system has a direct relationship to the problem-solving network. The problem-solver is the network member; problem solution is facilitated through the innovative system.

Another important point must be mentioned. Frequently, innovation as problem solving is largely ephemeral and of the moment. However, when minor problems proliferate or deepen, they usually indicate that more basic adjustments are necessary in the performance, informative, or transactional systems. Therefore any systems analysis and redesign becomes a function of the innovative system, the output of which may range from a subtle change to a pronounced restructuring of the organization.

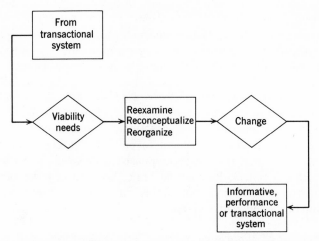

Figure 3.18. An innovative system. Refer again to the big black box, Figure 3.14. Viability needs (changes required for survival) are the inputs to this system. The process is essentially a hierarchy of (*a*) reexamination of existing systems; (*b*) reconceptualization of existing systems; and (*c*) reorganization of existing systems. The process is applied, in turn, to the informative, performance, and transactional systems. Each time a change is introduced, the total system is evaluated for adequacy. Whenever adequacy is reached, the innovative system ceases operation.

OUTPUT SYSTEM CONTRIBUTIONS TO THE ORGANIZATION

The output systems do different specific things within the organization, such as "tightening a screw" (performance system); "insuring that total department output is complete and well-balanced" (informative system); "shipping the services or items to the user—and receiving payment or evaluation therefrom" (transactional system); and "modifying the kind of things done or made" (innovative system). Stated in such a way, they are seen to provide something that users want. Stated in a more general way, they collectively provide for the four basic organizational necessities of *action, stability, environmental intelligence,* and *adaptation,* just as the networks previously considered did.

Contributions of Performance Systems. These arrange for, or facilitate, the accomplishment of basic organizational tasks. It can be seen that at one level of analysis the production of a tool may be basic, and at a different level the production of profit by an entire firm may be basic. However perceived, performance systems are meaningful only in relationship to one another and to the whole organization. The informative system provides this meaning.

Contributions of Informative Systems. Informative systems manufacture total meaning from the combined outputs of performance systems. They are concerned with the collective internal workings of the organization, not with relationships between the organization and its outside world. Such relationships are facilitated through the transactional system.

Contributions of Transactional Systems. These provide for interactions between the organization and entities in the environmental set. Depending on the level of analysis, the transactional system may be relating one firm to the industry, one department to part of a larger organization, or one culture to another. It must be emphasized, however, that even though the transactional system does provide interface between the organization and its environment, it does not supply any corrective mechanism. This is a function of the innovative system.

Contributions of Innovative Systems. Provisions for needed change are made by innovative systems. Whenever other systems are determined inadequate, that is, when there is an organization problem to be solved, the innovative system becomes the facilitating device to effect shifts in relationships or entities. It is of prime importance to organizational survival.

In summary, the output systems are seen to be interdependent and interlocking. Relations among the systems are shown in an abstract way in Figure 3.19. It is important to note that each type of system is completely differentiable from each other one; this contrasts with the kinds of networks, which allow multimembership. In other words, the systems are mutually exclusive entities; the networks overlap. Both are collectively exhaustive in that they consider every part and activity of the matter that falls in their frame of reference. The frame of reference for networks is the people involved; that for the systems is the things that are done or accomplished.

SUMMARY

Any organization can be viewed as a collection of personnel networks providing for needed membership activity and change, or as a collection of output systems providing for needed facilitating activity and change. Either model will provide the manager with a useful analytical pattern for his department or firm. And, as will be shown later in this book, considered together they provide an exhaustive scheme through which communication, problem-solving activity, and managerial success can be viewed.

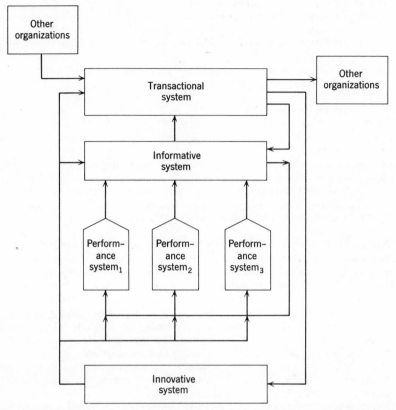

Figure 3.19. Relationships between systems. It is readily seen that the informative and performance systems provide intra-organizational balance. Through these two, the organization does its tasks and the tasks are kept in tune with each other. Through the transactional system the organization is kept in contact with other organizations, and by means of it both receives and transmits, recruits and ejects. The sole output of the innovative system is change, which it can provide by intervening into any other of the organization's systems. Importantly, then, the innovative system is designed for *internal* adjustment. (The organization interacts within its larger environment or culture through its transactional system.)

NOTES

[1] Thompson, James D., et al. *Comparative Studies in Administration.* Pittsburgh, Pa.: University of Pittsburgh Press, 1959, p. 6.

[2] Face-to-face activities do not exclude the kinds of "direct" communication that can be obtained through telephone, teletype, or video contacts. For example, much of the activity of ham radio operators can be called *social.*

3 They are at least largely incongruent by definition, since the associations emerge to satisfy requirements which are felt, but not provided for, in other parts of the organization's structure. They are *compatible* since, if they are not mainly so, mutual survival of the social networks and the host organization cannot be expected.

4 Compare Gouldner, A. W., "Cosmopolitans and Locals: Toward An Analysis of Latent Social Roles—I" *Administrative Science Quarterly, 2*, 281–306 (1957).

5 *Ibid.*

6 The analogy fits any level of organization, even where the "organization" in which the specialist finds himself is a department (and where his allegiance is to some larger scheme, such as the dispersed and scattered body of a professional intra-company staff).

7 Problems can legally be considered "resources" to an organization. For example, could individuals fulfill their needs singly, they would not band together; in this sense an individual need is a recruiting resource function. Other cases can easily be made. However, in a pedagogical sense, the two factors are dichotomized here since it is a bit easier for some readers to think of problems and resources as separate entities.

8 Transgression of social norms is "sinful," which limits social network members' interaction with others. Ignoring administrative routines is "illegal" and limits participation of certain bureaucrats in innovative situations. Overstepping professional dictates is unethical and prevents most professionals (specialists) from shifting into true bureaucratic or managerial roles without a revolutionary change in self-perception. The *manager* (when acting in a problem solving network) is either beyond such identifications or is operating on relatively trivial problems where conflict does not arise. Those who find themselves in this condition are probably very low in the hierarchy, or are in fact "supervisors."

9 A bank teller, who unilaterally improvises his own system of checking the validity of signatures on items presented for payment (thus ignoring time-tried, established practices), is probably guilty of dysfunctional innovation.

10 Anything that consists of parts connected together will be called a system. Beer, Stafford, "Systems and Related Concepts," *Cybernetics and Management*. London: The English Universities Press, 1959, pp. 9–12.

11 Compare McMillan, Claude and Richard F. Gonzalez. *Systems Analysis*. Homewood, Ill.: Richard D. Irwin, 1965, p. 3: "Subsystems of the firm might follow an identification of the major functional areas: production, personnel, accounting and distribution. We are not, however, restricted to this set of subsystems; the concept of system permits other meaningful subsystem identifications, such as the information system of the firm."

12 "The lines depicting the network of our system are in fact its *communications*. The state of the lines at any given moment reflects the amount of *information* in the system. The structure of the communications and the nature of the information which flows through them to one of the elements of the system will determine, at any given moment, whether this element is in a given state or not." Beer, *op. cit.*

13 The type of member generally employed is a human, often referred to as a manager, a researcher, or, more generally, a problem solver.

BIBLIOGRAPHY

Andrew, Gwen. "An Analytic System Model for Organization Theory," *Journal of Academy of Management,* 190–198 (September 1965). [22] *

Balderston, F. E. "Communication Networks in Intermediate Markets," *Management Science,* 154–171 (January 1958). [27]

Beer, Stafford. *Cybernetics and Management.* London: The English Universities Press, 1959.

Black, James Menzies. "Employee Communication: All Dressed Up and No Place to Go?," *Management Review,* 4–8 (July 1959). [13]

Boulding, Kenneth E. "General Systems Theory—The Skeleton of Science," *Management Science,* 197–208 (April 1956). [23]

Burlingame, John. "Information Technology and Decentralization," *Harvard Business Review,* 121–126 (November–December 1961). [16]

Cummings, Larry L. "Managerial Effectiveness I: Formulating a Research Strategy," *Journal of Academy of Management,* 29–42 (March 1966). [12]

Eckman, Donald P. *Systems: Research and Design.* New York: John Wiley and Sons, 1961.

Gouldner, A. W. "Cosmopolitans and Locals: Toward an Analysis of Latent Social Roles—I," *Administrative Science Quarterly,* II, 281–306 (1957).

Haire, Mason. *Modern Organization Theory.* New York: John Wiley and Sons, 1959.

Hormann, Aiko M. "Designing a Machine Partner," *Datamation,* 13 (2), 29–33 (February 1967).

Halterman, Carroll C. "Information Systems and Evidential Meaning." [21]

McMillan, Claude and Richard F. Gonzalez, *Systems Analysis,* Homewood, Ill.: Richard D. Irwin, 1965.

Shull, Fremont, Jr. "The Nature and Contribution of Administrative Models and Organizational Research," *Journal of Academy of Management,* 124–138 (August 1962).

Simon, Herbert A. *The New Science of Management Decision.* New York: Harper and Row, 1960.

Smith, Alfred G. "The Organization Man and the Research Man," *Communication and Status: The Dynamics of a Research Center.* Eugene, Ore.: University of Oregon, 1966, pp. 29–38. [25]

Stogdill, Ralph M. "Basic Concepts for a Theory of Organization," *Management Science,* Series B, B-666-B-676 (June 1967). [28]

Thompson, James D. et al. *Comparative Studies in Administration.* Pittsburgh, Pa.: University of Pittsburgh Press, 1959.

* Number in brackets refers to reading number in "Related Readings" section of this book.

4

PROBLEM DEFINITION

After studying the general concepts of communication, managers, and organizations in relation to control, we are now ready to explore in depth how these can be used for operational improvement. Essentially, this means relating this background information to the basic control dimensions mentioned in Chapter 2, problem definition, communication capability, and managerial competence. We shall do this by presenting detailed analytical models of each in the next three chapters, starting with problem definition.

By problem definition we mean the process by which the manager (*a*) perceives symptoms of actual or potential trouble; (*b*) puts the symptoms into useful syndromes or patterns; and (*c*) infers from the patterns the underlying problem or problems in a given situation.

It is obvious that a managerial problem is an interpretation or mental construct not directly observable by the manager. Indeed, the only valid test of the rightness or wrongness of the manager's identification of his problem lies in seeing whether symptoms are changed as desired when a given "solution" is tried. If the solution results in changing the symptoms in the direction desired by the manager, he can assume that he has rightly defined his problem; if the solution brings no change or worsens the symptoms, the manager can assume that his problem definition is wrong. He then tries again for better definition.

The analysis of problem definition involves the following dimensions: discrepancies; level of recognition; relationships established; and operationality of relations.

EVALUATION OF DISCREPANCIES

By discrepancies we mean any complaint, any trouble, any barrier to effective organizational functioning at any level. A discrepancy exists when something is less, or worse, than it ought to be. Sometimes called a symptom, a discrepancy is observable in the real world. Examples of discrepancies include inaccurate reports, high personnel turnover, high production rejects, and decreased sales revenue. Discrepancies are the indicators of managerial problems as well as the means of determining whether the manager has been successful in handling them.

An evaluation of discrepancies can be made by examining (*a*) number; (*b*) distribution in organizational units; (*c*) distribution in specialties; (*d*) distribution among topics; and (*e*) membership or output orientation.

Number. Since all organizations operate at less than ideal expectations, all organizations have discrepancies. The question here is to determine whether there are more than the normal number. By normal we mean the quantity of discrepancies which the firm can safely tolerate without impairing its products and services beyond a given level. This means that the organization should have *discrepancy norms,* and, where feasible, these norms should be categorized according to type and source (e.g., production, sales, personnel).

Further, some discrepancies should be examined against special circumstances. Seasonal fluctuations, equipment changes, or personnel turnover can make significant differences at times. Allowances for these can be made by: (*a*) deliberately ignoring special cases; (*b*) discounting a certain proportion of discrepancies in given areas; (*c*) considering them over a different time span; and (*d*) setting separate norms for special conditions.

In any event if the discrepancy number is exceeded, it is a direct indicator of the need for further analysis.

Distribution among Organizational Units. In this step the analyst is concerned with finding whether discrepancies are fairly evenly distributed or clustered in relatively few units in the firm. It is possible that a large proportion of the total may stem from two or three departments. Or it may well be that all departments are fairly equally involved. Again, it is possible that some units have a greater share of one type and a lesser share of some other. It is of course important that the analyst use the same criterion fix with all units.

Distribution among Specialties. At this point the analyst is ascertaining how discrepancies are spread among different specialized groups within the firm. By specialized groups we mean personnel networks involved in specific product and service activities. Examples include accountants, training personnel, engineers, shipping clerks, and salesmen. Depending on need, the groupings can be both broad or narrow. For example, "engineers" could be subdivided into "electrical," "mechanical," and "chemical." It is even possible to consider this distribution by levels within the organization (e.g., top management, middle management, first-line supervisors), using appropriate subcategories.

Clearly this step helps the analyst to pinpoint even more sharply the location of quantity and types of organizational deficiencies. It also helps to determine whether these exist in relatively isolated pockets of specialized personnel or in broader groupings in the total firm.

Distribution among Topics. Here the analyst seeks to find the most discrepant subject areas within the firm. Topical categories can be very general or very specific. It is probably more helpful to the analyst to work with general classes with useful subclasses under each. Subclasses should be as close to operational as possible.

As to general classes that may be used, there are several: traditional functional areas (production, sales, finance, etc.); categories emerging from analysis of specific discrepancies elicited from organizational personnel; department or division areas; and problem areas (budgeting, planning, staffing, etc.). Whatever the classification system, it must be (*a*) simple—but adequate; (*b*) clear and acceptable to the analyst; and (*c*) clear and acceptable to consumers.

Membership/Output Orientation. Based on our previous discussion of personnel networks and output systems, the analyst in this step is determining discrepancies related to both people and facilitating systems in the organization. Obviously, all foregoing steps will reveal discrepancies which fall into one or both of these categories; however, here the analyst goes farther by looking closely at the member-to-member, member-to-output, and output-to-output relationships in the firm. Do members interact with one another? Do specialists know important administrative policies and procedures? Do social networks act to thwart important managerial task accomplishments? Does the informative system adequately communicate to managers data concerning task performances? How is conflict handled? Between persons? Between managers? Between departments? Is conflict handled to produce progress? Or is it mishandled, and therefore disruptive to organizational goals?

Of course the analyst must get discrepancies from first-hand observation, but general questions along the lines of the preceding questions can furnish valuable guidelines for making his observations, as well as for arriving at classifications or groupings once the observations are completed.

EVALUATION OF LEVEL OF RECOGNITION

By level of recognition we mean the extent to which discrepancies are perceived, recorded, interpreted, and brought to the attention of responsible people.

An examination of level of recognition includes the following: (*a*) actual knowledge of discrepancies; (*b*) knowledge by appropriate organizational personnel and units; (*c*) knowledge by appropriate managers; (*d*) perception of gravity; and (*e*) procedures for recording and communicating to management.

Actual Knowledge of Discrepancies. The analyst should bear in' mind that discrepancies may be widespread in an organization without being so recognized. From the manager's viewpoint, unless symptoms are consciously perceived, they do not operationally exist.

If symptoms are not actually known, the analyst will probably need to look for reasons for the deficiency. Sometimes a lack of awareness may result from confusing symptoms of serious difficulties with normal conditions. Frequently personnel think that the troubles encountered are part of the natural order, that they are part of situations to be tolerated rather than conditions to be overcome.

Another factor contributing to lack of awareness is the absence of clear criteria. Organizational members should have some common view toward discrepancies. One inaccurate report may not be classed as a symptom; however, five or six of a given kind may be. On the other hand, one inaccurate financial report to stockholders may be a very significant symp-

Clear criteria should also include the means of observing symptoms. Some factors bearing on this are:

1. *Who* does the observing? For example, what personnel, what levels, what jobs, what departments are observing?

2. *How* are observations made? Are they made by one or several persons? One or several departments? On an ad hoc or a continuing basis?

3. *What purpose* does the observation serve? To monitor special situations? To keep tabs on the unit as a whole? To put administrative pressure on certain departments or people?

Yet another reason for lack of knowledge of discrepancies may be conscious or unconscious fear of actually recognizing them. Personnel may perceive that genuine awareness of troubles will be a threat to themselves.

Or they may fear reprisals from others if certain deficiencies are made known. Thus troubles may be conveniently overlooked rather than brought into focus.

Knowledge by Appropriate Personnel and Units. Even if discrepancies are known to some personnel and units, they may not be known to all proper people and units. Therefore the analyst should determine to what extent they are known to (*a*) originating personnel and units; (*b*) external personnel and units; and (*c*) responsible managers of administrative units.

Do those at the point of origin actually know that the symptoms exist? It is not uncommon for these people and units to be completely unaware that they are the source of troubles. And if they know, how clearly do they know the symptoms in question? Sometimes a discrepancy is only vaguely felt or dimly perceived, not consciously recognized. Do originators know the number, frequency, and type of symptoms? Are sources, both personnel network and output system, known? Are some symptoms perceived to the exclusion of others?

Next the analyst should determine how well the external personnel and units—other than those at the point of origin—recognize the discrepancies. It is not uncommon for outsiders to perceive symptoms of problems far more accurately than those on the inside. The reason is obvious: the outsider may be on the receiving end; he gets the adverse impact, therefore he is frequently more sensitive to the discrepancy than is the originator. Since it gets customer complaints, the sales department may see symptoms of manufacturing problems more readily than the production department. Since they must operate within them, workers may discern discrepancies in administrative policies far more readily than those who formulate those policies.

Do responsible managers and administrative units know symptoms? Even if both originators and outsiders know, it is clear that effective corrective action rests with organizational managers and administrative units. The manager must know in order to take the necessary innovative steps; the administrative unit must know in order to carry out the policies and procedures resulting from managerial decisions. All foregoing questions apply.

Perception of Gravity. In this step, the analyst is determining the seriousness of the perceived symptoms. Each should be ranked and weighted in terms of severity of impact. It is conceivable that three out of a total of fifty symptoms may be more important than all remaining forty-seven. The analyst can make his judgments concerning gravity from information gained in all preceding steps. He can supplement this by discussions with key personnel and units involved.

Procedures for Recording and Communicating to Management. The analyst needs to determine the means by which symptoms are recorded and brought to the attention of managers. What formal procedures are used to record symptoms? A suggestion system may be used by some organizations. Grievance procedures are frequently employed in organizations with unions. With crucial jobs, on-line monitoring may be required. For example, with tight production schedules, it may be necessary to know at a given moment where trouble is occurring; if there are key personnel shortages, it may be necessary to know immediately where problems arise in order to allocate people accordingly. Recording may be through direct observation by supervisors, use of performance profiles and logs, or a combination of these. Batching procedures may be used where periodic assessments are appropriate. These can include questionnaire surveys, interviews, formal reports, and staff meetings.

The analyst should note all recording procedures used and evaluate them for adequacy. In addition he needs to determine how the recorded data are communicated to management. First, he needs to examine the *means* by which the data are communicated. Are they by informal word of mouth? By written memoranda? By formal reports? By staff meetings? By ADP systems? By combinations of the preceding? In making the determination, the analyst should know whether the means are by design or by accident. In other words, are there explicated procedures, or do people merely follow their own ways in communicating symptoms?

Next the analyst needs to assess *organizational flow* of the data. Through and to what units do the data go? Are there clear distinctions as to which symptoms are to be routed to what organizational departments? Are both personnel networks and output systems specified? Are there channels for both routine and nonroutine functions? And, as in means, the analyst should determine whether or not there are explicit guidelines for organizational flow.

In addition the analyst needs to determine the adequacy of procedures for informing *key managers* about discrepancies. Are there specified ways to communicate with given managers about particular symptoms? If there are such guidelines, are they used? How do key managers actually know the symptom status in their respective spheres?

EVALUATION OF RELATIONSHIPS ESTABLISHED

By relationships established, we mean putting discrepancies into meaningful patterns or syndromes. Only when properly related can symptoms be useful in diagnosis of managerial problems.

An examination of relationships involves: (*a*) determining whether there are relationships; (*b*) determining whether they are related to problem areas; (*c*) determining whether they are perceived in the organization; (*d*) determining whether they are perceived at appropriate levels; and (*e*) determining whether they are perceived by appropriate managers.

Relationships between Discrepancies. Even if discrepancies are adequately recognized, it is obvious that this fact alone is insufficient. Proper patterns, or relationships, of discrepancies are necessary if they are to be made meaningful. The analyst should determine whether certain symptoms fall together, interconnect, or are interdependent. There are no easy rules; however, we offer the following sequence of questions as one way to proceed:

1. What *generalizations* can be made concerning discrepancies?
2. What *theories* can be constructed from the generalizations?
3. What *causal connections* can be inferred from the generalizations and theories?
4. What is the nature of, and what discriminations can be made, from each of the three?

By generalizations we mean the *extended* observations made of the actual symptoms. If, out of a total of fifteen reports of a given type, ten are observed to be inaccurate, then the generalization, "Two-thirds of this type of report is inaccurate," may be valid. Generalizations are useful to get a picture of the overall status of a situation.

Theories are attempts to *explain* generalizations in terms of *what is happening.* In one sense theories are "super-generalizations," that is, more abstract generalizations about lower-order ones. Properly constructed, theories allow an even more penetrating analysis of relationships between discrepancies.

Causal connections are attempts to determine *why* something happens or has happened. Stated another way, causal relations are generally inferred as reasons which acted to bring about present and past events.

The analyst may move to other approaches once he has completed this or a similar sequence. The actual situation will dictate the exact analytical pattern.

Relation to Problem Areas. The analyst is now ready to determine whether discrepancies are related to appropriate problem areas. Problem areas can be classified from any feasible viewpoint. Departmental classifications (marketing, sales, finance, production) are common. Hierarchical levels (top, middle, lower management), special program areas (sales campaigns, cost-cutting programs, safety programs), or significant problem areas (critical training needs, crucial recruitment problems) are other possibilities.

Another method of classification uses the three essential elements of managerial control: problem definition, communication capability, and managerial competence. These, together with the subcategories given in Chapters 4 to 6, can constitute very valuable groupings.

Perception in the Organization. Irrespective of the patterns of relationships established, it is clear that these perceptions must be properly observed within the unit or nothing of worth can ensue. The analyst may raise questions such as: Do people and units at the *points of origin* perceive the relationships? Do people and units at the *points of impact* perceive the relationships? Do people and units at *all appropriate levels* perceive the relationships? Do *managers,* in areas where the problems are of concern, perceive the relationships?

In getting answers to these questions, the analyst probably will need to make direct observations, talk with key people in the concerned units, as well as construct his own generalizations, theories, and causal connections.

EVALUATION OF OPERATIONALITY OF RELATIONS

By operationality of relations, we mean putting ideas into some useful *working* form. Generalizations, theories, and causal connections are helpful to the manager only when he can actually perceive the possibility of doing something with them to handle the problems which confront him.

An examination of operationality of relations involves answering questions along the following lines: Are relationships translated into real problems? Are problems stated to suggest solutions? Are problems stated with adequate precision and rigor? Can problems be resolved within available resources of the organization?

Translation into Real Problems. The term *real problem* refers to some observable discrepant situation; that is, a discrepant situation that exists in the real world. This definition casts aside many so-called problems with which some managers may feel concern. For example, "How can we improve managerial leadership?" is not a real problem simply because when stated this way it does not lend itself to observation. "How can we improve communication?" is of the same ilk.

On the other hand, "How can we get manager *A* to monitor production scheduling?" is a possible real problem. "How can we get certain messages from Department *A* to Department *B?*" is another potential real problem.

Along this line, the analyst needs to consider whether the problems are stated at the proper level of complexity. Overcomplicated problems pose unnecessary obstacles; on the other hand, oversimplification must also be avoided. Further, in order to be real to the organization and its members, problems should be stated in terms that are communicative to those units and people. And generally the more "practical" the statement of the problem, the better.

Suggestion of Solution. General statements of problems are useful as starting points; but general problems must be made susceptible to resolution. To determine whether this is done, the analyst should ask several questions.

1. Are problems put into *manipulable form?* That is, are problems broken into workable parts, are priorities established, and is a practical sequence of attack set forth?

2. Are there provisions for both *routine and nonroutine solutions?* Certainly solutions should be routinized as far as possible. But where necessary, nonroutine solution areas must be recognized and provision must be made for handling them.

3. Are both membership and output orientations given proper weighting? This refers once more to the two basic organizational models discussed in Chapter 3. In some instances output validity is more important than membership acceptance. In other cases, the opposite is true. In many situations, both will be equally important. In any event, the analyst must determine whether both factors are considered, as well as the bases upon which judged.

Precision and Rigor. Here we mean the accuracy and care with which problems are stated. The analyst can raise several questions to determine this.

1. Is *quantification* used where possible? All appropriate mathematical models and statistical tools should be employed as the situation allows. Properly used, these represent the most valuable means of exactitude and care in thinking.

2. Are problems adequately related to *past* and *present* organizational events? This means taking into consideration the real-world data of the organization. Are sales forecasts related to historical and current sales figures? Are new performance requirements arrived at after reflective consideration of former norms? Are future personnel needs hooked into real organizational experience?

3. Do solutions allow for *adjustment* in light of changes? A solution is a prediction. But any prediction is based only on what is known at the time made. Changing conditions therefore may require approaches different from the ones predicted. The analyst should determine whether these allowances are made, and on what bases.

Available Resources. Utopian solutions are worthless to managers. And any solution finally is no better than feasible existing or anticipated resources of the organization. To get at this facet, the analyst should raise these questions: Are solutions related to *monetary* resources of the organization? Are solutions related to *physical* resources (plant, equipment, etc.) of the organization? Are solutions related to *output capability* of the organization? (Here, of course, we refer to all the facilitating systems in the firm.) Are solutions related to the *membership capability* of the organization? (This means all the organizational personnel networks, including the problem-solving network with which the manager is primarily concerned.)

A PRACTICAL WORKING MODEL

To this point we have been concerned with a rather elaborate explanation of problem definition. This was necessary to gain understanding of the analytical components and their relationship to one another. With this background, we are now ready to present a working model which the manager, or another analyst, can use to make assessments of the level of problem definition in his organization.

A very practical approach is to put the dimensions into an algorithm, or sequence of steps. This can be done as illustrated in Figure 4.1.

Rationale of the Algorithm

A study of Figure 4.1 reveals several things. First, the factors of discrepancies, level of recognition, relationships established, and operationality of relations, respectively, are set forth in an ascending order of importance. Second, a total of 10 points is assumed, the 10 points relating to severity of problem definition. That is, "0" represents "optimum" problem definition; 10 represents the severest departure from optimum. Third, out of the total of 10 points, priorities are weighted as follows:

Discrepancies . . . 1
Level of recognition . . . 2
Relationships established . . . 3
Operationality of relations . . . 4

    Total . . . 10

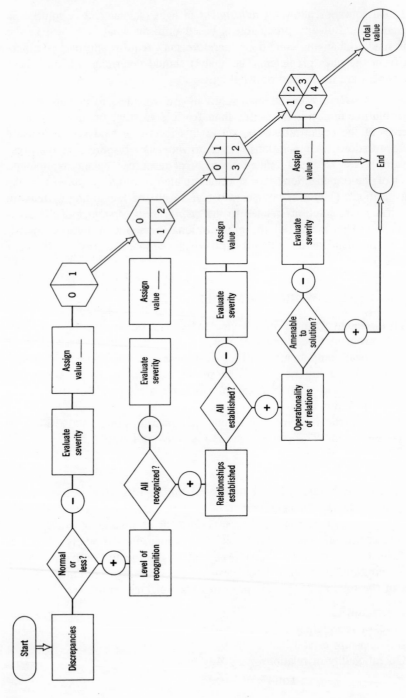

Figure 4.1. Algorithm for analysis of problem definition.

72

We explain our rankings and weightings in this way: Discrepancies either exist or not; they are merely to be observed. If they do not exist in sufficient number, there is no problem. This is the simplest and easiest step to determine, therefore it is given the lowest numerical rating, 1.

Level of recognition is a more complex step. Assuming sufficient severity of discrepancies, the determination of this factor involves the analyst in making inferences and judgments about the kinds and qualities of perceptions of organizational people and units. In analysis, it is considered more important than perception of discrepancies, because unless adequate recognition exists, the discrepancies do not *operationally* exist. This justifies its weighting of 2.

Relationships established is an even more sophisticated and important step. This involves putting the recognized discrepancies into some adequate patterns, constructs, concepts, so that the real underlying problems can be determined. It is therefore given the next highest numerical rating of 3.

Operationality of relations is given the highest weighting because this is the "payoff" for all the other steps. Unless problems are put into some feasible, some manipulable, form, so that they can be handled, then all preceding steps are futile. Its rating of 4 is justified accordingly.

Summating Values in the Algorithm

This is merely a matter of adding the "departure values" from each of the four steps in the algorithm. Since there are 10 points possible, the result is some proportion of that number. This is illustrated in the hypothetical example of Figure 4.3.

SUMMARY

Problem definition is the process by which the manager perceives symptoms, puts the symptoms into syndromes, and infers underlying problems. A useful approach to evaluating problem definition involves examining discrepancies, level of recognition, relationships established, and operationality of relations.

This chapter has offered a detailed explanation of how each of the four elements can be analyzed. We also set forth an algorithm which permits the analyst to make useful quantitative calculations of each dimension, as

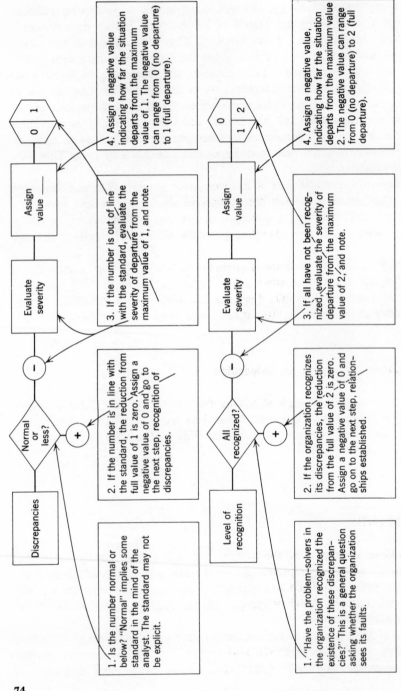

Discrepancies

Normal or less?

Evaluate severity

Assign value ____

| 0 | 1 |

1. Is the number normal or below? "Normal" implies some standard in the mind of the analyst. The standard may not be explicit.

2. If the number is in line with the standard, the reduction from full value of 1 is zero. Assign a negative value of 0 and go to the next step, recognition of discrepancies.

3. If the number is out of line with the standard, evaluate the severity of departure from the maximum value of 1, and note.

4. Assign a negative value indicating how far the situation departs from the maximum value of 1. The negative value can range from 0 (no departure) to 1 (full departure).

Level of recognition

All recognized?

Evaluate severity

Assign value ____

| 0 | 2 |
| 1 | |

1. "Have the problem-solvers in the organization recognized the existence of these discrepancies?" This is a general question asking whether the organization sees its faults.

2. If the organization recognizes its discrepancies, the reduction from the full value of 2 is zero. Assign a negative value of 0 and go on to the next step, relationships established.

3. If all have not been recognized, evaluate the severity of departure from the maximum value of 2, and note.

4. Assign a negative value, indicating how far the situation departs from the maximum value of 2. The negative value can range from 0 (no departure) to 2 (full departure).

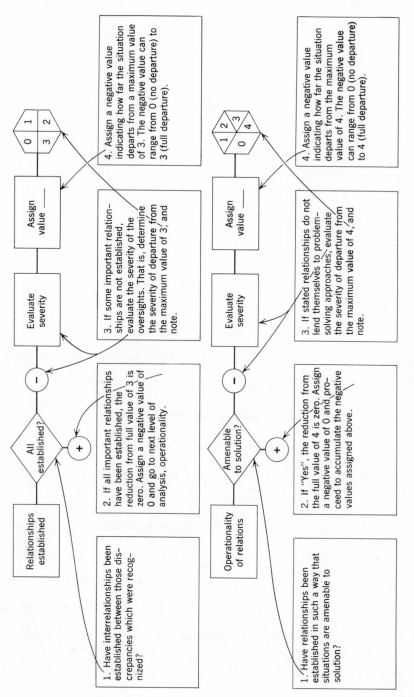

Figure 4.2. Use of the algorithm.

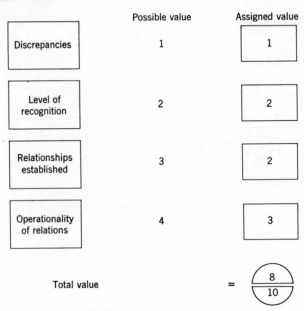

Figure 4.3. Summating values in the algorithm.

well as to arrive at an aggregative index of the degree of problem definition in the organization.

BIBLIOGRAPHY

Blau, P. M. "Formal Organization: Dimensions of Analysis," *American Journal of Sociology,* **63**, 58–69 (1957).

Bross, Irwin D. J. *Design for Decision.* New York: The Macmillan Company, 1953.

Burlingame, John F. "Information Technology and Decentralization," *Harvard Business Review,* 121–126 (November–December 1961). [17] *

Chandler, Margaret and Leonard R. Sayles. *Contracting-out: A Study of Management Decision-making.* New York: Columbia University, Graduate School of Business, 1959.

Dearden, John. "Myth of Real-time Management Information," *Harvard Business Review,* 123–132 (May–June 1966). [10]

Duckworth, Eric. *A Guide to Operational Research.* New York: Dover Publications, 1962.

Emery, F. E. and O. A. Oeser. *Information, Decision and Action.* Carlton: Melbourne University Press, 1958.

Hilgard, Ernest R. "Creativity and Problem-solving," in H. H. Anderson, ed., *Creativity and Its Cultivation.* New York: Harper and Brothers, 1959.

* Number in brackets refers to reading number in "Related Readings" section of this book.

Kepner, C. H., and B. B. Tregoe. *The Rational Manager*. New York: McGraw-Hill Book Company, 1965.

Kozmetsky, George and Irving J. Lieberman. "A Mathematical Model for Integrated Business Systems," *Organizing for Effective Systems Planning and Control, Special Report No. 12*. New York: American Management Association, 1956. [24]

Maier, Norman R. F. *Problem-solving Discussions and Conferences: Leadership Methods and Skills*. New York: McGraw-Hill Book Company, 1963.

Mander, A. E. *Logic for the Millions*. New York: Philosophical Library, 1947.

March, James G. "Business Decision Making," *Industrial Research* (Spring 1959).

Osborn, A. F. *Applied Imagination: Principles and Procedures*. New York: Charles Scribner's Sons, 1953.

Simon, Herbert A. *The New Science of Management Decision*. New York: Harper and Row, 1960.

Wertheimer, Max. *Productive Thinking*. New York: Harper and Brothers, 1945.

5

COMMUNICATION CAPABILITY

The term "communication capability" refers to the flow of material, information, ideas, perceptions, understandings, and conflicts between the various parts and members of an organization. This includes all the methods, means, and media of communication; all the channels, networks, and systems of communication; all the person-to-person interchange; and all the data and information necessary to carry out organizational tasks. Communication capability, then, encompasses the means by which the manager and his organization get inputs, process them, and critique outputs. As such, it is vital to managerial success and organizational survival.

The analysis of communication capability involves evaluating the dimensions of technology, organizational structure, interpersonal communication, and job-relevance of data.

EVALUATION OF COMMUNICATION TECHNOLOGY

"Technology" encompasses the communication *means,* including all hardware and software components. For example, typewriters, teletypes, calculators, overhead projectors, multiple-copy forms, and computers are hardware. Letter formats, sequencing of paper flow, methods of presentation, and methods of programming are software.

An examination of communication technology should proceed in the following sequence: (*a*) equipment; (*b*) methods; (*c*) modernity; (*d*) usefulness; (*e*) compatibility with organizational needs; (*f*) qualifications of using personnel; and (*g*) acceptability to users.

Equipment. What kinds of equipment are in use? For example, does the oganization depend on word-of-mouth, written memoranda, telephone and video contacts, a completely integrated computer-based system, or all of these? Regardless of the type of technology, it is most important that it be effectively and efficiently used. Availability does not mean proper usage. The key question should be, "Is it optimum for the firm?" Not every firm needs a computer; not every one can exist with a mere paperwork flow scheme.

Methods. Every communication system should be specifically tailored to the department or organization it serves. Is there evidence that all hardware and all personnel are fully integrated into the communication system, or is a complex group of facilities merely overlaid? Have all aspects been studied for proper method, proper logic, and proper flow to insure that the least costly and most efficient communication job can be accomplished? The existence of a systems analysis group in the organization *suggests* but does not guarantee that this is done.

Modernity. Certainly neither the hardware nor the software should be obsolete. Obsolete does not mean merely "old"; it means that the technology is too primitive for, or not equal to, today's job. Certain parts of an organization communicate quite well with rudimentary technology, for example, committee meetings or luncheon affairs. Others demand quite exotic and costly equipment, for example, research and development groups, telemetry systems, and minute-by-minute market monitors for stock index quotations.

Ease of Use. The communication technology should be such that an individual can enter the communication situation or get information from it with apparent ease. It must be accessible and available. It should not require undue ability on the part of the user, nor should it require an inordinate amount of training or indoctrination.

Compatibility with Organization. Are the types of methods compatible with the type of organization serviced? Does the organization have the talent, the procedures, and the need to use them? A useful question to ask is "How much better or worse off would the organization be without the present technology?" Organizations such as church groups, temporary organizations, or one-time activities should not incur the burden of complex equipment. They cannot stand the cost of purchase or lease, they cannot take the time to train operators, and they cannot undertake the chore of disposal. On the other hand, certain other temporary organizations, for example, those generated to predict elections, those prognosticating outcomes of war games, or one-time massive training operations, cannot possibly perform their duties without such equipment.

Qualifications of Personnel. Personnel must be knowledgeable, trained, and skillful in the use of whatever equipment and methods are prescribed.

For example, a great amount of training is necessary for a manager merely to represent himself properly to his superior and subordinates. And it requires top-grade skill for a secretary to be of value. A systems analyst must be very knowledgeable if he is to break down and to reconstruct an organization's channels to best effect. Where specific equipment is involved, training in its use is needed. Typewriters, calculators, copiers, drafting equipment, photo-reproduction and duplication units all require specialized training.

Acceptability to Users. Regardless of the potential value of a technology, it must be welcomed by its users. If not, much time will be spent rationalizing "why it won't work." Sabotage, in fact, has been observed on many occasions; and such behavior as overriding automated systems with manual controls is evidence that faith in the machinery has not been developed. Not only the hardware but the methods themselves must be "sold." Changing procedures from time-tried and time-tested familiar ways often results in rejection, or, in any case, lowered performance. It should be borne in mind that the customer of a business is a "user" of that business' systems. For example, many times a computer-produced billing or a form letter loses acceptance for the firm.

EVALUATION OF ORGANIZATION STRUCTURE

Organizational structure includes the complete set of relationships existing between the parts and the members. Let us be clear about what we mean by organizational structure. But first we want to emphasize what we do *not* mean. We are not referring to the more narrow view of structure as a mere set of formal relationships: relationships between hierarchical levels, between positions, between departments. We include all these to be sure, but our definition is far more encompassing.

When we use the term *organizational structure* we refer to the *total pattern of relationships between all organizational people, between all organizational parts, and between the organization and its whole environment.* We mean all those relationships discussed under personnel networks and output systems. Organizational structure, then, includes the total culture and climate of the manager's firm.

In a business organization there should be at least some sort of desired or "formal" organization chart. One should be able to see different levels of authority, different departments, and some differentiation of specialization or product. It is, of course, well-known that the formal organization chart does not represent all the real-world relationships. Social networks, informal associations, and professional groupings always develop in the administered organization. In charting or planning, the executive should always provide for the existence of both personnel networks and output systems.

An evaluation of organization structure can be made using the following foci: (*a*) discernible structure; (*b*) structure and organizational needs; (*c*) structure and organizational goals; (*d*) structure and individual goals; (*e*) understanding of organizational structure; and (*f*) acceptance of organizational structure.

Discernible Structure. Basic evidence of structure is the existence of an organization chart. If a chart is available, the analyst examines it for adequacy and representativeness. If no chart exists, the analyst has the task of determining what the firm's management thinks the shape of the organization is. The analyst can pose questions such as these: Is the structure, as represented, adequate in detail? Are there gaps or omissions? Does the structure suggest activities or relationships which are not there? The analyst should bear in mind that this step is directed to determining whether or not structure actually exists—not to determining whether such structure is optimum or best.

Structure and Organizational Needs. Structure can actually be harmful if it is at odds with the needs of the organization. The analyst can raise questions like these: How do people and units interact within the structure? Does the structure provide for handling conflict to insure organizational progress? Or does it seem to create continuing destructive repercussions? Is a service-type framework being employed for a product-type business? Is the unit broken up into geographical departments, when a functional or product differentiation may be more desirable? Has the structure kept pace with organizational growth? Is the structure in line with future organizational needs? Is it apparent that some functions needed are not adequately provided for, or, on the other hand, are there vestigial departments or committees that have long outlived their contribution?

Structure and Organizational Goals. As we detailed in Chapter 3, needs of the organization are related to both the products which come from it and the people who staff and comprise it. The structure must be compatible for both. The structure should be efficient, relatively streamlined, and tailored toward meeting the "total organizational purpose." Apart from the individual goals of its members, an organization has goals of its own; these must be accomplished if the organization is to justify its existence. Both the people and the parts of the firm must be logically related to each other as well as to the overall organizational goals.

Structure and Individual Goals. Very seldom are the goals of individual employees or members the same as the overall goals of the organization. Members have social needs, professional needs, actualization needs, all of which are important to them in their work. If the organization does not provide for these needs, adverse effects will follow. What appear to be superfluous items in structure, that is, items which at first glance do not seem to contribute to the output of the firm, may in actuality be fulfilling real personal needs of members. Their removal or incision may do far more harm than good. The analyst should evaluate structure accordingly.

Understanding of Organizational Structure. It is of crucial importance that members of an organization understand its structure and their place in it. Although the manager is himself a member, the first attention of the analyst should be directed toward the employees, the participants, the bulk of people involved in day-to-day operations. A starting point may include job and task descriptions, manuals for guidance, and process charts. Although their existence does not guarantee understanding, the average firm or organization seldom achieves employee knowledgeability without them. But, regardless of the stated tasks and responsibilities, do the members *really* understand how the organization works? Observation and discussion will bring this out. Another important principle to remember is that members understand better to the extent that they participate in defining organizational structure and how they fit into it. The analyst should ascertain the extent and type of ongoing membership participation; it will give significant insight concerning the degree of both manager and member understanding.

Acceptance of Organizational Structure. Do members agree with the logic and the rationale of the organization's shape? Is there evidence of either enthusiasm or antagonism? Is it overt or covert? Is it real? Acceptance or rejection of an organization may be the result of structure, good or poor management, or other conditions. It is futile to construct the "ideal" organization if nobody will accept the result. Along this line, members are more likely to be "sold" on the organization if they know that their ideas on structure are taken seriously by management. If management gives mere lip service to members' suggestions, automatic overt or covert rejection of organizational structure will follow. In the final analysis, the members must persuade themselves that the unit is best for itself and for them. Once again, what at first may appear to be an illogical and somewhat unsystematic structure may have significant trade-offs in terms of improved acceptance.

EVALUATION OF INTERPERSONAL COMMUNICATION

By interpersonal communication we mean all exchanges that take place between people. Such communication can be official or unofficial, formal or informal. It can take place by word-of-mouth, memoranda, through meetings, or over the telephone. Problems in this area stem from the fact that human beings see things differently, say things differently, interpret things differently.

An evaluation of interpersonal communication may use the following dimensions: (*a*) interpersonal cognizance; (*b*) interpersonal understanding; (*c*) interpersonal responsibility; (*d*) media and methods in interpersonal communication; and (*e*) relevance and balance in interpersonal communication.

Interpersonal Cognizance. Do the people involved actually know who other members of the organization are? How well do they recognize them, not only in terms of personal likes, dislikes, and abilities, but also in terms of the roles they occupy and the organizational functions they perform? How well are members of the organization acquainted with each other? Do they know only those in their immediate work or problem area, or do they also know how other more removed people fit into the picture? How well people know each other directly affects their success in communicating with each other.

Interpersonal Understanding. Are members speaking the same language within the organization? Is there evidence of mutual understanding throughout the diverse groups? Irrespective of whether agreement on activity or principle exists, is there evidence that ideas, concepts, problems, and procedures are passed on from one person to another? At a higher level, is there evidence of empathy among members? Are attempts made to try to understand each other? Frequently interpersonal understanding may be almost completely lacking among groups of different "cultures." A common example of this is where workers with different skill or training backgrounds interface. Differing departmental jargons or professional terms can erode interpersonal understanding. When there are differences in interpersonal understanding, is there evidence of constructive efforts and means for reconciliation? Or, through a laissez faire approach, or by deliberate intent, are these differences eroding the route to organizational progress?

Interpersonal Responsibility. To what level is there a conscious and demonstrable *mutual* responsibility for interpersonal communication? Are genuine, systematic attempts made to understand, to clarify, to restate issues, to assure that desired outcomes are attained? Interpersonal responsibility does not exist if superior-subordinate communication is merely one-way. Just as important, co-workers must question and answer, repeat, check, and restate until sufficient comprehension takes place. Where all parties have a deep and sincere interest in the organization and its goals, they will demonstrate active interpersonal responsibility. Generally this type of interest in organizational goals will be directly related to the degree and kinds of *commitment by the members* to organizational goals and objectives. This commitment is a direct result of the type of organizational climate and culture. The analyst must keep these principles in mind as he examines the very important element of interpersonal responsibility.

Media and Methods in Interpersonal Communication. Broadly speaking, the vehicles by which messages are carried are called media. For example, a printed page, a telephone system, and a video display are types of media. The ways in which these are used are termed methods. It is obvious that there are better and worse methods for each medium in a given situation. On a broad base, the media and methods for communication must be compatible with the structural needs and goals of the organization itself. Also, the goals must not be alien to the abilities of individuals to interact with them. General appropriateness of media was discussed under Technology.

Relevance and Balance in Interpersonal Communication. Communication among individuals should be pertinent to both the goals of the firm and the needs of the people. These two should have a fair balance. In examining the kinds of communication that take place, these two questions can be asked: "Is communication directed toward solving organizational goals?" and "Is interaction useful in solving personal problems?" Clearly, if neither of these is answered affirmatively, the communication is nonrelevant. Relevance in interpersonal communication involves (*a*) the right people in contact with each other; (*b*) the right subjects being discussed by the people involved; and (*c*) the right messages being delivered about the topics under discussion.

Just as important as relevance is balance. This means: Is too much interaction taking place about some items and not enough about others? Are some problems ignored—and others attacked—out of proportion to their importance? Does communication take place about output of the firm at the expense of ignoring problems of people? Do individuals spend too much time on personal troubles, fogging and clogging channels that need to carry trouble-shooting advice about the operations of the firm?

EVALUATION OF JOB-RELEVANCE OF DATA

Each task, duty, output, or function in an organization has communication requirements. These include such things as orders, directions, evaluations, feedbacks, and measurements. In raw form such communications are called "data." Data that contribute directly to furthering performance on the job are called job-related. Extraneous data are referred to as "noise." For example, much direction, which may be poorly stated, contains a large amount of noise. Poorly worded instructions, carelessly computed statistics, poorly run meetings, sloppy job descriptions, are all entropic, or poorly informative. When extraneous data are received, the effort of sorting, interpreting, and processing detracts from the user's output and efficiency. On the other hand, it is vital that all required data are furnished, for without adequate data, the job could not be done at all.

An examination of job-relevance of data can be made using these foci: (a) knowledge of data requirements; (b) adequacy of data; (c) providing for needed data; (d) quantity of data; (e) timeliness of data; and (f) credibility of data.

Knowledge of Data Requirements. When job descriptions, task specifications, and process requirements are spelled out, or enumerated, it can be inferred that data requirements probably have been considered. Where no such evidence exists, it is probable that adequate understanding of requirements is not known. Some operating specifications only imply the data need. Others explicate in detail, particularly in cases where full systems analyses have been made by the organization. Regardless of how well requirements are known by the analyst, it must be determined that the *users* understand them, and, in fact, that they do use them. It is important, then, that data requirements be understood at three different levels: (a) general requirements for the organization; (b) particular or peculiar requirements for subsystems or components; and (c) specific requirements for exact positions or jobs.

There must also be an understanding among the different hierarchical levels of the organization. For example, on a broad, general base, top management should be able to perceive general data requirements on which policy and long-range strategies are based. On the operating level, the managers must have available data useful for tactical, short-run decisions. On the factory floor, the individual processor, operator, or mechanic must get all necessary data for him to perform his job in the best way.

Adequacy of Data. If all jobs are being done at an adequate level, it can be assumed that adequate job-related data are being received. This may not be exactly true, because the possession of better data may reveal that the job could be done at a higher performance level, or done better in a different way. If jobs are not being accomplished according to demand, it can be assumed that data relevant to the job are inadequate. For example, if the operator were better informed about his performance, the criteria used to evaluate it, and what was generally expected of him, he would probably work at a higher level of acceptability. An approach to examining such a situation might be the following:

1. Make sure that the output measures are proper and correct.

2. Examine the information and materials being received to determine whether something is lacking.

3. Check the process itself to see whether it is the method rather than the data which is faulty.

Of course, if no one of these reveals trouble areas, the criteria may require adjustment. If this is the case, data adequacy should be evaluated according to the new criteria that emerge.

Providing for Needed Data. Data should be readily available. They should be brought to the area of requirement on the basis of anticipated needs. For example, certain kinds of materials are needed more frequently than others; other kinds of materials are cheaper to provide and store than to be without. When the risk or cost of specific action to search out needed data is greater than the cost of providing that which is probably needed, then the latter course of action should be followed. It should be noted that there are psychological and sociological problems attendant to one's not having data relevant to his job or position. The need for status knowledge, for information about one's performance level, is very significant to people. If job-relevant data are made difficult to obtain, both the personnel networks and the output systems of the organization suffer. In this respect it can be seen that much information should probably be furnished to members of the organization solely to satisfy their "need-to-know." Viewed coldly and rationally, this may be judged as superfluous and wasteful. In actuality such data are vital to the maintenance of a proper balance between personnel networks and output systems of the unit.

Quantity of Data. A certain amount of data is needed for any given operation; more than enough data, however, clouds the issue. Both empty channels and clogged channels are deleterious. Too much data result in extra processing time by either automatic equipment or individuals. Too little data mean that production time must be diverted to search and hunting activities when this time could be used for needed output. In the sense that data are input to a production process, the amount of production is bottlenecked by their lack. To the extent that data are quality control oriented, their lack increases the probability of rejection or failure. In the personnel networks of the organization, lack of data can result in inequity and improper rewards. Symptoms may be high attrition rates, poor morale, and high absenteeism. The costs of not having data are easy to see.

On the other hand, there is a point where the cost of additional data is higher than the expected return from it. For example, the cost of additional market analysis may not be justified by increased sales. The cost of additional communication to employees through a plant newsletter may not pay for itself in improved morale or output. The cost of an "absolutely correct" information processing system may eat up any and all savings in errors reduced.

Timeliness of Data. Data must be brought to the job at the time needed. They may be brought from some central storage or memory (either mechanical core or the mind of the operator, for example). Or they may be transported immediately (real-time) from the point of origin. Therefore it can be seen that getting required data to the job depends upon three things: (*a*) providing for data generation at the time required; (*b*) providing for memory or other storage of data; and (*c*) providing communication facilities to carry the data from the point of generation or storage to the point of operation.

Costs are involved in all three cases. First, there is a risk of not being able to obtain data if their need is not anticipated and storage is not provided. Second, memory is costly, whether it exists in a computer or mentally by a highly trained professional. Third, a large amount of redundance is required among the wires, cables, equipment, as well as people, in order to avoid saturation of the system. Fourth, guaranteeing against data distortion is an expensive proposition. Risks of data timeliness, then, must be balanced against costs.

Credibility of Data. For data to be useful at any point, they must be understood, believed, and accepted. This requires that the user be able to talk in the same language in which the data are expressed, that he have faith in the system by which they are communicated, and that he accept them as a base for action. Essentially these requirements speak for the need of *authority* in data. The user must either accept as valid a source of guidance and information (on its face), or he must know enough about the system, including the rationale behind its data gathering, so that he does not question his inputs. These factors speak to the need for (*a*) a system that is simple but adequate for the job; (*b*) personnel who are well-trained in the required skills and techniques; and (*c*) a willingness on the part of management to explain "how, what, and why" things are done.

It must be remembered that credibility of data does not depend on logic alone. Certainly there must be a conditioning of users to accept the data. Acceptance of constraint data (orders) may depend on the charisma of the supervisor, or the subordinate's perception of authority. Acceptance of performance requirements may depend on the professional outlook of the recipient, or perhaps on the esteem in which his actions are held by his peers. The acceptance of process data may depend on a history of past success, knowledge about a new system, or mere blind faith. In any event, the data must be seen as credible, otherwise they will not be made a part of the organizational process. They will be without proper impact.

ALGORITHM TO EVALUATE COMMUNICATION CAPABILITY

Following the same pattern employed with problem definition, we now present an algorithm which can be used to evaluate the level of communication capability in the organization (Figure 5.1).

Rationale of the Algorithm

As with the approach in problem definition, the algorithm for evaluation of communication capability sets forth dimensions in an ascending order of importance. And the factors are weighted from 1 to 4 in the same manner. We explain our weightings as follows: *communication technology* (1), including both hardware and software, can be observed and classed as adequate or inadequate in the organization. Although this is important, an organization sometimes can function quite effectively with "primitive" or apparently ineffective technological means; *organization structure* (2), is the context within which communication functions. This includes all the personnel networks and output systems of the organization. Since this represents the relationships in an organization, it is more important than technology. Still, some units with apparently poor organizational structure function quite well; it is, accordingly, not as important as the next element; *interpersonal communication* (3), represents all the personal interchange in the organization. It is clear that even with good technology and good structure, poor interpersonal communication can lead to organizational failure. And it is also clear that good interpersonal communication can exist in an organization with both poor technology

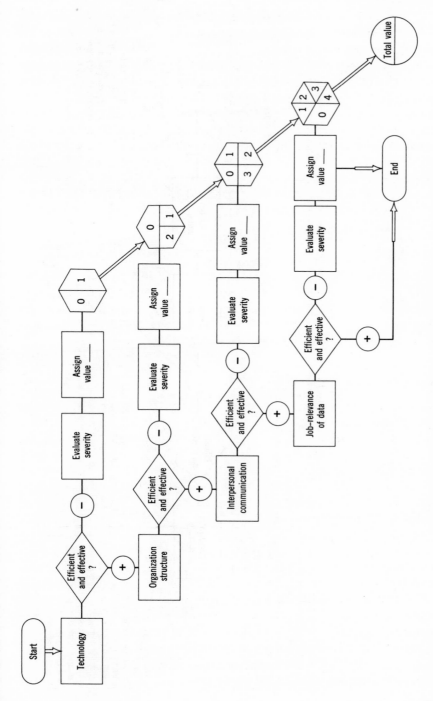

Figure 5.1. Algorithm for analysis of communication capability.

89

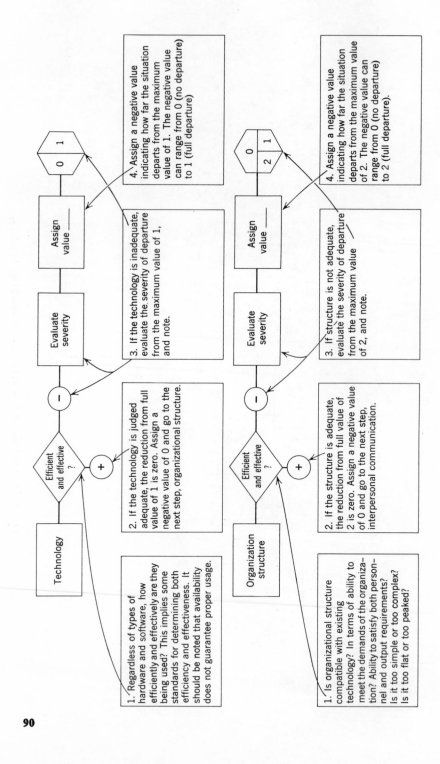

Technology

Efficient and effective ?

Evaluate severity

Assign value ___

0 | 1

1. Regardless of types of hardware and software, how efficiently and effectively are they being used? This implies some standards for determining both efficiency and effectiveness. It should be noted that availability does not guarantee proper usage.

2. If the technology is judged adequate, the reduction from full value of 1 is zero. Assign a negative value of 0 and go to the next step, organizational structure.

3. If the technology is inadequate, evaluate the severity of departure from the maximum value of 1, and note.

4. Assign a negative value indicating how far the situation departs from the maximum value of 1. The negative value can range from 0 (no departure) to 1 (full departure)

Organization structure

Efficient and effective ?

Evaluate severity

Assign value ___

0 | 1 | 2

1. Is organizational structure compatible with existing technology? In terms of ability to meet the demands of the organization? Ability to satisfy both personnel and output requirements? Is it too simple or too complex? Is it too flat or too peaked?

2. If the structure is adequate, the reduction from full value of 2 is zero. Assign a negative value of 0 and go to the next step, interpersonal communication.

3. If structure is not adequate, evaluate the severity of departure from the maximum value of 2, and note.

4. Assign a negative value indicating how far the situation departs from the maximum value of 2. The negative value can range from 0 (no departure) to 2 (full departure).

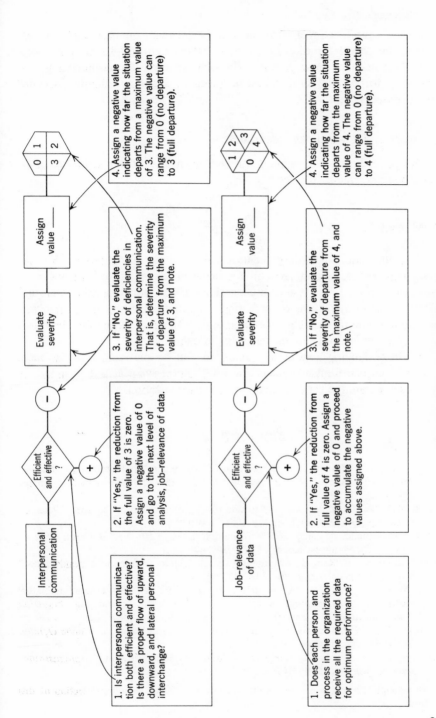

Figure 5.2. Use of the algorithm.

and poor organizational structure; *job-relevance of data* (4), is, of course, the payoff for the organization. Unless data get to the job at the right time, in the right way, and in the right amount, all the preceding elements are for naught. It is therefore given the highest weighting in communication capability.

Summating Values in the Algorithm

This procedure is the same as for that given in problem definition. Follow the steps given there.

SUMMARY

Communication capability includes all the flow of material, information, perceptions, and understandings between the parts and members of an organization. It is vital to managerial success and organizational survival. A useful approach to evaluating communication capability involves examining communication technology, organization structure, interpersonal communication, and job-relevance of data.

We have detailed how these dimensions can be analyzed. We also have set forth an algorithm for calculating each and arriving at a total index of the level of communication capability in the organization.

BIBLIOGRAPHY

Blake, R. R., J. S. Mouton, L. B. Barnes, and L. E. Greiner. "Breakthrough in Organization Development," *Harvard Business Review,* 133–155 (November–December 1964).

Cook, P. H. "An Examination of the Notion of Communication in Industry," *Occupational Psychology,* 1–14 (January 1961). [14] *

Daniel, D. Ronald. "Management Information Crisis," *Harvard Business Review,* 111–121 (September–October 1961). [15]

Davis, Keith A. "A Method of Studying Communication Patterns in Organizations," *Personnel Psychology,* 6, 301–312 (1953).

Day, Melvin S. "NASA's Developmental Program for Selective Dissemination of Information," *Proceedings of the 1964 Institute in Technical and Industrial Communications,* Colorado State University, pp. 35–39. [20]

Deutsch, Karl W. "On Communication Models in the Social Sciences," *Public Opinion Quarterly,* 16, 356–380 (1952).

Dorsey, John T., Jr. "A Communication Model for Administration," *Administrative Science Quarterly,* 2, 307–310 (1957).

* Number in brackets refers to reading number in "Related Readings" section of this book.

Fest, Thorrel B. "Closing the Communications Gap," *Proceedings of the 1962 Institute in Technical and Industrial Communications,* Colorado State University, pp. 93–99. [18]

Festinger, L. *A Theory of Cognitive Dissonance.* Evanston, Ill.: Row, Peterson, 1957.

Guetzkow, Harold and H. A. Simon. "The Impact of Certain Communication Nets upon Organization and Performance in Task-Oriented Groups," *Management Science,* I, 233–250 (1955).

Halterman, Carroll C. "Information Systems and Evidential Meaning," Reprinted by author's permission. [21]

Higham, T. H. "Basic Psychological Factors in Communication," *Occupational Psychology,* 1–10 (January 1957). [2]

Jackson, Jay M. "The Organization and Its Communication Problem," *Advanced Management,* 17–20 (February 1959). [16]

Odiorne, George S. "An Application of the Communications Audit," *Personnel Psychology,* 7, 235–243 (1953).

Paine, Frank T. "Management Perspective: Sensitivity Training: The Current State of the Question," *Journal of Academy of Management,* 228–232 (September 1965).

Schramm, Wilbur, ed., *The Process and Effects of Mass Communication.* Urbana, Ill.: University of Illinois Press, 1954.

Smith, Alfred G. "The Organization Man and the Research Man," *Communication and Status: The Dynamics of a Research Center.* Eugene, Ore.: University of Oregon Press, 1966, pp. 29–38. [25]

Stogdill, Ralph M. "Basic Concepts for a Theory of Organization," *Management Science,* Series B, B-666-B-676 (June 1967).

Vardaman, George T. "How to Develop a Communication System," *ICIE Reporting,* 10–11 (January 1964). [19]

Weisman, Herman M. "Problems in Meaning," *Proceedings of the 1964 Institute in Technical and Industrial Communications,* Colorado State University, pp. 115–124. [6]

6

MANAGERIAL COMPETENCE

Having examined problem definition and communication capability, we are now ready to look at the third control dimension, managerial competence. Here we are concerned with the manager himself. For, whereas problem definition and communication capability are fundamentally *impersonal* processes, managerial competence is directed toward those elements that comprise the manager as a person.

We should remember that it is the manager *as a person* who must make judgments about problems, who must decide on the communication means needed to handle them, and who must put together the plans and programs that will give continuing control in the area under his surveillance. Stated a different way, managerial competence includes the manager's perceptual capacity, conceptual capacity, and operating style. These refer, respectively, to the manager's ability to sense correctly what is going on, to interpret properly and to make sound judgments about ongoing events, and to take effective action to handle discrepant situations.

Managerial competence can be examined using the following analytical factors: (*a*) intelligence; (*b*) experience, education, and training; (*c*) demonstrated skill; and (*d*) meeting organizational demands.

EVALUATION OF THE MANAGER'S INTELLIGENCE

By intelligence we mean the capacity of the manager to deal with words, ideas, things, and people in ways that maximize his effectiveness. When true, across-the-board managerial intelligence exists, not only do we find verbal fluency and ability in technical problem solving, but we also see respect for, and a sensitive response to, the needs of other human beings. Intelligence, then, is basically concerned with the manager's ability to *sense* correctly *what is going on.*

The analyst has many possible sources of information concerning managerial intelligence. Data can be derived from the *backgrounds* of those concerned; from reviewing *instruments* such as intelligence tests, psychological reports, interview reports, and recruiter evaluations; from *job evaluations* by supervisors, peers, and subordinates; and from *scholastic records*.

The analysis of intelligence can proceed by looking at: (*a*) specification of intelligence requirements; (*b*) determination of needed intelligence levels; and (*c*) existing intelligence levels.

Specification of Intelligence Requirements. If jobs have been properly specified, the intelligence level required for each will be indicated. Often the requirement is a very broad one, and it may be more implicit than explicit. Interviews with others, a review of the level of operations commonly undertaken, and comparisons with jobs of similar nature (which may be specified) will reveal the degree to which the characteristic should be present. Stating or deriving the level should be done in terms of the kind of measurement employed. For example, if an IQ measurement is going to be made, the requirement should be stated in terms of level or interval of IQ. If measurement on a particular test or examination is to be made, the requirement should be given, or converted, to those score values. For example, a requirement of "brilliant," if meaningful, may be satisfactory for executive recruitment, but the specification of an "IQ of 120" may be far more worthwhile for evaluating a new trainee.

The most basic considerations in examining specification of intelligence requirements are:

1. Some determination of required intelligence levels is made.
2. The levels are meaningful.
3. The levels are expressed so that they can be compared.
4. The levels are acceptable to users.

It should be noted that specifying levels of intelligence among *jobs* is merely the first step to determining how well *job-holders* are meeting those requirements.

The analyst probably assumes that if managerial job descriptions include intelligence requirements, recruitment has been done using this guideline. But he should also assume that wherever there are no specifications, intelligence as a specific factor has been ignored.

Determination of Needed Intelligence Levels. The analyst should judge whether it is feasible for the organization to determine intelligence requirements for jobs. And, further, he should judge the feasibility of determining how well an individual fits the requirements. As stated, levels should be expressed in meaningful terms.

A few guidelines which the analyst will find useful follow. Requirements for the job stem from organizational characteristics; requirements for the individual stem from his own personality. Moreover, if records are kept, the analyst can consider this as evidence that efforts are made to determine intelligence requirements. Another point to bear in mind is that some managerial jobs are very broad and undefined; others can be precisely stated. Furthermore, the higher the performance requirements and the less specific the performances required, the higher the intelligence level needed to fill the slot. Again, intelligence becomes a most important factor in jobs which either cannot be, or are not, described in terms of activities. Such jobs are usually set out in terms of the results desired. On the other hand, if the results can be translated into desired performances, emphasis on selection and recruitment can be shifted to background or skill. Not only does this suggest better organizational planning, but it also gives higher reliability of selection relative to requirements. Finally, it should be remembered that intelligence, as we define it here, is probably the most costly of all managerial characteristics to purchase.

Determination of Existing Intelligence Levels. According to the needs of the organization, and according to the assessment of organizational managers, the analyst should be able to judge whether managerial intelligence is too high or too low. It should be noted that a man can be assigned to a job that is too small for him just as he can be assigned "over his head." This will be reflected in personnel costs. It goes without saying that a man assigned to what he perceives as a trivial job is a person likely to leave the organization. It is equally clear that a man who is over his head is a candidate for ulcers, defeat, and eventual loss. In the process he will no doubt cost the outfit money in poor decisions.

The analyst must be concerned also with how intelligence is allocated throughout the organization. Is it properly distributed? Are managers of high intelligence apparently wallowing in subordinate positions or departments of little consequence? Are important positions and departments staffed by those of lower potential? These questions take the long-range view. It is quite probable that in training programs, or in a period of crisis, talent may be assigned to projects or functions on a "crash" or vestibule training basis. In any event misallocation of talent throughout the organization is prima facie evidence that, somewhere at the top, management intelligence or skill is suspect; this is itself a symptom for serious concern.

EVALUATION OF EXPERIENCE, EDUCATION, AND TRAINING

It is apparent that more often than not individuals cannot be recruited on the basis of intelligence. Recruiting characteristics more frequently considered are experience, education, and training. By experience we mean that part of a manager's background covering past performance and activities bearing on job qualifications other than formal academic history. By education we mean formal schooling, such as whether the manager is a high school or college graduate or possessor of an advanced degree. Training refers to skill, job, or professional experience, usually related to a particular performance or a specific firm.

To be sure, there is some difficulty in separating the effects of experience, education, and training on an individual, and it is for that reason that we consider them as a group here. Further, there are some complementary contributions. A highly trained or well-educated man is of lesser value than another until he gains experience and makes meaningful that which he has learned. Moreover, recency of education is usually of greater value to a man who has had experience in the field than to another who is without it. For the analyst to evaluate adequately these three requires understanding trade-offs among them. To what extent is one more important than another? To what degree can education be substituted for training? Does existence of one characteristic suggest that risks can be taken on another, with the expectation that competence will routinely develop? Recruiters ordinarily do not hire new college graduates on the basis of their work experience. Neither does industry seek company directors on the basis of recency of their education. A reasonable balance must be determined.

In order to evaluate experience, education, and training, the analyst should examine (a) specification of requirements; (b) compatibility between requirements and organization needs; (c) existing levels; (d) balance throughout the firm; and (e) development and training for management.

Specification of Requirements. When considerable turnover in managerial positions has occurred, it generally results in organizational specification of required levels of experience, education, and training. Such specification is necessary for recruitment, promotion, and for training into jobs. Certain organizations with highly developed personnel servicing systems (e.g., those under Civil Service categories) are known for their careful and exact specifications. Within all organizations the lower-level jobs are likely to be better specified than those above them. It follows that older, more institutionalized firms are apt to have more carefully laid out descriptions. When requirements are adequately stated, the problem is merely one of reviewing them for adequacy and comparing them with the qualifications of the incumbents. When specifications are missing, it becomes the analyst's chore, through interview, job analysis, and further organizational review, to determine what they really are, or what they should be.

Compatibility between Requirements and Organization Needs. Certain managerial job requirements, particularly those in professional or technical areas, may be the result of pressure applied by specialist groups rather than the result of meeting bona fide organizational needs. In this respect it may be ultimately necessary to either bring the level down to earth or revise faulty management perspective.

Professional groups having their own requirements include engineers, accountants, attorneys, medical doctors, and dentists. In addition, unions and trade associations are able to mold certain jobs to an extreme degree. And, at other times, legal requirements as established by public laws or ordinances may take precedence over basic organizational demands. In any event the analyst must examine to what degree the requirement of all jobs is overstated or understated. Just as it is too expensive to meet artificially elevated requirements, so is it also fatal to ignore a requirement which is crucial to the firm.

Existing Levels. Having determined what levels are best and proper for the organization, one must next examine how well the requirements are fulfilled by people occupying the jobs. The basic question is "Are managers on the job underqualified or overqualified in terms of experience, education, and training?" In answering this question, the analyst should first compare personnel records showing each man's qualifications with the organizational chart enumerating what each job requires. Of course some judgment must be used in determining whether a certain deviation is critical, or whether one qualification may compensate for a shortage in another. Certainly for new, lower-level employees, one must expect a rather low experience factor. And for new manager-trainees being routed through a series of experiences which are to be of later benefit, underassignment or "overqualification on the job" is temporarily to be expected. There may also be situational requirements which result in occasional misplacements. What is important is not that a few such cases exist, but whether misassignment is the *rule*.

Balance throughout the Firm. Each individual manager should have a proper balance of experience, education, and training. Just as important, there should not be certain units that have the lion's share of talent while others are poor. Not only should this be true on the basis of *general* qualification levels, but also there should be balance among all three characteristics. For example, a department may have a staff of highly educated managers, but few with any experience. Another may have an experienced group, no members of which have had requisite recent training in current methods. Granted there are times when these conditions are in fact the best ones for the firm, which could rationalize such a distribution and thereby remove any stigma from the management who decreed it. However, we are here trying to determine the *evaluation* of the situation, and if the situation is bad simply because it cannot be improved, this does not make it good.

Development and Training for Management. Here the analyst raises this basic question: Is there a need for education, training, or development of organizational managers, and is that need being met? There is almost always a need for some sort of indoctrination, if only to integrate the individual into the firm. And, as the man develops, or as the firm develops new demands and goals, new training or development may be required. Promotions, transfers, and job changes generate the need for programs designed to facilitate the shifts.

Therefore, training and development programs should meet both present and anticipated needs of the firm. These programs must also be seen as beneficial by the trainees themselves and must be demonstrated to be so. It is far too costly to train where training is unnecessary, or to train in the wrong direction, but it is probably more costly to incur obsolescence among managers, upon whose performance survival of the organization depends to a large degree. The existence of a well-developed program is evidence in itself that management at some level has examined its needs, and that it has taken steps to meet them. And this is a mark in its favor. Where no program exists, the analyst must determine whether one is really needed, and, if so, the nature and seriousness of the omission.

EVALUATING DEMONSTRATED SKILL

By demonstrated skill we refer to the manager's showing (*a*) how well he works with, and listens to, people; (*b*) how well he works with the techniques and tools necessary to his job; and (*c*) how well he works with the ideas and concepts needed for his firm's survival. More familiarly, this can be broken down into the *administrative activities* expected of him: planning, organizing, staffing, directing, and controlling. True, some authorities add to or delete from this list, but it is essentially complete. For how well a man plans depends on his skill with people, ideas, and tools; and how well he controls depends on the same triad. It is most common to judge and evaluate managers on the basis of their demonstrated activities, and most rating scales include the five functions listed.

Of course, skill cannot be divorced from intelligence, experience, or training. However, skills are more readily observable and measurable. Furthermore, a manager's skill is directly tied to his day-to-day success or failure. Estimates of intelligence are broad and indirect; the value of experience, education, and training can be only approximate. But any experienced executive can estimate the skill levels of his people with a fair degree of confidence. Thus the evaluation of managerial skill, man by man, is operationally possible and is commonly done. Why? Because it results in a computation that is understandable in terms of getting the job done. Skill, then, is reflected in a manager's success in planning, organizing, staffing, directing, and controlling. It is simply a judgment about how he performs managerial tasks.

An analysis of demonstrated skill involves examination of records, validity of evaluations, recorded adequacy, and specific deficiencies.

Records. Managers' personnel records should include an estimate of the level of their managerial skills. How well does the manager carry out his functions of planning, organizing, staffing, directing, and controlling? This is a question which inevitably forms a part of every periodic evaluation, and it is the recorded answers that are sought here. Managers should be individually evaluated at every organizational level. The absence of evaluations may be a two-pronged problem: (*a*) the organization, at some levels, is not exercising control, and (*b*) the analyst's job of evaluating general skill levels is made infinitely more difficult.

Validity of Evaluations. How well do existing evaluations actually represent the skill levels in the organization? There should be some relationship between high skill levels and effective performance, or between low skill levels and problematic results. Such a relationship is only suggestive of validity, however. Since it is very difficult to determine the absolute validity of the evaluations, it is probably better for the analyst to determine first whether evaluations are performed in a *systematic,* reasonable fashion. Does halo effect appear to exist? Is there evidence of rater bias in any particular group of ratings? Can the analyst ascertain departmental differences which are out of line with probability? If the manner of making the estimates is sound and in accordance with standard personnel practices, a certain amount of validity can probably be assumed.

Recorded Adequacy. A given manager's record may show him to be average, suitable, or adequate so far as his skill levels are concerned. Yet he may not be doing the job expected of him by the organization. This may be because he is incompetent, or because he is unaware of how he is doing, or because he has not been inspired to develop himself. Regardless of the reason behind it, the important symptom here is that the manager's actual skill performance (regardless of his skill qualifications) is not being made a matter of record. Here, too, a lack of records of skill performance is basic evidence of inadequate control on someone's part, pointing, perhaps, to other areas of managerial problems. A running record of skill deficiencies throughout the organization is an invaluable tool: it may act to revise recruiting or training needs; it may point to different types of skills needed; or it may suggest that the wrong types of individuals are managing or being managed.

Specific Deficiencies. The total balance sheet of skills and needs within the unit may show no glaring deficiencies. But the analyst must examine the situation more closely. The assignment of personnel to accomplish managerial tasks may cause some departments, some projects, or some levels of organizations to be underqualified or overqualified. Often managers who are particularly skillful are channeled into staff or headquarters locations, leaving operational areas relatively barren of qualified supervision. Then, too, there may be a hoarding of skills in some department or committee group, especially where an executive of some power has the ability to do this. Furthermore, some departments or units, which once competed poorly for talent, may not attract highly skilled managers. These factors, among many others, act to skew the apportionment of managerial skills throughout the organization.

Particular attention should be given to the allocation of *needed* managerial skills throughout the firm. Different areas and different levels require different kinds of skills. For example, there are needs for highly developed personal skills where face-to-face dealings among individuals are common. And there are needs for highly developed conceptual skills among certain types of staff. In evaluating the severity of a deficiency, the question to be asked is: Are the skills present in the managers and in the departments in the proportions needed?

EVALUATION OF MEETING ORGANIZATIONAL DEMANDS

In the last analysis, managerial success must be measured in terms of how well a manager meets the needs of his organization. Irrespective of how well he measures up on intelligence or experience, education, and training or demonstrated skills, the acid test of a manager's merit is whether he is successful in promoting the organization and its goals. An analysis of meeting organizational demands may be made by looking at these dimensions: organizational specification; success and failure records; informing managers of success and failure; and meeting all demands.

Organizational Specification. What are managers expected to do? If organizational demands are specified, either in terms of results expected or in terms of the people and tasks required to meet ends, it is a fairly good indication that an effective approach is taken to meet them. If demands are not set out, or if they are stated in vague, amorphous, nonoperational terms, one can almost guarantee that they are going to remain unsatisfied.

The demands an organization makes on a particular manager, when properly stated, become in fact a statement of that manager's job. And since the manager himself is usually in the best position to know what is required, the statement of demands on him is even better if he has participated in the interpretation and communication of organizational expectations. In any event an organization that does not know what it requires from its managers cannot judge their performances. As far as the analyst is concerned, if specification of demands is lacking, further evaluation of managers' successes or failures is very uncertain.

Success and Failure Records. Assuming that the purposes and specific goals of the organization are clearly stated, there should also be a box score of how well each manager is meeting his goal or target. If records are not kept, it may well be that standards are not understood, and this in itself is evidence that management deficiencies exist somewhere up the line. This should alert the analyst to other possible problem areas.

Success and failure records can be very valuable. Totaling up the success/failure rate from period to period is therapeutic to a manager: it helps in motivation; it is educational; and it points to areas of needed training or help.

Informing Managers of Success and Failure. The analyst's basic question here is: Are managers kept informed about their successes and failures in meeting organizational demands? Records of managerial accomplishments are largely academic if the managers are not made aware of them. But when properly communicated to managers, these records become the means whereby good performance can be recognized and poor performance can be improved. Furthermore, the very process of informing managers about their performance partly assures a refinement of the statements about their work.

Where no communication appears to exist between managers and their supervisors, the analyst should suspect a deficiency in personal or technical skills at upper levels. Indeed, he may properly conclude a real gap in organizational communication, for feedback to managers about their performance is essential if a unit is to maintain proper control. And it goes without saying that failure to tell people where they stand will result in apprehensions, lowered performance, and high attrition rates. The analyst will almost invariably find a high correlation between these symptoms and a lack of information by managers about their meeting organizational demands.

Meeting All Demands. Does the manager meet the demands of *all* members of the organization? That is, does he fulfill the needs not only of his superiors but also of his peers, co-workers, and subordinates? An organization is an aggregation of different demands, each of which must be met in context with the others. Thus the manager who optimizes the complete complex of pressures placed upon him is the successful manager.

The manager who optimizes is the one who satisfies each demand to the extent that total organizational requirements are best met. For example, certain demands of stockholders may take precedence at one time but not at another. Or an emergency may dictate that standing orders should be temporarily waived. Or personal requirements of large, socially oriented groups may change the complexion of administrative directions, or even cause them to be interpreted differently according to the circumstance. And, of course, the manager who optimizes must recognize and meet the demands of both the personnel networks and output systems in the organization.

In a word, the *sine qua non* of the manager's success is his ability to satisfy the total complex of organizational demands placed upon him, and to be so perceived by those with power to sanction.

ALGORITHM TO EVALUATE MANAGERIAL COMPETENCE

As with both problem definition and communication capability, we present in Figure 6.1 an algorithm for use in evaluating the level of managerial competence in the organization.

Rationale of the Algorithm

As with the two preceding algorithms, the algorithm for evaluation of managerial competence places elements in an ascending order of importance. The factors are weighted from 1 to 4 in the same way. The weightings are explained as follows: *intelligence* (1) at an optimal level either

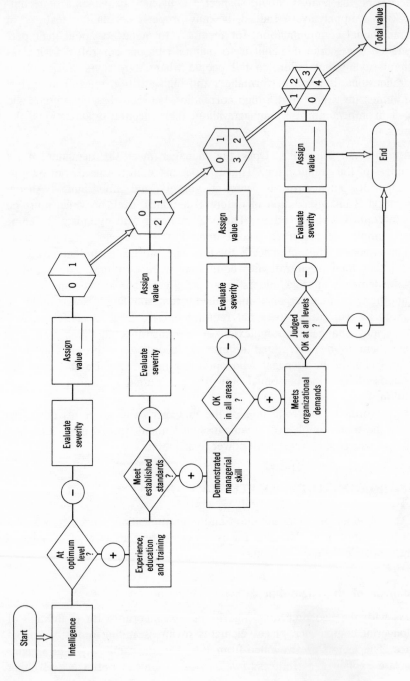

Figure 6.1. Algorithm for analysis of managerial competence.

exists or not. Standards are relatively easy to specify and to use in order to discern whether the organization possesses this managerial characteristic as required; *experience, education,* and *training* (2) constitute the means by which intelligence can be fashioned to meet organizational needs. This dimension is more important because it puts the person closer to the operational needs of the organization; *demonstrated managerial skill* (3) means that the manager can actually show adequacy in performing necessary functions, and this step is even closer to the operational needs of the organization. Meets *organizational demands* (4) has the highest weighting because this is the payoff. Since the manager either does or does not meet the operational needs of the organization this is the real measure of managerial success.

Summating Values in the Algorithm

Summate, using the same procedures given for the preceding algorithms.

SUMMARY

Managerial competence includes the elements by which the manager as a person defines problems, brings to bear the necessary communication capability, and executes control to accomplish his objectives. Managerial competence can be evaluated by considering intelligence; experience, education, and training; demonstrated skill; and meeting organizational demands.

We have explained here how all of these can be examined. We have presented an algorithm for evaluating each, together with the method to arrive at a total index of the level of managerial competence in the organization.

BIBLIOGRAPHY

Andrew, Gwen. "An Analytic System Model for Organization Theory," *Journal of Academy of Management,* 190–198 (September 1965). [22] *

Argyris, Chris. *Personality and Organization.* New York: Harper and Brothers, 1957.

Barnard, Chester I. *The Functions of the Executive.* Cambridge, Mass.: Harvard University Press, 1938.

Burack, Elmer H. "Technology and Some Aspects of Industrial Supervision: A Model

* Number in brackets refers to reading number in "Related Readings" section of this book.

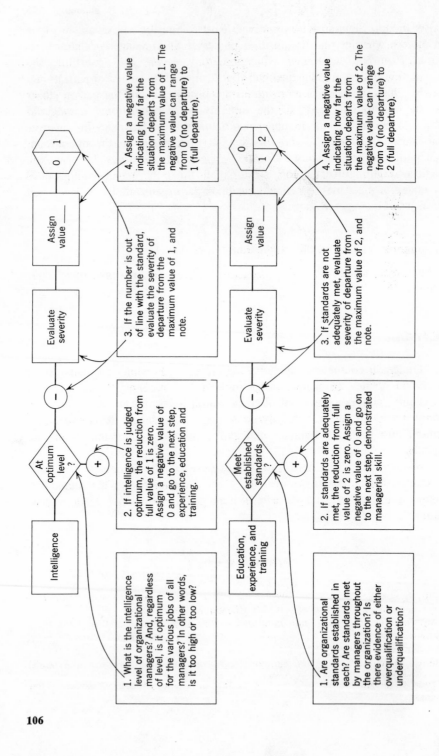

Intelligence

At optimum level?

1. What is the intelligence level of organizational managers? And, regardless of level, is it optimum for the various jobs of all managers? In other words, is it too high or too low?

2. If intelligence is judged optimum, the reduction from full value of 1 is zero. Assign a negative value of 0 and go to the next step, experience, education and training.

Evaluate severity

3. If the number is out of line with the standard, evaluate the severity of departure from the maximum value of 1, and note.

Assign value ___

0   1

4. Assign a negative value indicating how far the situation departs from the maximum value of 1. The negative value can range from 0 (no departure) to 1 (full departure).

Education, experience, and training

Meet established standards?

1. Are organizational standards established in each? Are standards met by managers throughout the organization? Is there evidence of either overqualification or underqualification?

2. If standards are adequately met, the reduction from full value of 2 is zero. Assign a negative value of 0 and go on to the next step, demonstrated managerial skill.

Evaluate severity

3. If standards are not adequately met, evaluate severity of departure from the maximum value of 2, and note.

Assign value ___

0
1   2

4. Assign a negative value indicating how far the situation departs from the maximum value of 2. The negative value can range from 0 (no departure) to 2 (full departure).

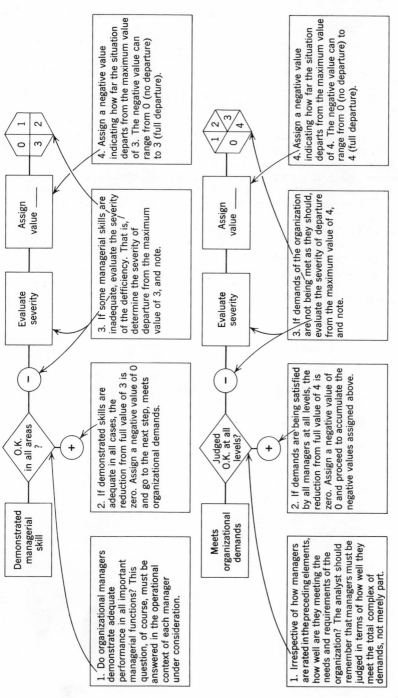

Figure 6.2. Use of the algorithm.

107

Building Approach," *Journal of Academy of Management,* 43–66 (March 1966). [26]

Cummings, Larry L. "Managerial Effectiveness I: Formulating a Research Strategy," *Journal of Academy of Management,* 29–42 (March 1966). [12]

Dale, Ernest. *Management Theory and Practice.* New York: McGraw-Hill Book Company, 1965.

Haberstroh, Chadwick J. "Control as an Organizational Process," *Management Science,* 165–171 (January 1960). [8]

Mayo, Elton. *The Social Problems of an Industrial Civilization.* Boston, Mass.: Graduate School of Business Administration, Harvard University, 1945.

Roethlisberger, F. J. and William J. Dickson. *Management and the Worker.* Cambridge, Mass.: Harvard University Press, 1939.

Rubenstein, Albert H. and Chadwick J. Haberstroh, Eds. *Some Theories of Organization.* Homewood, Ill.: The Dorsey Press, 1960.

Simon, Herbert A. *Administrative Behavior.* New York: The Macmillan Company, 1957.

Smith, Alfred G. "The Organization Man and the Research Man," *Communication and Status: The Dynamics of a Research Center.* Eugene, Ore.: University of Oregon: 1966, pp. 29–38. [25]

Thompson, Victor A. *Modern Organization.* New York: Alfred A. Knopf, 1961.

Urwick, Lyndall F. *The Pattern of Management.* Minneapolis, Minn.: University of Minnesota Press, 1956.

7

THE MANAGER: ORGANIZATIONAL
DIAGNOSIS AND DESIGN

REVIEW

Before moving ahead we shall briefly review some ideas of the preceding chapters. This will help the reader to refresh his memory; further it will give an integrated base from which to proceed to the focal point of this chapter: the manager in organizational diagnosis and design.

This book attempts to do what has not been adequately done before: to put into systematic and operational form many disparate and discrete thoughts vital to an understanding of managers, communication, and control in organizations.

It is a truism that managers control organizations to the extent that communication permits, but such a statement needs further definition. *Managers* are those who allocate or allot resources. *Communication* is the flow of material, information, perceptions, and understandings between the various parts and members of an organization. *Control* includes the planning, adjustment, and correction of parts in a situation in order to achieve ends or objectives. In short, managerial activity is dependent on an organization's total communicability to provide problem solving and guidance. Through such an intimate and delicate relationship is control maintained.

Theories Underlying Managerial Control. To fully describe the place of management, communication, and problem solving in organizations, it is necessary for several theoretical areas to be combined into a conceptual framework. These areas are *problem theory and practice, communication theory and practice,* and *managerial theory and practice.* Together they subsume a large number of specific approaches such as decision making, system and process theory, and human relations. Most schools of manage-

Major Theoretical Areas	Subdivisions
I. Problem theory and practice	Generalized faculty Prescribed patterns Mathematical models Machine systems
II. Communication theory and practice	Personal communication Mass communication Organizational communication Communication systems
III. Managerial theory and practice	Administrative activities orientation Task orientation Human relations orientation Organizational orientation

Figure 7.1. A conceptual framework for managerial activity.

ment thought draw heavily on the various ideas outlined in Figure 7.1, although they see them in different configurations. Some ways in which theoreticians believe them to interact are shown in Figure 7.2. The authors believe that schemes that are restricted to fragmentary parts of the three basic areas explain incompletely how managerial problems in organizations are identified and solved.[1]

Figure 7.2d best represents a unified theory of management. Managerial control properly occupies a position of centrality since it is the manager who makes things happen. It is not easy to explain how he does this, but a first step should point out the sensitive relationship between

1. The manager's perception of a situation.
2. His plans and procedures to handle it.
3. The communication necessary for him to understand and direct ongoing activities.

A second step is to recognize that a competent manager addresses himself unashamedly to the following questions:

1. How do materials, information, perceptions, and understandings flow between the various parts and members of my organization?
2. In what way do the characteristics of participants affect organizational communication?
3. How are the arrangements of the parts (including the members) important?

Answers to such vital queries—important if the manager is to maintain control—are made easier to obtain through the medium of a "networks/

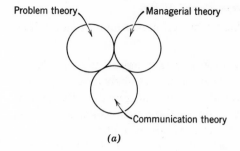

Problem theory

Managerial theory

Communication theory

(a)

Figure 7.2. Theories of management.

(a) A traditional approach to management. The traditional approach treats the areas discretely and assumes that the manager will understand organizations if he understands the areas separately. Little attempt is made in the literature to show more than tangency of the areas of interest.

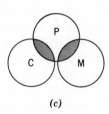

(b)

(b) The human relations approach to management. Here much is made of the relationship between the manager and how he communicates in terms of human problems. Concern centers on *personal relationships* (from communication theory), and on *generalized faculty* (from problem theory), both of which are handled through *administrative activities* (managerial theory).

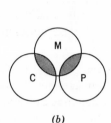

(c)

(c) The systems approach to management. Most of the literature dealing with the "systems approach" concerns itself with the relationship between *communication systems* (from communication theory) and *machine systems* (from problem theory), in an *organizational orientation* (from managerial theory). The manager is implicitly recognized to be involved in problems, but since he is difficult to deal with as a system entity, his presence is only cursorily treated.

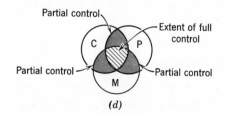

Partial control

Extent of full control

Partial control

Partial control

(d)

(d) An integrated approach to management. Each of schemes a to c presents a limited perspective of managerial activity. The idea this book advances is that all aspects of the three conceptual ideas must be interrelated.

111

systems" model of organizations. Such a model aids in understanding how organizations work.

Theories Underlying Organizations. A *networks* model assumes an organization to be a constellation of person-to-person networks, whereas a *systems* model views an organization as an integrated collection of mechanical schemes. Emphasis of a *networks* model is placed on the characteristics and attributes of *members*; in a *systems* model attention is directed to the *output facilitated* by each arrangement. Networks are classified as *social, specialist, administrative,* and *problem-solving;* systems are called *performance, informative, transactional,* and *innovative.* It is important to note that the networks, which are collectively exhaustive, are not mutually exclusive. Systems, on the other hand, are both mutually exclusive and collectively exhaustive.

Understanding Organizations Through the Model. To one peering from the networks perspective, an organization is seen in terms of its personnel interaction patterns. Here the analyst focuses on the communication activity of individual participants and on their psychology and sociology, since the application of such a model centers on humans as network nodes.

Alternatively, from the systems perspective an organization is conceived as an integrated set of input-process-output arrangements, each making its own demands on and contributions to total unit activity. Here the communication activities under scrutiny are largely those of material *flow:* they focus on inputs and outputs, operations, the adequacy of channels, and the mechanical relations between the parts.

Membership and Structure in the Model. As stated, the focus of the networks model is on the human factors therein. In contrast, the systems model highlights the structural aspects of organization. This is not to say that there are no structural features to the networks, for there are; and it is not to say that there are no human entities as parts of systems, for there are these also. But the two concepts of *membership* and *structure* characterize different halves of the dichotomy.

At the risk of oversimplification, the networks outlook may be said to follow the outlook taken by industrial social psychologists, and the systems outlook follows that taken by information theorists and rhochrematicians.[2] The analogies, admittedly incomplete, are meant to illustrate major differences, not to provide descriptions.

Assessing the System State (Measuring Managerial Control)

The preceding theories aid the analyst in understanding organizations better and guide him in intelligent diagnosis and design. But when is di-

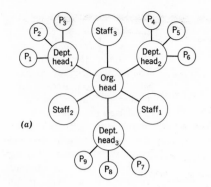

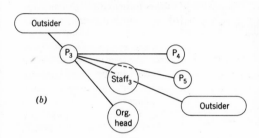

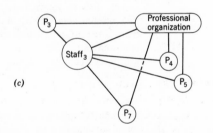

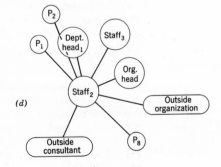

Figure 7.3. Components of the networks model.

(a) *An administrative network.* This chart shows, in a simplified way, the "official" relationships of people in an organization. It shows all members as they relate to each other so long as they act in their prescribed roles.

(b) *A social network.* This shows the interaction pattern between members in, say, a bowling team. Although most of the members are members of the larger organization, there are two "outsiders" involved. In this social net it is apparent that P₃ is the leader, even though the team contains others with higher "official" statuses.

(c) *A specialist network.* Here is shown the interaction pattern between members who are, say, clinical psychologists in the larger organization. Staff₃ appears to be the leader. However, the common contact with the outside professional organization implies a greater allegiance. Importantly, this connection provides for transaction between the larger organization and others.

(d) *A problem-solving network.* Here is shown an interaction pattern between a problem-solver and others who have a contribution to the problem's solution. It is apparent that Staff₂ is the leader, or problem-solver, and that he is soliciting from and directing others, including some outside contacts and the organization's administrative head.

113

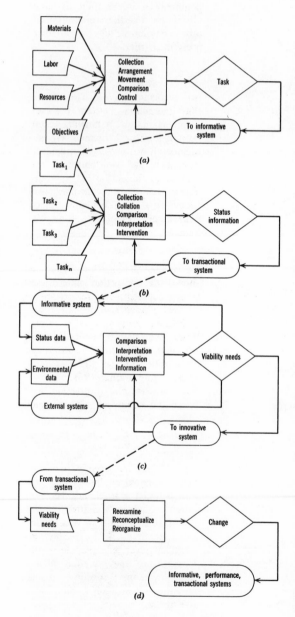

Figure 7.4. Components of the systems model.

(*a*) *A performance system.* As inputs the performance system has one or many of such things as materials, labor, resources. These inputs are converted into some task. This output is fed into the informative system where it is collated and compared with other performance systems' outputs. Adjustment of each performance system can be made by the informative system.

(*b*) *An informative system.* Tasks from individual performance systems provide inputs to the informative system. These inputs are converted into internal organizational balance (or awareness of its lack). Internal status information is fed into the transactional system.

(*c*) *A transactional system.* Inputs from the informative system (about internal activity) are combined with data from other organizations (the environment). These inputs are processed into outputs of "awarenesses of needed change." These *viability needs* may trigger demands of the informative system, or of external systems or both. If these systems are incapable of adequate response, the innovative system is set into motion.

(*d*) *An innovative system.* Viability needs (changes required for survival) are the inputs here. The process is essentially a hierarchy of (1) reexamination of existing entities; (2) reconceptualization of existing entities; and (3) reorganizing existing entities. The process is applied, in turn, to the informative, performance, and transactional systems. Whenever adequacy is reached the innovative system ceases operation.

agnosis required? When is managerial activity necessary in a particular situation? How urgently are correctives needed?

The state of a system determines the amount and kind of intervention to be taken. To see whether managerial activity is required, and if so, what kind, the manager should determine the level of control that exists. Fortunately, by computing a control index, this is made a relatively simple matter.

Variables Relevant to Determining Control. Problem definition, communication capability, and managerial competence are the three basic variables to be weighed in determining whether any administered organizational requires adjustment.[3] Taken together, they are able to serve as a measure of the control state of the organization. The validity of the control index concept does not depend on acceptance of the networks/systems model of organization, but it is entirely compatible with it, as will be seen later.

Managerial Competence as a Variable. Whether the analyst sees an organization as a collection of networks or as a hierarchy of systems, managerial problem solving is of prime concern. For the *manager* (as an allocator, problem solver) enjoys membership in the problem-solving network—when seen from the one approach—and operates in the innovative system—when seen from the other.

Communication Capability as a Variable. Communication, further, is another central variable, governing both how well members relate to each other in networks and how well systems correlate in their arrangements and flows.

Problem Definition as a Variable. Last, it is crucial both to understand the drives motivating the formation of interpersonal patterns and to define the underlying situations calling for specific outputs of systems. In other words, the *definition of problems,* along with the *manager* and *communication,* form the triad of general variables in any control scheme.

Assessment of the control variables is done by evaluating observable process dimensions as shown in Figure 7.5. In simple situations the analyst may assign values directly. In complex ones he utilizes additional shredouts of the dimensions shown. Thus it is feasible to compute an index of organizational efficiency by determining the joint relationship among *managerial competence, communication capability,* and *problem definition.* This can be done for any collectivity, whether it is a firm, a department, or a total administered organization. Comparison of the index with the evaluator's expectations tells him whether he has a situation meriting still deeper investigation and repair. If he has such a situation, the

Variable Being Assessed	Observable Process Dimensions
Managerial competence	Perception, conception, style
Communication capability	Cueing, carrying out, critiquing
Problem Definition	Symptoms, syndromes, problem defining

Figure 7.5. Components of control index computation.

theoretical areas of problem theory, communication theory, and managerial theory will furnish further guides to his performance.

What Information a Control Index Provides. A control index may be computed at two different levels. A rough aggregative index, such as would result from attention only to the broad process dimensions indicated in Figure 7.5, gives the manager a gross measurement of his control. Yet even at this level a number of required adjustments become obvious. A more precise figure, such as that which can be arrived at through more rigorous auditing methods, provides information for finer and more complex organizational adjustments.

Certainly, if an index figure is below what has been determined to be safe, there is an indication that change is needed. In addition, some general areas of weakness can be inferred. For example, if *problem definition* has earned a value at or near perfect, attention should probably be first directed toward managers or communication. On the other hand, if *communication capability* has earned a perfect or nearly perfect score, it is unlikely that significant gains in control will be made by focusing attention in that direction. Conversely, if an area earns a very low score, it may well be that major faults exist there.

Index values, then, suggest where the manager may make his most significant gains. They aid him in attending promptly to areas most needing his concern.

THE RELATIONSHIP OF MEMBERSHIP AND STRUCTURE TO FACTORS OF CONTROL

As mentioned, a control index can be computed either for a total organization or for each of its parts. Comparisons show where and how priorities for further in-depth managerial activity should be established. In other words, the index values tell the analyst

1. Certain organizations or departments need servicing more urgently than others; and

2. Within those organizations or departments, certain broad areas are of most immediate concern.

Should further in-depth analysis and design be required, it must be done through a practical system having a valid theoretical foundation. The basis for such a system is found in the relationships between the control index variables and the networks/systems model, as shown in Figure 7.6.

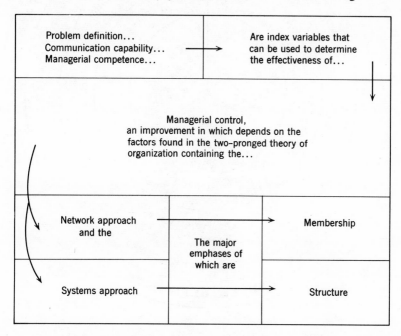

Figure 7.6. Control related to organization theory.

Interrelationships Among the Index Variables

As shown in Figure 7.6, the index variables can be used to determine the effectiveness of managerial control. We now describe each variable and relate each to the attributes of *membership* and *structure*. Figure 7.7 shows the factors of control in such a way that the evolutionary logic connecting the variables is apparent. The verbal descriptions are attempts to further clarify and rationalize those relationships.[4]

Managerial Competence. This basically depends on the sensitivity of the problem solver to the environment around him. This sensitivity is

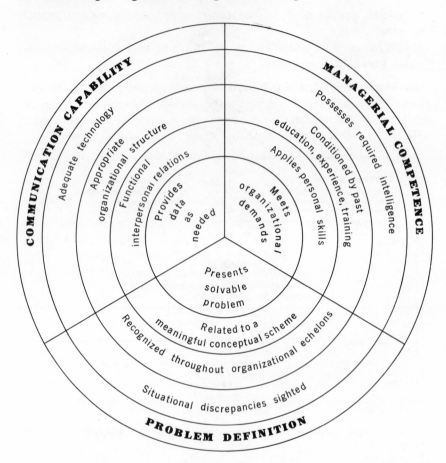

Figure 7.7. Interrelationships among the control index variables.

called *intelligence*. A manager's intelligence is further conditioned by his education, experience, and training in a way that should improve his on-the-job potential. But these potentials—until made real by action—are only attitudinal. There is an acid test of "how well the manager performs" that is reflected in his observable skills. And regardless of all else, he must meet the organization's demands—demands of peers, supervisors, subordinates—to be fully successful.

Communication Capability. Communication capability rests on the organization's technology. This can be thought of as the "wherewithal" by means of which data may be conveyed. How this technology is exploited depends greatly on how efficiently the parts of the organization are related or *structured*. And since the critical nodes within a human organization are the humans themselves, only some constructive interpersonal relations will prevent dysfunctional bottlenecking of data, regardless of the adequacy and sophistication of the technology and shape. Finally, data must be brought to and from the necessary locations, for what good are data about one problem if they are available only at the site of another?

Problem Definition. This depends upon discrepancies first being sighted. If they are never seen, nothing more will be done. After they are sighted, they must be recognized for what they are (discrepancies); and they must be recognized both wherever and whenever they occur. Yet all of this still signifies little unless these symptoms are made meaningful by collation and relation to a conceptual scheme. In other words the symptoms must be made *informative*. Further, any problem recognized must ultimately be stated in some solvable form. For if it remains so vague that the manager —the organization's problem-solver—can do nothing with it, it will never be corrected.

Thus it can be seen that these "factors of control" are logically related in a sequence of (*a*) a solvable problem, together with (*b*) data adequate to solve it, to which is added (*c*) a problem solver capable of action. The factors of control are also intimately related to the concepts of membership and structure, two primary features of the network/systems organizational model, in an input-output orientation. A discussion of this relationship follows.

Factors of Control and Process (Input-Output Orientation)

The manager is related to the real world through the problem and pertinent data. He is part of a *process,* converting input (a problem) to output (a solution, or change). This input-output orientation is a meaningful one, and it adequately shows the manager's place in problem solving. But the same approach can be used to demonstrate how *intelligence, technology,* and the *situation*—the three inputs to managerial control—are converted through the organizational media of "structure" and "membership" to the ideal outputs of *solvable problems, needed data,* and *meeting organizational demands.* The relationships are shown in Figure 7.8.

Inputs and Outputs Related to Membership and Structure

Much of the preceding material dealt with how an analyst, or manager, could determine levels of performance or effectiveness within a particular organization. Our focus now shifts to a much higher level of abstraction, and the three control factors are shown to be variables interacting with

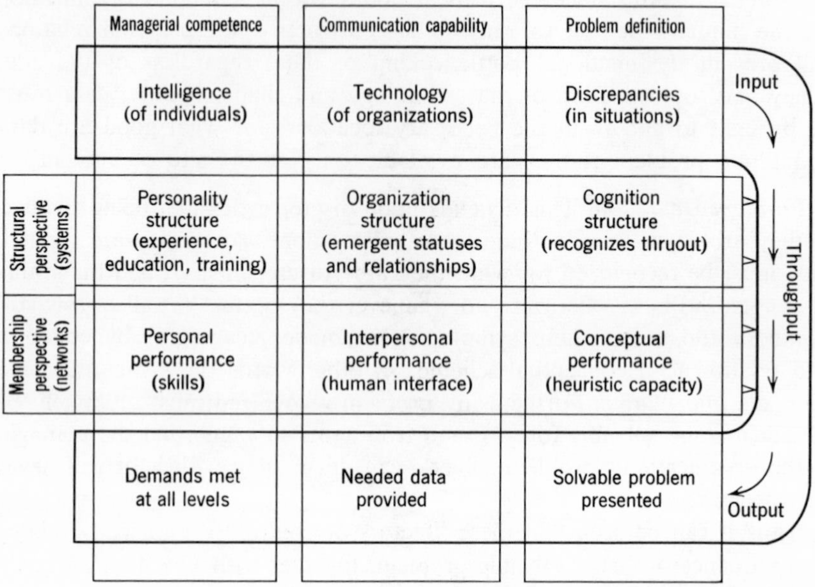

	Managerial competence	Communication capability	Problem definition	
	Intelligence (of individuals)	Technology (of organizations)	Discrepancies (in situations)	Input
Structural perspective (systems)	Personality structure (experience, education, training)	Organization structure (emergent statuses and relationships)	Cognition structure (recognizes thruout)	Throughput
Membership perspective (networks)	Personal performance (skills)	Interpersonal performance (human interface)	Conceptual performance (heuristic capacity)	
	Demands met at all levels	Needed data provided	Solvable problem presented	Output

Figure 7.8. Input-output orientation of the control index factors.

membership and *structure*. This awareness broadens our evolving conceptual base which (*a*) is rooted in problem, communication, and managerial theories; (*b*) is made meaningful and pragmatic in the relationships between managerial competence, communication capability, and problem definition, and (*c*) is now put in context with the organizational attributes of membership and structure.[5]

Inputs Related to Membership and Structure. The raw materials, or inputs, to organizational activity consist of members in a certain cultural setting and in a particular situation. In other words we have (*a*) individuals of certain intelligence, (*b*) a certain level of technology available to the collectivity, and (*c*) a situation more or less discrepant. It should not be necessary to suggest that a nondiscrepant situation will not motivate action. Situations we are interested in are those from which managerial activity develops, so we will assume that change is desired.

Process (Throughputs) Related to Membership and Structure. The impact of structure is felt in all three areas. For example, the structuring of the problem solver (i.e., his experience, education, and training) affects his activities; it facilitates and/or impedes his approaches. The structuring of the organization (including both the formal or "desired" arrangements and the informal or "emergent" relationships) enables and/or impairs goal-related activities. And the degree of congruence between the discrepancy patterns and the cognitive structure employed throughout the particular unit determines how well the situation is apprehended and cognized.

The impact of membership, or "human characteristics," is also felt in all three of the areas. For example, a manager will have a "performance personality"; that is to say, he himself—as a human being—is an intervening variable between his experience and training and the demonstrated performance of his skills. Variations in the interface efficiency among different humans are readily admitted. Each member is unique (despite common referents) and brings this unique contribution to the communication process. With regard to the conceptual performance necessary to convert recognized symptoms and syndromes to a meaningful problem, little need be said. Here is "thinking" at its most basic; here is the application of heuristic capacity which as of today only the "human" element can provide.

Outputs Related to Membership and Structure. What is the result of all this arrangement? Simply this: intelligence, technology, and discrepancies are processed under both the structural constraints and the membership constraints of the organization. Resulting from the type of throughput are (*a*) a solvable problem, (*b*) data brought to bear on it, and, finally, (*c*) the demands or needs of the organization being met.

THE RELATIONSHIP OF MEMBERSHIP AND STRUCTURE TO DIAGNOSIS AND DESIGN OF ORGANIZATIONS

Having considered the factors of control in relation to each other—and in relationship to membership and structure—we are ready to complete the picture by putting them into context with the combined networks/systems model. The first step is to relate the theoretical model to different kinds of organizations. The second step is to relate diagnosis and design to managerial perspective. From such vantage points we can then look at the operational procedures which make up managerial activity.

As has been stated, the networks/systems model avoids some conceptual limitations inherent in some other models which attempt to describe organizations by combining only *parts* of personnel models with *parts* of structural ones. In addition; either half of the networks/systems model provides a high level of analysis, since each accounts for an understanding of the four basic organizational needs: (*a*) accomplishing required activities; (*b*) maintaining unit stability and insuring continuance; (*c*) relating the unit to the world around it; and (*d*) adjusting things as needed for the organization's survival.

Yet, even more usefully, the two halves combined provide a higher level of analytical insight than either does separately. For example, an organization can be analyzed as a constellation of personnel networks, each with its own facilitating systems. Other applications are apparent.

The major contribution of the combined model is a better understanding of how organizations work. Still, it is also a keen analytical tool, which permits operationally specifying how the planning for and management of complex organizations relate both to human membership needs and to organizational output requirements.[6]

The Model Applied to Different Kinds of Organizations. The complexity of organizations is tied both to their purposes and to their resources. Simple, uncomplicated units, where well-established methods are employed, and where objectives are well-defined, present a trivial problem to the analyst. On the other hand, complex organizations with loosely defined or amorphous objectives are a major challenge.[7] Figure 7.9 depicts these ideas.

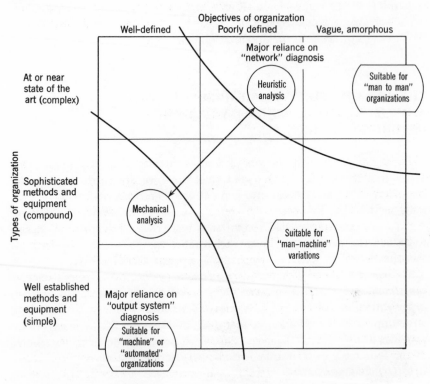

Figure 7.9. How the model applies to different kinds of organization.

DIAGNOSIS AND DESIGN OF ORGANIZATIONS

The primary approach to diagnosis and design of an organization must be consistent with the type of organization under surveillance. If the manager believes his organization is basically "a collection of people" he should approach it primarily as a biological fact. If he perceives his organization as basically a "structural entity" he should approach it as he would a machine.

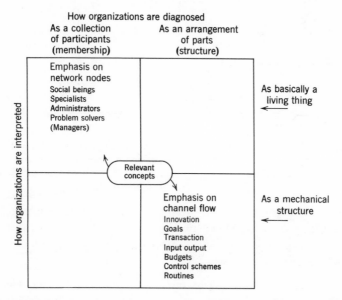

Figure 7.10. Managerial perspective and diagnosis. There are two logical approaches to organizational analysis. If only one is used, the method of interpretation must be compatible with the view taken. Ideally, both should be combined.

Approaches to Diagnosis. Figure 7.10 suggests how the manager should approach diagnosis. It implies that understanding man-to-man type organizations results mostly from heavy emphasis on *network analysis,* whereas understanding automated firms rests largely on an *output system* approach. The reader will rightly infer that many 50-50 situations require a balance of both. This shows that although there are some types of organizations where fairly adequate *analytical* insight may be attained through either approach, *design* demands more conceptual skill.

Approaches to Design. The means by which the manager should approach design are suggested in Figure 7.11.

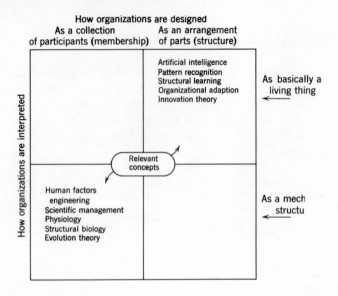

Figure 7.11. Managerial perspective and design. There is no single logical approach to designing organizations. They must be perceived as either living structures or man-machine situations. Theories underlying these approaches must be the bases of action.

Diagnosis Related to Design. From the foregoing it can be seen that for the manager to do a complete job, he must consider the organization as networks of human interaction in a constellation of adaptable systems.[8] This is demonstrated by Figure 7.12.

Summary of Significant Relationships. A number of new ideas have been established thus far. First, it was brought out that any adequate conceptual scheme for understanding management control in organizations must be erected on the three basic theoretical areas of problem theory, communication theory, and managerial theory. Within this framework a networks/systems model of organizations was described as the most adequate springboard for effective diagnosis and redesign. Then an evaluative device, the control index, was introduced as a vehicle available to the analyst to determine the adequacy of control—in other words, the tolerability of the present system state. That the three ideas were compatible was demonstrated by relating the various concepts to the organizational attributes of *membership* and *structure*. This interaction among control, membership, and structure is significant. It is basic to understanding the proper procedures for the analysis and redesign of organizations.

Although the preceding material has prepared the analyst for *measuring*

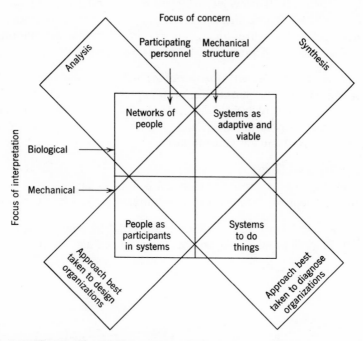

Figure 7.12. Diagnosis related to design. The complete scope of communication activity in administered organizations can be grasped by examining its two subsets present: (1) networks of people, and (2) systems of parts. On the other hand, in attempting to design communication systems for organizations, one must perceive units both (1) as adaptive and viable systems and (2) as people participating in this arena of systems.

his control level (and determining whether action is required) and has provided him with conceptual tools for *understanding* organizational activity (through the networks/systems model), it has not provided him with the requisite procedural guidelines for the necessary *approaches* (managerial activity) he must take. The following ideas are directed toward that need.

A Methodology for Diagnosis and Design

Earlier in this book it was pointed out that it is the manager who "makes things happen." But it was readily admitted that it is not easy to explain how he does this. At that time, the authors posited a sensitive relationship between the manager's perception of a situation, his plans and procedures to handle it, and the communication necessary for him to understand and direct ongoing activities. Following that, a number of ideas were presented which provided strong clues to understanding managers and organizations. Those theoretical insights must now be related to the sequence of activity which the manager—in allocating or allotting resources—follows in his process of diagnosis and design.

The General Sequence of Managerial Activity. The manager, in his diagnosis and design of organizations, draws upon all of the ideas previously introduced: the control index, the networks/systems model, and the underlying concepts of membership and structure. Essentially, the following questions are asked and answered in turn:

1. Is there a problem?
2. Which type of organizational model is appropriate?
3. In what sequence should the organizational entities be examined?

Is There a Problem? This question is answered by computing a control index. A flow chart of the operation looks something like Figure 7.13.

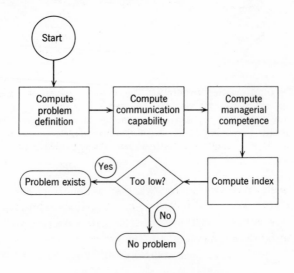

Figure 7.13. Is there a problem?

Recomputation of the index is not a major problem. When the index items are examined for the first time in a particular organization, a great deal of effort and care will be necessary. However, subsequent examinations will be shorter for the following reasons: (*a*) many items will change but little, and the changes will be easier to assess; (*b*) some items, historical in nature, will not change at all; and (*c*) familiarity with the organization, and its data sources, will tell the analyst where to look efficiently in subsequent assessments.

Which Type of Organizational Model is Appropriate? To answer this question sensibly, the manager simply determines whether he is dealing with an automated or an incompletely automated organization. If the unit under scrutiny is automated, the bulk of his problem is probably in the output systems. However, since no organization will be *completely* automatic, there is a high probability that network dysfunction will be found.

Logic suggests that system diagnosis take precedence if the answer to the question "Is the organization completely automatic?" is "Yes."

However, even if the answer to the question of automaticity is "No," logic still dictates first attention to system diagnosis and adjustment, with provision for subsequent attention to networks. Figure 7.14 suggests the rationale for this approach.

A COMPLEX ORGANIZATION

IF AUTOMATED (MACHINE ONLY)				IF INCOMPLETELY AUTOMATED (MAN-MACHINE)			
HAS SYSTEMS				HAS SYSTEMS			
Per-formance	Informa-tive	Trans-actional	Inno-vative	Per-formance	Informa-tive	Trans-actional	Inno-vative
WHICH MAY OR MAY NOT HAVE THEIR OWN SUBSYSTEMS				*and* HAS NETWORKS			
				Social	Special-ist	Adminis-trative	Problem-Solving
				EACH OF WHICH HAS ITS OWN SYSTEMS			
but HAS NO NETWORKS				Per-formance	Informa-tive	Trans-actional	Inno-vative
				EACH OF WHICH MAY OR MAY NOT CONTAIN PEOPLE IN OTHER NETS			

Figure 7.14. Which Type of Organizational Model is Appropriate?

If the organization or unit is completely automated:
- · It has systems
- · which may or may not have subsystems
- · but it has no networks.

If the organization is incompletely automated:
- · It has systems
- · and it has networks
- · each of which has its own systems
- · each of which may or may not contain people in other nets.

If the unit is really *completely* automated, a solution can be reached by systems analysis alone. Otherwise it will require successive iterations of system diagnosis and network diagnosis, in turn. Completely automated situations are rare.

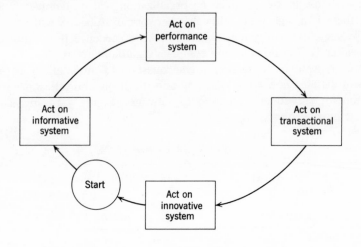

Figure 7.15. System diagnosis and design.

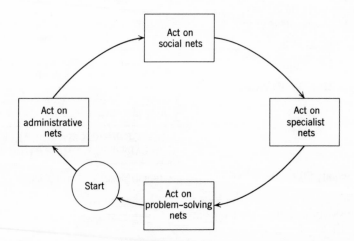

Figure 7.16. Network diagnosis and design.

In What Sequence Should the Organizational Entities be Examined?
The answer to this question follows naturally from the answers to the two preceding. Figure 7.15 shows the sequence of managerial activity followed when examining the organization's systems. Figure 7.16 shows the sequence followed when examining its networks. Figure 7.17 relates (*a*) control

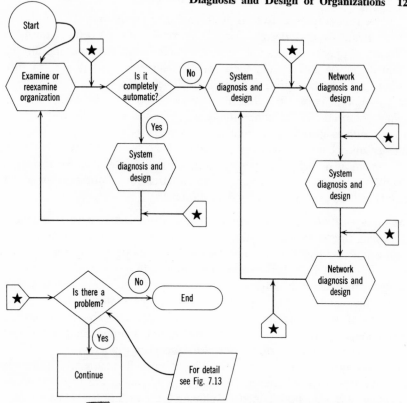

Figure 7.17. A master plan for managerial activity.

index computation, (b) systems diagnosis and design, and (c) networks diagnosis and design, into a master plan of managerial activity. Probably the most subtle but important implication made here is that the manager must shift back and forth from a structural perspective to a membership perspective as appropriate.

System Diagnosis and Design Sequence. System diagnosis and correction proceeds through the sequence shown in Figure 7.15.

Network Diagnosis and Design Sequence. Figure 7.16 shows the sequence of network diagnosis and correction.

A Master Plan for Managerial Activity. Managerial activity is tied together into the sequence shown in Figure 7.17. The manager starts by exploring his situation. Through computing his control index, he answers the question: Is there a problem? (It should be noted that what is a problem to a manager at one level in the organization may not be a problem to a manager at another.) Next he identifies his organization type in order to gain a proper perspective. If it is completely automatic, he relies on system diagnosis and design, looping through this procedure until the problem disappears. If it is not completely automatic, he proceeds through system diagnosis and design, then network diagnosis and design, in turn, continuing the process until at some point he can answer "No" to the original question. It is possible that after several loops he will decide that his original determination of automaticity was erroneous, and he will redefine his approach accordingly. Common sense suggests that at some time the manager must cease correctives even though he may not have eliminated the problem as he originally perceived it. This implies a need for change in objectives, a different perception of the situation, or a modification of criteria. These are expected and legal developments.

Summary of Managerial Activity. The control index, system diagnosis and design, and network diagnosis and design have been tied together into a pattern of management events. Since the manager makes these events happen, they can be called *managerial activity.* It is worth noting that the manager proceeds with diagnosis and design by first examining structural aspects, then membership aspects, through as many iterations as are required. In each of these investigations he is aided and abetted by his understanding of managerial, problem-solving, and communication theories.

Managerial activity is directed toward instituting a change in a situation, directing, correcting, or remodeling it until it adequately meets the manager's criterion. Whenever the change is adequate, the manager stops. Adequacy may also be attained by changing the criterion against which a situation is judged.[9]

MANAGERIAL PROBLEM-SOLVING AND INNOVATION

It has been explained that managerial activity consists of (*a*) giving attention to situations needing change (problem definition); (*b*) drawing out the data required and issuing appropriate directives (exploiting communication capability); and (*c*) making decisions with regard to what, in one's best judgment, is necessary adjustment (exercising managerial competence). A sequence of such activity was developed in a broad general way.

The most critical aspect of a manager's activities is the *innovation* in which he must engage; this is usually the most difficult part of his activity to make explicit. Fortunately, the models we have examined facilitate understanding how a manager proceeds, both in the areas of routine problem-solving and in the "twilight zone," which he must frequently explore. The following explanation first deals with problem-solving in general, then treats the details of problem-solving applied in the processes of diagnosis and design. But, more important, it describes how the manager must proceed when standard problem-solving methods are inadequate. The explanation recognizes the centrality of the manager, whether the perspective taken is one of networks or systems.

Managerial Problem-Solving. Essentially, the manager is engaged in problem-solving. In the process he is buttressed by his understanding of problem, communication, and managerial theories, but the process itself —whether he is engaged in the diagnosis and design of a network or analyzing and reshaping part of a system—is simply one of applying managerial effort to a discrepant situation to arrive at a better solution. This effort, which includes allocation and intuition, is described next.

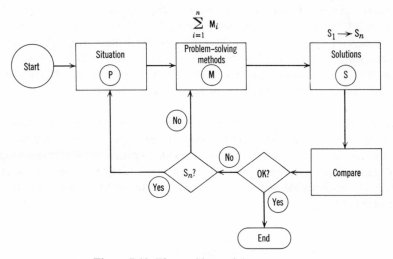

Figure 7.18. The problem-solving sequence.

The Problem-Solving Sequence Is Universal. To any situation "P" there are a number of standard problem-solving methods "M" that can be employed. As a result, a certain number of solutions "S" are possible. As each solution is obtained, it is compared with a criterion to see whether a satisfactory result is reached. Whenever a solution is unsatisfactory, the question is then asked: Is this the last possible solution? And, if it is not, a new method is employed. If it *is* the last possible solution, then the problem-solver must take another look at the situation in order to see if he can better define it. This "new look" is described as the *reexamination, reconceptualization,* and *reconstruction* phases of his activity.

It is important to realize that the problem-solving approach just described is universal. That is, this is the general approach taken by the manager whenever he must act. Specifically, whenever such phrases as "Act to Correct," "Respecify Network," and "Reconstruct System," appear, this sequence is the first one followed by the manager in an attempt to accomplish such a desired end. (The specifications above are in reality statements of *criteria*, to the extent that they establish the kind of output which forms a desirable solution.)

The Manager is Central to Problem Solving. As we have mentioned, the manager (problem solver) appears in our networks model as a member of each problem-solving network. Since it is largely this particular network's activity that is being described when problem-solving is discussed, the problem-solving network will not be shown as one of those under diagnosis and design. The reader should understand that this net, as an *extension* of the manager, is *performing* managerial activity.

Problem solving is also a major function of the innovative system. Whenever an organization is perceived from this viewpoint (as a set of systems), it is therefore the innovative system—of which the manager must be a part—that is actually performing the analysis and intervention. For this reason, the innovative system is never shown as one under scrutiny.[10]

Both problem-solving networks and innovative systems require intuitive capability, which is the key contribution of managers to organizations. If one recognizes that the sole source of heuristic capacity is the human mind, it is reasonable that there must be both an intelligent human member central to each problem-solving net and human intelligence involved in each innovative system.

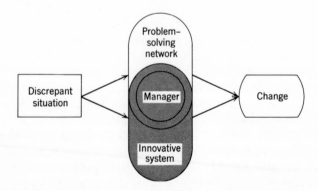

Figure 7.19. The manager as an organizational component. It is through the manager's action—whether as a member of the problem-solving network or as an entity of the innovative system—that change occurs.

SPECIFIC MANAGERIAL PROCEDURES AND ACTIVITIES

Up to this point the book has covered the entire range of managerial activities in organizations. However, prior emphasis has been on methodology, that is, on a general conceptual approach. How is this methodology made operational? How does the manager actually proceed? The rest of this section is directed to answering such questions. The ensuing figures illustrate specific managerial procedures and activities.

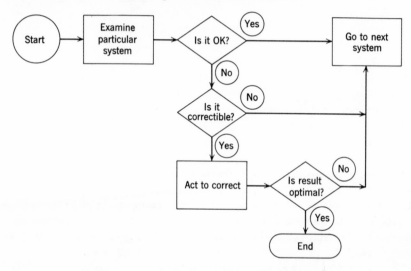

Figure 7.20. System diagnosis and design sequence.

System Diagnosis and Design Procedure. How does the manager proceed in his analysis of systems in an organization? His basic approach is shown in Figure 7.20. Essentially, the manager examines a *particular* system, proceeding to the next system if no discrepant situation exists. Should a problem exist, he must ask the question: Is the problem correctible? If the answer is "Yes," he takes action. If the answer is "No," he proceeds to the next system to see what improvement can be made there. After each segment of managerial activity, he tests to see whether his collective result to that point is optimal for the whole organization. Whenever his actions are rewarded by an "optimal" collective result, he terminates activity.

The loop in Figure 7.20 refers only to one such investigation, but a similar sequence is followed for each one.

Network Diagnosis and Design Procedure. In most cases system diagnosis and design will be followed by network diagnosis and design. The sequence for this kind of activity is shown in Figure 7.21. Essentially, the

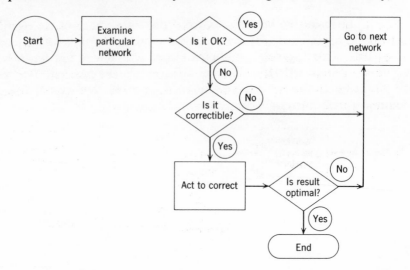

Figure 7.21. Network diagnosis and design sequence.

manager examines a *particular* network, proceeding to the next network if no problem exists. Should a problem exist, he must ask the question: Is the problem correctible? If the answer is "Yes," he takes action. If the answer is "No," he proceeds to the next network to see what improvement can be made there. After each corrective action, he tests to see whether his collective result is optimal for the whole organization. Whenever his actions are rewarded by an "optimal" collective result, he terminates activity.

The loop above refers only to one network, but a similar sequence is followed for each one.

Managerial Innovation

What specific managerial activities take place in the process of diagnosis and design? As was pointed out earlier such acts as "correct," "redesign," and "reconstruct" suggest that a problem-solving sequence is invoked. But what takes place when this sequence is inadequate? What does the manager do when his standard routines for problem solving fail? As is shown in Figure 7.22, whether he is performing system diagnosis or network diagnosis (and design), he eventually proceeds through a sequencing of reexamination, reconceptualization, and reconstruction of the organiza-

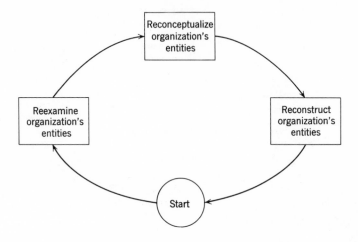

Figure 7.22. General innovation sequence.

tional entities under his surveillance. Very basically, this calls for (a) a careful survey of all the critical variables, (b) an attempt to view them in a new light (see them in some new way), and (c) the taking action to mold things into a new shape.

This aspect of managerial activity is expanded into more detail in the next four figures.

The Manager Must First Reexamine. When standard routines for adjustment do not produce results, managerial activity enters a reexamination phase. This approach is shown in Figure 7.23. First, the manager examines the criteria, then he examines the objectives, next the methods employed, and finally his resources, in that order. In the light of his findings he takes another look at the situation. Does it now appear to be the same situation that he first saw? If the answer is "It is different," he then reverts to standard problem-solving methods in his search for rapid solution. If after reexamination, the situation has *not* changed, then his only hope for improvement is by moving on to the reconceptualization phase.

The Manager Must Next Reconceive. When reexamination activity fails to produce acceptable results, the manager enters the reconceptualization phase, as shown in Figure 7.24.

Whereas the reexamination phase was essentially a search and identification procedure, this activity requires a more intuitive, or "brainstorming" approach. In turn, *new conceptions* of the resources, employable methods, appropriate objectives, and allowable criteria are sought. Consequently, the situation is reexamined. Is it now tolerable? If so, terminate.

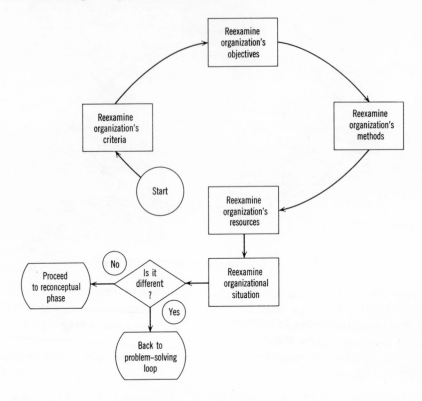

Figure 7.23. Reexamination phase.

If the situation is not one that the analyst can live with, he must then proceed to the reconstruction phase.

The Manager Must Finally Reconstruct. When both the reexamination and reconceptualization activities fail to produce acceptable results, the analyst enters the first half of the reconstruction phase. The priority given to this half recognizes that logically the organization's *systems* are given first attention. The sequence is shown in Figure 7.25.

Attention is first given to the informative system since it is the key to total internal status of the organization; next, one or more of the performance systems are attended to; finally, the transactional system (that which relates the organization to its environment) is reconstructed or adjusted. After any or all of this activity, the situation is referred to again. Is it within limits—tolerable? If so, end the activity. If it is not tolerable, the manager must ask: Has the situation changed? If the situation has not, he then proceeds to the second half of the reconstruction phase (giving attention to the networks). If the situation *has* changed, he then reattacks the

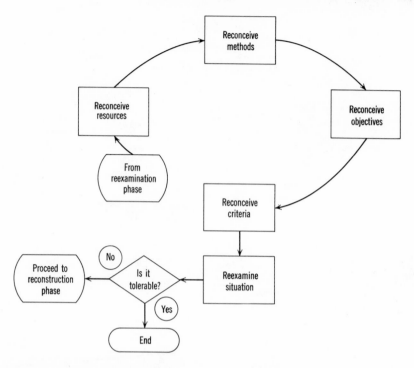

Figure 7.24. Reconceptualization phase.

new situation with those standard methods in his problem-solving kit.

This second half of the reconstruction phase is entered into when a tolerable situation has not been reached by the end of systems adjustment. Here attention is directed to the *networks,* in turn, in the sequence shown in Figure 7.26.

Attention is first given to the administrative network, the set of formal relationships among organization members. Next, social network activity it attended to, then specialist networks, in turn. After any or all of these efforts, the situation is reexamined, and, if it is tolerable, managerial activity comes to an end. At the end of this phase, even if the situation has *not* changed, the manager's attempts must now terminate, for nothing can be done since all avenues of repair have been exhausted. However, if the manager does have a new situation, he attacks it by means of standard problem-solving methods, hoping for a routine solution.

Summary: Specific Managerial Procedures and Activities

Whether we view an organization as a constellation of human networks or as a set of mechanical systems, it is the manager who acts, intuits, ex-

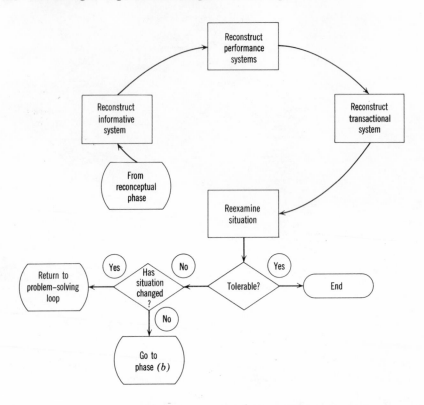

Figure 7.25. Reconstruction phase (a).

ercises control. The manager (or a manager) is present in each problem-solving network, and managers (human intuition) contribute the necessary heuristic capability to the innovative systems in organizations.

Most problems in organizations are solved by a routine problem-solving sequence of applying standard methods to discrepant situations to produce solutions. The solutions are examined for acceptability and the process is iterated until a tolerable result is attained.

In complex organizations a manager frequently reaches the end of his standard problem-solving repertoire before he has reached an ideal solution. This requires his engaging in a general "innovation" sequence of reexamination, reconceptualization, and reconstruction. The first step is essentially search and identification, the second a series of intuitive, conceptual efforts; the last is a sequence of adjustment, test, and readjustment, in a sort of "sensitivity-analysis" approach. It is really in this innovative type of managerial activity that one's theoretical backgrounding about problems, communications, and management provides him strongest support.

The reexamination phase consists of the manager's attention being directed to criteria, objectives, methods, and resources, in turn. This is a kind of "redefining" activity, and roughly compares to the idea of *problem definition,* identified as a central variable of control.

The reconceptual phase consists of the manager's attempts to derive

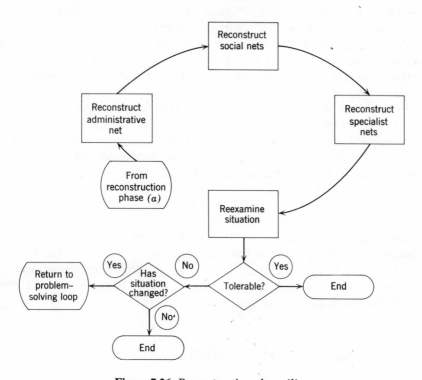

Figure 7.26. Reconstruction phase (*b*).

new meaning, form additional feasible relationships, and take new perspectives toward resources, methods, objectives, and criteria, in that order. This is largely an intuitive activity, and roughly compares to the idea of *managerial competence,* identified as another central variable of control.

Reconstruction, in both its phases, exploits the possibilities in rearranging (*a*) the systems in the organizations and (*b*) the network configurations. Central to this activity is an awareness of the relationships—the interactions—among the parts being adjusted. Such adjustment affects the way the parts relate and roughly equates to redetermining the *communication capability* of the unit, the final variable of control.

CONCLUDING REMARKS TO THE TEXT

This book has treated a number of ideas central to managerial control. We have stated that the level of managerial control can be determined by assessing existing degrees of managerial competence, communication capability, and problem definition. We have further shown that managerial activity is central to organizational viability; fundamentally, this activity is problem solving: managerial allocation and readjustment of entities important to the unit.

From what we have said, it can be seen that managerial problem-solving is not trivial. In order to gain and maintain control in complex organizations, the manager must constantly revert to such innovative activities as reexamination, reconceptualization, and readjustment of organizational parts. We have presented, as a logical approach to this activity, a combined networks/systems model.

Underlying our whole thesis is the assumption that a manager's success depends on how well he is grounded in current theories about problems, communication, and managers. This is why we have presented significant concepts and principles from these fields of study. And it is why we include in the "Related Readings" section and in bibliographical references extensive outside sources that the reader may find helpful in supplementing his understanding of the ideas we have presented.

NOTES

1 Compare with William G. Scott, "Organizational Theory: An Overview and Appraisal." *Journal of the Academy of Management, 4,* (1), 7–26 (April 1961). Scott says: "Human behavior in organizations, and indeed, organization itself, cannot be adequately understood within the ground rules of classical and neoclassical doctrines."

2 Rhochrematics deals with materials flow. Richard Johnson, Fremont Kast and Jim Rosenzweig. *The Theory and Management of Systems.* New York: McGraw-Hill Book Company, 1967, pp. 172–194.

3 Administered organizations are defined as: "Collectivities which exhibit sustained activity; are part of a larger system; have specialized purposes; and are dependent upon interchange with the larger system." James D. Thompson, et al. *Comparative Studies in Administration.* Pittsburgh, Pa.: University of Pittsburgh Press, 1959, p. 6.

4 Compare, Joseph A Litterer, *Organizations: Structure and Behavior.* New York: John Wiley and Sons, 1963, particularly pp. 28–38.

5 *Ibid.,* specifically Figure 4, p. 37. Litterer is exemplary of current theorists, in that

he recognizes well the variables and activities of interest. The authors do not allege to have created any new variables; their main contribution is claimed to be a more useful conceptual scheme.

[6] In Scott's words, the authors believe they are "uniting what is valuable in classical theory with the social and natural sciences into a systematic and integrated conception of human organization." Scott, *op. cit.* The model also is believed to be complete—one adaptable not only to complex units but also to organizations of any size, duration, and description.

[7] Adapted from an approach suggested by Aiko M. Hormann, "Designing a Machine Partner," *Datamation,* **13**, (2), 29–33 (February 1967).

[8] Compare Philip Selznick, "Foundations of the Theory of Organization," *American Sociological Review,* **13**, 25–35 (February 1948). Selznick says: "On the one hand any concrete organizational system is an economy; at the same time it is an *adaptive social structure.*" Frank J. Jasinski sets out a similar idea somewhat differently in his classic "Adapting Organization to New Technology," *Harvard Business Review,* **37**, (1), 79–86 (January–February 1959). His thesis is that *"a change in production or technology affects organizational relationships."* The dual perspective is basic.

[9] This book deals with *Managerial Activity,* which many writers have differentiated completely from Organization Theory. Most, in making this differentiation, posit a *normative* focus (in Managerial Theory) as against a *descriptive* perspective (in Organization Theory). The authors suggest this to be a false dichotomy: the manager (allocator, intervener, rearranger) is simply an organizational member interested in introducing change. As such, he is best understood in the context of organization theory, to which his activity relates.

[10] What is meant here is that the manager does not scrutinize the problem-solving network *while he is acting as the central member of it,* or the innovative system *while he is functioning as its intuitive source.* Managers may analyze subordinate, superior, or ancillary problem-solving nets (or innovative systems). When they do this, however, these entities become part of a "situation" toward the investigation of which some other problem-solving network or innovative system is being invoked.

BIBLIOGRAPHY

Hormann, Aiko M. "Designing a Machine Partner," *Datamation,* **13** (2) (February 1967).

Jasinski, Frank J. "Adapting Organization to New Technology," *Harvard Business Review,* 79–86 (January–February 1959).

Johnson, Richard, Fremont Kast, and Jim Rosenzweig. *The Theory and Management of Systems.* New York: McGraw-Hill Book Company, 1967.

Litterer, Joseph A. *Organizations: Structure and Behavior.* New York: John Wiley and Sons, 1963.

Scott, William G. "Organizational Theory: An Overview and Appraisal," *Journal of the Academy of Management,* **4** (1) (April 1961).

Selznick, Philip. "Foundations of the Theory of Organization," *American Sociological Review,* **13**, 25–35 (February 1948).

Thompson, James D. et al. *Comparative Studies in Administration.* Pittsburgh, Pa.: University of Pittsburgh Press, 1959.

2

RELATED READINGS

INTRODUCTION

SECTION 1: INTERPERSONAL COMMUNICATION

This section deals with issues related to communication between people. In "Management Perspective: Sensitivity Training: The Current State of the Question" Frank T. Paine examines the value of studying this controversial area. He concludes that although its effectiveness has not been demonstrated in on-the-job settings, T-group training for executives should be continued with self education as an objective. "Basic Psychological Factors in Communication" by T. M. Higham concerns some of the more important psychological research findings related to communication behavior. Higham concludes that careful placement of key personnel—personnel who command trust and respect—is the way to successful communication in an organization. In "The Receiving End of Communication—Listening" Percy A. Field defines listening, sets forth some things known about it, and relates listening to learning. Roy C. Nelson's article, "Transcultural Communication," deals with the proposition that the world population explosion makes it imperative that communication be improved in order to create tolerable conditions for people and their societies. In "A Dynamic Theory of Communications" C. Merton Babcock discusses the framework of socio-linguistic behavior and sets forth the variants to determine communication effectiveness. In "Problems in Meaning" Herman M. Weisman reviews several important current theories of meaning. He then develops a model relating the process of communication to the transference of meaning.

1

MANAGEMENT PERSPECTIVE: SENSITIVITY TRAINING: THE CURRENT STATE OF THE QUESTION *

Frank T. Paine

For years, it has been suggested that increases in interpersonal competence significantly improve organizational performance.

Ideally, each member achieves a high degree of self-acceptance. Each is able to create conditions such that acceptance of self and others increases. This tends to lower external dependency. Members are free to accept new ideas and thoughts. This leads to increased experimentation and risk taking with new thoughts. Such patterns of behavior aid the organization in keeping pace with today's fast moving economic and technological developments. Measured both in organizational and individual well-being, these outcomes have been considered by many difficult to obtain but desirable. Clearly, all is not so easy.

One proposed solution in widespread use has been sensitivity training or education. Not education in the ordinary sense, sensitivity training is process oriented rather than content oriented. It is concerned with the process of human relations through actual emotional experiences. Sensitivity training is also structured around the trainee. He, not the trainer, is the focal point. Leadership and rewards and penalties are largely controlled by the trainees. The trainees are supposed to learn new modes of "authentic" interpersonal behavior through interaction and "non-evaluative" feedback in partially unstructured situations.

* Reprinted from *Journal of Academy of Management,* September, 1965, pp. 228–232.

ARMCHAIR ARGUMENTS—CON

Recently there has been some criticism of sensitivity training. Odiorne, for example contends that there is a definite relationship between sensitivity training and the fable of the emperor's new clothes, i.e. few dare to criticize the training process for fear that they will appear to be insensitive and antihuman-relations oriented.[1] Of the many possible criticisms, probably these two are most telling.

1. There is a denial that "authentic" relationships are desirable in all organizations. In one case where managers of an engineering firm were given T-group training, the result allegedly was dissolution of a previously quite successful company.

2. There is also a contention that training does not change the interpersonal relationships in a durable manner.

Before dealing with scientific evidence on the results of training, let us raise some questions about the practice itself.

Do the trainers have complete control over the learning process; are the trainers sure of the terminal point in training? Are some of the trainers incompetent, and some of them relying on ultradramatic pedagogical methods? Some trainees reported a case where one of their number received a bogus telephone call from his mistress in which the mistress threatened to reveal all to the trainee's wife.[2] Another question—is there no criterion for admission to a training session save money? Thus may unstable trainees be subjected to a situation that they may be unable to handle? (The result might be a nervous breakdown.) A final question is based on a criticism of participative management. Is T-group training a kind of therapy in which the trainees are made to see that participation is a great cure for management problems?

ARMCHAIR ARGUMENTS—PRO

These questions should not go unanswered. The idea is rejected that the T-groups are uncontrolled, at least in a general way. The groups do have objectives; all is not aimless talk. The standards for admission and for trainers should be high, of course. The claim though that sensitivity training is dangerous is discounted in that only four breakdowns have occured among the 10,000 people who have participated in programs.[3] Still that is four individuals.

The notion that T-group training is participative management brain-washing is false. The purpose is to make the trainee ask questions of himself. Furthermore, sensitivity training is not therapy in the true sense of the word. Real therapy would involve deep clinical insights developed through an intimate therapist-patient relationship. This relationship cannot exist in the T-group situation.

Nevertheless some aspects of sensitivity training practice limit its value. Effective management behavior is a function of several variables and increased sensitivity is not the whole answer to the problem. Moreover, feedback under T-group conditions may not always be helpful, since it is not related to the actual job situation. Unrealistic group norms, role definitions and individual expectations may result. In addition the trainees are not always equipped to give feedback in a benevolent, nonevaluative and skillful manner. Research by competent social scientists has not unearthed many valid generalizations. Therefore, untrained executives should not be expected to do so. However, we should not condemn the movement. We would recommend that emotional responses be carefully observed in the future to prevent psychiatric damage and executives should be informed of the possible consequences of T-group training.

Further, if sensitivity training actually changes behavior, certain types of organizations (as well as individuals) should be warned against it. In these organizations: the desire is to remain highly directive; money, threats, and promotional opportunities are felt to be the only motivations; managerial views are more exclusively production-centered; and, reactions to training are lukewarm. In short, if an organization feels that it should not adopt some such motivational management theory as Likert's, it should not bother with sensitivity training.[4] Perhaps its members cannot and should not be expected to sacrifice their high need for power and aggression. Their needs and those of the organization may be best expressed and best realized in a bureaucratic mechanism.

RESEARCH ON EFFECTIVENESS

Although sensitivity training has actually been used since 1947, there is little scientific research evidence that the training experience actually changes executive behavior. Returning trainees seem to feel that they have benefitted, but they cannot be specific about the changes.[5] However, some research has been done in the area of the results of sensitivity training. Some of the published studies will be examined.

Miles has traced the improvement in what he calls the three predictor variables in interpersonal performance: sensitivity, the ability to listen and communicate; diagnostic ability; and action skill, the ability to maximize personal and group satisfaction.[6] With on-site testing and interviews, he found that 73% of the trainees showed a statistically significant improvement in these three areas. He found that the greatest improvement came in the sensitivity area.

Bass traced the before and after reactions of 34 trainees to the film "Twelve Angry Men," which concerned the deliberations of a murder trial jury.[7] He found that after T-group training the men showed a significant increase in awareness of the feelings and ideas of the men in the film.

Burke and Bennis (1961) have studied perceptual changes arising from sensitivity training.[8] To do this they gave before and after Semantic Differential Tests to 84 trainees at Bethel, Maine.[9] It was postulated that training would not change a person's conception of ideal behavior to a great degree. However, it was thought that perceived behavior would become more congruent with the ideal. In other words increased profile similarity was expected. The tests bore this out with a high level of confidence. Since one of the goals of sensitivity training is self-acceptance, it would seem that this test speaks well for sensitivity training. However, increased profile similarity weakens the benefits postulated by the optimum stress theory, which states that there should be an optimum divergence between ideal behavior and self-perceived actual behavior. Therefore, it could be argued that trainers should not aim for too high a level of profile similarity.

It was also postulated that the perceptions of others would become more congruent with self perception, and that the change in others' perception would be greater than the change in self perception. Both of these hypotheses were supported. Essentially, others' perceptions, self perception and the ideal were brought into closer alignment. This would indicate greater self-acceptance and greater acceptance by others. This is one of the goals of sensitivity training.

ON THE JOB BEHAVIOR CHANGES

All of the above tests were confined to the laboratory environment. They indicate at least temporary perceptual changes which may or may not be related to effective management behavior.[10] They do *not* demonstrate that sensitivity training is better than other methods. They do *not* demonstrate that on the job behavior has been changed for the better.

Bunker made a study of on the job behavioral changes.[11] This involved sending questionnaires to former trainees and an untrained control group eight to ten months after the training period. Questionnaires were also sent to fellow workers and superiors. Special pains were taken to obtain a high level of response. Over three-fourths of the former trainees, two-thirds of the control group and five-sixths of the describers returned the question-naire.

There were three categories of ratings: overt changes (e.g., communi-cation), inferred changes (e.g., awareness of group behavior) and global, general judgments. It was reported that the former trainees experienced more changes in the first two categories than the control group. There was not much difference between the two groups with respect to the third cate-gory, since these responses tended to be vague and general. It was also found that the answers given by fellow workers and superiors supported the changes observed in the first two categories. One might say this study proves that sensitivity training does result in on the job behavioral changes. However, the results may represent only a desire on the part of former trainees and their colleagues to report change even if none occurred.

One must conclude that there has been no substantial evidence presented that proves: that sensitivity training actually changes on the job behavior; or, that as yet changes are, in fact, durable and definitely related to more effective management.[12]

CONCLUSION

Sensitivity training is not an organizational panacea. All organizations and all managers should not use it even if it is really effective. In fact its effectiveness has not been proven in on the job setting. Many of the aspects underlying T-group training practice are subject to doubt. It is clear that much research is needed to test the assumptions and the actual results of T-group training. Some of the more important variables to consider in the research design are as follows:

1. long-term results;
2. related to effectiveness of management behavior;
3. comparing different training methods (e.g. role of trainer or content emphasis versus process); and,
4. their effect on different personality types.

It may be that subsequent research will discover that sensitivity training is unable to make any durable improvement in managerial performance. If this turns out to be the case, new avenues will have to be explored.

In the meantime it has been shown that, when properly conducted, sensi-tivity training can demonstrate to executives that there are different modes of interpersonal behavior. Even if this does not cause the executive to alter his behavior, the training experiences will allow the executive to be criti-cally aware of himself in his relations with others. Assuming this to be an important requirement for effective management in certain organizations, T-group training is a valuable educational experience. Therefore, T-group training should be continued with self education as its chief goal.

NOTES

[1] Odiorne, G. S., "The Trouble with Sensitivity Training," *Training Directions,* Vol. XVII, Oct. 1963.

[2] *Ibid.*

[3] Argyris, C., "A Comment on George Odiorne's Paper," *Training Directions,* Vol. XVII, Oct. 1963.

[4] Likert, R., *New Patterns of Management,* New York: McGraw-Hill, 1961.

[5] There is a substantial amount of anecdotal evidence which we will not report here. It consists of post-training testimony, casual observation and recall. Scientific evidence is developed from controlled, systematic investigation and objective analysis. An assessment of statistical significance is frequently made. A few other scientific studies are presently in progress.

[6] Miles, M. B., "Human Relations Training: Processes and Outcomes," *Journal of Counseling Psychology,* Vol. VII, No. 4, 1960.

[7] Bass, B. M., "Reactions to Twelve Angry Men as a Measure of Sensitivity Training," *Journal of Applied Psychology,* No. 3, July, 1962.

[8] Burke, H. L. and Bennis, W. G., "Changes in Perception of Self and Others During Human Relations Training," *Human Relations,* Vol. XIV, 1961.

[9] No control group was used as was the case in the two studies above. Therefore it was impossible to isolate the variable of sensitivity training.

[10] Bunker, D. R., "The Effect of Laboratory Education Upon Individual Behavior," pre-publication draft, Harvard University, 1963.

[11] The Miles study did include some interviews outside the laboratory. The behavioral changes were reported by others (that were subjects) who presumably knew of the training.

[12] Most management training programs and, in fact, many of our educational programs suffer from this lack of scientific evidence.

REFERENCES

Argyris, C., "A Comment on George Odiorne's Paper," *Training Directions,* Vol. XVII, October, 1963.

———, "In Defense of Laboratory Education," *Training Directions,* Vol. XVII, October, 1963.

———, *Interpersonal Competence and Organization Behavior,* Irwin, Homewood, Ill., 1962.

———, "T-Groups for Organizational Effectiveness," *Harvard Business Review,* March–April, 1964.

Bass, B. M., "Mood Changes During a Management Training Laboratory," *Journal of Applied Psychology* No. 5, 1962.

———, "Reaction to Twelve Angry Men as a Measure of Sensitivity Training," *Journal of Applied Psychology* No. 3, July, 1962.

Bradford, L. P., Gibb, J. R. and Benne, K. D. (Eds.), *Laboratory Education and T-Group Method,* New York: John Wiley and Sons, 1964.

Bunker, D. R., "The Effect of Laboratory Education Upon Individual Behavior," pre-publication draft, Harvard University, 1963.

Burke, H. L. and Bennis, W. G., "Changes in Perception of Self and Others During Human Training," *Human Relations,* Vol. XIV, 1961.

House, R. J., "T-Group Training: A Review of the Scientific Evidence and an Appraisal," unpublished paper, University of Michigan, 1963.

Klaw, S., "Two Weeks in a T-Group," *Fortune,* August, 1961.

Likert, R., *New Patterns of Management,* New York: McGraw-Hill, 1961.

Miles, M. B., "Human Relations Training: Processes and Outcomes," *Journal of Counseling Psychology,* Vol. VII, No. 4, 1960.

Odiorne, G. S., "The Trouble with Sensitivity Training," *Training Directors,* Vol. XVII, Oct. 1963.

Tannenbaum, R., Weschler, I. R. and Massarik, F., *Leadership and Organization,* McGraw-Hill, New York, 1961.

This, L., and Lippitt, G. L., "Managerial Guidelines to Sensitivity Training," *Training Directors,* April, 1963.

2

BASIC PSYCHOLOGICAL FACTORS
IN COMMUNICATION *

T. M. Higham

A celebrated authority on Canon law and mediaeval universities, Dr. Hastings Rashdall, was one of those who could ride, but not understand a bicycle. One day, for example, having had a puncture in his front tyre, he was found vigorously pumping up the back one; when a passer-by pointed this out to him, he remarked, "What? Do they not communicate?" I sometimes wonder whether, in our present-day eagerness to "put people in the picture," we do not behave rather like Dr. Rashdall, strenuously pumping in information at one end of a firm, in the hopeful expectation that it will somehow find its way to the other. Perhaps we too ride, but cannot understand.

In the last few years, a great deal has been written on this topic of "communications," mainly to the effect that communication must be "two-way," a comment of unstartling originality, as anyone familiar with the derivation of the word must realise. Today you can hardly open one of the many journals, English or American, in the personnel field, without finding some article on the subject, or some review of the latest authoritative work on it; there is even a "Communications Training Centre" in existence, and one firm, at any rate, now has its "Communications Manager"; Technical Colleges, Evening Institutes and other organizations run courses in clear expression, and the art of speaking or writing; you can be trained in running a meeting or leading a conference. Training Officers and others make increased use of visual and other aids, as a help in putting their teaching across; industries make use of suggestion schemes, joint consultative committees, broadcast address systems and similar devices to try to ensure that

* Reprinted from *Occupational Psychology*, January, 1957, pp. 1–10.

information reaches to all levels in the business and is fed back again to the top. But, as P. H. Cook (1951) has said:

"There is as yet no firmly-established theory of communication which can provide guiding principles guaranteeing that effective communications will be achieved. As a result much communication practice is dependent on unconfirmed hypotheses, personal hunches and techniques and tricks of doubtful merit."

The nearest approach to a theory of communications has probably come from students of cybernetics and information theory. The new science of "Communication Engineering," as Professor Meredith (1955) pointed out recently, is so highly developed that "we are strongly tempted to use it as a ready-made frame of reference, and to fit all our ideas about communication into this frame." That I believe to be a mistake—not so much because it is difficult to see what relevance a man-made machine has in considering the problems of a God-made man, but rather because, in everyday life, at home, in industry, in social life generally, the problems of communication (that is, of the transmission of ideas and attitudes) between people and groups are not those which can be solved, or even greatly understood, by means of a knowledge of information theory. Until such time as a machine is developed which can not only interpret information, but also convey its like or dislike of its informant, I believe we should do well to stick to our knowledge of human and animal psychology in trying to understand the problems and workings of communication between individuals and groups.

In most of the studies of communication between individuals and groups which I have come across, scant recognition is given to what is, perhaps, the one fact which we do know from experience about it—that if a person dislikes or mistrusts us, he is not likely to be receptive to what we have to say, and his version of our words is likely to be distorted by his personal opinions of us, or his preconceived notions about our motives. For that reason a study of communication could well begin with an examination of the problems of the reception of information—that process by which we perceive what is said against a background of who says it. It is there that the work of animal psychologists, and the many experimental studies of perception, can help us.

The experiments of Schelderup-Ebbe (1935) with hens, Maslow (1936) with apes, and Lorenz (1954) with dogs have shown clearly that a sizing-up process goes on when two animals meet, which subsequently merges into a dominance-submission relationship. Of these, the most vivid is probably Lorenz's description of the encounter of two adult male dogs:

"Two adult male dogs meet in the street. Stiff legged, with tails erect and hair on end, they pace towards each other. The nearer they approach, the stiffer, higher and more ruffled they appear, their advance becomes slower and slower. . . . They do not make their encounter head to head, front against front, but make as though to pass each other, only stopping when they stand at last flank to flank, head to tail, in close juxtaposition. Then a strict ceremonial demands that each should sniff the hind regions of the other. Should one of the dogs be overcome with fear at this juncture, down goes his tail between his legs and he jumps with a quick, flexible twist, wheeling at an angle of 180 degrees, thus modestly retracting his former offer to be smelt. Should the two dogs remain in an attitude of self-display, carrying their tails as rigid as standards, then the sniffing process may be of a long protracted nature. All may be solved amicably and there is still the chance that first one tail and then another may begin to wag with small but rapidly increasing beats and then this nerve-racking situation may develop into nothing worse than a cheerful canine romp."

Apart from the fact that such encounters take place primarily on a symbolic level, is the encounter between two humans so very different? When two individuals meet for the first time, there is usually a rather more refined process of "sniffing over"—an interchange of neutral information (the weather, for example, or a search for mutual acquaintances) which serves the same purpose. An attempt to set up a dominance-submission relationship also emerges on some occasions, as Maslow (1937) has shown. Pear (1955) has explored with skill the part played by voice and social differences in the same situation. The fact that this process may be going on below the level of consciousness is a further factor: there are still, for example, some managers who sit with their backs to the light, in a chair just a little higher than that of their visitors, and continue to write after someone enters their office; but luckily their numbers are dwindling. But these, unlike the Admiral's gold braid and the peacock's tail, are more often than not uncoscious ways of conveying an impression of importance. None the less, their effect on recipients is much the same.

What has not yet been satisfactorily demonstrated is the opposite of that—the approach or manner which makes for confidence and an easy reception. If there are mannerisms which tend to put the recipients of information in a subordinate position, by conveying an attitude of superiority, are there other ways in which an atmosphere of trust and confidence can be built up without loss of status by either party?

If we recall the two dogs sniffing each other over, I believe we can say that such a situation is possible—and in fact many well-trained interviewers and counsellors are creating such a situation every day. Every interviewer is taught to "put the candidate at his ease"—in other words to make him receptive, whether it be to questions about himself or to advice and guidance. The exact ways in which this is done vary, but the essential part has been well put by Oldfield (1941):

"The adoption of an appropriate *general attitude* at the outset of the interview is a matter of greater importance than the maintenance of an effort to *behave* appropriately throughout its course. As an eminent psychologist remarked apropos this question, 'each interview is a world to itself. One hour I am a schoolmaster, the next a parson.' "

It seems clear that to ensure good reception, you must create the right atmosphere. This is, perhaps, the one prerequisite for effective communication. Where it does not exist, communication will be difficult, and all that is said is likely to be distorted. A further complication is that two people, or two groups, rarely if ever meet with what is called an "open mind." Each comes together, instead, with preconceived ideas about the other, and about the other's preconceived ideas about them.

During the preliminary "sniffing over," any small clues that can be fitted into the pre-existing picture will be readily grasped. The ingenious experiments of Asch (1946) demonstrate this point neatly. It will be remembered that he read two lists of personality traits to two different groups of people. The first group's list was "Kind, Wise, Honest, Calm, Strong." The second group's list was "Cruel, Shrewd, Unscrupulous, Calm, Strong." The last two epithets in both lists were the same. After hearing the lists, separately, the two groups were told, "Suppose you had to describe this person in the same manner, but without using the terms you heard, what other terms would you use?" The first group, who heard the list "Kind, Wise, Honest, Calm, Strong," gave the following synonyms for "calm"—soothing, peaceful, gentle, tolerant, mild-mannered. But the second group, who heard "Cruel, Shrewd, Unscrupulous, Calm, Strong," produced synonyms for "calm" like cold, frigid, calculating. Similar results were got from the two groups with synonyms for "strong"—the first group listing such terms are fearless, helpful, just, forceful; the second group giving ruthless, overbearing, hard, inflexible, dominant. Both groups on hearing the first few epithets, got a fixed idea about the sort of person described; the later terms were merely fitted into the existing pattern.

This is not merely an academic point, illustrated by carefully controlled laboratory experiments; it is a very real factor in communication, simply because "the past in the worker's mind," as Zweig (1952) calls it, is so strong and potent a factor in his reactions. The truth of that is seen in the study made recently by the Acton Society Trust (1952) of communications in the coal mining industry. In an attempt to raise the output of coal, many attempts were made to tell the miners why a higher output was necessary; pamphlets, magazines, even a personal letter from the then Prime Minister, Mr. Attlee, were employed. But, as the report makes clear:

"The mere provision of information . . . does not reduce proneness to prejudice . . . it does not succeed in modifying the underlying attitude of mistrust upon which credulity seems to be based."

In a later report, *Management under Nationalisation,* the Trust (1953) quote the comment of an Area Manager in the Coal Industry, pointing out that he:

"can never forget that the (Coal) Board's biggest headache is the attitude of the miners and their misconceptions about the work the Board and its staff perform, and, perhaps most important, about the need for economic efficiency."

Then follows the comment of the Area General Manager:

"We have issued booklets, but nobody bothered to read them. We had a few questions when we started joint consultative committees, but even these have now petered out. We have tried to put explanations into the minutes and put them up on the notice-board, but nobody bothered to read them. It is no use trying to put it over at the lodge meetings of the union, for only a few miners attend them. This is really our major difficulty, how to put this information across and how to rid the minds of the men of misconceptions."

The pathetic notion that you can improve communications by giving more and better information should surely be allowed to die a natural death; you will not get any reception if you are not trusted; but if relations are good, then there is a good chance that what you say will be received, and that you will get co-operation in return.

But even where trust and mutual confidence do exist, that tendency to come to an interview, meeting or conference with preconceived notions is still found, and we cannot afford to forget that the same situation is almost always seen in different ways by different people, depending on their personal capacities, inclinations and background. Zangwill's (1937) experiment on *"Aufgabe"* showed the importance of that. Two groups of subjects were shown, separately, a vague, ill-determined inkblot. They were not told what it represented, but one group was told that it might be like an animal; and the second group was told that it might resemble a landscape. Both groups drew and described what they had seen. The first group all drew cats, rabbits, or similar animals, while the second group drew mountains and hills. The same stimulus confronted both groups, but their preconceived ideas about it determined their reactions to it.

I believe, therefore, that in trying to understand human communication, we would be well advised to study the basic mental processes that underlie so much of everyday human behavior—the study of perception in particular, and the many experiments on *"Aufgabe"* and attitude formation.

But further problems arise. Suppose that a person to whom we wish to communicate something has sniffed us over asking unconsciously, "Is he friendly, can I trust him?", and decided that he is disposed to listen to us, we still need to know whether what we say will be understood, and if so, whether, at a later date, it will be recalled or repeated accurately. So I would suggest that comprehension and recall are legitimate subjects for research and study when considering human communications.

Both of these, as it happens, have been studied fully in recent years. I should like, therefore, only to point out a few of the researches or experiments which seem to me to throw light on how we succeed or fail in comprehending information and recalling it accurately.

Bartlett (1951) has suggested that one of the chief functions of the mind, when it is active, is "filling up gaps"; that is, it is constantly trying to link new material into the pattern of older material, in order to make it meaningful. Our minds seem to prefer the simple and regular to the complex and irregular, and to organize what is received into tidy, meaningful bundles. That is why it is so difficult to get a new idea across; for a new idea has to be fitted into the existing structure in the mind, and it is often quite a struggle to do so. A simple demonstration of that difficulty was given by Wertheimer; to give you an example of it, suppose you look at these four words:

MAN   TABLE   KNIFE   CLOTH

You can, without much difficulty, form some kind of mental picture out of them. If I add the word TROLLEY, you can probably fit that in quite easily to your already established picture. But if I now add the words:

SURGEON   BLOOD   ANAESTHETIC

you will probably have a few puzzled moments before you are able to reorganize the picture in your mind. The meaning of the isolated words changes as the pattern alters, so that the table, once laid for a meal, with a knife handy for cutting a cake, becomes an operating table, with the knife poised over the man who a few moments earlier was sitting down to his tea.

Our mental habits persist and may help or hinder us; they will only do the former if we can link what we have to say onto what our listeners already know; for in that way, the new can be assimilated to the old.

But there is more to comprehension than mental habits; the interest of the subject matter and our own intelligence are also involved. Some idea of the extent of these factors can be seen in two very detailed and careful experiments carried out by the BBC Audience Research Department (1950, 1951, 1952).

The first of these researches was an attempt to assess the intelligibility of a series of Forces Educational Broadcasts; the second was concerned with the comprehensibility of the five minute programme "Topic for Tonight" which follows the 10 o'clock news. What was particularly striking about both these researches was that they demonstrated that understanding was largely based on intellectual capacity—not perhaps a very new finding, but an interesting one because it showed the extent to which comprehension relies on intelligence. To quote from the report:

"It would seem that the talk which is couched at a level of difficulty appropriate to the top third of the population can rarely convey much to people of even average intelligence and little or nothing to the backward quarter (of the population)."

But something else came out of the first research too; that was the finding that, apart from intellectual capacity, comprehension was "profoundly influenced by the extent to which (people) are interested in the subject, or have their interest in it aroused. The greater the listeners' interest, the greater their understanding is likely to be, and vice versa." This factor of interestingness was more important for intelligibility than any factor of style, language, and delivery. Certainly, such factors as limiting the number of main points, providing clear summaries, a lucid and lively style, concrete treatment, and the illustration of abstract points all *make for* intelligibility —the research proved that—but they do not *guarantee* intelligibility; they only come into play if the talk is interesting in the first place.

Although these studies are of great value in showing just how complicated a matter it is to get information across that will be remembered with any accuracy, a broadcast talk is not the same as face-to-face contact; there are, unfortunately, to my knowledge, no scientific studies of the intelligibility of personal talks to an audience as compared with broadcast talks. The nearest approach to such an investigation is the series of experiments conducted by Lewin (1947) on the respective values of lectures and group discussions in changing food habits. It will be remembered that the latter proved far more effective because the audience participated in a decision. They were, in fact, "ego-involved." I should like to suggest that it is that factor of ego-involvement which lies behind the importance of interest in the subject matter of a talk, which was so well shown in the BBC researches.

Some years ago, I carried out some experiments on the transmission of rumour (Higham, 1951). The method I used was to get someone to recount a short tale to a second person, who repeated it to a third, and so on; each version of the story was recorded on a recording machine, so that a permanent record was available; by those means the successive reproductions could be analysed to see what changes had taken place in the narrative. I used different types of story and different groups of subjects; one day, quite by accident (as I must admit), I made up a short tale about a professor discussing the prospects of his students in their forthcoming examinations; I tried this out on just such a group of his students as might be involved in this sort of discussion. To my surprise, I found that reproduction of the story showed few changes and comparatively small loss of detail, whereas all the other stories produced many changes and a great loss of content with successive reproductions. Applying an appropriate statistical technique, I found that such a result was unlikely to have happened by chance. The explanation was that the students were personally involved in the story; it was about something that affected their interests; and for all they knew it might have been true, or a prophetic warning! Because of this personal interest they remembered it better.

Joint Consultation, particularly through Works' Councils, shows this sort of thing well: matters which management thinks of burning interest are passed by almost without comment; but if an announcement is made that the price of tea in the canteen is going up, discussion is animated and prolonged. People will show most interest in things which concern them personally, or which are linked to their basic needs; that is perhaps why discussion methods seem to be more successful in bringing about change than are formal lectures, for if you take part in a discussion you become involved in it, and it means more to you.

None the less, I think we would be unwise to neglect the importance of the personal factor even in the comprehension of information. For, as many will testify, a good speaker can arouse interest in his audience, even if he breaks every known rule of lecturing. Professor Meredith (1950) has given an excellent example of this in a talk he gave some time ago:

"I am not a theologian, but I was once privileged to attend, at a weekend conference, a lecture by a professor of theology. It was twenty-five years ago and it is still vivid to me today. The subject was Amos, of whom I previously knew precisely nothing. By the end of the lecture I had not only a dynamic impression of the character and message of the prophet but also a clear and colourful picture of the contemporary economic, political, and social structure of the people of Israel. The professor used no notes. He padded round the room, with his hands behind his back, and wearing felt slippers. From time to time he raised one foot to scratch the calf of the other leg. Now and then he looked at one or other of us directly in the eyes, with a kind of challenging glare. At other times he gazed through the window into the extreme distance, as if looking at Palestine, and describing what he saw, taking our gaze with him. I recall that he pronounced Jahweh with the sort of sound one makes in clearing one's throat."

Later Professor Meredith gives his views on why the professor of theology, and other lecturers he had heard, succeeded in communicating to their listeners. He says:

"You can wander about, you can indulge in irritating mannerisms, you can hum and haw, you can remain glued to a desk, you can twiddle your fingers, you can commit all the crimes on the statute book (the latter would make entertaining reading if someone would write it: 'The Deadly Sins of the Lecture Theatre'), and you can get away with all of them if only you have the one supreme virtue. What is that virtue? The name I would give it is *vitality*. This was the common factor in all my remembered lectures."

I suggested earlier that the recall of information was a part of the process of communication which could well be studied. Indeed it has been thoroughly explored, notably and perhaps primarily by Sir Frederic Bartlett (1932) whose book *Remembering* is still the classic on that subject. Later work by Allport and Postman (1948) and others on rumour has supported these earlier findings. The factors of interest and personal involvement, which I mentioned earlier, are important in recall, because we tend to remember better and more accurately those things in which we have been personally interested; but with matters less personal, or less interesting, our minds tend to transform what we have heard, until our final recollection may be quite different from what actually took place. This is an important factor in two way information, because if, for example, a Works' council holds a meeting, it is attended by delegates from different sections of the organization, who have to report back to their constituents; and it is in this reporting back that mistakes and falsifications—albeit involuntary ones—are apt to occur.

Another BBC experiment has shown the importance of some other factors in recall as well. This experiment (1954) was about the immediate memory of a feature programme, one of the "This is the Law" series, in which the script was enlivened by dramatisation, and by being cast in the form of a continuous story. In addition the subjects were all personally invited to the BBC to take part in the experiment. Under such conditions about 80 percent of the story was recalled accurately, with the same variations according to intelligence, occupation, etc. as had been found previously. What is interesting, though, is that the material—a connected story, dealing with everyday people and incidents in everyday language—"lent itself to quick and easy assimilation." But illustrations and dramatisations cannot just be left to make their point; as Vernon has pointed out (1946) they must be related to the subject matter as a whole, otherwise the point is apt to be forgotten.

Here, as in the other aspects of communication which I have touched on, much work remains to be done. So much of what passes for "communication theory" (in the non-engineering sense) is based on hunches and prejudices that further careful experiments are needed. It is the importance of the personal factor in communication that particularly needs to be examined. Simply because we almost all have to live and work among other human beings, we all tend at times to be like the character in Shaw's "Fanny's First Play," who was asked to comment on a production. "You don't expect me to know what to say about a play," she said, "when I don't know who the author is, do you?"

If subjective evidence is acceptable, we have the testimony of teachers, sages and others over the centuries, that people tend to weigh up who we are before listening to what we have to say.

St. Thomas Aquinas warned his pupils *"Non respicias a quo sed quod sane dicetur memoriae recommenda."* Dr. Johnson said of someone, "What you have to say about Aristotle tells me very little about Aristotle, but a great deal about you." Emerson put it more forcefully, "What you are sounds so loudly in my ears that I cannot hear what you say." In many speeches, talks, and other forms of communication, it is often the character of the man that shows through the words he uses, as for example in Sir Winston Churchill's war-time speeches. What is said, and how it is said, often matter less than who says it. As Lord Rosebery said of William Pitt the Elder: "It is not merely the thing that is said, but the man who says it that counts, the character which breathes through the sentences."

There needs to be some degree of warmth in a personal relationship for real communication to exist. When people in conference or consultation have built up stable and firm relationships, then communication is not only easier but, usually, better. As Sir Geoffrey Vickers (1954) has put it:

"Consider how much easier it is to communicate on a standing committee, the members of which are used to deliberating together, than on an ad hoc committee which has never met before. Consider also, how, if the atmosphere of a conference begins to deteriorate, all the experienced members will set to work to put it right again, that is, to recreate the mutual attitudes without which it is a waste of time to confer."

So I should like to suggest to you that successful communication will come about by careful placement of key-men—men, that is, who command trust and respect, who are sympathetic and intelligent; they are your eyes and ears, the people through whom information will flow to you and from you.

As to most operatives, the foreman, not the Board of Directors, *is* the firm, it means careful selection and training of your supervisors. On a higher level, it means equally careful selection and training of junior staff. But a fundamental attitude of "consistent and fair treatment of employees, pursued in good times and bad, and humour and common sense in day to day relationships," as John Marsh of the Industrial Welfare Society put it recently, is not something you can just lay on; it is not a technique; it springs from qualities of character and personality, which is why selection is so important. As Marsh (1954) says:

"The fully fashioned personnel or welfare service cannot be effective unless the foreman—who is 'the firm' to most employees—is efficient, just and consistently humane in his leadership. One knows of instances where the results of years of patient endeavour in building up morale have been dissolved within a few hours of a manager losing his temper. All this goes to show that there are no final answers to human relations questions."

And if at times we tend to forget that last sentence, and to think that we really have at last found the means to cure the human ills of industry once and for all—and judging by the rise and fall in the popularity of such means to that end as welfare schemes, joint consultation, communications and co-partnership, at times we all do think that—then we would do well to remember the warning of Sir Thomas More:

"It is not possible for all things to be well unless all men are good, which I think will not be for these many years."

REFERENCES

Acton Society Trust (1952): *The Worker's Point of View.* London: Acton Society Trust, 39, Welbeck Street, W.1.

Acton Society Trust (1953): *Management under Nationalisation.* London: Acton Society Trust.

Allport, G. W. and Postman, L. (1948): *The Psychology of Rumour.* New York: Holt.

Aquinas, St. Thomas (?1260): *De modo studendi.* Oxford: Blackfriars.

Asch, S. E. (1946): Forming Impressions of Personality. *J. Abnorm. Soc. Psychol.,* **41,** 258–290.

Bartlett, F. C. (1932): *Remembering.* London: Cambridge University Press.

Bartlett, F. C. (1951): *The Mind at Work and Play.* London: Allen and Unwin.

Belson, W. A. (1952): *An Inquiry into the Comprehensibility of "Topic for Tonight."* Audience Research Department Report. London: British Broadcasting Corporation.

Cook, P. H. (1951): *The Productivity Team Technique.* London: Tavistock Institute of Human Relations.

Higham, T. M. (1951): The Experimental Study of the Transmission of Rumour, *Brit. J. Psychol. (General Section)*, **42**, 42–55.

Lewin, K. (1947): Frontiers in Group Dynamics (II). *Hum. Rel.*, **1**, 143–153.

Lorenz, K. (1954): *Man Meets Dog*. London: Methuen.

Marsh, J. (1954): Human Relationships in Industry. *Financial Times*, 30 September.

Maslow, A. H. (1936): The Dominance Drive as a Determiner of the Social and Sexual Behaviour of Infra Human Primates I–IV. *J. of Genet. Psychol.*, **48** and **49**.

Maslow, A. H. (1937): Dominance-feeling, Behavior and Status, *Psychol. Rev.*, **44**, 404–429.

Meredith, G. P. (1950): The Art of Lecturing. *Brit. Med. J.*, 26 August.

Meredith, G. P. (1955): The Flow of Information. *Occup. Psychol.*, **29**, 99–103.

Nias, A. H. W. and Kay, H. (1954): Immediate Memory of a Broadcast Feature Programme, *Brit. J. Educ. Psychol.*, **24**, 154–160.

Oldfield, R. C. (1941): *The Psychology of the Interview*. London: Methuen.

Pear T. H. (1955): *English Social Differences*. London: Allen and Unwin.

Schelderup-Ebbe, T. (1935): The Social Behaviour of Birds. In Murchison, C., *A Handbook of Social Psychology*. Worcester: Clark University Press.

Silvey, R. (1951): The Intelligibility of Broadcast Talks. *Public Opinion Quarterly*, Summer.

Vernon, P. E. (1946): An Experiment on the Value of the Filmstrip in the Instruction of Adults. *Brit. J. Educ. Psychol.*, **16**, 149–162.

Vernon, P. E. (1950): *An Investigation into the Intelligibility of Broadcast Talks*. Audience Research Department Report. London: British Broadcasting Corporation.

Vickers, C. G. (1954): Human Communication. *Brit. Management Rev.*, **12**, 71–79.

Zangwill, O. L. (1937): A Study of the Significance of Attitude in Recognition, *Brit. J. Psychol.*, **28**, 12–17.

Zweig, F. (1952): *The British Worker*. London: Penguin Books.

3

THE RECEIVING END OF
COMMUNICATION—LISTENING *

Percy A. Field

"It takes two people to say a thing—a sayee as well as a sayer. The one is as essential to any true saying as the other."

The sayee is the person at the receiving end of communication. He is the listener. Because of the feedback mechanism, his role is by no means a passive one. Just how well the sayee assimilates information, however, does depend on many factors, some of which form the subject of the rest of my talk.

LISTENING DEFINED

In an article on listening that appeared in the *General Electric Review* in 1958 C. J. Dover defined listening as follows:

"The act of listening includes the assimilation and interpretation of visual stimuli received in context with sound stimuli."

I am not going to deal with the semantic aspects of this definition for there are others of equal importance. Because of this I have, in a broad sense for this talk, taken listening to mean

> Aural, visual and sensory perception as recorded and then interpreted in the mind of the listener.

Note that, for the purposes of this talk, I have included sensory perception in its broadest sense as an act of listening. This would include smell,

* Reprinted from *Proceedings of the 1962 Institute in Technical and Industrial Communications,* Colorado State University, pp. 32–43.

taste, touch, response to heat and cold, and so on. By stretching a point one could also include extrasensory perception insofar as the rather meagre information on this matter indicates that it does appear to have some aspects of reality.

Although the bulk of human communication is carried by sound and sight, in its more subtle aspects a nod of the head, shrug of the shoulders, raised eyebrow or flicker of an eyelid can convey as much information as a thousand words or several pages of pictures. Such common expressions as "speaking with his tongue in his cheek" or "with his fingers crossed" indicate to the listener that he must interpret what he sees or hears according to the extent of "finger crossing" or "tongue cheeking" engaged in by the sender. And it was Victor Hugo, I believe, who said that a man, when conversing with a woman, should listen to what her eyes are saying.

Other aspects of perception, although difficult to define, are understandingly implied when someone is said to "listen with an inner ear" or "listen with the heart," or to "see with an inner eye" or "with his mind's eye."

It is also quite common to refer to human responses in terms of tactile sensations, so that almost everyone knows what is meant when someone (the listener) is said to be "touchy," or is a "soft touch" or an "easy touch" or has the "common touch." We also speak of "hot news" or "hot off the press," and at times may describe someone as a "cold fish."

All life and all progress, in the sense implied in this talk, is totally dependent upon effective listening, for without the ability to listen life would cease. The sensory organs detect and enable living matter to seek out and use light, water, food and the other essentials of life. They also warn of danger and play an important role in adaptation to environment.

WHAT WE DO KNOW ABOUT LISTENING?

Everything we know has been learned through listening. We first learn to speak by listening to our parents and then by repeating the words and simple phrases that attract our attention. Our sensory organs are always alerted and ready to "listen" and the sensations and experiences we undergo as the result of our exposures to many forms of stimuli are recorded in our memory and form part of the learning process as we progress through life. And it was Epictetus, the Greek philosopher and stoic, who remarked that man was given two ears, but only one mouth, that he might hear twice as much as he speaks. It is surprising, therefore, that until recently very little formal attention has been devoted to the listening process.

It is even more surprising when we are told by the people who have studied these matters, that most people, in their work-a-day lives, spend from forty-five to seventy-five percent of their time in listening. In a great many cases this listening is done at about one-quarter to one-third of its possible efficiency. A long hard look at this, in many instances, could suggest that many people are actually earning only about a half of the salary they are paid to do their jobs.

This is something that perhaps time will cure, for as the importance of listening becomes recognized, and as efforts are made to improve listening skills, it is only a matter of time before this matter is attacked at the school level where it should receive as much attention as does speaking, reading and writing.

At the present time some of the things that are known about listening include the following:

(*a*) Listening skills vary greatly among individuals.

(*b*) There is a deterioration in listening attention from kindergarten through high school.

(*c*) Males are better listeners than females.

(*d*) People listen much faster than they can talk.

(*e*) Listening takes energy.

(*f*) Listening skills can be improved greatly.

(*g*) There are many obstacles to effective listening.

(*h*) On the average people listen at a low level of efficiency.

(*i*) Bad listening habits result in an emphasis on the faults and a decrease in listening ability.

(*j*) Men are attracted to women who listen interestingly.

(*k*) Listening skills can be taught.

(*l*) The average person remembers very little of what he takes in.

Not only do listening skills vary greatly among individuals but there is also a noticeable difference in the performance of males and females at listening tasks. Tests at the University of Minnesota and elsewhere showed consistently that although females achieved better intelligence scores than did males, the males were by far the best listeners. This does not necessarily imply that there is a direct relation between intelligence and ability to listen. A poor listener is not necessarily stupid. In fact egocentric persons are often poor listeners even though they may be quite gifted intellectually.

The deterioration in listening attention as a pupil progresses through school is well known to teachers. Children in their early school years pay a lot of attention to what the teacher is saying or doing. As they get older their attention tends to wander and to become fixed on other things. This, again, has been investigated and established as one of the facts of life with which teachers have to contend.

One reason, in listening, why attention tends to wander is that people can think much faster than they can talk. Because of this they also listen much faster than they can talk. On the average, thoughts tend to move along at a rate of four hundred to five hundred words a minute (on the assumption, of course, that most thoughts are formulated in terms of the words we know), while people speak at perhaps one hundred to one hundred and twenty-five words a minute, in English. Under stress, or when excited, speech rate often increases, but so does the rate of thinking so that when people say that their thoughts are just racing along they may be thinking at word rates of perhaps seven to eight hundred words a minute.

It is hardly necessary to explain why men are attracted to women who listen with interest. It may be apropos, however, to quote one Chicago newspaper writer (Sydney J. Harris) who in one of his daily columns said that "the trouble with most conversations between the sexes is that women can listen so much faster than men can talk."

Just as a television or radio receiver require to be turned on and connected to a source of power before they are able to pick up programs, so also do the human sense organs consume energy when they are in a state of alertness and ready to receive information. Anyone who has listened to an important speech or lecture for any length of time, particularly if there are distractions in the environment, may feel exhausted at the end of the program. He does not have to be told that his close attention to what the speaker had to say has consumed a lot of energy. Likewise, long sessions of study that involved the assimilation of information through reading may leave one with a wrung-out feeling. Under stress, in times of danger, excitement, or worry, when more than one of the sense organs is at a pitch of alertness, large amounts of energy are consumed, factors which may leave the people involved utterly exhausted later on.

Although poor listening habits are common-place, it does not necessarily follow that people are born that way and that their listening abilities may not be improved. Where deliberate attempts have been made to improve listening skills the results have been very worth-while, so much so that improvements of from twenty-five to fifty percent have been achieved after various periods of training. Because training of this sort has been shown to be well worth-while some schools, colleges and universities now provide courses of training in listening.

To a considerable extent effective listening depends upon the ability to surmount the many obstacles commonly encountered. We have mentioned distractions in the listening environment, and to these should be added emotional factors such as prejudice, dislike of the speaker or his subject, worry, anger, fear, grief, joy, self-consciousness, the style or format of a piece of writing, the use of emotion-laden words, deliberate attempts to confuse or mislead through false premises, and the many other traps of this sort that await the unwary. All of these degrade one's ability to take things in effectively or without distortion. The failure of a speaker or writer to sufficiently orient his hearers or readers, or to speak in terms that they understand, so that his message does not tie in with their background of experience, establishes in many cases an almost insurmountable obstacle to understanding and effective listening.

Among the many undesirable characteristics that human beings acquire are those that may be termed bad listening habits. These commence in infancy and tend to follow us throughout our lives. They result in an increase in the faults and a decrease in listening ability. Bad listening is often rampant in many organizations where many of the men near the top know very little of what is *really* going on at the lower levels of their establishments. This situation develops most frequently because the people who should keep their ears open to what is going on have never really learned to pay attention to what the lower echelons are saying. It is quite common to hear of an executive being referred to as "having an open door and a closed mind." He has simply detuned his hearing mechanism into another channel.

THE PROCESS OF LEARNING

Earlier in this talk we mentioned that people learn through listening. It may seem surprising, therefore, to be told that even the most careful listeners forget more than half of what they hear or read shortly after the event. In fact, in about two weeks most people have forgotten about seventy-five percent of what they hear or read. Perhaps this may justify "cramming" for an examination shortly before it occurs! Not only do most people forget quickly, but in tests where stories involving people are passed through another group of people by word of mouth, the most frightful distortions are likely to occur, so that "what went in there" is often the exact opposite of "what comes out here."

The process of learning is really a process of learning and then forgetting much of the original information, but with each repetition of the information being learned, more and more of it is retained until eventually much of it becomes fixed in the memory. The way in which learning normally progresses is shown in Fig. 1.

The amount of information learned is related to the amount of effort devoted to the learning process. Fig. 1 shows that learning progresses quite rapidly at first and then slows down for a while. Interest flags, the mind and body tire, and this results in a slowing down of progress. But later on the task is taken up again with renewed vigor and progress accelerates. Still later it again slows down and then, after a time, it speeds up again. Progress finally levels off near the optimum amount of learning acquired for each individual item concerned.

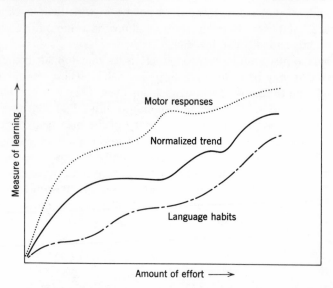

Figure 1. How learning progresses.

There is some disagreement among the people who investigate these matters about the difference shown between motor responses and language habits. Because we, as writers, editors, and communication specialists, deal with language and are only too well aware of the difficulties encountered by many people in learning satisfactory language habits, it seems reasonable to assume that the difference shown does exist, and that more difficulty occurs in learning to speak and write effectively than exists in learning motor habits such as, for instance, in learning how to skate or to swim. I leave out for obvious reasons such abilities as are involved in violin playing, because this involves high motor skills combined with the ability to interpret musical symbols (language) and convert these into pleasing music.

As we have just said, learning progresses in steps of learning-forgetting, learning-forgetting, over many cycles of effort. The normal rate of forgetting is well established and is shown in the curves in Fig. 2. From these it is at once evident that the amount of information retained normally declines very rapidly soon after first learning it. Half of it is forgotten by the next day and in two weeks only about one quarter of the original information is retained in unmodified form. After that the progress of forgetting proceeds much more slowly and the amount of information retained levels off, nearly, so that some memory of the event is likely to remain for many years.

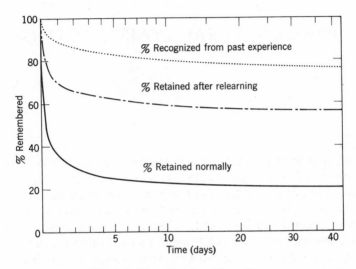

Figure 2. The progress of forgetting.

On the other hand, a recurrence of the original event, or further study, so that, in effect, some degree of relearning occurs, results in a re-engraving on the memory of the original information, after which forgetting progresses much more slowly than originally, as shown in the percent retained after relearning curve of Fig. 2.

The percent recognized from past experience relates to the many things that one encounters in one's daily life. We recognize the chirping of a robin, the shape of a chair, the smell of a flower, the taste of a mint, the feel of silk and so on from past experience. These are things that form part of our daily lives. We are not likely to forget these very quickly. People who have become blind, or have lost their hearing or sense of smell still recognize what these are like when the things to which they pertain are mentioned. These former sensations are so engraved on their memories that the percent recognized from past experience is likely to be high. Their listening senses relate the event almost instantly to a similar event in past experience, which is the process of recognition.

4

TRANSCULTURAL COMMUNICATION *

Roy C. Nelson

There are a great many forces loose in the world today. The collective pull of these forces is resulting in rapid and unprecendented change. Societies are being remolded; existing power structures are breaking up; new alliances are being formed; technology with its concomitants is invading all parts of the world and profoundly affecting the basic existence of man. Events follow each other with such speed, that it is difficult to make predictions, to pass judgment as to whether what is happening is beneficial or detrimental, or even to set up standards to evaluate what is called progress. The only thing we can be certain of is that unremitting change will go on and this Humpty-Dumpty world will never be put back together again as it existed yesterday, or last week, or a year ago. We are in fact in a perpetual state of transition.

The chief cause of the transitory nature of our time is an exploding body of information, powerful as an atomic bomb but different. Like an atomic bomb it has deposited culturally radioactive materials in almost all areas of the world on the winds of change—communication.

FOR PEOPLE

At this point, then, I should like to examine some of the broad implications of communications, their relationships with cultural systems and the impact communications are having on man and his societies. Communication always involves people, whether we refer to two people engaged in a friendly interchange of gossip or whether our reference points to

* Reprinted from *Proceedings of the 1964 Institute in Technical and Industrial Communications,* Colorado State University, pp. 63–67.

a complicated system of communication in a governmental agency or an industrial complex. Communication can be oral or written, technical or non-technical, processed by a mechanical device, utilize the mass media, and be local or world-wide in scope, yet in each case it has implications for people. This categorical assertion is true, because all communication derives from a source—a human being, and it is ultimately perceived by a receiver—another human being. If I belabor the obvious, it is because the obvious so often eludes us. The Communications network, including media, techniques, and mechanical devices, fascinates us so much that we often neglect the character and content of the message and its effect in human terms. The typewriter, for example, has been an invaluable invention for speeding and making more legible many forms of correspondence and writing. But our interest in the typewriter is not primarily, or at least should not be on the mechanical principles controlling the machine, the metal from which it is fashioned, or its ink processes. Rather our concern should be with the person composing at the typewriter, the rhetoric he creates, and the ultimate influence his message will have. The same emphasis should be apparent in transcultural communications.

In international communication, we can marvel at transoceanic cables, global radio networks, intercontinental television, translation services and computers, international editions of newspapers and periodicals, and communication satellites, but we also need to concern ourselves with the flow of information over these instruments, the impact which the signals and symbols are having on individuals and societies, and the purposes, problems and failures associated with the message content. I approach the study of communication then as a humanity, for man is never quite as human as when he is communicating with his fellowmen. Especially when we observe men reaching across cultural barriers to make contact with other human beings do we gain insight into an understanding of, and appreciation for the many faces of man—his needs, his aspirations, his failings, his problems, and perhaps his tragic nature.

To reiterate, communication and culture are intimately concerned with people. And the number of people we have on this earth at this moment is staggering. Demographers estimate that there are three billion, two hundred million persons populating the earth in 1964. More overwhelming are the prospects for the future; *homo sapiens* is reproducing himself more rapidly than any other of the higher animal forms, and in fact may be driving many of them into extinction. If present population trends continue, by the year 2000 A.D. or in thirty-six more years the present number of people will double and seven billion persons will compete for the available space on this little globe. If natural or man-made catastrophes do not intervene, many of you . . . will be alive in 2000 A.D. Even if you abhor congestion

and crowded conditions today, you will have to content yourself on a pro-
portionate basis with just one half as much space as you have in 1964.

This brings me to the thesis I wish to support . . . : the population explosion, like the information explosion, commands that we improve communication if this planet is to support tolerable conditions for humans and
their societies. Burgeoning births and fewer deaths are forcing the elbows
of masses of people closer together and leaving much less room in between.
Judging by the past, irritations, conflicts, and strife will increase unless
more effective communications bridge the gap between societies, make possible better problem solving and decision making, and replace suspicion
and distrust with understanding.

CULTURE

In order to develop my thesis I should like to examine in a broad and
general way the phenomenon called culture, to determine the restraints it
has put on communications, and to suggest a few principles which may assist in spanning some of the cultural clefts which separate men.

Someone has said that communication is culture, but this is only a partial truth. Rather I believe culture is the residue of an endless flow of communication which has accumulated in the nervous systems of a people
within a particular group. Culture has its outlet in music, art, philosophy,
religion, language, and technology, but more importantly is reflected in the
habits, beliefs, customs, interests, aspirations, and ways of perceiving reality of the persons within a particular cultural community.

A variety of cultures exist—rather than one world culture—for the reason that communication has been inverted, confined to the group, and re-
strained from infusing other groups. In other words, a culture results from
a kind of communicative inbreeding. As soon as the individuals of a culture
begin to communicate with individuals of another group, their culture
changes and aspects of the second culture are adopted by the first group.

This cultural in-group feeling can be traced to conditions in the ancient
world of our ancestors. In the long ago, in order to survive, the individual
was compelled to identify completely with his own people. Outside his own
group everything was different, strange, and hostile. The tribe living across
the river or the city-state on the other side of the peninsula was not to be
trusted. Warfare and an uneasy peace between the clans precluded all but a
modicum of friendly discourse.

Culture—Natural Factors

Much of this group-patriotism persists today in varying forms and degrees. The three billion inhabitants of this planet Earth are still divided into
many cultural groups—this despite the shrinking of the globe, revolution-

ary advances in communicative technology, and a new mobility which brings the ordinary traveler to places visited only by the daring adventurer a short while ago. Although terrestrial distance has all but disappeared, the cleavages among men in many cases have become wider, and the social distance between human groups much longer.

Geography, the physical feature of the planet, man's nature, and a combination of natural and man-made events have conspired to divide and sub-divide, to erect communicative barriers, and to establish layer on layer of cultural strata. To begin with, a global map of the Earth shows five continents, nicely grouped into two hemispheres. If a political map is superimposed on these physical features, we see a patchwork of 120 nation states. In a few cases such as between Canada and the United States, an imaginary line separates one nation from another. Quite often, however, barbed wire, brick walls, and concrete bunkers reinforce the boundary. In other cases, geographical regions are off-limits to members of another nation, as Larimer County surrounding Fort Collins is to the Russians and all of Red China is to citizens of the United States. Now if we superimpose an ideological overlay on the political map, the acetate will highlight the grouping of nations adhering to socialistic or capitalistic economics and democratic or autocratic forms of government. Still another grouping can be made on the basis of economic development, delineating the have and have-not nations. If we let black represent total poverty, we should have to color almost half of the land surface dark gray to represent less than adequate food, clothing, and shelter for people residing in these areas.

Temperature, rainfall, and altitude are among natural elements which tend to stratify and assign people to culture. Man's relation to his environment profoundly affects his interests and more importantly how he views reality. People have always talked about the weather, because weather profoundly affects their lives. For example, the experiences of desert nomads are intensely different from the Eskimos. Dwellers in the high dry Andes have learned to respond to the universe in dissimilar ways from those who live in the humid, tropical jungles of the Congo. People who live close to earth develop a different culture from those who live in crowded urban areas. Geography and climate also tend to determine how people make a living, how they cultivate the soil, where they build their cities, the nature of their industrial developments, and the amount of wealth they accumulate. All of these effects then become causes to orient further people to distinctive cultural societies.

Culture—Human Factors

Let us turn now from natural elements to the human elements, which have been responsible for restraining communication and thereby molding cultural patterns. Perhaps the most ancient of the human factors is man's conceiving gods or a deity and then formulating doctrine to govern his relating to that deity. The three billion people of the world, if we disregard sects and minor denominations, adhere to less than a dozen great religions. History tells the story of many bloody religious wars. It is therefore encouraging to note in modern times a growing religious tolerance and a respect for the many faiths and ways men worship. But religion still remains a dominant culture factor and an obstacle to communication in many sections of the world. Religion is one factor behind the bitterness between Israel and the surrounding Moslem Arabic states; Hindu India and Moslem Pakistan fear and distrust each other with as much fervor as the Christian nations of the West abhor the state atheism of Soviet Russia.

But the most disruptive human factor to communication, and yet the most superficial, is the degree of pigmentation in a man's skin. Even in a country like the United States, where the mass media dominate our lives and where a more massive movement of information is occurring than in any other time or place, the most critical problem of this year has been the lack of interracial communication. Recent events in St. Augustine, Florida, and Philadelphia, Mississippi are evidence that even in highly civilized countries there are those who are committed to keeping the races separate. While the problem has been most intense in the South, the devices to keep the colored people from communicating with the whites such as restrictive covenants, segregated schools, discriminating labor practices, off-limit playgrounds and parks, and prejudice are national in scope. A Civil Rights Law can, of course, alleviate some of the most flagrant abuses to interracial communication, but it cannot eliminate prejudice, enforce respect for the basic dignity of another human being, or bring about genuine communication; at best it can only create conditions where these values can grow and flourish. In the United States, the colored people are a minority of one to ten; but of the three billion people in the world, they are an overwhelming majority. The club, the bulldog, the fire hose, and the electric prod are hardly the communicative tools on which to bring about racial understanding. The two-thirds majority of the three billion people in the world who are colored are unlikely to be impressed by these desperation measures, either here or by the apartheid policy of the Republic of South Africa.

LANGUAGE

Now I should like to consider a human invention which is more closely associated with culture than any of the other factors I have mentioned. I refer to language. Language acts not only as a cohesive agent within a group but as an insulator of the group against alien ideas, attitudes, and concepts. Language, even more faithfully than climate, race, or religion, classifies the three billion into specific cultural groups. Consisting of a code of symbols to which meaning has been arbitrarily assigned by a particular group, language permits individuals to say something about that part of the universe they observe and how they observe it. As I have previously said, human experience depends upon environment. A cowboy herding cattle in Texas, for example, experiences a cluster of sensations quite different from a sailor crossing the Pacific Ocean; however, if they have a common vocabulary, they can each vicariously relive the experiences of the other. Language, then, reflects human experiences and the manner perceiving reality. Language, therefore, is the most accurate index of people's culture as well as a dependable regulator of communication. Sophistication in using language also determines the forms of communication which can be comprehended. The illiterates, a billion or more strong in the present world, are limited to the spoken word or immediate communication; they cannot store information by writing for use at some future time; neither do they have the freedom to be enriched by ideas their fellow men have recorded on the printed page.

Language is also a great divider. The three billion people of the world, unless they are multi-lingual, are separated into 3000 language groups. The great modern state of India alone is handicapped by fifteen language systems. One of the disunifying problems for the emerging nations of Africa is the multitude of language and tribal dialects which bar an easy transmittal of information from one area of that continent to another. Although the Europeans have carried their language systems to all parts of the world, Europe which has been a virtual breeding ground for language, has not been able to achieve any degree of linguistic unity.

THE "TWO CULTURES"

Even before the Roman classes of plebians and patricians or the caste system of India, societies were stratified into classes—usually determined by accident of birth. More recently, possession of wealth and economic status have become the determinants of class. Although in many countries of the world, culture differs from class to class, in the United States, at least, class culture has deteriorated and has been replaced by mass culture —stimulated and nourished by the mass media. But as economic class fades, another threat to communication has appeared.

A new division, here and in Europe, has developed among the intellectuals who pursue different disciplines—namely the sciences and the humanities.

In 1959, the English physicist and novelist, C. P. Snow, called attention to this phenomenon with the warning that men educated in the humanities have little understanding of developments in the physical and biological sciences; and correspondingly that the mathematician and scientist have little to say to their counterparts in the humanities about art, literature, and philosophy. Margaret Mead supports Snow's view with this observation:

"We are, in fact, in danger of developing as other civilizations before us have developed, special esoteric groups who can communicate only with each other and who can accept as neophytes and apprentices only those individuals whose intellectual abilities, temperamental bents, and motivations are like their own."

Miss Mead goes on to say,

"Now we must find new educational and communicative devices that will not sacrifice this new high level of specialized communication and yet will protect our society and all the intellectual disciplines within it from the schismatic effects of too great a separation of thought patterns, language, and interest between the practitioners of a scientific or humane discipline and those who are laymen in each particular field."

Other critics see the two polar groups formed around these two different educational pursuits repelling each other more and more with the intensification of specialization. The scientists seek to understand the world; and in so doing they are, through applied science, reframing society itself. The non-scientific intellectual, on the other hand, influences the decisions which go on in the framework. Failure of these two groups to communicate may well result, as Snow points out, in dire consequences for civilization as we know it.

REMOVING BARRIERS TO TRANSCULTURAL COMMUNICATION

These represent some of the cultural strands which have had a major influence in fixing social origins and caused groups of men to travel slightly different paths. A continuum of societies from the most primitive to the most advanced could be constructed from groups now living in various parts of the world. Should our goal be to amalgamate all of the differing communities into one massive, monolithic world society? I think not. Even if such a condition could be brought about, it would not be desirable. Each cultural community is a laboratory in humanity and an experiment in living and the findings of each, if properly communicated, can enlighten and enrich the relationships of men everywhere. We need only look to the development of our own nation for evidence that unity can grow out of diversity, and that the "unum" can be achieved without sacrificing the "pluribus." It is possible, I believe, through more effective communication to multiply the interests of groups of individuals and to introduce more variation into the subject matter which concerns human beings.

Fully realizing the immensity of the task and the character of the obstacles which stand in the way of its accomplishment, I should, nonetheless, like to state some broad objectives for the improvement of communication that this nation and especially those of us involved in the communication arts and sciences might dedicate ourselves to and hopefully achieve.

First, artificial, unnatural barriers to communication must be leveled wherever they exist. I refer to iron curtains, brick walls, jamming of radio broadcasts, distortion, deception, and secrecy. To put it more positively, the increasing amount of information now being generated must be made available to a larger per cent of the three billion inhabitants of this globe. Those who are rich in knowledge and skills must undertake a global effort to diffuse and disseminate information to the poor in knowledge and the unskilled. If environment is to be better controlled, hunger and want alleviated, disease wiped out, and a richer material life made possible for the two-thirds of the world's population who barely subsist, then useful knowledge in the sciences and technology should circulate freely to all areas of the world. But this knowledge should only be disseminated with full awareness of the context of a thousand cultures and an understanding of the impact this knowledge will have on the audiences who receive it. Failures and difficulties associated with efforts in the past to effect technological development can be traced in large part to a neglect of social factors and human relations. Science and technology cannot be disassociated from human affairs. The humanist and the scientist, therefore, must begin a meaningful dialogue and join forces; the message of each bears on the message of the other, and together on the welfare of all.

Second, our communications must be a two-way street. By this, I mean that we should endeavor to know as much about other peoples as we desire them to know about us. A Good Neighbor Policy or an Alliance For Progress will remain an empty gesture if we ignore the arts, literature, and philosophy of our friends to the south. Neither will there be a true meeting of the East and West if we fail to read the great books, look upon the oriental religions with contempt, and are too blind to the expectations and aspirations of the so-called teeming masses; and if we look upon ourselves as superior, these feelings of supremacy must be supported by something more substantial than the color of our skins, the shape of our noses, or any other hereditary feature. As we begin to study other cultures we will benefit by forming more profound insights into our own. We should also be aware that whether or not we are communicating to children or adults of this or any other culture, we can talk to them only in terms of what makes sense to them.

A WORLD LANGUAGE

Third, we should work vigorously to establish a better linguistical medium of exchange—an exchange worldwide in scope. Such a language should not be Esperanto or Interlingua or any of the other artificial languages but most logically, English. To be adopted widely, an international language should have certain qualities: It should have a phonetic system which can be easily mastered; its rules of grammar and syntax should be easily learned; its code of symbols should be free from ambiguity and cause a minimum of semantic confusion; and it should have stability enough to resist fad but flexible enough to incorporate new words into its lexicon to reflect new concepts, new inventions, and new scientific discoveries in a changing world.

Despite the fact that English does not rate very high when subjected to these criteria, nevertheless, I recommend English as a world language for the reasons that it is most widely used language in the world, it is already being taught as a second language in many countries of the world, and it is the language of science. In making this suggestion I do not propose to eliminate the other 3000 languages; rather I believe that those of us who speak English have a greater obligation to overcome our linguistic provincialism by studying other languages. The effectiveness of anyone working and living in another country is greatly curtailed if he cannot speak the tongue of those about him. More than any other component, language is the looking glass of culture, for the difficulties of learning a second language are not necessarily found in grammar or pronunciation but rather in its social and cultural features. The second language will often be based on a whole new way of looking at reality, demand new habits of observation, and reflect new attitudes and values.

IN MINDS OF MEN

Fourth, the content of our international communication, should ordinarily carry affection, respect, encouragement, and appreciation for the cultures of other people even though we may not approve of their government. The transmission of hate, animosity, and belligerent threats has not been effective in improving human relations. The best hope for peace in our time rests firmly on the premise that communications can reduce fear and tension and promote good will throughout the world.

In the preamble of the UNESCO charter is the assertion that wars are made in the minds of men. Conversely, peace is also made in the minds of men. There have been warlike cultures and peaceful cultures; in each case these mental states were determined and reinforced by content of the communication which flourished in each group.

Communication and tension also operate in a circular process. As tension subsides between two hostile cultures, rents begin to appear in the curtains and cracks in the walls which have acted as barriers. As tension rises, communication tends to dry up.

In the decades ahead, the pressures of an increasing population will multiply and magnify conflicts and cause new problems which cry for new solutions. These problems can and will be solved but only if pertinent data are gathered and communicated and the rational rather than the emotional dominates the rhetoric of exchange.

INTERNATIONAL COMMUNICATIONS

With these broad objectives in mind, let us examine the apparatus of international communications. In terms of involvement of people, international communication forms four levels and takes the form of a pyramid. The first level making up the apex of the pyramid is the diplomatic corps, including representatives of the government such as ambassadors, delegates to the United Nations, and treaty negotiators. The next level might be termed the subdiplomatic or official. It is made up of international business, cultural and athletic exchanges, Fulbright scholars and students, scientific meetings and conferences, AID Missions, and Peace Corps. Even though these groups do not make high level policy, they usually have the sanction of the government. The third level affects more people and consists of the communications media such as newspapers, radio and television, books, periodicals, and films. The final level at the base of the pyramid is composed of the people-to-people contacts and includes the ordinary tourists and visitors who are physically present in another culture. These four levels are not mutually exclusive and each level relates to the other. Peace Corps volunteers, for example, are trained and supervised by the government, but the magnificent accomplishments of the volunteers are traceable to the direct communication they have had with the people of the host country. The USIS, another agency of the government, operates the Voice of America, circulates books and magazines in its overseas libraries and teaches classes to citizens of the host country in its binational centers.

Looking at the growing size of the communications pyramid at every level, we are led to conclude that the gigantic efforts this nation is engaging in assures a glowing future for all mankind. Leadership in the United Nations, for example, has encouraged the General Assembly to emerge as a forum wherein the newest delegate from the newest, tiny African state can debate issues with representatives from nations long established. We are sending students, scholars, technicians to almost all of the developing nations of the world, and our universities and colleges, no matter how small or where located, are educating students from these same countries. Our books, periodicals, and films are in demand and are circulating more freely than ever before. About one per cent of our population, including students, business men, the families of military personnel, and tourists will spend some part of 1964 in other countries. Although difficult to measure, thanks to better communication techniques at all levels of the pyramid, people round the world are better informed, more capable of dealing with ideas, and more skilled in relating to other people than at any other period of time.

ARE WE DOING ENOUGH?

But before becoming too optimistic about present trends, we must ask ourselves if what we are doing is enough, if we are moving as rapidly as the world situation demands, and whether our action programs are qualitatively sound. Let me cite some disturbing examples.

Seven-hundred million people in Red China are not represented in the United Nations, have little communication with Western nations and almost none with the United States. Although we have more than a million overseas Americans, only a small part of them make significant effective people-to-people contacts. Our 8000 Peace Corps volunteers have been effective in this respect, but 8000 persons among three billion are less than the proverbial drop in the bucket. Much of what we export about ourselves over communication media is cheap and tawdry; because of language difficulties and widespread illiteracy our written material can have no reception at all; television is too expensive for the underdeveloped areas of the world where even private radios are uncommon. It has been estimated that an additional 100,000 people obtain proficiency in English each day, but the world population is increasing twice as fast or by 200,000 each day. Our domestic violence receives more attention abroad than does our idealistic talk about peace, brotherhood, and equality. The gap between our stated beliefs and our day-to-day action lead many people to question our moral purpose. The staggering quantity of scientific facts and data has often been considered a commodity, an end in itself, something to be computed, stored, and retrieved, with little relationship to the human beings whose lives are drastically altered by this information.

These are just some of the dilemmas and paradoxes which color the problem of communication in a changing world. They should not, however, be viewed through the dark glasses of defeatist pessimism or the rosy spectacles of an easy optimism but with clear-eyed realism.

THE HOPE AND MEASURE

As I have pointed out, mankind is the sum of many parts, varied, different, and separated by cultural residue deposited by ages of history. Because of the tremendous rate at which population is increasing, these many parts must be integrated in a harmonious whole by vastly improved communications at all levels of the pyramid if diverse societies are to continue to coexist side by side and to promote the material welfare and humane values of the individuals who reside in each. I believe we have no other option but to accept this goal. Anthropologists tell us that the human race hasn't changed fundamentally from its cavemen ancestors and technology really hasn't changed us but only altered our environment and given us some new thoughts. If that be true, we must remember that we no longer live in a series of isolated caves but in one big cave. And we have learned to use a new kind of fire—capable of killing almost everyone and making the cave uninhabitable.

But we have also advanced from the crude picturegraphs carved on stone to pulsating electronic signals capable of symbolizing all of the thoughts of man. The hope and measure of our future depend on the ideas we create, our skill in encoding and decoding them, and the sense of responsibility by which we communicate them to our fellow men.

5

A DYNAMIC THEORY
OF COMMUNICATION *

C. Merton Babcock

Communications courses, ostensibly geared to the demands of our time, are frequently administered and taught by individuals with doubtful convictions concerning the efficacy of a functional approach to language studies. Traditionally trained instructors tenaciously cling to a regal, time-honored doctrine of prestige and authority, which assumes a hierarchal social structure incompatible with democratic social theory or the observable facts of twentieth-century American society. The unjustifiable analysis of language into stratified levels of usage, apparently arranged to coincide with fictitious levels of society, has been properly exploded.[1]

The nineteenth-century doctrine of usage represented an initial revolt against authoritative dicta in matters of language utility. At the beginning of the present century, language scholars defined a doctrine of appropriateness in an attempt to find a practical and realistic method of determining verbal effectiveness. This doctrine relates effectiveness to such factors as characteristics of the language, peculiarities of persons engaged in communication, psycho-social needs of the communicatee, emotional attitudes of communicator and communicatee, and controlling purposes for which communication is initiated.

Recognition of the primary importance of language as an instrument of communication in a democratic society follows logically enough cognizance of the glaring "misuses" for which it may be employed. Educators have been made aware of the potency of language in the personal, intellectual, and social development of individuals. Some have conceived the potentialities of language as an indispensable instrument for solving inter-

* Reprinted from *The Journal of Communication,* May, 1952, pp. 64–68.

cultural, -political, -social, and -national problems of the people of the world. Too many, however, have misinterpreted the "signposts," or have been unable to discount their unrealistic, traditional training in language and scarcely know how to approach the problems of instruction from a functional-dynamic point of view.

The belief that communicative effectiveness is relative to interrelated and interacting variables in a given dynamic social configuration may be called a field theory of communication. The purposes of the present paper are to conceive a framework within which socio-linguistic behavior can be explained and to define variants which may determine effectiveness in a given communication field. The proposed formulation is based on the assumptions that social and linguistic changes are co-relative, that language is a psycho-social characteristic of human behavior in a state of incessant flux, and that a complex pattern of interrelated variables in a given socio-linguistic configuration is unique.

Five "master terms," said to adequately represent the limitations of a given statement of motives, are utilized for the present architectonic. These terms are Act, Scene, Agent, Agency, and Purpose.[2] A communication event incorporates all five of these terms or determinants.

The event is the entire drama to which attention is directed, a set of social circumstances arbitrarily isolated from a stream or context in which it can be defined, a dynamic multivalence of forces, observable and unobservable, apparent and transcendent, in process. From a communication point of view, the event may be observed in the employment of symbols (act), under specific circumstances (scene), by an individual or individuals (agent), using selected media (agency), for defined ends (purpose). This is a way of saying that any event is arbitrarily bounded by the limitations of what, who, when, where, how, and why. These determinants commingle, unite, overlap in the event, and are in the strictest sense inseparable, in that no one of the terms can be defined adequately without mention of all the others.

ACT

The communicative act, which has been here defined as the employment of symbols, can best be understood as a mutually reciprocal procedure: at once assimilative and disseminative. An individual collects facts, experiences, observations, etc. which he combines and organizes into ideas, thoughts, insights, revelations. He then translates these insights into meaningful verbal symbols, which he disseminates or transmits to other individuals. This sensory-cortical-linguistic-social process is the communicative act, and may be thought of as a spontaneous and inevitable emancipation or release of fluid forces or tensions in the social event from which it develops and in which it can be defined. This definition of an act does not include the employment of symbols for the mere sake of employing symbols, but assumes a dramatic, social situation in which there is not only transmission but also reception of ideas. The act, then, is a sort of socio-linguistic synapse.

The relative effectiveness (success or failure) of the communicative act is dependent upon innumerable "immanent" factors and combinations of factors which are virtually impossible, by current research methods, to control. A speaker who gives the same speech on many occasions can testify to the varying enthusiasm with which different audiences, under various circumstances, receive the communication. The actual words employed perhaps have no more to do with the audience responses than do other factors. The same is true of written messages. Many a reader has reversed, after a second reading, his initial judgment of the pleasure or profit derived from a particular book.

Verbal meaning derives, not from the isolated word in its conventional, historical, traditional, or etymological dimensions, but from the context, both social and verbal, in which the word appears. Isolation, separation, or disengagement of the word from these contexts strip it of meaning, value, currency, or efficacy.

SCENE

The scene of a communication event is made up of the unique set of circumstances or conditions in which the act develops. The precise limits of the scene or frame of reference are arbitrarily fixed or established by the observer. The scene is limited, not only by time and place, but by innumerable social, economic, political, psychological considerations. These considerations may be combined in the expressions *culture* or *civilization* or *context*. Whatever set of values may most appropriately be used as a yardstick for the determination of the relative success or failure of a specific *communiqué* is implicit in the frame of reference or context. When the scene changes, the system of values changes and a new yardstick becomes necessary.

The unwillingness of many students of language to accept the theory that social changes are reflected in changes of language partially accounts for the existing state of confusion regarding usage. It seems utterly absurd to pay homage to the disengaged word, to depend upon dictionaries for word meanings and pronunciations, and to determine "correctness" by imposed criteria. When Calvin Coolidge announced his 1927 political intentions in the words, "I do not choose to run!" hundreds of people vainly attempted to corner his meaning in the dictionary rather than in the political-social scene in which the verbal act developed.

No formula for effectiveness can be derived that will allow for the changed and changing conditions of society. Social norms are irreducible to closed equations. Teachers and students of language must persistently scrutinize their axiomatic assumptions if they are sincerely concerned with the effectiveness of their communicative endeavors. A certain linguistic mobility and adroitness is necessary if social communication is to relate to experience and the demands of our time, rather than to the dictates of authority, reason, logic, or consistency. The effective communicator, then, would be impelled to familiarize himself with the values and taboos of the society of which he is part, rather than the dogmas of a society which has ceased to exist.

AGENT

A successful agent of the group's interests is not imposed upon, but rather emerges from the group he identifies. The unique qualifications of such an agent or spokesman are not in any sense fixed. He is a "functional exuberance," which is born of "instantaneous intensities" in a group configuration. His voice is an affinity of heterogeneous voices, his diction the resultant of many contradictions.

The agent's first responsibility is to the group he represents and addresses. His task is to efficiently communicate an idea or ideas to this group. His effectiveness as a communicator is determined by this group. His qualifications are not then predetermined. Since students have been almost invariably taught to imitate and emulate the "great minds," the "successful artists," the "master wits" of the writing and speaking traditions, the schools may be said to produce men and women relatively incapable of making necessary adjustments to existing individual differences among audiences and readers. The results may be decorous even though ineffective. Communication is often blocked, clogged, glutted by the very speakers who are applauded for their "fine" words and impressive delivery. The fact that, in most institutions of learning, students are coerced into making speeches or writing papers on assigned subjects may partially explain the apparent "language distress," the communicative inefficiency of such students.

AGENCY

The selected media by which thoughts, ideas, convictions, insights are transmitted from the writer-speaker to the reader-listener is here termed the communicative agency. Symbolic language is thought to be the most effective, precise, and efficacious of the several agencies employed in the communication of ideas. Although the appropriateness of media is certainly relative to the nature and purposes of the communication, the present concern is solely with the written and spoken word, or what is generally referred to as diction.

Word choices defended by dictionary definitions or by eminent authorities may be determined to be precisely "correct" by several criteria, but hopelessly inappropriate, and therefore ineffective, as far as the auditors and readers are concerned. That such choices should be preferred to words which would carry a "Message to Garcia" with utmost efficiency and dispatch is ridiculous.

The student of speech or composition, in many schools, is early apprised of the "inadequacy" and "inferiority" of his habitual word choices. He sets half-heartedly about the business of finding more suitable and acceptable words, and becomes convinced somehow that there exists one most suitable and "correct" combination of words by which to express his idea. Rather should he practice giving expression to his idea in various ways, adjusted to a variety of "real-life" situations. At present, most high school and college "themes" are written with no particular reader in mind, except possibly the instructor. Continuance of such an impractical, unrealistic, artificial practice will doubtless result in consistently ungratifying "efforts" at effective writing and speaking. Good language, in the final analysis, is language which gets the desired effects with a minimum of friction and difficulty for both speaker-writer and reader-listener.

PURPOSE

The adequacy of communication may be defined as the extent to which the precise purposes of the communicator are realized with respect to the communicatee. This is another way of saying that the success or failure of a given set of words in a specific social context alters with the uses to which the words are put. Any classification of the various uses for which language may be employed is strictly arbitrary and of necessity highly abstract. The complexity of the pattern of motivations—psychological, social, economic, political, ethical, etc.—operating in a given communication configuration is unique and defies analysis or standardization.

The crux of the matter is simply that there is no magic formula for communicative effectiveness. A dynamic theory of communication offers a major challenge to educators and research specialists to devise means of measuring the relative effectiveness of specific communiqués within a framework of ever-changing circumstances.

NOTES

[1] John S. Kenyon, "Cultural Levels and Functional Varieties of English," *College English X* (October 1948), pp. 31–36.

[2] Kenneth Burke, "The Five Master Terms," in W. S. Knickerbocker's *Twentieth Century English* (New York: Philosophical Library, 1946), pp. 272–288.

6

PROBLEMS IN MEANING *

Herman M. Weisman

My youngest daughter, Abbi, aged 2, is learning to talk. She is receiving expert help from her 8-year-old sister, Lise. Abbi learns through the pedagogical techniques of demonstration and imitation. Lise points to things and pronounces their names. Abbi mouths the words after her. Lise has experienced the frustrations of many teachers. Early in her school experience, Abbi called all frisky, moving things "kittycats"—even when they were birds or moths. While Abbi was quick to learn and point to a horse and call it "horsey" she, at first, also called cows and sheep "horsey."

One day Harlan, Abbi's and Lise's 11-year-old brother, complicated matters. Abbi and Lise were visibly enjoying an object of instruction. Each had half of a red, succulent apple. "Apple! Eat apple," said Lise. "Eat apple," imitated Abbi. "Apple, red," said Lise, holding her half up in demonstration. "Apple, red," said Abbi. Lise then used the index finger of her other hand and pointed to the bright red skin of the apple and said, "Red." Then she pointed to Abbi's rocking horse and said, "Red." Then she pointed to Abbi's tricycle and said, "Red." Abbi said, "horsey, bicycle." "No," said Lise, "red, red."

"You're confusing her," interrupted Harlan. "She doesn't know what you mean by red. Besides not all apples are red." "This one is," said Lise. "Not all apples are red," said Harlan. "That's not the way to make her understand."

"It is so," said Lise.

"It is not!" retorted Harlan with the superior conviction of an older brother. "She doesn't know the meaning of apple, red or *anything* the way you're teaching her," he said.

* Reprinted from *Proceedings of the 1964 Institute in Technical and Industrial Communications,* Colorado State University, pp. 115–124.

190

"How would *you* explain to a baby the meaning of apple, the meaning of red?" asked Lise.

Harlan thought a moment, then said, "Why don't you look it up in the dictionary?"

Lise got the dictionary out of the bookcase and read: "Apple. Firm-fleshed, smooth-skinned, round or oblong pome fruit of the tree of the genus Malus, varying greatly in shape, size, color and degree of acidity."

"You see," said Harlan, "it can have various kinds of colors."

"But, I don't understand the meaning," said Lise.

"Now, do you know what apple means?" asked Harlan of Abbi.

"Let's look up red," said Lise. "A primary color or any other spread of colors at the lower end of the visible spectrum, varying in hue from that of blood to that of pale rose or pink," she read. "I don't think Abbi would understand this either," said Lise. "And I think *my* way of explaining is better," she added.

"Too late now," observed Harlan. "She ate up your explanation."

This little episode demonstrates why the concept of meaning has plagued not only 2 year olds, 8 year olds, and 11 year olds, but has plagued and confused philosophers from the time of Plato to the present and why many American linguists have thought it the better part of valor to cast out meaning from their consideration of language. As Mario Pei has observed:

". . . a truly complete system of meaning involves an analysis of the universe. All that the linguist can do is to deal with language, based only upon the analysis of the universe which is completed during the life of the individual speaker or, at the most, of the speaking community.

"The meanings of a linguistic community . . . include the total experience of that community: arts, sciences, practical occupations, amusements, personal and family life. . . .

"No two individuals have precisely the same life-experience. Even granting that they have at their disposal the same equipment of semantic expression (sounds, words, grammatical and syntactical forms), these means of expression will fail to coincide to approximately the same degree as the individual experiences differ. A word or sentence is not merely a bundle of sounds; it is also a bundle of associations. These associations are not quite identical for any two speakers; neither will the words or sentences hold for them exactly the same semantic content." (18:118–119)

Moreover the word, *meaning,* represents a great range of diverse matters, such as: denotation; connotation; neuro-muscular and glandular activity; usefulness; value; conceptual implications; to what the interpreter of a symbol refers; what the interpreter of a symbol ought to be referring; to what the user of a symbol wants the interpreter to infer; or for that matter, any object of consciousness whatsoever. Ogden and Richards in their book *Meaning of Meaning* have identified 16 different groupings of meaning and the existence of 23 meanings of meaning (16:186-187). Charles C. Fries (7:104) has noted identification of more than 50 different senses of the term, meaning. Often these various meanings are grouped under two main general headings: (1) *Referential,* or tangible to things, situations, events or ideas; and (2) *Expressive,* or the emotive, non-cognitive kinds of meaning.

Not only linguists have avoided and tried to divorce themselves from the consideration of meaning, but also information theorists. From the time Claude E. Shannon first propounded communication theory, information theorists have indicated that their fundamental concern is the measurement of information content of messages; they contend that information must not be confused with meaning. Two messages one of which is heavily loaded with meaning and another which is utter nonsense hold equivalency as far as transmission of information is concerned. The semantic aspects of communication are irrelevant to engineering aspects and the word information in Shannon's communication theory relates not so much to what you do say as to what you could say. (26)

However, meaning is *fundamental* to human communication. Communication, to use Warren Weaver's widely accepted definition, includes all procedures by which one mind affects another. This involves not only oral and written speech, but also music, the pictorial arts, the theatre, the ballet and, in fact, all human behavior. The word communication is derived from the Latin *communis,* meaning common. When we communicate, we are trying to establish a *commonness* with someone. In the human situation, communication involves the sharing of experience with others through formal or informal languages or through signs and symbols. (27:17–20) *So when communication is effected, there has been a transference of meaning.* Since all human behavior is involved in the communication process, meanings are transferred through the various modes whereby one mind affects another; and *no communication can take place without the transference of meaning.* (Please note that I have been careful to say *transference* of meaning rather than *transmission* of meaning. This point will be discussed further.) The science of transference of meaning is known as semantics. So basic to communication is the process of meaning that the two terms are frequently interchanged. We say, "Tell me what you mean," "Write clearly so the reader knows what you mean," "Do you know what Picasso is trying to communicate in his paintings?" *"Finnegan's Wake* says nothing to me," etc.

Meaningfulness may be achieved in a number of nonlinguistic ways. But meaningfulness alone does not constitute language. Yet language, according to Mario Pei, to be worthy of the name must be meaningful. Sounds, words, grammatical forms, syntactical constructions are the tools of language, and meaning is language's avowed purpose. Because meaning and its transfer are indissolubly linked with the human mental processes, linguists have often considered meaning outside of their boundaries and have directed their concern to components of language, such as phonetics, phonemics, morphology, grammatical forms, syntax, lexicology, word history, and even literary style. (18:81, 118)*

We will not be limited by the boundaries imposed upon themselves by linguists in our considerations of meaning . . . , but we will begin with some general linguistic considerations, because the major mechanism by which meanings occur are through words or language. Humans, as semantists have pointed out, live in two worlds—the world of direct experience and the world of words. Between the world of experience and the world of language, between things and words, between events and speech, certain relations have been established. These relations are governed by the rules that are in part arbitrary, and in part dictated by the nature of common human experiences. The form of the rules—grammar and syntax—varies from language to language. I'm not going to be concerned with these variations. The significant fact is that all human societies use some kind of language and have done so from earliest times. Aldous Huxley has observed that language permits human beings to behave with a degree of purposefulness, perseverance and consistency unknown among other mammals. Human behavior, as we know it, became possible only with the establishment of relatively stable systems of relationships between things and events on one hand and words on the other. In societies where no such relationship has been established—where there is no language—behavior is nonhuman. Language makes it possible for man to build up a social heritage of accumulated skills, knowledge, and wisdom; it enables us to profit by the experiences of past generations; each generation does not have to begin over again. Huxley has said that, "Words and meanings of words are not matters merely for the academic amusement of linguists and logisticians, or for the aesthetic delight of poets; they are matters of the profoundest ethical significance to every human being." (10:3–4–12)

The number of theories of meaning is vast; so is their variety. In the limited time I have, it would be an impossible task to trace them. But I think it would be fruitful to examine some of the issues in the various theories, and as we explore in the maze of arguments, and counterarguments, we will come up with insights which will be helpful to our understanding of this

---

* Typical of the linguistic approach is to look on meaning from the viewpoint of language structure as: "The linguistic meaning of *'the happy boy'* in the sentence the *'happy boy is playing in the pond'* as nominative substantive form class." (17:285)

most fundamental of processes in communication, and perhaps out of these insights might come a unity.

PRELINGUISTIC MEANING

Is there meaning in things that are not words? Shakespeare found "tongues in trees, books in running brooks, sermons in stones." The rate of pulse or heartbeat provide a physician meaning. Thirsty cattle "know" that low, thick foliage "means" water. Newly hatched chicks, after picking indiscriminately at various caterpillars, come upon the cinnabar caterpillar which is bitter to their taste. After a few pecks by the chick, the markings become decidedly meaningful, and the chick avoids the cinnabar caterpillar.

James J. Gibson has speculated on the pre-linguistic capacity for meaning of primitive man:

"Let us consider . . . one of our very early ancestors some five or ten million years ago . . . He was no longer living in trees. . . . Since he probably had little or no language, he had no names for things and we shall never know what his ideas or conscious experiences were. But we do know this. He discriminated among the variations of his retinal images and could therefore react differentially to the objects of his environment. . . .

"Judging from his probable behavior, primitive man discriminated the solidity, separateness, and spacing of things with great accuracy. In his place, we would say that he saw a visual world. But he also behaved toward things with circumspection, for he saw a world of meanings. Speculative as all such accounts must be, it is reasonably certain that our primitive ancestor got about in his environment, and knew one object from another.

"His behavior was based on locomotion and recognition: it was adjusted to space, and at the same time it consisted of reactions to objects. Vision provided him both guidance for his actions and cues for his actions. Presumably, then, an object like the sabre-toothed tiger was both localized and meaningful in his experience since he reacted to both its distance and its significance. . . .

"Our own experience of the visual world can be described as extended in distance and modelled in depth; as upright, motionless as a whole, and unbounded; as colored, textured, shadowed, and illuminated; as filled with surfaces, edges, shapes, and interspaces. . . . No less than our primitive ancestor we apprehend their uses and dangers, their satisfying or annoying possibilities, and the consequences of actions centering on them. Surfaces and shapes are in actuality perceived as ice, apples, fur, fences, clouds, shoes, people, and so on. . . .

". . . . There are meanings when one surface touches another or collides with another, or when one object produces an action in another. There is also the whole range of social meanings, facial expressions, gestures, persons and actions between persons. The visual world (as well as the entire environment as may be perceived by the full modality of senses) is saturated with many kinds of meaning, and it seems to get fuller with meanings as we live year to year." (8:197–199)

In the primitive world and in the animal world, meaning is largely "instinctive." The "signs" of meaning are attached to the thing they signify. Meaning is a cue for action and is not a relation of a sign to the thing it signifies. In human society on the other hand, signs—language—are mobile and detachable. Semantic meaning differs fundamentally from meaning as a cue to action. In human society, as Wilbur Urban has observed, language "makes it possible to be always passing from what is known to what is yet to be known. There must be a language whose signs—which cannot be infinite in number—are extensible to an infinity of things. This tendency of the sign to transfer itself from one object to another is characteristic of human language" . . . This phenomenon of transference performs the simple act of linguistic meaning. (25:107–108, 111)

We are now getting at the heart of the consideration of the transference of meaning—how communication takes place. As I said before, theories of meaning are numberless. Philosophers, linguists and psychologists have been examining the nature of meaning since Plato. A number of scholars have made some notable contributions—John Stuart Mill, Bertrand Russell, Ludwig Wittgenstein, Wilbur M. Urban, Ogden and Richards, Adam Schaff, Charles Osgood and others. The nature of meaning has many hazy aspects and no theory or explanation has wide acceptance. We might examine some of these contributions.

John Stuart Mill

Mill was responsible for the concepts of denotation and connotation. But more fundamentally, he approached the notion of meaning lexically. From a logician's viewpoint, he felt that just as we have to learn the alphabet before we can begin to spell, so it is natural for us to suppose that the meanings of sentences are put together from their components; and meanings of sentences are derived from their ingredient words. He considered word meanings atoms, sentence meaning molecules. What a sentence means is decomposable into the set of things which the words in it stand for. Mill assumed that words were names of things or ideas; that they denoted things or persons; and also, that words connoted or signified simple or complex attributes which the thing or person denoted.

Bertrand Russell

Bertrand Russell took up where John Stuart Mill left off. Russell indicated that the meaning of many kinds of expressions are matters not of naming things but of saying things. To know what an expression means, involves knowing what can (logically) be said with it and what cannot(logically) be said with it. Russell introduced a distinction between two kinds of meaning: *expression* and *indication*. Every sign that indicates also expresses, but some signs that express don't indicate anything. Logical words like "or" and "not" express a state of mind, but do not indicate an objective state of affairs.

Ludwig Wittgenstein

Wittgenstein was both a pupil and mentor of Bertrand Russell. His contributions to the nature of meaning have been significant. He saw that all words and phrases that can enter into sentences are governed by rules which he called logical syntax or logical grammar. Picking up where Russell left off, Wittgenstein said, don't look for meaning, look for use. He saw a significant analogy between expressions and chess pieces. The significant meaning of an expression (word or phrase) and the powers or functions in chess of a pawn, a knight, or the queen have much in common. To know what the knight can or cannot do, one must know the rules of chess as well as be familiar with various kinds of chess game situations. What the knight may do cannot be determined from the material or shape of the piece of which the knight is made. Similarly, to know what an expression (word or phrase) means is to know how it may or may not be used and the rules governing its use (logic, grammar, and syntax). This viewpoint was contrary to the denotationist's assumption that almost all words or phrases and even all sentences are alike and have the one role of naming. Wittgenstein's analogy of language to chess called attention to the fact that there are many kinds of words, phrases and sentences and that there is an infinitely large variety of the kinds of roles performed by words, phrases and sentences. Adjectives do not do what adverbs do nor do all adjectives do the same sort of things, nor mean in the same way, as one another.* Some

* Rulon Wells provides an excellent illustration: " 'Big' and 'little' seem like typical adjectives; so do 'grey', 'sweet', 'loud'. Yet there is an important difference between 'little' and 'grey' for example . . . we can argue: 'An elephant is a grey animal,' but we cannot similarly argue: 'An elephant is an animal, therefore a little elephant is a little animal.' . . . Wittgenstein would call this difference a difference in . . . logical grammar." (29:280)

nouns are proper names, but most are not. The sort of thing that we do with sentences are different from the sort of things that we do with most single words. And the capacity of different sentences is different. There is no one basic mold which can be imposed on expressions for meaning. Commenting on this insight of Wittgenstein, Gilbert Ryle has said that "Learning the meaning of an expression is more like learning a piece of drill than like coming across a previously unencountered object. It is learning to operate correctly with an expression and with any other expression equivalent to it." (21:162)

PSYCHOLOGICAL CONSIDERATIONS OF THE NATURE OF MEANING

The previous views were theoretical contributions by philosophers. Psychologists have brought many significant insights to the nature of meaning. Both philosophers and psychologists have been more interested in semantic meaning than in syntactic meaning. Psychologists have been interested in understanding the process of human behavior which occurs in an organism whenever a sign is received (decoded or produced). However, psychologists, as would be obvious, disagree among themselves as to the nature of meaning in the behavioral processes. Charles E. Osgood has defined the psychological problem as that of the sign or symbol never being identical with the thing it signifies. As for example, the *word* hammer is not the same stimulus as the *object* it signifies. Therefore, the word does not elicit behaviors which are the same as the object would elicit. (17:3–4) Psychologists are, therefore, interested in determining under what conditions a stimulus which is not a significate becomes a symbol of the significate. Now let us examine some psychological views of meaning.

Mentalistic View

This psychological school of meaning is dualistic; it seeks a correlation between material and nonmaterial events: It looks on meaning as a "mental" event. The stimuli of meaning—both symbols and the objects which they represent—are "physical" events. At the core of all mentalistic views is an association between symbols and "ideas." In essence, this view is that something which is not the signification becomes a symbol for the signification if it gives rise to the idea or thought of that signification. Ogden and Richards' approach in the *Meaning of Meaning* is probably the most refined expression of the mentalistic view. (17:4)

Substitution View

Early behavior psychologists, influenced by Pavlov, proposed a theory of meaning that expressed the view that meaning was achieved simply by conditioning. Their view was that whenever something which is not the object evokes in an organism the same reactions evoked by the object, it is a symbol of it—it means that object. (17:4–5) Meaning is a reflex action within the human organism to the symbolization of the object.

Dispositional View

Though Charles Morris might be classified as a philosopher, well trained in the tradition of Charles Peirce, his approach is of behavioral psychology. He defined meaning as: Any pattern of stimulation which is not the object becomes a symbol of the object if it produces in an organism a "disposition" to make any of the responses previously elicited by the object. (17:5)

Representational Mediation Process

Charles E. Osgood has modified Morris's theory of meaning. Words, according to his view, represent things because they produce in human organisms some replica of the actual behavior toward these things, as a mediation process. The mediational process is the mechanism that ties particular symbols to particular objects rather than to others. The mediation mechanism includes some part of the same behavior produced by the signification of the symbol. The presence of the particularistic property depends upon previous contact of non-significate and significate patterns of stimulation in the experience of the organism. (17:5–8)

Osgood says that the vast majority of signs or symbols used in ordinary communication are *assigns*. Their meanings have been "assigned" to them by way of associations with other signs rather than by way of direct associations with the objects signified. For example, the word *zebra* is understood by most children, yet few of them have had any experience with zebras. In learning to read, the child deals with *assigns*. The printed markings on the page are seldom associated directly with the objects signified, says Charles Osgood, but are associated rather with auditory signs created by the child and teacher as they verbalize.

Meanings which different individuals have for the same symbols will vary to the extent that their behaviors toward the things symbolized have varied. This is so because the representational process—the meaning of the symbol—is entirely dependent upon the nature of the total behavior occurring while the signs are being established. Given the essential sameness of human organisms and the stability of physical laws, the meanings of most primary perceptual signs should be constant across individuals; as is, for example, the significance of the visual cues arising from the apple object. Given stability of learning experiences within a particular culture, Osgood says, meanings of most common verbal symbols will be highly similar; for example, the adjective *sweet,* will be used in much of the same type of total situations regardless of the individual in our culture. On the other hand, the meanings of many symbols will reflect the idiosyncrasies of individual experiences; as for example, the common nouns "father," "mother," "poet," —"technical writer" or "professor." (17:8–9)

Charles E. Osgood and his associates at the University of Illinois have been responsible for one of the more interesting and productive experimental methods attempting to measure meanings by a *semantic differential* process. Their process of measurement is based on an index of connotation— how a given word is understood, and how it is being actually used by those who speak the language in question. Their research is based on the assumption that context influences meaning and that meanings are internal judgments. The semantic differential instrument utilizes the fact that words are not only denotative but are also connotative. Osgood found that there are three principal connotative factors in almost all words. These are the evaluative (good/bad) factor, the potency (strong/weak) factor, and the activity (active/passive) factor. Osgood assumes that words touch off connotative mediating responses within the individual, as well as denotative. Whenever an individual transmits a verbal message, his receiver responds to its denotation, but he also responds in a "customary" way to the connotation.

The Semantic Differential measuring instrument is a combination of word associations and scaling techniques. The subject is given a word, concept or object such as Barry Goldwater, for example, and a number of polar adjective pairs, such as Statesmen-demagogue, strong-weak, energetic-passive. A scale is provided in this fashion:

Barry Goldwater Statesman:—:—:—:—:—:   :Demagogue

The subject is asked to check the direction and intensity of his association. If he has a favorable attitude toward Goldwater he will place a check mark to the left of midpoint, the nearness to "good" indicating his degree of favorability. The opposite association would be recorded by a check mark to the right. A check midpoint would indicate the association was mixed or that no association was produced. See Fig. 1.

Barry Goldwater

Statesman :__:__:__:__:__:__:__:__:__:__:__:__:__: Demagogue

Strong   :__:__:__:__:__:__:__:__:__:__:__:__:__: Weak

Energetic :__:__:__:__:__:__:__:__:__:__:__:__:__: Passive

Figure 1. Osgood's Semantic Differential measure of meaning instrument.

As you would infer, the Semantic Differential technique has proved a useful measuring instrument of attitudes as well as meaning. (17)

The Triadic Concept of Meaning (Ogden and Richards)

The Meaning of Meaning by C. K. Ogden and I. A. Richards has been one of the most influential books in the study of meaning, language and communication. Ogden and Richards' triangular diagrammatic illustration of the operation of meaning has become classical. It is interesting to note that both Bertrand Russell and Charles Peirce had previously made observations of the triadic character of meaning.

The most obvious way to conceive meaning is as a two-way relationship, between a symbol and an object—the term that means and the object that is meant. Ogden and Richards saw a triadic relationship in the operation of meaning. The relationship was analyzed as a conjunction of two dyads: one holding between the symbol and interpretant; and the other between the interpretant and the object. This relationship has been diagramed in Fig. 2.

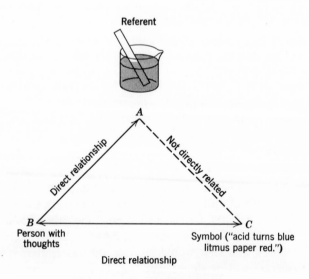

Figure 2. Triangle of meaning.

The dotted line indicates that there is no direct connection between the symbol and the referent. The connection between the word and object is always arbitrary and conventional. It corresponds to nothing in the external world. I will be returning to the triangle of meaning diagram a little later.

MEANING AS A SOCIAL RELATION BETWEEN MEN WHO COMMUNICATE (Adam Schaff)

Adam Schaff is a Polish philosopher and a Marxist. His book *Introduction to Semantics,* was recently translated into English. It is a searching and thorough analytical examination of semantics, the elements of communication, sign, meaning, language, and logic. Marxist philosophy colors Adam Schaff's analysis but does not vitiate his critical considerations.

Adam Schaff observes that the problem of meaning appears whenever we use signs (symbols) in the process of human communication. Meaning occurs as a definite social relation between men who communicate. He explains social relations as:

"Someone wants to incite someone else to action, to inform him about his thoughts, feelings, etc., and with that end in view resorts to a sign—a gesture, a word, an image, etc. If the intended effect has been achieved, i.e., if the appropriate thoughts have in fact been conveyed to the other party . . . the meaning of the sign has been understood by the hearer or reader." (22:265)

Adam Schaff has revised Ogden and Richards' triadic relationship of meaning; he identifies the following three elements as indispensible in the transference of meaning:

1. two persons who communicate with one another;
2. a referent;
3. the sign by which thoughts are conveyed.

He emphasizes that material objects or events become signs only when they enter into definite, intricate relations with men who use them as signs (symbols). It is only in such a context that an object or event has a meaning. Adam Schaff says, similarly, human cognition (thinking) is a social relation, since it is a relation between the person who does the thinking— shaped by life in society—and the object of the thought. (22:265)

Schaff emphasizes, also, that meaning is a system of relations between men on a psychological plane because the relation is between men who act, feel and who communicate with one another. For Schaff, meaning belongs both in the sphere of human action and in the sphere of human thought. He holds that these two spheres are inseparably connected. The thought processes of an individual are determined by the social and cognitive processes of that individual's society. Therefore, language operates on the social level. Communicator *A* has similar thought processes with communicator *B* and the social processes determine their interactions. Meaning, understanding and, consequently similar thought processes, as well as behavioral reactions are interconnected. Thus, says Adam Schaff, meaning is molded in the process of reflection of objective reality in the human mind. Meaning is the cognitive process of reflection in the human mind of the object to which the signs refer. But, at the same time, it is an element and even an instrument of the process since without the sign (symbol) there is no communication. So meaning is genetically conditioned by social practice. The social experience of a given society is transmitted through language to a member of that society.* (22:265–267,271)

MEANING AS AN OPERATION

The chief proponents of this approach are the late P. W. Bridgman, Nobel prize physicist, and Anatol Rapoport, a mathematician and general semanticist. According to this approach, meaning is equal to the sum of the operations to be found in what one does and not in what one says. This view is similar to Wittgenstein's approach of *usage* of a term. A question has meaning when one can point to the operations resulting in an answer to that question. Bridgman has written that:

"We evidently know what we mean by length if we can tell what the length of any . . . object is, and for the physicist nothing more is required. To find the length of an object we have to perform certain physical operations . . . by which length is determined. . . . We mean by any concept nothing more than a set of operations; *the concept is synonymous with a corresponding set of operations.* If the concept is physical, as of length, the operations are actually physical operations, namely those by which length is measured; or if the concept is mental, as of mathematical

---

* This viewpoint is not far from the "Dispositional" view of the American psycholinguist, Roger Brown, who says, "Within a linguistic community there are standards . . . for the usage of an utterance and for total behavior with reference to the utterance. These standards define appropriate behavior, the conventional disposition. A child born into the community does not at first conform to these standards but he eventually does so and is then said to speak and understand the language." (5:105)

continuity, the operations are mental operations, namely those by which we determine whether a given aggregate of magnitudes is continuous." (22:253)

SUMMARY OF THEORIES OF MEANING

In the limited time that I have, I can at best identify some of the possible interpretations of meaning:

1. Meaning is identical with the object of which a given expression is the name. (The view of G. Frege and John Stuart Mill.)

2. Meaning is an inherent property of the object to which the symbol refers. (John Stuart Mill.)

3. Meaning is an ideal entity. (E. Husserl)

4. Meaning is a relation
   a. between symbols (Syntactical meaning)
   b. between the symbol and object (Lexical meaning)
   c. between the symbol and the thought about the object (Logical meaning)
   d. between the symbols and human action (Behavioral psychology)
   e. between men who communicate with one another by means of symbols (Adam Schaff)

Meaning has logical, psychological, and sociological aspects. Psychologically, any item that is to have meaning must be a sign or symbol to someone. Logically, it must be capable of conveying a meaning. And, sociologically, the user operates within an environmental matrix which influences both psychological and logical aspects. Susanne K. Langer claims that there is no basic quality of meaning. Its essence lies in the realm of logic, where one does not deal with qualities but with reactions. She says it is more appropriate to say meaning is a function of a term. A function is a pattern viewed with reference to one special term around which it centers. This pattern emerges when we look at the given term in its total relation to other terms about it, and the total may be quite complicated. The meaning of the term rests on the pattern in which the term itself holds the key position. (12:56) See Fig. 3.

Meaning is not transmittable. It's not a label tied around the neck of the word, sign or symbol. It's more like the beauty of a face, says Colin Cherry, which lies altogether in the eye of the beholder. (6:115) Meaning, as Roger Brown has indicated, is the property of mutually relevant people, things and events in a situation. Some of the events are the noises made by the speakers, but it is important to realize that meaning is just as much a

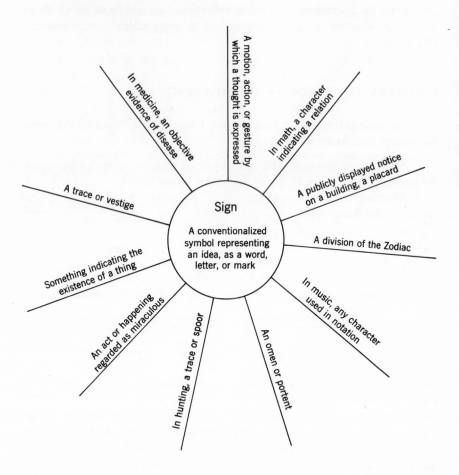

Figure 3. A diagram illustrating functional pattern of meaning of a term—(Sign in present instance)—viewed with reference to one special term around which it centers. The pattern emerges when we look at the term in its total relation to other terms around it.

property of the people, their "sets," their specific behavior, the things and events of the situation as of the noises made. (28:141)

TOWARD A UNIFIED THEORY OF COMMUNICATION AND MEANING

Despite the multiplicity of theories of meaning, there is no satisfactory and universally accepted explanation of the operation of meaning. This is

due, I believe, to a gap in theoretical thought between the relation of meaning to communication. Communication, as I have indicated earlier, is
effected by the transference of meaning. Linguists, philosophers, psychologists and information theorists have approached the problem of meaning
from the orientation of their own disciplines. Within their own disciplines,
the problems of meaning have presented perplexing and profound questions. They have apparently not wished to complicate their probings by
going beyond the compartments of their own fields of interest, and, while
much pay dirt has been found in the diggings within their own scholarly
investigations, there is a need for an overview theory unifying communication and meaning. In the little time remaining, I shall attempt to outline the
elements which might compose such a unified theory. To do this, I will try
to relate communication theory to meaning theory. In the interest of time
and convenience, I shall do this by a series of diagrams which I believe will
provide the tools for my probings.

Please consult Fig. 4 which is a model of the human communication situation. (23:4) This model has been borrowed from the Claude E.

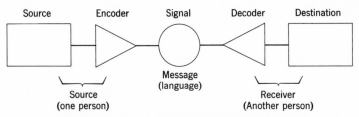

Figure 4. Human communication model.

Shannon information theory model. As you can see there are three basic
elements in human communication: the source or sender; the message or
signal; and the destination or receiver. The source may be a person speaking, writing, typing, drawing, gesturing; it may be a communication organization such as a newspaper, magazine, book publisher, radio or TV station,
technical publication section in a company, or a motion picture studio. The
message may be in the form of writing, Braille, printed characters, diagrams or pictures on paper, sound waves in the air, a gesture, or a grimace,
bells, flags, or smoke signals in the air, or any form of signal capable of
being interpreted meaningfully. The destination may be a person listening,
watching, reading, perceiving by any or all of his senses. (27:19–20)

What happens when communication takes place? First, the source en-
codes his message; that is, he takes the information or thought or idea he
wants to share—taking it from a stockpile of possible messages—and en-
codes or expresses it in a form that can be transmitted. The coding process
is the thought or formulation process which takes place in the mind of the

source for translation into signal, message, or symbolic means to enable sending. The message or symbol is sent in the form of gestures, grimaces, speech, written words, drawn diagrams, pictures, or radio pulses. The message is received by the decoder in the human communication system, which is, of course, the cerebral perception system of the individual receiving the message. The decoder can translate the message only within the framework of his own stockpile of experience and knowledge. The source can encode and the destination can decode only within the experience each has had. Let us add to our mode: Fig. 5 illustrates this. If the circles do not meet, there is no common experience or empathic psychological sets, then communication is impossible. (27:20)

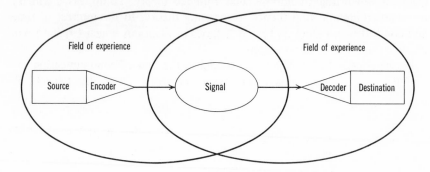

Figure 5. Commonness of experience necessary for communication.

In the human communication system, just as in the radio or telephone model, the operation can be no better than its poorest link. To use engineering terms, there may be noise, (a disturbance which does not represent any part of the message) filtering, (abstraction or abridgement) or distortion (perversion of meaning) at any stage in the communication process. If the person sending the message does not have adequate or clear information, the message is not formulated or encoded adequately, accurately, or effectively for the transference of meaning. If the intent of the message is not transmitted accurately enough, despite interference and competition to the desired receiver, if the message is not coded in a manner which corresponds faithfully to the encoding, and if the person receiving the message is unable to handle the decoded message so as to produce the desired response, then there is a breakdown in the communication system. (27:20–21)

Each person in the communication process is both an encoder and decoder. He receives and transmits. The communicator gets feedback of his own messages by listening to his own voice as he talks or by reading his own message as he writes. Thus, we are able to correct mispronunciations as we listen to ourselves talk or catch our mistakes in our writing, as we read what we have written or add information as we recognize an omission. Feedback enables us to catch weaknesses in communication links where they may occur. (27:23–24)

Now, with this in mind, we might redraw the communication model to show two humans conversing. Figure 6 might represent *A* trying to com-

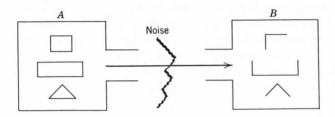

Figure 6.

municate to *B* his ideas represented by the square, the rectangle, and the triangle. Without feedback, *B* would get distortions of the ideas *A* has in mind. Figure 7 provides the feedback and shows that *A* and *B* are both

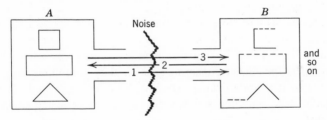

Figure 7. Feedback in two-person communication.

senders and receivers. Thus, 1 is a stimulus message which is followed by a response 2 from *B*. This message is a corrective to *A* who sends 3. *B* responds to 3 by correcting the originally received message. He then transmits the shapes of the correction back to *A*, who sends another message, and so on. (3:7–8)

Now let us examine the operation of meaning through its most traditional diagraming. When we speak or write to one another, we transmit our thoughts through physical signals. Properly constructed and organized these signals become messages of orderly selected signs and symbols. The symbolization is the physical embodiment of our messages or thoughts. Ogden and Richards identified three elements involved in the transference of meaning. (1) thought; (2) symbol; (3) referent. The three elements are represented by 3 corners of a triangle as is shown in Fig. 2. The symbols or words have no direct relationship to their referents and cannot be identified with the physical fact they symbolize except indirectly through the reader's mental processes. Line *AC* of the triangle becomes a direct relationship only after the reader pronounces the word symbols of the fact. The symbolization (the sentence, "Acid turns blue litmus paper red.") becomes identical (means the same thing in the mind of the reader) with the act it represents.

Words represent facts. A person perceives the fact that acid turns blue litmus paper red. The person selects the proper words to form a message which will designate (mean) the fact or thing perceived (the referent). Words, then, refer through the mind to facts. Past experience through memories and through external environment influences the proper selection of the symbolic response to the referent by the person encoding and sending the message. (27:32–33)

This diagram is not a full explanation of the operation of meaning. It may illustrate perhaps some of the operations in the decoding or encoding process. Missing from it is the diagrammatizations of the transference of meaning to communicators. Nothing is revealed of the intricate process of what happens in the transference of meaning between speaker and listener or between writer and reader. The triangle, of course, is inadequate because in the meaning situation, there are requirements for geometrical configurations which have a greater potential for illustrating the many operations than the triangle has to offer. In the communication situation, minimally, there must be persons who communicate with one another; there must be the object concerning which they communicate; and finally there must be the symbolization which is the vehicle for the final element—the thought—the encoding and decoding by means of which communication takes place.

The full process of the act of communication cannot lend itself to a simple geometric figure. I have attempted to diagram in Fig. 8 the communication process in the transference of meaning. My diagram is an attempt, too, to show the many variables in the operation of communication. While I find it more satisfactory than the triangle of meaning conceived by Ogden and Richards and than the diagram adapted from Shannon's communication model, it is by no means entirely to my satisfaction. It is presented as a *tentative* diagram for your consideration and comments and as a stimulant for further development.

At the present, in my estimation, there is no comprehensive, unified theory of human communication. Shannon's communication theory is more accurately a theory of information, although it has been extremely influential in the theorizing of the processes behind the human communication situation. Many of its elements are applicable, as can be seen from the earlier diagrams. However, Shannon himself eliminates the fundamental compo-

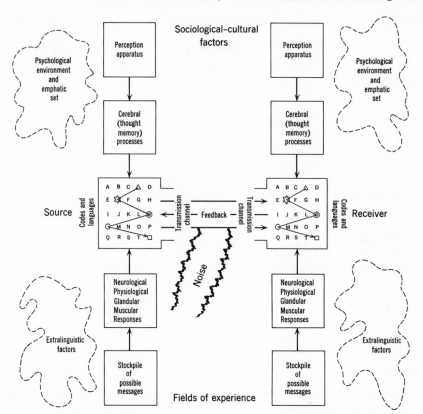

Figure 8. Process of communication and transference of meaning.

nent *meaning* from his information theory. Any human communication theory which eliminates meaning, the consummation of the communication process, from its considerations as irrelevant is not only inadequate, but invalid.

A valid communication model which would show the process of communication and the consummation of the transference of meaning needs to illustrate in the communication chain that every sender and receiver is an encoder and decoder. It must show the communicators operating within fields of experience, and within empathic sets, and show the influence of extra linguistic phenomena, as well as the influence of language—the code of their communication vehicles. The model must also provide for their feedback mechanism, as well as for the psychological, sociological, and perception modalities, and physiological sequences in operation. It's a tall order. This is what Fig. 8 attempts to do. I leave it with you for your consideration.

APPENDIX

DEFINITIONS

Code

A set of unambiguous rules whereby messages are converted from one representation to another.

Communication

The word is derived from the Latin *communis,* which means common. When we communicate, we are trying to establish a commonness with someone. A giving and receiving of meaningful information, signals, or messages by talk, gestures, writing, signals or symbols.

Decode

"Translate" into comprehensible "language" or communicative code.

Encode

To formulate or to transform from one representation to another, into a communicative code.

Grammar

A system or habitual way of speaking or writing a language.

Language

A body of words, signs, symbols and methods for putting them together in order to convey meaning.

Linguistics

The scientific study of language.

Message

An encoded selection of symbols intended to communicate information.

Phoneme

A variety of sounds in a given language which the speakers of that language choose to regard as a single sound. The sounds of *k* in "kin" and "skin" are different; "kin" has a puff of breath after the *k*, "skin" has not. In many languages (Sanskrit for example) the 2 sounds of *k* would be considered as separate, and would give rise to semantic confusion if they were interchanged.

Referent

That which a sign or symbol "refers to" or "stands for."

Semantics

A systematic branch of study concerned with meanings of words, signs and symbols. (General Semantics: "The study and improvement of human evaluative processes with special emphasis on the relation to signs and symbols, including language.")

Sign

A conventional symbol representing an idea, as a word, letter or mark; a motion, action, or gesture by which a thought is expressed, or a command, or wish made known.

Signal

A sign, event or watchword, which has been agreed upon as the start for concerted action; signals announce the presence of things rather than serving as reminders of things.

Signification

The object or idea being signified or meant.

Symbol

That which suggests something else by reason of relationships, association, or convention; a written or printed mark, word or emblem used to represent or stand for an object or idea; in writing or printing, a conventional sign such as a character, a letter or an abbreviation used instead of a word, or words, as in mathematics, physics, chemistry, music, phonetics, etc. to represent operations, quantities, spatial position, elements, relations, qualities, sounds, etc.

Symbology

The art of expression by symbols; also the study of interpretation of symbols.

Syntax

In grammar, the arrangement of words as elements in a sentence to show their relationship; sentence structure.

Word

The smallest unit of speech that has meaning when taken by itself.

REFERENCES

[1] Berlo, David K., *The Process of Communication,* New York: Holt, Rinehart and Winston, Inc., 1960.

[2] Birdwhistell, Ray L., "An Approach to Communication," ms. of paper presented to the American Orthopsychiatric Association, April 24, 1962.

[3] Birdwhistell, Ray L., "Communicating on Purpose," ms. of Keynote Address to VPGA, March 21, 1963.

[4] Bloomfield, Leonard, *Language,* New York: Holt, Rinehart and Winston, 1962.

[5] Brown, Roger, *Words and Things,* Glencoe, Illinois: The Free Press, 1958.

[6] Cherry, Colin, *On Human Communication,* New York: The Technology Press of Massachusetts Institute of Technology and John Wiley and Sons, Inc., 1957.

[7] Fries, Charles C., "Meaning and Linguistic Analysis," in *Readings in Applied English Linguistics,* Harold B. Allen, Editor, New York: Appleton-Century-Crofts, 1958.

[8] Gibson, James J., *The Perception of the Visual World,* Boston: Houghton Mifflin Company, 1950.

[9] Hughes, John P., *The Science of Language,* New York: Random House, 1962.

[10] Huxley, Aldous, "Words and Their Meaning," in *The Importance of Language,* Max Black, Editor, Englewood Cliffs, N. J.: Prentice-Hall, Inc., 1962.

[11] Kecskemeti, Paul, *Meaning, Communication and Value,* Chicago: The University of Chicago Press, 1952.

[12] Langer, Susanne K., *Philosophy in a New Key,* New York: A Mentor Book, the New American Library, 1961.

[13] Malmberg, Bertil, *Structural Linguistics and Human Communications,* New York: Academic Press, Inc., Publishers, 1963.

[14] Mill, John Stuart, *A System of Logic,* London: Longmans Green, & Co., 1889.

[15] Morris, Charles, *Signs, Language, and Behavior,* New York: Prentice-Hall, Inc., 1946.

[16] Ogden, C. K., and I. A. Richards, *The Meaning of Meaning,* New York: Harcourt, Brace & World Co., Inc., 1956.

[17] Osgood, Charles E., and George J. Suci, and Percy H. Tannenbaum, *The Measurement of Meaning,* Urbana: University of Illinois Press, 1957.

[18] Pei, Mario, *The Story of Language,* New York: A Mentor Book, The American Library, 1960.

[19] Russell, Bertrand, *An Inquiry into Meaning and Truth,* Baltimore: Penguin Books, 1962.

[20] Ryle, Gilbert, "The Theory of Meaning," in *The Importance of Language,* Max Black, Editor, Englewood Cliffs, N. J.: Prentice-Hall, Inc. 1962.

[21] Saporta, Sol, Editor, *Psycholinguistics,* New York: Holt, Rinehart and Winston, 1961.

[22] Schaff, Adam, *Introduction to Semantics,* Translated from Polish by Olgierd Wojtasiewicz, New York: The Macmillan Company, A Pergamon Press Book, 1962.

[23] Schramm, Wilbur, "How Communication Works," in *Process and Effects of Mass Communication,* Wilbur Schramm, Editor, Urbana: University of Illinois Press, 1955.

[24] Upton, Albert, *Design for Thinking: A First Book in Semantics,* Stanford, California: Stanford University Press, 1961.

[25] Urban, Wilbur M., *Language and Reality,* New York: W. W. Norton & Company, Inc., 1941.

[26] Weaver, Warren, "Recent Contributions to the Mathematical Theory of Communication," in *The Mathematical Theory of Communication,* by Claude E. Shannon and Warren Weaver, Urbana: The University of Illinois Press, 1949.

[27] Weisman, Herman M., *Basic Technical Writing,* Columbus, Ohio: Charles E. Merrill Books, Inc., 1962.

[28] Weisman, Herman M., "Symbols and Meaning," in *Proceedings, 6th Annual Institute in Technical and Industrial Communications,* Herman M. Weisman, Editor, Fort Collins, Colorado: Colorado State University, 1964.

[29] Wells, Rulon, "Meaning and Use," in *Psycholinguistics,* Sol Saporta, Editor, New York: Holt, Rinehart and Winston, 1961.

[30] Wittgenstein, Ludwig, *Tractatus Logico-Philosophicus,* London: Kegan, Paul, Trench, Trubner & Co., Ltd., 1933.

[31] Wooster, Harold, "A Web of Words," in *Proceedings of 6th Annual Institute in Technical and Industrial Communications,* Herman M. Weisman, Editor, Fort Collins, Colorado: Colorado State University, 1964.

RELATED READINGS

SECTION 2: COMMUNICATION AND MANAGERIAL CONTROL

Section 2 presents a variety of viewpoints concerning communication and managerial control. In "Limitations of Managerial Control" Morris A. Savitt discusses the concept of dynamic management in relationship to the concept of control. He suggests that dynamic management should be paralleled by dynamic managerial controls. "Control as an Organizational Process," by Chadwick J. Haberstroh, reports research concerning the application of the theory of self-regulation systems in an industrial plant. Haberstroh concludes that feedbacks of information on performance and objectives had much influence on certain types of managerial decision processes. In "Data Systems that Cross Company Boundaries" Felix Kaufman points up the potential impact of data systems which transcend a given organization. There are some important implications for managers in both large and small organizations. John Dearden, in "Myth of Real-Time Management Information," contends that a real-time system cannot be used in management control. He also argues that a real-time system is of only marginal value in other areas of top management concern. In "Computer Effect Upon Managerial Jobs" Joseph P. Schwitter reports the results of a survey concerning changes in managerial jobs due to the introduction and use of computers. He concludes that, contrary to other predictions, middle management jobs of the future will require more initiative, vision, and knowledge. "Managerial Effectiveness I: Formulating a Research Strategy" by Larry L. Cummings reviews an array of research on the prediction of managerial success. It points out the need to examine dimensions which are not included in most prior studies.

7

LIMITATIONS OF
MANAGERIAL CONTROL *

Morris A. Savitt

There is increasing evidence of fundamental changes in the managerial process.[12,15,22] In a previous period of change related to the days of the "efficiency experts," there were managerial malpractices which seriously hindered our development in this process. It is the purpose of this paper to focus attention upon a way of thinking which, hopefully, will enable managers to go forward more rapidly than has heretofore been the case.

Specifically, a current trend in managerial theory is briefly examined. A quick look is then taken at the related concept of managerial control. Finally, the limitations of managerial control are reviewed, and a suggestion is offered as to how the limitations might be eased.

In 1927 Follett wrote that the right kind of functional relating will create a unity which will produce a value beyond the mere addition of its parts.[18] This could be termed the dynamic (versus the "either-or") approach to decision-making. For some time the Follett thesis did not receive too much attention, but more recently there has been a renewal of interest in the dynamic route to managerial decision-making.[11,25]

HORIZONTAL VERSUS VERTICAL

Our special concern is with a logical expansion of the dynamic decision-making principle to an area not usually characterized by this approach. To illustrate, recourse to the controversy concerning the span-of-control concept is appropriate. Note that Simon has criticized this principle, pointing

* Reprinted from *Advanced Management,* April, 1962, pp. 20–23.

out there is another, contradictory proverb of administration which renders the span-of-control principle useless.[21] The contradictory proverb, according to Simon, states that administrative efficiency is enhanced by minimizing the number of organizational levels through which a matter must pass before action is taken. The conflict appears to be between the relative merits of the horizontal versus the vertical forms of organization.

Suojanen has criticized the span-of-control principle on the ground that recent insights into the nature of group coordination reveal such a high degree of self-control within the group that the area of effective supervision is much larger than that predicted by the span-of-control notion.[23]

Urwick has defended this precept.[24] He says that the span-of-control concept applies primarily to subordinates whose work interlocks. Where there is no interlocking there is less need for more levels of control. Therefore, if the principle is correctly applied, many objections to it will disappear.

The dynamic approach to the managerial process suggests there is no real difference here. The Urwick course appears to be quite valid for the moderately-sized organizations found in a situation of the sort which brought forth the theory when Graicunas first developed it and Urwick first presented it in formal fashion. The later approach seems pertinent to those more recently evolved conditions which have led to the development of modern industrial giants.

It is not a matter of either the one or the other. Rather, since there is likely to be a side-by-side existence of both types of organization for some time to come, why cannot each principle be applied as the circumstances require?

CONTROL CONCEPT IN BROADER SENSE

A major aspect of dynamic management, and paralleling its development in many ways, is the control concept in its broader generic sense. Traditional ideas concerning the meaning of control usually imply seeing to it that action follows the plan. This leads to the establishment of so-called controls and infers a degree of coercion by the manager or executive. More recent thinking emphasizes the logic of the over-all situation which itself calls for voluntary human action.[7] The problem, as I see it, is to discern, not decide, what is needed.

In any case, no matter where else they may differ, students of the control concept in management seem to agree that there are generally three factors involved: (a) standards or objectives as a basis for control, (b) the comparison of actual with planned behavior—which involves an information system of some sort, and (*c*) human beings.

There are at least two difficulties involving standards with which we shall be here concerned. The first has to do with the definition of the basic unit to be utilized as an expression of performance. The second has to do with the terms in which the basic unit is to be measured.[8]

WHAT IS BUSINESS INCOME?

To illustrate: A basic unit in the determination of business enterprise success is business income. Now what exactly is business income? A study group including lawyers, economists, businessmen, and accountants reviewed this problem under the aegis of the American Inst. of Certified Public Accountants and the Rockefeller Foundation for about three years.[6] The group found that business income is defined differently for different purposes.

Business income is one thing when the object is determination of tax on income, interest on an income bond, or management compensation. It is another thing when the purpose is to ascertain the shares of a year's products that have been received by capital and labor. It is thought of in still another way when the new investor is involved. What has been described as the case with such a fundamental standard as business income is not too different from the situation found with other business standards such as cost and profit.

Now suppose an aspect of business income is defined acceptably to all concerned. What shall be the basis for income measurement? The various bases for valuing the dollar as a monetary unit are widely known.

ADMITS POSSIBLE MULTIPLICITY

My personal belief is that, here again, there is no real conflict in any of this. Dynamic management admits of a possible multiplicity of sometimes similar goals or standards (definitions), each with its own rationale (form of measurement). With this in mind it becomes easier to set more accurate, realistic standards for more effective managerial behavior.

To keep this paper within practicable boundaries, let me state, simply, that an information system will be thought of as involving written accounting, statistical, or other numerical data.

1. Accountancy. In a very real sense, accountancy is a language form used to reflect the behavior of the enterprise. The need for an accurate or relatively true picture of reality as a prelude to effective executive behavior need not be belabored. Our job, then, is to determine whether accountancy develops important distortions in the image it is designed to convey.

What many regard as a fairly precise method for collecting and transmitting information is, according to some authorities, actually subject to indecisive thinking and serious obscurities if not downright (although unintended) deceptions.[2,4,5] A form of organizational language, generally supposed to be accurate, is criticized as being characterized to an appreciable extent by apparently random and often contradictory principles.

To illustrate: One of my earlier efforts disclosed at least three distinct forms of accounting theory.[20] The sole proprietary form was developed in the days when the small proprietorship was the dominant form of business enterprise. The corporate entity form of accountancy was developed when it became evident that proprietary accounting was subject to major deficiencies in its efforts to furnish even relatively accurate information about the modern corporate form of enterprise. The third form of accounting theory, the fund approach, while used in specific business applications, is generally associated with governmental and eleemosynary institutions.

Each of these three forms of accounting theory leads to differences in statement presentation, underlying methodologies, and to subtle but important differences in interpretation. When, in the collection and presentation of accounting information, there is an unrecognized shifting back and forth among the three systems, the end results are bound to be confusing, to say the least. Unfortunately the critical attitude toward accounting information is therefore all too often justified.

But it need not be so. In terms of this study, the illness and the cure parallel those described in the discussion of standards. That is, there appear to be several similar but not identical information systems, each of which has a specific application. Why not recognize and accept this concept? It will then be possible to utilize each version of the language more consistently and intelligibly.

One does not, of course, overlook the judgment factor in accountancy as practiced by the professional accountant. But this is precisely the point. Individual judgments are subject to much variation. Witness, for example, legal proceedings with respect to taxes, estates, etc., with equally eminent and qualified accountants on opposing sides. A procedure which may provide a common base for more consistent judgments has much to recommend it.

2. Statistics. Statistics as a communication mechanism is being used widely in organizations of all types. Yet a widely known statistician-scientist recently wrote that it is not without reason the professional philosopher and the plain man can now make common cause in a suspicious attitude toward statistics.[13] According to this statistician, the term has at least four different meanings in the context of statistical theory alone. Each of these four has its unique concepts and methodologies and is suited to the solution of particular, separate sets of problems. The difficulty and the remedy are as proposed in the discussion of accountancy.

3. Mathematics. Concern with mathematics as an information system in business is occasioned by rapid developments in the area of operations research. This comparatively new approach to decision-making in organizations is based in large part upon mathematical applications.[19]

By this time, one might suspect that even the Queen of the Sciences is subject to limitations like those suggested above. One is not disappointed. According to one writer there are three main schools of mathematical philosophy (the logistic, the formalist, and the intuitionist), each with its own concepts, methodologies, and applications.[3] Another writer distinguishes among five characteristic positions as to the object of mathematical inquiry.[14]

IMPORTANT DIFFERENCE TO BE NOTED

There is, however, an important difference to be noted as between mathematics on the one hand and, on the other, accounting, and statistics. Stated simply, there does not seem to be as much confusion in the application of mathematical principles as in the other areas. An explanation may be found in the greater age of the field of mathematics and therefore the longer time available for the development of a systematized application of its theories and interpretational systems. It is suggested that development in the other areas may be deliberately hastened to achieve the level attained in mathematics. All segments may then move forward more quickly than has been the case heretofore.

It is not the purpose here to repeat criticisms directed in recent years at practices in personnel management and human relations in business. The suggestion is offered that the problem, in principle, is like that discussed in the case of standards and information systems.[1,9,10,16,17] And the remedy is similar.

A FRUITFUL BEGINNING

It is suggested that a dynamic approach to management and managerial controls could do much to reduce present difficulties involving certain emergent managerial concepts and methods. It is further suggested that there is enough now known about standards, information systems, and people, under conditions of organizational control, to make possible a fruitful beginning to systematization along the lines indicated herein. It is suggested, finally, that recognition and acceptance of the historic approach to the review and study of the management of organizations could do much to improve managerial performance.

REFERENCES

[1] Chris Argyris, *Personality and Organization: The Conflict Between System and the Individual* (New York, Harper & Bros., 1957)

[2] As reported in *The Executive,* Baker Library, Harvard Univ., Vol. 3, No. 9 (1960), pp. 7–9.

[3] Max Black, *The Nature of Mathematics: A Critical Survey* (London, Routledge and Kegan Paul, 1958), pp. 7–11.

[4] Albert J. Bows, "The Urgent Need for Accounting Reforms," *N. A. A. Bulletin,* Sec. 1 (Sept. 1960), pp. 43–52.

[5] R. J. Chambers, "Measurement and Misrepresentation," *Management Science,* Vol. 6, No. 2 (Jan. 1960).

[6] *Changing Concepts of Business Income: Report of Study Group on Business Income* (New York, The Macmillan Co., 1952).

[7] C. West Churchman, Russell L. Ackoff, and E. Leonard Arnoff, *Introduction to Operations Research* (New York, John Wiley & Sons, Inc., 1957), pp. 3–9.

[8] C. West Churchman and Philburn Ratoosh (editors), *Measurement: Definitions and Theories* (New York, John Wiley & Sons, Inc., 1959), pp 3–94.

[9] James Howard Cooper, "The Crisis in Human Relations," *Readings in Human Relations,* Keith Davis and William G. Scott, editors (New York, McGraw-Hill Book Co., Inc., 1959), pp. 446–455.

[10] Peter F. Drucker, *The Practice of Management* (New York, Harper & Bros. Publishers, 1954), pp. 273–288.

[11] Jay W. Forrester, "Industrial Dynamics: A Major Breakthrough for Decision Makers," *Harvard Business Review* (July–Aug. 1958).

[12] Arthur J. Goldberg, "Challenge of Industrial Revolution II," *The New York Times* (Apr. 2, 1961).

[13] Lancelot Hogben, *Statistical Theory: The Relationship of Probability, Credibility, and Error* (New York, W. W. Norton and Co., Inc.) pp. 13–30.

[14] Louis O. Kattsoff, *A Philosophy of Mathematics* (Ames, Iowa, The Iowa State College Press, 1948), pp. 8–15.

[15] Harold J. Leavitt and Thomas L. Whisler, "Management in the 1980's," *Harvard Business Review* (Nov.–Dec. 1958).

[16] Douglas McGregor, *The Human Side of Enterprise* (New York, McGraw-Hill Book Co., Inc., 1960).

[17] Malcolm P. McNair, "What Price Human Relations?" *Harvard Business Review* (Mar.–Apr. 1957).

[18] Henry C. Metcalf and L. Urwick, editors, *Dynamic Administration: The Collected Papers of Mary Parker Follett* (New York, Harper & Bros. Publishers), pp. 200–201, 295.

[19] Maurice Sasieni, Arthur Yaspan, and Lawrence Friedman, *Operations Research: Methods and Problems* (New York, John Wiley & Sons, Inc., 1959).

[20] Morris Aaron Savitt, *Introduction to the Fund Theory of Accounting,* unpublished Master's thesis, New York Univ. (1950).

[21] Herbert A. Simon, *Administrative Behavior,* 2nd Edition (New York, The Macmillan Co., 1958).

[22] Herbert A. Simon, *The New Science of Management Decision* (New York, Harper & Bros. Publishers, 1960).

[23] Waino W. Suojanen, "The Span of Control—Fact or Fable," *Advanced Management* (Nov. 1955), as quoted in *Readings in Management,* Max D. Richards and William A. Nielander, editors (Cincinnati, Southwestern Publishing Co., 1958), p. 564.

[24] Lyndall F. Urwick, "The Manager's Span of Control," *Harvard Business Review* (May–June 1956), pp. 39–47.

[25] Raymond Villers, *Dynamic Management in Industry* (Englewood Cliffs, N.J., Prentice-Hall, Inc., 1960).

8

CONTROL AS AN
ORGANIZATIONAL PROCESS *

Chadwick J. Haberstroh

The study of self-regulating systems, now generally known as cybernetics, explores the ways in which some output of a dynamic system can be maintained in a more-or-less invariant equilibrium, or steady state, in the face of disrupting external forces.[1] The most general answer to this question is that the system must somehow be supplied with information about the disrupting forces that is used to offset their effect. A common way of supplying this is by means of a feedback of information on the deviations of the output from equilibrium. This information flow causes the equilibrium to be restored in some appropriate manner.

Even assuming that one does know the feedback channel used and understands the laws through which the feedback restores equilibrium, he still has a right to ask how it is that the system exists at all, and why it tends to an equilibrium at that particular value and not some other. In the case of engineering control systems the answer to this question is simple and direct: the designer intended them to perform in the way they do. Thus, there is a purposive element in these control systems resulting from an *a priori* selection of the equilibrium to be obtained. If one asks the same question, however, about naturally self-regulating systems, such as homeostatic mechanisms in the living organism or ecological balances in a community of organisms, the answer is neither simple nor direct. The equilibria found and the mechanisms for attaining them have come about by the process of natural selection in the context of a particular environment. If we put the same question in the case of organizational systems, the answer is even less

* Reprinted from *Management Science,* January, 1960, pp. 165–171.

direct and more complicated, involving as it does a multitude of designers each consciously striving to realize his own objectives, in the context of an environment and of selection pressure arising from the limitation of resources as well.

In organizations the conscious intentions of the participants are an important factor. In order to explain the gross behavior of an organization, these intentions must be measured and brought into relation with the other aspects of the organization's functioning. The existence of stable organization implies a degree of harmony and co-ordination among the participants, a sharing of intention. In order to secure this, participants communicate with each other and in doing so construct a common symbolic picture of the goals they have set for the organization and the means by which they intend to attain the goals. This picture, or representation, of the means and ends of organization (the "task analysis") is implicit in the verbal communication inside the organization. It can be measured by the use of content-analysis techniques. I have attempted to apply these techniques to a sample of communication from an integrated steel plant operated by one of the American companies.[2] This case will be used as an example in exploring organization purposes and other organizational characteristics affecting control processes.

Goal formation is influenced by the intentions of the individual participants and by the environmental constraints under which they operate. Both can be sources of conflict. The emergence of stable, enduring patterns of organization is in part a process of conflict resolution. The necessity of reducing conflict to manageable bounds tends to direct the organization's efforts toward a small number of goals and a small number of means activities for achieving them, relative to the number of alternatives that might be conceivable. It is to be expected, therefore, that the number of independent goals turned up in the task analysis will be rather small. Conflict reduction is facilitated if these goals are formulated in terms of acceptable levels, rather than in terms of optima,[3] and if the criterion of goal achievement is external and objective, rather than subjective and open to dispute. If members measure goal achievement objectively and perceive means to attain them, the goals are termed "operative."

In the case of Integrated Steel, four goals were discovered. These relate to cost reduction, production level, safety, and medical care. The safety and production goals are formulated in terms of acceptable levels set by an external office. Performance is measured in terms of tonnage produced and frequency of injuries, and an elaborate technology exists for goal achievement. In the case of safety, this task analysis was measured in detail. The goal of providing adequate medical care was departmentalized in a plant hospital; and a standard cost system and various cost reduction programs were in operation. Neither the hospital nor the cost system was investigated, however.

If the process of goal formation results in a small number of operative goals, as it did at Integrated Steel, the basis for a feedback of information on deviations of performance from the established goals is already apparent. To affirm the existence of a control system we need only verify that this information is reported to executive centers and that the executives respond so as to achieve the goals. The task analysis comprises a program of means activities understood by the participants to lead to goal achievement. One way of responding would be to adjust the level of resource use in these means activities. Let us refer to this as "routine control." Another way of responding would be to look for a better way of achieving goals. This type of activity could take the form of inventing new means activities or of altering the system of executive organization (i.e., changes in personnel or in allocation of functions). It might be expected that this type of activity would occur only in a case of extreme or repeated failure. Let us call this "non-routine control." Sufficient pressure might even lead to modification of goals in order to assure survival of the organization. Normally, however, the evolved structure of goals and means activities determines what the participants do; communications channels carrying information on performance influence when and how much they do.

In the case of Integrated Steel's safety program the type of means activities which have been developed to implement the safety objective are accident investigations, safety conferences with workmen, implementation of safety work-orders, special inspections, clean-up work, etc. The execution of each of these activities is in some way conditional on the occurrence of injuries in the plant. Other activities are also carried on which are independent of the occurrence of accidents. These include routine inspections, training and screening procedures for new employees, safety clearance of engineering proposals, job analysis, publicity campaigns, etc.

The formal communication channels on safety performance begin with injury reports made by the plant hospital. This information is collated and distributed daily throughout the plant's executive organization in detail and in statistical summary. This information cues the line supervision to investigate injuries; alerts the plant safety staff to inspect for similar hazards and to assist in accident investigations; and, in summary figures, provides the basis for broader types of corrective action such as the study of classes of jobs for hazards, the issuance of special instructions to employees, and evaluation of supervisors. The same reports when aggregated into divisional and plant injury frequencies serve as an indicator of the plant's overall performance relative to its safety goals.

The routine control processes discussed above are not the only, or even the most important, means of control used at Integrated Steel. The non-routine control processes, changes in personnel and in the institutional structure within which the participants operate, take precedence. The very nature of the accident process (i.e., the importance of human failure, rare events, conjunction of circumstances, and the randomness of occurrence of injuries) make for a different degree of reliability on the technological side from that encountered in connection with, for instance, production matters. Because the coupling between the program of means activities and the degree of safety performance is not fully determined, there is a need for relatively tight control over the programs themselves. This is achieved by response of the top plant management to deviations of the plant and departmental injury frequencies from the objectives set for them at the beginning of the year. These yearly objectives are set by company officers above the plant level, although the plant management has discretion to aim at a more difficult target if it chooses.

Figure 1 is a block diagram of the control structure discussed above. The input (I) is the annual safety objective which is compared with the

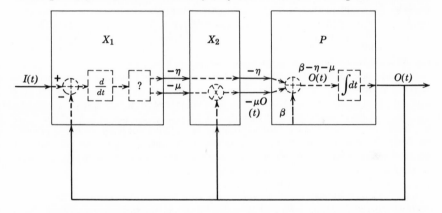

Figure 1. Control flow chart of safety functions at Integrated Steel.

performance of the plant (O) by top management. The result of the non-routine control functions of the top executive organization (X_1) may be expressed as the two parameters of the routine control system: the intensity of response to injuries (μ) and the level of independent safety activity (η). A complete model of the top executive function was not constructed, although there seems to be evidence [4] that it responds to changes in the degree of error (a differentiating operator). Other than that it appears possible to say only that its effects are intermittent, rather than continuous, and respond only to error in excess of a certain threshold. It is therefore a non-linear operator. In the case of the routine control function (X_2), however,

TABLE 1   INNOVATION * AND PERFORMANCE AT INTEGRATED STEEL

Year	Average All Plants	Disabling Injuries					Total Injuries			Innovation *
		Error	ΔError	Plant Performance	Error	Target	Plant Performance	Error	Target	
1	5.29	.98	.98	6.17			357			moderate
2	4.95	.13	—.85	5.08			422			none
3	5.41	1.77	1.64	7.18			407			heavy
4	4.66	1.24	—.53	5.90			302			none
5	3.66	.67	—.57	4.33			244			none
6	3.55	.65	—.02	4.20	.46	3.74	210	0	238	light
7	3.00	.83	.18	3.83	.50	3.33	196	0	210	moderate
8	2.38	.81	—.02	3.19	.72	2.47	183	11	172	light
9	2.07	.63	—.18	2.70	.54	2.16	133	0	168	none
10 [a]	1.93	.91	.28	2.84	.80	2.04	128	0	133	heavy

[a] At time major decisions were taken.

* Level of innovation in the plant-wide safety program was rated by the author on the basis of a survey of plant safety files. The information found consisted of a description of the innovations made. This information is briefly summarized below.

In the first year studied the safety staff recommended and received management approval of a job analysis program which was to provide the basis for strict enforcement of safe working procedures. They also requested regular physical examinations for all employees.

In year two, no safety innovations were discovered.

In year three, one of the plant manager's top staff assistants announced to division managers the inauguration of an extensive program of job analysis and indoctrination of workmen in safe procedures. He also urged the division managers to inaugurate the practice of having foremen make thorough investigations of all minor injuries as a basis for corrective action. This was to be coupled with a program of training foremen in the responsibilities which would be placed upon them in these two programs, and also the formation of division safety committees at top division management level to expedite safety recommendations. He also announced inauguration of a plant-wide safety committee.

In years four and five no new activity was discovered.

In year six a proposal was made by the safety staff for transfer of some functions so as to improve the coordinating service of the safety staff and shift more executive responsibility on to the line organization. There was a new program of statistical reporting of injuries classified by types of accident.

In year seven management inaugurated a revised system of job analysis, appointed a new plant-wide advisory committee, inaugurated an annual conference of all division managers for the purpose of setting objectives and reviewing the safety program, and also ordered the universal replacement of a hazardous type of crane controller in use through most of the plant.

In year eight a new statistical basis for the reporting of injuries was inaugurated.

In year nine no innovations were discovered.

In year ten a revised and greatly expanded program of job analysis was instituted, with a number of executives re-assigned to safety responsibilities exclusively. Procedures for top level reporting and evaluation of safety performance were revised to place greater emphasis upon safety.

a linear model seems appropriate. Executives appear to proportion their influence on the injury rate to the magnitude of that rate plus a constant. The "program" operator (P) relates the control activities to the actual performance of the plant, adding and integrating the safety efforts $(\mu O + \eta)$ and the exogenous load of new hazards (β).

Table 1 contains data on injury rates, safety objectives, and innovations in the safety program for a 10 year period. The changes in organization made by top management in year 7 did not take effect until year 9. Thus, during the period beginning with year 3 and ending with year 8, the routine control system operated with constant parameters μ and η. Under this assumption, the injury rate $[O(t)]$ is given by

$$O(t) = \int [\beta - \eta - \mu O(t)]dt \qquad (1)$$

or equivalently

$$O'(t) = \beta - \eta - \mu O(t). \qquad (2)$$

Solving this differential equation,

$$O(t) = \frac{\lambda}{\mu} + \left[\hat{O} - \frac{\lambda}{\mu} \right] e^{-\mu t} \qquad (3)$$

where $\lambda = \beta - \eta$ and $\hat{O}$ is the initial level of the injury rate.

This equation implies that first differences in injury rates tend to decrease by a constant ratio from year to year. The performance data for years 3 to 8 in Table 1 is fairly consistent with this.

Another principle of control, important in the case of organization, is that of factorization. Ashby has shown [5] that if trial-and-error changes are relied upon for control (compare the operator X_1 at Integrated Steel), a large system cannot practically be stabilized unless its output can be factored into a number of independently controlled information sources. At Integrated Steel, the safety objective was broken down by divisions and injury rates were reported on that same basis. Part of the nonroutine control activity occurred at the division level. Innovation in divisional programs initiated by division management was correlated with the division's performance error.

This, of course, bears on the subject of decentralization in organizations. Meaningful decentralization is probably impossible without a resolution of the goals into nonconflicting, operative subgoals so that these can be placed under independent control. On the other hand, there is probably a size for organizations at which goal attainment becomes impossible without factorization, even though the method used may not resemble current definitions of "decentralized authority." The plant production, cost, and safety goals at Integrated Steel appear to represent just such a factorization of the company goals.

In summary, the characteristics postulated by cybernetic theory for self-regulating systems have their correlates in human organizations. In the case of Integrated Steel, the theory points up the influence of information feedbacks upon the actions of the executives in attempting to realize the organization objectives. Of particular importance are the role of the higher echelons of executives in controlling the mode of response of the lower echelons and the use of multiple feedbacks in the design of the executive system.

NOTES

[1] Wiener, N., *Cybernetics,* Wiley, N.Y., 1948; Ashby, W. R., *An Introduction to Cybernetics,* Wiley, N.Y., 1956.

[2] This research was carried out at the Graduate School of Industrial Administration, Carnegie Institute of Technology, under a grant from the Ford Foundation for research on human behavior in organizations. A full report of the methods and the results of this investigation, as well as a more thorough discussion of the topic of the present paper, is contained in my doctoral dissertation, *Processes of Internal Control in Firms,* University Microfilms, Inc., Ann Arbor, Michigan, 1958.

[3] Simon, H. A., *Models of Man,* Wiley, N.Y., 1957, page 241.

[4] Compare columns 4 and 11 in Table 1.

[5] Ashby, W. R., *Design for a Brain,* Wiley, N.Y., 1952.

9

DATA SYSTEMS THAT CROSS
COMPANY BOUNDARIES *

Felix Kaufman

Recent developments in data processing technology permitting some computers to communicate directly with each other have brought us to the point where broad new areas of information consolidation appear to be feasible—and may, in fact, be imminent. We are now witnessing the prospective development of systems broad enough to cut across company boundaries. Obviously such systems can have a profound impact on the way business and commerce are conducted.

This preamble is stated with the full knowledge that management, during the first decade of the computer, has generally faced major problems in introducing electronic data processing into relatively simple systems environments. So far, attempts to achieve highly integrated, companywide, so-called "total systems" have been largely unsuccessful, although the concept is useful and provides a practical goal for many data processing programs. In fact, as the second computer decade begins, some authorities are sufficiently disenchanted to reject the "total system" approach outright as unsound, recommending instead concentration on more limited but probably more manageable consolidations.

Nevertheless, major new technological developments are confronting us with the possibility that our earlier "total system" thinking may have fallen short conceptually of the real meaning of "total." Notwithstanding past experience with intracompany integration, there would now appear to be broader, but still practical, systems which are worth considering. All business is involved in constant interconnection and intercommunication with other organizations—whether suppliers, customers, or competitors. In

* Reprinted from *Harvard Business Review,* January–February, 1966, pp. 141–155.

effect, each company system functions within a still larger "total system." [1] Thus company boundaries are not the only, or even the most meaningful, system boundaries. Therefore, even though internal systems may still be far from totally integrated, perceptive management needs to begin to consider the new possibilities for co-ordinating data processing *outside* its own organizational limits.

Why is a broader kind of "total system" forthcoming? What are some of the forms which it may take?

COMPUTER COMMUNICATION

As suggested, the feature of the new technology that opens the door for broader systems is *communication between computers* and related developments in computer time sharing. We are already witnessing high-speed, efficient, accurate communication between machines, as will be discussed. It is the prospect of developing this ability further that makes the concept of broader systems practical.

Machines communicate by means of networks of decentralized computers. The same effect is obtained in a single system through time sharing, or simultaneous service from a central computer to multiple users. Time sharing, in particular, may offer management unprecedented flexibility in its utilization of information resources. Systems formerly based on separate computers may now communicate with one another within the same machine system.

Computer Network

What is the nature of a computer network? . . . Each installation may be connected with some other installation or, in the extreme case, with all others by communications connections that can range from full-time use of leased lines to as-required use of the public dial telephone system. Since the majority of computers now in use are dissimilar in model or manufacture, communications between them have been fairly limited, consisting chiefly of simple structured messages, such as inventory interrogations (as opposed to the remote implementation of complex programs). However, when the network links *similar* computers, as is beginning to happen, processing capabilities increase tremendously. For example:

One aircraft manufacturer has transmitted both data and computer programs between similar installations linked by a microwave network. The network has been able to level the entire system's work load; if one computer is overloaded, part of its data and program load can be transmitted automatically to another installation with the available capacity.

The new developments in computer manufacture are tending increasingly to emphasize compatibility between competitive models and systems. Since future networks will therefore more likely consist of compatible machines, their communication can become more versatile and efficient.

Time Sharing

How does time sharing work? This method links a network of remote input-output stations with one central computer. . . . Each remote station has unrestricted access to the central machine; its input-output devices provide a means for entering data into the computer and for displaying or transmitting the answers received. Each remote station enters data whenever it chooses, and information is stored in the central computer, character by character, according to the station number from which it is received. Messages can be received concurrently from any number of stations, and then put on the job queue. When the job is completed, results are transmitted to the originating station. In many time-sharing systems, only a few seconds elapse between the completion of the input messages and the print-out of the results.

Time sharing is, of course, economical for intracompany use. For instance:

The worldwide facilities of a large oil company communicate by TWX network with a computer in the home office. Information about problems can be received from the most distant stations, and results returned within a few seconds.

A computer service company provides similar capability for solving larger problems:

Several clients of the service are using small computers, rather than teletype-writers, as high-speed input-output terminals for entering data and receiving results from the larger central installation. For each client, the net cost of such time-shared problem solution is lower than if equally powerful equipment were rented full-time.

The potentialities of intercompany time sharing are even more interesting than are those of networks. As time sharing develops further, a central computer may process data for two entities affected by a single event. Or it may communicate directly and instantly with another time-sharing center involving another entity.

Implications of Trends

Both of these trends—networks of computers and large time-shared central computers—are continuing. In a sense, they are not too different.

Technically, a network of compatible computers can be replaced (without too much difficulty) by substituting for each computer in the network an input-output device connected to a large central computer. The long-range implications of this fact are interesting, as this case demonstrates:

Computer Networks Created. About 10 years ago, the nation's airlines began installing electronic systems for maintaining their inventory of seats. After several years, each line had its own system, with inputs to each central installation by way of "agents sets" in sales offices.

However, controlling seat inventory on its own planes solved only part of a line's ticket-selling problem. As a result of the common practice of passengers' buying a ticket involving flight legs on several lines, carriers were in frequent contact with one another to make reservations or to sell space for themselves. It was realized that it would be more efficient if such communications did not require manual contact. Since each trunk line had an electronic space accounting system, linking all of them would provide each carrier with convenient communication access to the others (an example, incidentally, of a network of independently controlled computers).

Airline reservations are now reaching the point of such extraorganizational, intersystem communication. One large trunk carrier maintains inventory records for a feeder line; therefore, communication between these two systems is possible. In another case, a communications equipment manufacturer provides switching arrangements for several carriers through the use of the manufacturer's common facilities. In a third instance, large trunk lines have set up regular communications circuits between their respective electronic reservations systems. . . .

Growing Burden. But this concept of a network of electronic seat inventory systems may well become increasingly impractical. One of the problems is the large number of airlines. There are now some 12 major U.S. trunk airlines and over 20 U.S. feeder airlines. In addition, there are over 20 foreign airlines serving the United States, plus about 60 intrastate helicopter, freight, and air taxi lines. Considering that a passenger's ticket may cover various combinations of these types of airlines, it is apparent that the communications lines connecting one to another could get quite complicated.

Possible Solutions. While it is too early to say how this system will be simplified, it serves the purposes of this article to consider a possible solution. In this system, one computer is used for interline reservation processing and is connected to each airline's individual systems. This central computer might maintain its own inventory records (space "loaned" to the central system by each of the airlines), or it might interrogate each of the affected airlines' systems for a given inquiry; system operation would probably be faster if it maintained its own inventory records.

Though such a solution probably would be an improvement over the existing system, it would not be optimal. One significant shortcoming might occur with respect to "loaned" or "blocked" space, which might lead to cases where flights appeared to be sold out when in fact they were not. Another shortcoming might be that the airlines would continue to use noncompatible systems. For example, even now, while some airlines are maintaining complete passenger records by the computer (passenger's name, address, complete itinerary, and so forth), other airlines are maintaining just their seat inventory on their computer.

The most efficient—and technically feasible—solution would be to have one central system serving all airlines on a time-sharing basis. . . . Such a system would maintain all records in a standard manner and would avoid many of the problems of "loaned" space. It could evolve from the present systems if there is economic pressure for it to evolve. The system boundaries in such a case *would differ markedly from organization boundaries;* there are fundamental reasons for designing the scope and breadth of a data system independently of the corporate operating structure.

. . .

CONCLUSION

The various illustrations in this article underscore the need to adopt broader systems in order to obtain certain advantages.

Through an examination of these advantages we can clearly discern at last the fundamental criteria which govern the design of information systems. Apparently, one effect of greater technological power is that it advances our perceptiveness in discerning fundamental criteria and permits us to define the basic postulates which will ultimately dictate the size of an information system.

These postulates are as follows:

· The extensive duplication of data in files frequently is an extra-organizational condition. The minimization of redundancy requires "thinking beyond total systems," requires crossing company or entity boundaries.

· The elimination of repetition in the transcription of source data cannot be completely accomplished on an entity basis. (One man's output is another man's input.)

· Files organized on an entity basis frequently do not include all of the data needed to control the object which is the subject of the file (an employee, for example).

· The best data processing is none at all. To achieve this, one needs to be able to comprehend both sides of an event (that is, to let one data processing unit handle the event's impact on two or more entities).

Theoretically, an end result of the kind of system thinking described in this article might be a single data processing system for all the affairs of our economy. Clearly—and fortunately, from many points of view—there are many obstacles to the achievement of such a system.

Short of this, what is really practical and logical? The answer probably is that we could have much larger legal entities. A provocative possibility is that the forces described will produce new advantages for larger economic units and provide additional motivation for mergers.

This tendency, of course, may appear to be alien to the socioeconomic character of free enterprise. Is it not possible, however, that as time sharing makes the most sophisticated programs available to the small user as well as the large one, data processing and some of its related control functions (e.g., inventory control) will not remain in the arena of competitive activity? Information handling could become neutral ground. Information processes could be conducted at a uniformly high level of efficiency, with all users having equal access to the lowest-cost service. Perhaps users could purchase such services from data processing utilities.

To use an analogy, if each business had to provide independently its own electrical power capability, some would do it better than others and give themselves a competitive advantage. When companies purchase from a utility, however, differences exist only as to the efficiency of consumption and not as to the cost of the service. So it may be also for information processing.

In any event, the "total system" concept as described in this article should bring obvious benefits to all users. The challenge to large companies is to not be blinded by their size, but to think beyond even their own expansive and far-flung organizational boundaries to the possibilities of extracorporate systems. The challenge to smaller companies is to not be blinded by the advantages of complete autonomy and independence, but to take into account also the very real benefits of working agreements with other organizations even if management's freedom of action is somewhat curtailed thereby. As John W. Gardner stated in his book, *Self-Renewal:*

"It is becoming increasingly doubtful that a large number of small, unaffiliated operators can survive in a world of gargantuan organizations. Thus it becomes critically important to explore any possible arrangements

by which the individual or small organization can enjoy some of the benefits of large-scale organization without any substantial loss of autonomy." [2]

NOTES

[1] See Seymour Tilles, "The Manager's Job—A Systems Approach" (*HBR* January–
February 1963), p. 73.
[2] New York, Harper and Row, 1964, p. 85.

10

MYTH OF REAL-TIME
MANAGEMENT INFORMATION *

John Dearden

The latest vogue in computer information systems is the so-called real-time management information system. The general idea is to have in each executive's office a remote computer terminal which is connected to a large-scale computer with a data bank containing all of the relevant information in the company. The data bank, updated continuously, can be "interrogated" by the manager at any time. Answers to questions are immediately flashed on a screen in his office. Allegedly, a real-time management information system enables the manager to obtain complete and up-to-the-minute information about everything that is happening within the company.

The purpose of this article—aimed at a time span of the next five to seven years—is to raise some serious questions concerning the utility of a real-time information system for top management. I will try to show that it would not be practicable to operate a real-time *management control* system and, moreover, that such a system would not help to solve any of the critical problems even if it could be implemented. I will also try to show that in other areas of top management concern a real-time system is, at best, of marginal value. It is my personal opinion that, of all the ridiculous things that have been foisted on the long-suffering executive in the name of science and progress, the real-time management information system is the silliest.

* Reprinted from *Harvard Business Review,* May–June, 1966, pp. 123–132.

MEANING OF REAL-TIME

One of the problems in any new field of endeavor is that there is frequently no universally accepted definition for many of the terms. It therefore becomes nearly impossible to question the validity of the concepts underlying the terms because their meanings are different to different people. The term "real-time" is no exception. In fact, in a single issue of one computer magazine, back-to-back articles defined real-time differently; and one example, cited in the first article as an illustration of what real-time is *not,* appeared in the second article as an illustration of what a real-time system *is.*

SEMANTIC CONFUSION

One concept of real-time is demonstrated by these two quotations:

· "A real-time management information system—i. e., one that delivers information in time to do something about it." [1]

· "A real-time computer system may be defined as one that controls an environment by receiving data, processing them and returning results sufficiently quickly to affect the functioning of the environment at that time." [2]

The problem with both of these definitions is that they are too broad. *All* management control systems must be real-time systems under this concept. It would be a little silly to plan to provide management with budget performance reports, for instance, if they were received too late for management to take any action.

The following is a description of real-time that comes closer to the concept of real-time as it is used by most systems and computer people:

"The delays involved in batch processing are often natural delays, and little advantage can be obtained by reducing them. But elimination of the *necessity* for such delays opens new and relatively unexplored possibilities for changing the entire nature of the data processing system—from a passive recorder of history (which, of course, is valuable for many decisions) to an active participant in the minute-to-minute operations of the organization. It becomes possible to process data in *real-time*—so that the output may be fed back immediately to control current operations. Thus the computer can interact with people on a dynamic basis, obtaining and providing information, recording the decisions of humans, or even making some of these decisions." [3]

. . .

REAL-TIME PRACTICALITY?

. . .

1. Management Control

I do not see how a real-time system can be *used* in management control. In fact, I believe that any attempt to use real-time will considerably weaken even a good management control system. (In setting objectives or budgets, it may be useful to have a computer available at the time of the budget review to calculate the effects of various alternatives suggested by management. This however, is not a real-time system, since a computer console need be installed only for the review sessions.)

Calculating Performance. In the area of performance evaluation, real-time management information systems are particularly ridiculous. When a division manager agrees to earn, say, $360,000 in 1966, he does not agree to earn $1,000 a day or $1,000/24 per hour. The only way actual performance can be compared with a budget is to break down the budget into the time periods against which performance is to be measured. If the smallest period is a month (as it usually is), nothing short of a month's actual performance is significant (with the exception of the events picked up by the early warning system to be described below). Why, then, have a computer system that allows the manager to interrogate a memory bank to show him the hour-to-hour or even day-to-day status of performance against plan?

Even assuming objectives could logically be calendarized by day or hour, we run into worse problems in calculating actual performance, and worse still in making the comparison of actual to standard meaningful. If the performance measures involve accounting data (and they most frequently do), the data will never be up-to-date until they are normalized (adjusted) at the end of the accounting period. I will not bore you with the details. Suffice it to say only that a real-time accounting system which yields meaningful results on even a daily basis would be a horrendous and expensive undertaking.

Let us go one step further. Performance reports, to be meaningful, must include an explanation of the variances. This frequently involves considerable effort and often requires the analyst to spend time at the source of the variance in order to determine the cause. Would this be done every day or oftener? Ridiculous! There is one more thing about performance reports.

The important message in many reports is the action being taken and the estimated effect of this action. In other words, the projection of future events is the important top management consideration. Will this be built into the real-time system? Since this involves the considered judgment of the subordinate and his staff, I do not see how this could possibly be done even on a daily basis.

Early Warning. How about real-time for providing an early warning? Here, also, I do not see how it could be of help. Early warning has not been a problem in any top management control system with which I have been acquainted. In most instances, when situations deteriorate to the point where immediate action is required, top management knows about it. As the manager of a division ($100 million a year in sales) said to me, when I asked him how he knew when things might be out of hand in one of his plants, "That's what the telephone is for."

In any case, it is possible to prescribe the situations which management should be apprised of immediately, without even relying on a computer. Furthermore, the important thing is to bring the situation to top management's attention *before* something happens. For example, it is important to inform management of a threatened strike. Yet a real-time management information system would pick it up only *after* the strike had occurred.

In summary, then, early warning systems have been put into operation and have worked satisfactorily without a real-time system. I see nothing in a real-time management information system that would improve the means of early warning, and such a system would certainly be more expensive. (Note that here I am talking about management control systems. The early warning techniques of many logistical control systems, in contrast, could be greatly improved by real-time systems.)

My conclusion on management control is that real-time information cannot be made meaningful—even at an extremely high cost—and that any attempt to do so cannot help but result in a waste of money and management time. Improvements in most management control systems must come from sources other than real-time information systems.

2. Strategic Planning

Since strategic planning largely involves predicting the long-run future, I fail to see how a real-time management information system will be of appreciable use here. It *is* true that past data are required to forecast future events, but these need hardly be continuously updated and immediately available. Furthermore, much of the preparation of detailed strategic plans is done by staff groups. While these groups may on occasion work with computer models, the models would certainly be stored away, not maintained on line between uses.

Perhaps the most persistent concept of a real-time management information system is the picture of the manager sitting down at his console and interacting with the computer. For example, as a strategic planning idea comes to him, he calls in a simulation model to test it out, or a regression analysis to help him forecast, some event; or, again, he asks for all of the information about a certain subject on which he is required to make a decision.

It seems to me that the typical manager would have neither the time nor the inclination to interact with the computer on a day-to-day basis about strategic planning. Problems requiring computer models are likely to be extremely complex. In most instances, the formulation of these problems can be turned over to staff specialists. Furthermore, I think it would be quite expensive to build a series of models to anticipate the manager's needs.

Under any conditions, strategic planning either by the manager alone or by staff groups does not appear to be improved by a real-time system. Models can be fed into the computer and coefficients can be updated as they are used. Between uses, it seems to me, these models would be most economically stored on magnetic tape.

3. Personnel Planning

A real-time management information system does not help the top manager to solve his problems of personnel planning, although the computer can be useful in certain types of personnel data analysis. About the only advantage to the manager is that information becomes available somewhat more quickly. Instead of calling for the history of a particular individual and waiting for personnel to deliver it, the manager can request this information directly from the computer. Therefore, while a remote console device with a visual display unit *could* be used for retrieving personnel information, the question of whether it *should* be used is one of simple economics. Is the additional cost of storing and maintaining the information, plus the cost of the retrieval devices, worth the convenience?

4. Coordination

The coordination function is very similar to the management control function with respect to potential real-time applicability. A manager wants to know right away when there is an inter-departmental problem that will require his attention. As is the case with early warning systems developed for management control, a real-time system is not necessary (or even useful, in most cases) to convey this information. Further, I cannot see how a real-time management information system could be used in the solution of these coordination problems, except in unusual cases.

5. Operating Control

There is no question that real-time methods are useful in certain types of operating systems, particularly in logistics systems.[4] To the extent that a top executive retains certain operating control functions, there is a possibility that he may be able to use a real-time information system. Because of the necessity of doing other things, however, most executives will be able to spend only a limited amount of time on operating functions. This means generally that they must work on the "exception" principle. Under most conditions, therefore, it would seem much more economical for a subordinate to monitor the real-time information and inform the top executives when a decision has to be made.

It is very difficult to generalize about this situation. Here, again, it appears to be one of simple economics. How much is a real-time system worth to the manager in relation to what it is costing? I cannot believe that there would be many instances where a manager would be concerned with operating problems to the extent that a real-time information system operating from his office would be justified.

REPORTING BY COMPUTER

In recent months, there have been experiments to replace traditional published reports by utilizing consoles and display devices to report information directly to management. Although these techniques, strictly speaking, are not real-time, they bear such a close relationship to real-time systems that it will be useful to consider them here.

Modus Operandi

The general idea is that the information contained in the management reports would be stored in the computer memory so that the manager could ask for only the information he needed. This request would be made from the computer console, and the information would be flashed on a screen in his office. For example, a manager could ask for a report on how sales compared with quota. After looking at this, he could then ask for data on the sales of the particular regions that were below quota and, subsequently, for detail of the districts that were out of line.

The benefits claimed for this type of reporting are as follows:

· The manager will receive only the information he wants.

· Each manager can obtain the information in the format in which he wants it. In other words, each manager can design his own reports. One manager may use graphs almost exclusively, while another may use tabulation.

· The information can be assembled in whatever way the manager wants it—that is, one manager may want sales by areas, and another may want it by product line. Furthermore, the manager can have the data processed in any way that he wants.

· The information will be received more quickly.

Important Considerations

Before installing such a system, it seems to me, a number of things should be taken into account.

First, what advantage, if any, does this system have over a well-designed reporting system? Since the storage and retrieval of data in a computer do not add anything that could not be obtained in a traditional reporting system, the benefits must be related to convenience. Is there enough additional convenience to justify the additional cost?

Second, is it possible that for many executives such a system will be more of a nuisance than a convenience? It may be much easier for them to open a notebook and read the information needed, since in a well-designed system the information is reported in levels of details so that only data of interest need be examined.

Finally, will the saving in time be of any value?

It seems to me that the two main considerations in installing such a system are the economics and the desires of the particular executive. There is one further possibility, however, that should be carefully considered. What will be the impact on the lower level executives? If these people do not know the kind of information their superiors are using to measure their performance, will this not create human relations problems?

Without going into the details, I can see many problems being created if this is not handled correctly. With a regular reporting system, the subordinate knows exactly what information his superior is receiving—and when he receives it—concerning his performance. Furthermore, the subordinate receives the information *first*. Any deviations in this relationship can cause problems, and the use of a computer to retrieve varying kinds of information from a data base is a deviation from this relationship.

THREE FALLACIES

If management information on a real-time basis is so impractical and uneconomic, why are so many people evidently enamored with this concept? I believe that the alleged benefits of real-time management information systems are based on three major fallacies.

1. Improved Control

Just about every manager feels, at some time, that he does not really have control of his company. Many managers feel this way frequently. This is natural, since complete control is just about impossible even with the best management control system. Since most companies have management control systems that are far from optimum, there is little wonder that a feeling of insecurity exists. In the face of this feeling of insecurity, the promise of "knowing everything that is happening as soon as it happens" has an overpowering appeal.

As explained previously, real-time will not improve management control and, consequently, will not help to eliminate the insecurity that exists. What is usually needed is a combination of improved management control systems and better selection and training of personal. Even at best, however, the executive will have to accept responsibility for what other people do, without having full control over their actions.

2. "Scientific Management"

There appears to be considerable sentiment to the effect that the scientific way to manage is to use a computer. This fallacy implies that the executive with a computer console in his office is a scientific manager who uses man-machine communication to extend his ability into new, heretofore unavailable, realms of decision making.

I believe that it is nonsense to expect most managers to communicate directly with a computer. Every manager and every business is different. If a manager has the necessary training and wishes to do so, it may be helpful for him to use a computer to test out some of his ideas. To say, however, that *all* managers should do this, or that this is "scientific management," is ridiculous. A manager has to allocate his time so that he spends it on those areas where his contribution is greatest. If a computer is useful for testing out his ideas in a given situation, there is no reason why he should have to do it personally. The assignment can just as easily be turned over to a staff group. In other words, where a computer is helpful in solving some management problems, there is no reason for the manager to have any direct contact with the machine.

In most instances, the computer is of best use where there are complex problems to be solved. The formulation of a solution to these complex problems can generally be done best by a staff group. Not only are staff personnel better qualified (they are selected for these qualifications), but they have the uninterrupted time to do it. It seems to me that there is nothing wrong with a manager spending his time managing and letting others play "Liberace at the console."

3. Logistics Similarity

This fallacy is the belief that management control systems are merely higher manifestations of logistics systems.

The fact is that the typical real-time system, either in operation or being planned, is a *logistics* system. In such a system, for example, a production plan is developed and the degree of allowable variances established in a centralized computer installation. The actual production is constantly compared to plan; and when a deviation exceeds the established norm, this fact is communicated to the appropriate source. On receiving this information, action is always taken. Either the schedules are changed or the deficiency is somehow made up.

Notice that speed in handling and transmitting vast amounts of information is essential. This is the critical problem that limits many manual logistics systems; and the computer, particularly with real-time applications, goes a long way toward solving the speed problem.

In contrast, speed in processing and transmitting large amounts of data is *not* a critical problem in *management control* systems. Consequently, the improvements that real-time techniques may effect in logistics systems cannot be extrapolated into management control systems.

The critical problems in management control are (*a*) determining the level of objectives, (*b*) determining when a deviation from the objective requires action, and (*c*) deciding what particular action should be taken. The higher in the organizational hierarchy the manager is positioned, the more critical these three problems tend to become. For example, they are usually much more difficult in planning divisional profit budgets than plant expense budgets. In some instances the computer can help the manager with these problems, but I do not see how it can solve them for him. Furthermore, the use of computers in solving these problems has nothing to do with real-time.

SHORT-TERM VIEW

While real-time management information systems may be very useful in improving certain kinds of operating systems, particularly complex logistics systems, they will be of little use in improving management control. This is particularly true in the short-range time span of the next five to seven years.

The following is a checklist of questions that I believe the manager should have answers to before letting anyone install a remote computer terminal and a visual display screen in his office:

1. What will the total incremental cost of the equipment and programming be? (Be sure to consider the cost of continuing systems and programming work that the real-time systems will involve.)

2. Exactly how will this equipment be used? (Be sure to obtain a complete description of the proposed uses and the date when each application will become operational.)

3. Exactly how will each of these uses improve the ability to make decisions? In particular, how will the management control system be improved?

With precise answers to these three questions, it seems to me that a manager can decide whether or not a remote terminal and visual display device should be installed. Do not be surprised, however, if the answer is negative.

LONG-RANGE OUTLOOK

What are the prospects of real-time systems, say, 15 or 20 years from now? Some experts believe that, by that time, staff assistance to top management will have largely disappeared. Not only will the staff have disappeared, but so will most of the paper that flows through present organizations. A manager in the year 1985 or so will sit in his paperless, peopleless office with his computer terminal and make decisions based on information and analyses displayed on a screen in his office.

Caution Urged

It seems to me that, at the present time, the long-term potential or real-time management information systems is completely unknown. No one can say with any degree of certainty that the prediction cited above is incorrect. After all, 15 or 20 years is a long time away, and the concept of a manager using a computer to replace his staff is not beyond the realm of theoretical possibility. On the other hand, this concept could be a complete pipe-dream.

Under any circumstances, many significant changes in technology, organization, and managerial personnel will be required before this prediction could be a reality for business in general. As a result, if such changes do occur, they will come slowly, and there will be ample opportunity for business executives to adjust to them. For example, I believe there is little danger of a company president waking up some morning to find his chief competitor has installed a computer-based, decision-making system so effective that it will run him out of business.

I believe all executives should be open-minded to suggestions for any improvements in management information systems, but they should require evidence that any proposed real-time management information system will actually increase their effectiveness. Above all, no one should rush into this now because of its future potential.

The present state of real-time management information systems has been compared to that of the transportation field at the beginning of the Model-T era. At that time, only visionaries had any idea of how transportation would be revolutionized by the automobile. It would have been foolish, however, for a businessman to get rid of his horse-drawn vehicles just because some visionaries said that trucks would take over completely in 20 years.

It seems to me that this is the identical situation now. Even if the most revolutionary changes will eventually take place in management information systems 20 years hence, it would be silly for business executives to scrap present methods until they are positive the new methods are better.

NOTES

[1] Gilbert Burck and the Editors of *Fortune, The Computer Age* (New York, Harper and Row, Publishers, 1965), p. 106.

[2] James Martin, *Programming Real-Time Computer Systems* (Englewood Cliffs, New Jersey, Prentice-Hall, Inc., 1965), p. 378.

[3] E. Wainright Martin, Jr., *Electronic Data Processing* (Homewood, Illinois, Richard D. Irwin, Inc., 1965), p. 381.

[4] See Robert E. McGarrah, "Logistics for the International Manufacturer," *HBR* March–April 1966, p. 157.

11

COMPUTER EFFECT UPON
MANAGERIAL JOBS *

Joseph P. Schwitter

Concerning the impact of automation on managerial jobs, the following prediction is provocative. "By 1985, we will possess the technical capability required to handle most managerial jobs with machines." [1] Leavitt and Whisler foresee as a consequence of automation an increasing gulf between the few middle managers that are left over and the top executives.[2] These statements seem to foreshadow widespread technological unemployment for numerous managers. They also suggest that the content of managerial jobs will become simpler. On the other hand, MacNiece, speaking of "automatic computers" in connection with the production control manager's job, predicts a change toward greater difficulties and complexities.[3]

Such conflicting predictions call for empirical studies. More facts should be known about the extent and the characteristics of changes in managerial jobs due to the introduction and use of computers. This would help in recruitment, training, payment, and the establishment of performance standards.

ORGANIZATION AND METHOD OF RESEARCH

This project was designed to answer the following questions: has the content of managerial jobs changed due to the use of computers? Secondly,

* Reprinted from *Journal of Academy of Management,* September, 1965, pp. 232–236.

NOTE: This study has been made possible through the cooperation of Stephen D. Adams, Fred Jackson, Ray Neid and Harry Ruth. They deserve my gratitude. I am also thankful to my colleague Dr. Arlyn Melcher, Assistant Professor of Management, for his constructive criticism.

which managerial jobs have been affected? Job content changes can be either qualitative in nature such as increasing or decreasing responsibility, complexity, training, or quantitative such as more or less duties or subordinates.

The data were obtained by sending a questionnaire to forty-seven firms located within the highly industralized area of Northeastern Ohio. The questionnaire consisted of an open-end list of jobs in top, middle, and lower management. Changes in job content were indicated as plus, minus, or equal to pre-computer conditions. An increase in job content was specified as the condition where more subordinates or subordinates with higher knowledge and training requirements were given to supervise, more mathematical techniques were used in planning and controlling, new duties were added and a more technical knowledge and judgement were required. The same characteristics were used to indicate a decrease in job content.

After the return of the questionnaires, eighteen interviews were conducted with a different set of firms in the same area. The interviewees were mostly the controllers and wage administrators. The purpose was to obtain further information that would complement the questionnaire answers. For these semi-directive interviews the same definitions of job content were used.

SUMMARY OF QUESTIONNAIRE SURVEY

The survey yielded thirteen useable returns of forty-seven mailed questionnaires. One fifth wrote that they had installed computers only recently and were unable to say whether changes in managerial jobs had occurred. The findings are therefore based on the thirteen.

Only two of the thirteen reporting companies indicated a change in the content of *top* management jobs. And only two of six jobs listed on the questionnaire had undergone an increase in job content. The jobs of controller and vice president in charge of purchasing had changed. No significant changes occurred in the presidency and the vice presidencies in charge of manufacturing, sales and finance.

Concerning *middle* management jobs, seven firms reported changes. The ten jobs affected by the computer are listed in Table 1.

No change at all was reported for the jobs of the quality control manager, traffic manager and R & D manager. The sample indicates a stronger tendency toward increasing rather than decreasing job content. Specifically, jobs most directly related to the factory operations have become more difficult and complex.

TABLE 1.   NUMBER OF TIMES A JOB WAS
REPORTED TO HAVE INCREASED OR
DECREASED IN CONTENT

Managerial Job	Increase	Decrease
Plant Manager	1	—
Production Supervisor	2	—
Production Control Manager	2	2
Chief Engineer	3	—
Chief Accountant	3	2
Credit Manager	1	1
Sales Manager	1	—
Data Processing Manager	2	—
Systems and Procedures Manager	3	—
Industrial Engineer	1	—

The survey also revealed that the jobs of the manager of data processing, and the manager of systems and procedures have increased in difficulty. Seven out of thirteen companies reported a change in the content of lower management jobs. Table 2 indicates a trend towards decreased content for some jobs and increased content for others. Generally the functions performed with the help of the computer become less demanding, while the functions of systems and communications become increasingly more demanding.

TABLE 2.   NUMBER OF TIMES A JOB WAS
REPORTED TO HAVE INCREASED OR
DECREASED IN CONTENT

Managerial Jobs	Increase	Decrease
Stores Supervisor	1	1
Payroll Supervisor	1	3
Supervisor of Time Keeping	—	2
Standards Supervisor	2	—
Systems Analyst Supervisor	1	—
Supervisor of Programming	2	—
Machine Accounting Supervisor	1	—

Comparing the changes of the three job levels it can be concluded that *top* managerial jobs were the least affected by computers. The *middle* management jobs revealed slightly more increases than decreases in job content, while the *lower* management jobs (except those associated with data processing and standards) showed definitely a decrease in job content.

RESULTS OF THE INTERVIEWS

The results of the interviews did not fully confirm the findings of the survey. Concerning *top* management jobs, two of eighteen companies indicated an increase in job content. This tends to substantiate that the computer had little effect on the jobs on the top level.

Six out of eighteen firms reported a change in content of *middle* management jobs, three positive and three negative. This confirms only partly the findings of the survey which showed a stronger tendency toward increased job difficulty and complexity.

Related to the *lower* management jobs, six of eighteen interviewees reported a negative change. This verifies in part the survey findings.

The interviewed companies had used the computer long enough to observe changes and had used them extensively. Those companies that reported positive or negative changes were able to substantiate such changes with detailed examples. Some of these respondents felt, however, that job content changes were not exclusively related to the computer use.

CONCLUSIONS

Relatively few changes were reported in the survey and only one third of the interviewees had observed changes. This could mean that the computer's effects upon the job content are minor and slow. It could however, also mean that many firms are not alert to such cause and effect relationships.

The findings do not show strong trends (marked and uniform job changes) in either of the three managerial job levels. They do not support the conclusion that middle management jobs would become "more specialized and highly programmed." [4] The results, especially those of the survey, seem rather to support Hutchinson and others who predict that middle management jobs of the future would require more initiative, vision and knowledge.[5]

ADDITIONAL REFERENCES

Melvin Anshen, and G. L. Bach, *Management and Corporations: 1985* (New York: McGraw-Hill Book Company, 1960).

Gilbert Burck, "The Boundless Age of the Computer," *Fortune,* Vol. 69 (March 1964), p. 230.

"Computer, Promise or Threat?" *Credit and Financial Management,* Vol. 64 (November, 1962), pp. 20–22.

D. W. Dobler, "Implications of Parkinson's Law for Business Management," *Personnel Journal,* Vol. 42, No. 1 (January, 1963), p. 10.

John T. Dunlop, (ed.), *Automation and Technological Change,* The American Assembly, Columbia University (Englewood Cliffs, New Jersey: Prentice-Hall, Inc., 1962).

R. J. Eggert, "Creative Admen Fear Robots Will Displace 'em," *Advertising Age,* Vol. 31 (March 14, 1960), p. 82.

J. R. Fransica, "Electronic Data Processing and Its Significant Impact on Management," *National Underwriter,* Vol. 66 (January 19, 1962), p. 11 or *National Underwriter (Life ed.)* Vol. 66 (February 17, 1962), p. 8.

E. Graham, "Is the Computer Seizing the Creative Man's Job?" *Printers' Ink,* Vol. 274 (February 24, 1961), pp. 56–57.

C. L. Kobrin, "Computer; Its Impact on Management," *Iron Age,* Vol. 189 (March 8, 1962), pp. 65–72.

A. J. Krout, "How EDP is Affecting Workers and Organizations," *Personnel,* Vol. 39 (July 1962), pp. 38–50.

Albert Kushner, "People and Computers," *Personnel,* Vol. 40, No. 2 (January–February, 1963), p. 27.

Floyd C. Mann, and K. Williams, "Observations on the Dynamics of a Change to Electronic Data Processing Equipment," *Administrative Science Quarterly,* Vol. 5 (September, 1960), pp. 217–256.

G. J. McManus, "Are Computers Taking Over Management's Functions?" *Iron Age,* Vol. 187 (March 30, 1961), pp. 69–71.

P. W. Melitz, "Impact of Electronic Data Processing on Managers," *Advanced Management,* Vol. 26 (April, 1961), pp. 4–6.

"Middle Management and Technological Change," *Management Review,* Vol. 10 (October, 1963), p. 55.

Donald M. Michael, *Cybernation: The Silent Conquest,* (Santa Barbara, California, Center for the Study of Democratic Institutions, 1962).

G. M. Stilian, "Impact of Automation on the Manufacturing Executive's Job," *Management Review,* Vol. 47 (March, 1958), pp. 19–23.

Edward Weber, "Change in Managerial Manpower with Mechanization of Data Processing," *The Journal of Business,* (April, 1959).

Thomas L. Whisler, *Executives and Their Jobs: The Changing Organizational Structure,* (Chicago, Illinois: Graduate School of Business, University of Chicago, Selected Papers), Number 9.

M. D. Witty, "Obsolete at Age 29," *Computers and Automation,* Vol. 7 (December, 1958), pp. 26–28.

NOTES

[1] Melvin Anshen and G. L. Bach, *Management and Corporations: 1985* (New York: McGraw-Hill Book Company, 1960) p. 201. Also Donald M. Michael, *Cybernation: The Silent Conquest* (Santa Barbara, California: Center for the Study of Democratic Institutions, 1962) p. 18.

[2] Harold J. Leavitt and Thomas L. Whisler, "Management in the 1980's," *Harvard Business Review,* Vol. 36 (November–December, 1958) pp. 41–48.

[3] E. H. MacNiece, *Production Forecasting, Planning and Control,* 3rd ed. (John Wiley and Sons, Inc., New York, 1961) pp. 60–61.

[4] Gilbert Burck, "The Boundless Age of the Computer," *Fortune,* Vol. 69 (March 1964), p. 230.

[5] Loren K. Hutchinson, "Architects of Decisions," *Manage,* Vol. 16 (May 1964), p. 14 and 18.

12

MANAGERIAL EFFECTIVENESS I: FORMULATING A RESEARCH STRATEGY *

Larry L. Cummings

The purposes of this article are: (1) to set forth the various dimensions of the over-all research effort; (2) to present a review of the research on the prediction of managerial success or effectiveness; and, (3) to establish the focus for a second paper subsequently to appear in the *Academy of Management Journal* describing the results and implications of an intermediate research effort.

DIMENSIONS OF THE PROJECT

The primary, but general, objective of the research project consists of the identification, measurement and prediction of managerial effectiveness. There exists ample evidence that studies with this general orientation should be, at their best, longitudinal in nature.[1] In order to communicate the nature of the over-all study, it will be necessary to divide the presentation into several dimensions. In terms of some temporal perspective, these dimensions can be thought of as a series of phases as indicated in Fig. 1. This article will outline three of these dimensions, describe one in detail and set the stage for the second.

A healthy amount of research effort has been devoted to the study and prediction of managerial effectiveness. It is obviously mandatory that we review this research for its perspective and meaning. One of the salient points emerging from the review that follows is the frequently noted desire

* Reprinted from *Journal of Academy of Management,* March, 1966, pp. 29–42.

Phase I	Phase II	Follow-up Phases
A. Outlining the Basic Problem Area	A. Identification and Measurement of Independent Dimensions of Graduate Student Performance:	A. Conceptually and Statistically Identifying Several Dimensions of Managerial Effectiveness.
B. Reviewing the Previous Work in the Area: The Need for Longitudinal Research	1. Academic Performance	B. Relating the Data of Phase II to the Managerial Effectiveness Criteria
C. Designing the Longitudinal Strategy	2. Leadership Behavior in Decision Making Groups	C. Developing the Implications of the Results
	B. Prediction of These Dimensions Utilizing Cognitive, Attitudinal, Personality and Biographical Data	
	C. Accumulation of These Phase II Data on a Large Sample of Subjects	

TIME

Figure 1. The research strategy.

for, but far too little effort devoted to, a longitudinal or follow-up study of managerial success—particularly a study incorporating both academic and "real-life" or managerial performance dimensions on the same subjects.

A second dimension of the project, to be reported in a later article, concerns the building of a large sample of subjects (MBA candidates in the Graduate School of Business, Indiana University) and the measurement of various dimensions of their academic and leadership behavior while in graduate school. This phase utilizes new measures of leadership behavior and academic performance as criterion variables and relates a multiple predictor battery to these intermediate criteria through correlational and factor analytic designs.

The third dimension of the project will involve a follow-up study on these subjects with particular emphasis on the measurement and prediction of the long-range criterion variables; i.e. dimensions of managerial effectiveness. In this stage, the aforementioned intermediate criteria become important predictor variables thereby allowing one to study the relationship between various dimensions of graduate student performance and measures of managerial effectiveness.

The remainder of this article reviews the research on the measurement and prediction of managerial effectiveness or executive success so providing a focus for the next phase of the study to be reported in a second paper.

REVIEW OF THE LITERATURE

Harrell has presented the most comprehensive summary of research in this area as of 1961.[2] Since his work is readily available, only a brief summarization of his most important references will be presented here. This will be followed by a description of several publications which Harrell did not review as well as several recent studies which are major contributions to this area of research.

Work Reported by Harrell

Harrell reports that Havermann and West[3] found the following interesting items in a survey made by *Time* and analyzed at Columbia University: (1) men who worked their way through college did not do so well in business (in terms of earned income) as those who were family supported: and, (2) there was a difference in the percentage of graduates who become managers depending on religious preference; i.e. 34% of the Protestants, 33% of the Jews, and 26% of the Catholics became proprietors, managers, or executives.

Harrell reports that Husband[4] found that several dimensions of college performance correlated with success 30 years after graduation (Dartmouth, class of 1926). Husband found:[5]

1. Being outstanding in college in anything was associated with higher earnings, and being outstanding in more than one thing made financial success even more probable.

2. College grades were generally associated with earnings. Men with the highest grades . . . had the highest average earnings. . . . Those with the lowest grades . . . had the lowest median income.

3. . . . although men with (the) lowest intelligence scores had low earnings, so also did the men with the highest intelligence test scores.

4. Extracurricular activities also were associated with higher earnings in the study of Dartmouth students although not quite as much as were grades. Men with no extracurricular activities had median earnings of $13,840 versus $20,000 and over for those with outstanding success in extracurricular activities. Those who had participated moderately in extracurricular activities had intermediate incomes.

5. Athletes who had won their letters had incomes higher than those

who had not, although again the difference was not as great as for the extremes in grades. . . . Husband reported contrary findings by Tunis who had reported that although good scholars had high earnings, athletes from Harvard had relatively low earnings.

6. Those who had been editors or held top staff jobs in literary or musical organizations in college had somewhat higher earnings than the average. . . .

7. Political activities as shown by being a member of leadership organizations which included most of the class offices also were correlated with earnings.

Harrell also reports one of the early studies in this area done for the Bell Telephone System.[6] Men who had been in the top third of their graduating class had 48% of their numbers in the highest third of their salary group and 27% in the middle third salary group five years after graduation. Of those in the bottom third of the graduating class, only 22% were in the top third with respect to salary. Statistical contamination is a possibility here since the college grades of the subjects were available to their employers.

Harrell reports two more recent studies using Harvard and Stanford MBA's as subjects.[7] Both of these studies are unpublished and the Harrell reference is the only published information available on these studies. Ward related several predictors to the salaries of five classes of MBA's from Harvard. (The first class was that of 1948 and the other four were of succeeding years.) [8] Ward found the correlations reported in Table 1 between the predictors and salaries.

TABLE 1. CORRELATIONS BETWEEN SELECTED PREDICTORS AND SUBSEQUENT SALARY

	Salaries	
Tests or Grades	1955	Starting
Personnel Problems (AMP Differential Key)	.35	.24
Individual Background Survey (MBA Differential Key)	.30	.24
Emotional Maturity Rating	.27	.33
Administrative Practices Grade	.26	.33
Caution Score on Business Problems Test	−.21	.03
Objectivity Score on Guildford-Zimmerman	.20	.36
Productivity of Ideas on Imagery Events Test	−.13	−.22

Source: Harrell, *op. cit.,* p. 59.

The AMP Differential Key for the Personnel Problems Test, according to Harrell, "was based on answers by members of the Advanced Management Program, differentiating the most able from the least able . . ." [9]

Harrell also reports that the MBA Differential Key for the Individual Background Survey was based on answers of the MBA's. The actual background data collected were not noted. The Emotional Maturity Rating was made by the research staff on all information available at the time of graduation. Again, the exact nature of the information utilized is not recorded. The Administrative Practices Grade is a grade in a human relations course.

Williams has reported the following correlations relating the listed predictors to earned income (after 15 or more years) of Stanford MBA's: [10]

Predictor Variable	Correlation Coefficient
Number of offices as an undergraduate	.24
Grade point average in elective graduate courses	.22
Masculinity Scores on the Strong Vocational Interest Test	.19
Ratings by undergraduate professors	.18

This completes the summary of the work reported by Harrell. There are several other studies of major significance in this field that should be reviewed.

OTHER SIGNIFICANT WORK

American Telephone and Telegraph Company has in recent years engaged in an extensive examination of the relationship between college achievement and progress in management within the Bell System.[11]

Research in the Bell System

This study is based on 17,000 college graduates employed within the Bell System. The study utilizes, as the criterion measure, the annual salary earned by a manager as compared to that earned by others with the same length of service in the company.[12] The salary distribution for each length of service was divided into thirds. It was then possible to say for each graduate in the study whether he fell into the top, middle, or bottom salary third of all the college graduates in the System who had the same length of service.

This report relates rank in college graduating class to salary progress in the Bell System. In summary form, these results are as follows: [13]

	Top Salary Third	Middle Salary Third	Bottom Salary Third
Top Tenth of Class	51%	32%	17%
Top Third of Class	45%	34%	21%
Middle Third of Class	32%	36%	32%
Bottom Third of Class	26%	34%	40%

There seems to be a positive relationship between rank in graduating class and progress (in terms of salary) in the Bell System.[14]

This report also attempted to relate participation in collegiate extracurricular activities to salary progress. The subjects were classified into three groups according to the extent of their achievement in extracurricular activities.[15] The results indicated that extracurricular achievement was related to salary progress. In all scholarship groups, those subjects with substantial extracurricular achievement fared better than the others. With regard to the importance of extracurricular achievements, the study reports two general conclusions for which data are not offered: (1) extracurricular achievement is *somewhat* compensatory for lower academic rank; and, (2) consideration of a man's campus achievements is helpful in predicting his probable success in the System, but it is not by any means as strong a predictor as his scholastic achievement.

Two other relationships were studied: (1) that between degree of self-support while in college and salary rank; and, (2) that between college major (arts-sciences, business administration, or engineering) and salary rank. Neither yielded significant relationships.

Even though this study is not statistically sophisticated, the results have had substantial impact on the recruiting and selection policies and procedures of the Bell System.[16]

A Seminar on "Assessing Managerial Potential"

During March, 1957, the Foundation for Research on Human Behavior conducted two seminars on "Assessing Managerial Potential." [17] The purpose of these seminars was to review present practices and knowledge in appraising and predicting the effectiveness of executive personnel. Representatives from both academic institutions and industrial organizations participated in each of these seminars. The over-all report of the two seminars contains a wealth of practical experience and impressions on various ways of predicting and developing future managerial effectiveness. A number of abilities, attitudes, values, interests, and past experiences were mentioned by the participants as characteristics that they had observed to be associated with executive effectiveness in their own organizations. This investigator's concern with this particular report centers on two pieces of research reported therein *which had not previously appeared in the literature.*

Representatives from Sears, Roebuck and Company reported a series of studies being conducted within their organization, aimed at identifying the personality characteristics, attitudes, and values of executives which are associated with successful performance. Among the criteria of managerial success were morale among subordinates and actual promotion records. Among the important attributes revealed to be characteristic of successful executives in their organization were the following: mental abilities, personal values of a practical and economic nature, high general activity, emotional stability, self-confidence, objectivity, social skills, cooperativeness, and persuasiveness. Quantitative results and the methodology of the Sears study are not reported in the seminar proceedings. It is, therefore, difficult to judge the general applicability of the reported findings.[18]

A second piece of research reported at the Seminar was from the Employee Relations Department of the Standard Oil Company (New Jersey). Representatives reported on a long-term research project that they were conducting at the time of the seminar. As suggested by the title, "Early Identification of Management Potential," their purpose was to obtain information which would permit early identification of those persons who have the greatest potential for becoming successful managers in their company. In order to find clues to characteristics differentiating those persons who eventually become successful from those who do not, these investigators were making an intensive study of two groups of men. One group was composed of approximately 300 executives drawn from top management. In selecting this group the investigators started at the very top and went down in level and into affiliated companies until they accumulated their desired sample size.[19] The other group was a control group.[20] It consisted of men who were matched with members of the top managerial group on a number of relevant variables, such as: length of service, educational level, phase of the business started in and so on. Each man in the control group was selected to be at least two steps down the management scale from his counterpart in the top management group. It was reported at the seminar that the men of both groups were being given a comprehensive battery of psychological tests, including the following:

   a. general attitude questionnaire
   b. Guilford-Zimmerman Temperament Survey
   c. a non-verbal reasoning test
   d. the ETS—Picture test (work scene variety of the Thematic Apperception Test—TAT)

  e. a judgment test (work and non-work items)

  f. a multiple-choice individual background survey

  g. the Miller Analogies Test

At the time of the seminar, the Standard Oil (New Jersey) representatives reported that the data analysis was only beginning, and that no specific findings could be reported. They did indicate, however, that preliminary indications led them to expect that significant differences between the top management group and the control group would be found.

The Continuing Research of the Standard Oil Company (New Jersey)

Since the 1957 seminar, Standard Oil (New Jersey) has continued its research interest in the identification of management potential and has published at least one brief report on this topic.[21]

The following comments by Dr. Laurent describe the basic aims and assumptions of the over-all study; [22]

"This report describes the research which has been conducted during the past six years (1955–61) in Jersey Standard and affiliated companies with headquarters in the New York geographical area. The research was based on the beliefs (assumptions) that there are individual differences between the more successful and less successful members of management, that these differences can be measured early in the careers of employees, and that a candidate for a management position will have a better chance of being successful if his own characteristics are like those of the more successful managers."

As noted previously, the original intention was to utilize 600 subjects (two groups of 300 each). The final number was reduced to 443 managers at all stages of the management hierarchy.[23] All subjects volunteered for the research project and were assured that none of the information collected would be used for administrative purposes.

The predictors used in this study covered many sources of information about the managers including company personnel records and interview data as well as tests and questionnaires. The set, or battery, of predictor instruments developed required approximately eight hours for administration. These standardized predictors were administered:

1. Miller Analogies Test (MAT). This is a test of general intellectual functioning which emphasizes verbal abilities. The Advanced Personnel Test, a form of the MAT designed for use in industry, was included in the predictor battery.

2. Non-Verbal Reasoning Test. This instrument was a non-verbal test of general mental ability published by Richardson, Bellows, Henry and Company. This test uses geometrical figures as the basis for problems to test the examinee's ability to reason without using words.

3. The Guilford-Zimmerman Temperament Survey. This personality inventory measures ten different personality characteristics, some of which could be expected to be present in successful managers. Examples of these characteristics are emotional stability, objectivity, and friendliness.

Other predictors, referred to as experimental, were developed by the researchers:

1. Individual Background Survey (IBS). This consisted of a series of questions concerning an individual's background. The IBS covered the areas of home and family background, education, vocational planning and experience, financial background, leisure time activities, health history, and social and community relations.

2. Management Judgment Test. This test described problem situations and presented several choices for action or decision. The purpose of the test was to determine the examinee's judgment insofar as managerial problems are concerned and to compare his judgment with that of other executives.

3. Survey of Management Attitudes. This attitude inventory was included in the battery in an attempt to determine whether it could distinguish between various groups of managers in their attitudes toward the social conditions of the business and industrial world.

4. Self-Performance Report. Each manager completed a report describing his own performance to determine whether differences in these self-ratings were related to differences in managerial success.

5. Projective Technique. This instrument (using TAT pictures) went into the experimental battery in an attempt to measure differences among managers in their drive, their motivation for personal achievement in the company, and similar characteristics.

The researchers utilized the following additional sources of information: (1) the cumulative personnel record of each participant (including numbers and kinds of assignments in and out of the company, proportion of domestic and overseas assignments, and the functional activities in which the manager had had experience); and, (2) an interview in which each manager provided information on three areas of his life (his most critical period in planning his career before entering the company, the most critical period of his advancement in the company, and the person in the company who contributed most to his advancement). Immediately following the interview, the interviewer completed a check-list on the human relations skills exercised by the manager during the interview as well as a check-list covering the above four areas.

With respect to the criteria of managerial success, three were used in the Standard Oil (New Jersey) study: (1) position level within the organization, (2) salary, and (3) rated managerial effectiveness.

With regard to *position level,* several factors were considered, e.g. size of company, the organizational level of the position within that company, positions held previously by the incumbent, and grade established for compensation purposes. The inclusion of this positional criterion was obviously based on the assumption that the managers who had advanced to the higher levels had demonstrated greater managerial ability.

With regard to *salary,* three separate criteria were developed: (1) an index of salary progression, adjusted for inflation, which indicated those people who had achieved salaries significantly greater than the average of their colleagues for any given year, (2) an index with the effects of age eliminated, and (3) a measure of salary progress—defined as the difference between the age and inflation—adjusted index for 1950 and 1958 for each manager.

With regard to *managerial effectiveness,* lists of managers at like positional levels in the company were prepared and submitted to individuals within the company who had had an opportunity to observe the work performance of the managers (mostly their present or former superiors). An attempt was made to obtain three or more rankers for each list of managers. The rankers used the alternation-ranking method to rank order the managers. The managerial effectiveness criterion for each manager was the average of the rankings assigned by the rankers.

These researchers found considerable overlap among the criterion measures—particularly the position level and salary indices. Some method was needed to combine the various measures of success. They used factor analysis. Starting with a 71-variable matrix, they extracted 11 factors. The strongest factor, in terms of the amount of common variance accounted for, had high loadings on the primary criteria—position level, salary, and rankings of effectiveness. This factor was, therefore, designated as the success criterion. This served as the general criterion of managerial success in evaluating the usefulness of the predictors. However, the managerial effectiveness criterion differed sufficiently from the success criterion to make a separate analysis worthwhile.[24]

In summary form the results of this Standard Oil (New Jersey) study were as follows:

1. In terms of prediction of the over-all success criterion, the following predictors were significantly correlated at the .05 level.[25]

Variable	r
Individual Background Survey (experience items—after age 22)	+0.64
Management Judgment	+0.51
Individual Background Survey (early items—before age 22)	+0.40
Survey of Management Attitudes	+0.25
Self Performance Report	+0.24
Interview Check List	+0.21
Non-Verbal Reasoning	+0.20
Interview Check List on Human Relations Skill	+0.19
Miller Analogies	+0.18
GZTS—Emotional Stability	+0.14

These predictors were combined into a multiple regression equation. The multiple R's were +0.71 and +0.70.[26]

2. The relationship of the test scores to the managerial effectiveness criterion, while of significance statistically, was lower than in the case of the over-all success criterion. In general the same predictors correlated significantly (.05 level) with the managerial effectiveness criterion as with the over-all success criterion; e.g. individual background survey, interview check lists, masculinity, objectivity, and emotional stability scores on the GZTS, management judgment, non-verbal reasoning, and the MAT. The multiple R's were +0.56 and +0.48.

In conclusion, this investigator feels that the research of Standard Oil (New Jersey) on the identification and prediction of managerial potential and success is probably the best recent study dealing with this area of investigation. That work has dealt with many of the major conceptual and methodological problems. All of the details and sophistications of the research design have not been reported here. These researchers have implied that one of the major advances yet to be made in this area is a longitudinal study of potential managers across several types of organizations.[27] Such a study is one of the contributions toward which the research to be reported at a later date is aimed.

University of Minnesota Management Development Laboratory [28]

The work of Mahoney, et al. sought the identification of predictors of managerial effectiveness applicable in a variety of managerial staffing situations. The basic question of the study was, "What are the personal characteristics which differentiate between the more effective managers and the less effective managers?" [29] This study did not use a longitudinal approach, (i.e. it involved the simultaneous measurement of personal characteristics and managerial effectiveness). Thus this approach assumed relatively little change in measured personal characteristics between the time of managerial selection and the actual time of measurement.

The design of the study involved two types of analysis. *First,* measures of personal characteristics and managerial effectiveness were obtained for 468 managers in 13 different companies. The relationships between the measures of personal characteristics and managerial effectiveness were determined with one sub-sample of managers and a method for the prediction of effectiveness was developed on the basis of these relationships. *Second,* the prediction method was then applied to those managers in the second sub-sample in a cross-validation study. The latter part of the over-all study by Mahoney et al. is most appropriate to the research interests of this investigator. Therefore, the identification of the predictors used by Mahoney et al. and their relationship to the criterion of managerial effectiveness will be the major concern here.

The following tests and questionnaires were utilized by Mahoney et al. as predictors to measure the indicated personal characteristics: [30]

1. Intelligence. The Wonderlic Personnel Test (Form B); a twelve minute test used widely in industry as a short measure of general intelligence;

2. Empathy (awareness of the likes and dislikes of other people). The Empathy Test by W. A. Kerr and B. J. Speroff; this is an untimed test requiring the examinee to estimate the musical, literary, and social tastes of specified groups of people;

3. Vocational Interests. These were measured by *The Strong Vocational Interest Blank for Men;* this is an untimed questionnaire which compares individual likes and dislikes with those of norm groups of successful people in more than forty occupational groups;

4. Personality. Personality characteristics were measured by the California Personality Inventory by H. G. Gough; this is an untimed questionnaire concerning personal habits and attitudes. Scores were obtained for 13 scales measuring responsibility, tolerance, flexibility, status capacity, dominance, sociability, conversation, resourcefulness, self-assurance, self-control, self-acceptance, conformity, and self-satisfaction; and,

5. Biographical Experience. These were measured by a Personal History Questionnaire designed by the Management Development Laboratory staff to obtain information about behavior, experiences, and personal and family circumstances prior to age 25. The assumption underlying the use of this instrument is that much of the information obtained in the form of experience probably reflects various personal characteristics.

A total of 98 measures were obtained on each of the subjects through the use of these instruments.

Two criterion measures were utilized in attempting to ascertain the managerial effectiveness of a given manager. One dealt with the organizational level of the position held by the manager. The second was the rated managerial effectiveness (defined very broadly) of each manager. One to six of the manager's superiors (past and present) rated the managers with whom they were familiar using an alternation ranking method. The relationship between effectiveness rankings and organization level was analyzed to determine the desirability of combining these measures. Results of this analysis failed to indicate any consistent relationship between the two criteria. The two measures appeared to be measuring different phenomena. When these findings were discussed with executives in the participating companies, they generally expressed greater acceptance of the effectiveness ranking as a valid criterion of managerial effectiveness.

Through logic not made completely explicit, Mahoney et al. conclude the following with respect to the criterion measure: [31]

"The effectiveness ranking was selected as the criterion of managerial effectiveness for use in this study on the basis of its demonstrated reliability, practicality, the absence of identifiable bias, and the greater acceptance of those concerned."

The managers were then segregated into thirds according to their ranking, within their company,[32] on the effectiveness criterion. The middle third was dropped due to the unreliability associated with rankers placing subjects in this middle category.

Relationships between each of the 98 measures of personal characteristics and the two levels of effectiveness were tested for statistical significance. Relationships associated with 18 of the 98 measures were significant (not necessarily positive) at probability levels of .10 or less.[33] These 18 measures were: [34]

A. The Vocational Interest Blank Scores
1. Dentist
2. Veterinarian
3. Printer
4. Carpenter
5. Vocational Agricultural teacher
6. Farmer
7. Sales manager

   8. Purchasing agent
   9. President, manufacturing firm
   10. Occupational level
B. Personnel Test
   11. Total score corrected for age
C. The California Psychological Inventory
   12. Dominance
D. Personal History Questionnaire
   13. Number of memberships in high school organizations
   14. Number of sports and hobbies at age 25
   15. Number of offices in fraternal and professional organizations
       at age 25
   16. Highest educational level attained
   17. Wife's highest educational level attained, and
   18. Number of years worked by wife after marriage.

As noted previously, the next step taken by Mahoney et al. was to combine the above into a prediction procedure.[35] Generally, they classified the predictors into six groups on the basis of "judged" similarity.[36] They then established a "cut off" or passing score for each predictor by comparing the percentile distributions of scores of the "more effective" and "less effective" groups of managers. The cutting score on each measure was set at the point of greatest difference between these two distributions. For each *group* of predictors, a required number of measures within the group had to be "passed" in order to pass that group. Furthermore, the number of groups that had to be "passed" in order to be a "predicted effective manager" could be arbitrarily varied. So, in general, the prediction procedure involved a multiple cut-off approach. This prediction system successfully predicted the effectiveness criterion from consideration of personal characteristics for 71% of the managers in the first sample. In the cross-validation sample, the prediction scheme successfully predicted the effectiveness criterion of 66% of the managers.

Comparing this study with the work of the researchers at Standard Oil (New Jersey) we can note the following similarities and differences: (1) the Standard Oil (New Jersey) study utilized subjects within a single organization while the Minnesota study was multi-organizational; (2) the Standard Oil (New Jersey) study utilized a multiple regression prediction scheme; (3) the Standard Oil (New Jersey) study utilized a two-dimensional criterion whereas the Minnesota study used an appraised managerial effectiveness criterion; and (4) both studies found intelligence, several personality characteristics, and certain biographical information to be predictive of the criterion (a) used.

The Wider Perspectives of Dill, Hilton, and Reitman [37]

Dill et al. have provided a broadened perspective for the study and analysis of managerial effectiveness. They provided the needed function of reminding us that the job environment, in all its many dimensions, can play a significant role in conditioning the success of the manager.[38] They studied intensively the development of three young managers as they interacted with and influenced their job situations.

The major relevance of their work for the present study is their reminder that the relationship between a manager's personal characteristics and his managerial performance is conditioned by a multitude of factors which tend to be neglected in studies such as those reviewed previously. If one is to achieve balance in the study and prediction of managerial effectiveness, these conditioning factors must be considered. Dill et al. suggest that some of these factors might be: (1) the personality characteristics and actions of the manager's peers; (2) the personality characteristics and styles of leadership typical of the manager's superiors; (3) the opportunities for action and feedback provided by the manager's job environment; and (4) the general philosophy of management characterizing the manager's organization.

. . .

NOTES

[1] T. W. Harrell, *Manager Performance and Personality* (Cincinnati: South-Western Publishing Co., 1961).

[2] Harrell, *op. cit.*

[3] Havemann and P. S. West, *They Went to College* (New York: Harcourt, Brace and Co., 1952).

[4] R. W. Husband, "What Do College Grades Predict?" *Fortune*, Vol. 55 (June, 1957), pp. 157 ff.

[5] Harrell, *op. cit.*, pp. 57–58.

[6] W. Gifford, "Does Business Want Scholars?" *Harper's Magazine*, Vol. 156 (1928), pp. 669–674.

[7] Harrell, *op. cit.*, pp. 59–60.

[8] L. B. Ward, "Tentative Summary" (unpublished, Harvard Graduate School of Business Administration, 1958), cited by Harrell, *op. cit.*, p. 59.

[9] Harrell, *op. cit.*, pp. 59–60.

[10] F. J. Williams, "Predicting Success in Business" (unpublished Ph.D. dissertation, Graduate School of Business, Stanford University, 1959), cited by Harrell, *op. cit.*, p. 60, and F. J. Williams and T. W. Harrell, "Predicting Success in Business," *Journal of Applied Psychology*, Vol. 48 (June, 1964), No. 3, pp. 164–167.

[11] F. R. Kappell, "From the World of College to the World of Work," *Bell Telephone*

Magazine (Spring, 1962), pp. 3–21. This is a reprint of the John Findley Green Foundation Lecture given by Mr. Kappel at Westminster College, Fulton, Missouri on April 5, 1962. This investigator wishes to express his gratitude to Mr. Jess Overman, Supervisor of Employment, Indiana Bell Telephone Company, for calling his attention to this piece of research.

[12] Corrections were introduced to adjust for differences between salary levels in different parts of the country and between different departments.

[13] Kappel, *op. cit.,* p. 18.

[14] Two possible qualifications seem relevant here: (1) statistical contamination may be operative here if the class rankings of the subjects were available to those responsible for making promotional and salary decisions; and, (2) the data are not reported in a fashion which permits the testing of the significance of these results.

[15] Hopefully, achievement in extracurricular activities was not defined solely in terms of the number of such activities engaged in; i.e., some consideration should be given to (1) the importance of the activity and (2) the significance of the subject's position in this activity. It is impossible to ascertain from the data whether such factors were considered and evaluated.

[16] Extensive, personal conversations with Mr. Jess Overman, Supervisor of Employment, Indiana Bell Telephone Company.

[17] "Assessing Managerial Potential," Report of a Seminar conducted by the Foundation for Research on Human Behavior, Ann Arbor, Michigan, 1958.

[18] Further elaboration of the design and results may be found in *Research Toward the Development of a Multiple Assessment Program for Executive Personnel:* prepared by Psychological Research and Services Section, Sears, Roebuck and Co., June, 1965.

[19] It should be noted that both the Sears and the Standard Oil (New Jersey) studies utilize as subjects managers within a single company. The longitudinal dimensions of the author's research will study managers in several different types of industries, firms, and departments. This obviously makes the collection of the data more difficult; but, on the other hand, it adds to the potential general applicability of the findings.

[20] This matched-pair methodology was discontinued in the continuing research endeavors by Standard Oil (New Jersey), cf. next section.

[21] H. Laurent, "Early Identification of Managers," *Management Record,* Vol. 14 (May, 1962), No. 5, pp. 33–38.

[22] *A Summary of the Early Identification of Management Potential Research Project* in the Standard Oil Company (New Jersey) and Affiliated Companies, prepared by the Social Science Research Division of the Employee Relations Department, Standard Oil Co., (New Jersey), August, 1961, p. 1.

[23] Job re-locations, foreign assignments, illness, the pressure of business, and lack of interest were responsible for the reduction in the sample size. As mentioned previously, these factors made the matched-pair methodology impossible. A correlational analysis was used.

[24] The loading of the managerial effectiveness rankings on the success factor was .46.

[25] The critical r at the .05 level $= \pm 0.13$. These correlations listed are those on the cross-validation sample.

[26] A double, cross-validation study was done with two randomly composed subgroups.

[27] Personal correspondence with Dr. H. Laurent, Employee Relations Department, Standard Oil Company (New Jersey), September 10, 1963.

[28] The most comprehensive description of this research is contained in: T. A. Mahoney, T. H. Jerdee, and A. N. Nash, *The Identification of Management Potential*

—*A Research Approach to Management Development* (Dubuque, Iowa: Wm. C. Brown Co., 1961).

29 *Ibid.*, p. 14. Also see T. A. Mahoney, T. H. Jerdee and A. N. Nash, "Predicting Managerial Effectiveness," *Personnel Psychology*, Vol. 13 (1960), No. 1, pp. 147–163, and T. A. Mahoney, W. W. Sorenson, T. H. Jerdee, and A. N. Nash, "Identification and Prediction of Managerial Effectiveness," *Personnel Administration*, Vol. 26 (1963), No. 4, pp. 12–22.

30 *Ibid.*, p. 20. The authors justify their choice of variables as those most likely to be related to managerial effectiveness.

31 *Ibid.*, p. 28.

32 This means that the somewhat undesirable procedure of combining managers from different companies, rated by different superiors, was practiced. That is to say, the ranking of a given manager was made relative only to those other managers in his company ranked by a common judge(s). Yet, the results combine all managers who were thus ranked in the top third or the bottom third and labeled these the high and low criterion groups.

33 Probability levels were obtained with the Chi-square test of relationship.

34 Mahoney *et al.*, *op. cit.*, p. 31. Mahoney *et al.* suggest the following general description of the "more effective" manager. "The more effective manager tends to be more intelligent than the less effective manager; his vocational interests are more similar to those of sales managers, purchasing agents, and manufacturing company presidents; and less similar to the interests of men in the biological sciences and technical crafts such as dentistry, veterinary medicine, printing, carpentry; . . . he tends to be more aggressive, persuasive, and self-reliant; he has had more educational training and was more active in sports and hobbies as a young man; and his wife has had more educational training and worked less after their marriage." Mahoney *et al.*, *op. cit.*, 40.

35 The remaining 80 measures of personal characteristics were discarded from further analysis because of their lack of relationship with the criterion.

36 They did not run the correlations among the predictor measures.

37 W. R. Dill, T. L. Hilton, and W. R. Reitman, *The New Managers: Patterns of Behavior and Development* (Englewood Cliffs: Prentice-Hall, Inc., 1962).

38 A stimulating nonempirical, descriptive account of the role of the executive and the sources of his success has been presented recently by D. Braybrooke, "The Mystery of Executive Success Re-examined," *Administration Science Quarterly*, Vol. 8, (March, 1964), No. 4, pp. 533–560.

RELATED READINGS

SECTION 3: COMMUNICATION AND ORGANIZATION

The readings in Section 3 relate to organizational communication, with ideas ranging from the theoretical and general to the applied and specific. In "Employee Communication: All Dressed Up and No Place to Go?" James Menzies Black, after pointing out some dangers of many communication programs, sets forth some questions and guidelines for good organizational communications. "An Examination of the Notion of Communication in Industry" by P. H. Cook traces events leading to recognition of the importance of communication in industry. He analyzes trends indicated in the literature, pointing out some deficiencies needing correction, and then sets forth a theory of communication to act as a guide. Cook concludes by discussing communication in relation to organizational objectives. D. Ronald Daniel's article, "Management Information Crisis," discusses the need for relevant management information systems for changing organizational structures. Daniels presents reasons for the problem, pointing out that information must be related to planning and control; he then deals in depth with the planning function. In "The Organization and Its Communications Problem" Jay M. Jackson analyzes communication problems in organizations in terms of characteristics of organizations, research findings regarding communications flow, consequences of communication and communication problems as symptoms of other human relations problems. In "Information Technology and Decentralization," John F. Burlingame looks at the impact of information technology on middle management and decentralization. He concludes that the role of the middle manager and the process of decentralization will increase in the future. "Closing the Communications Gap" by Thorrel B. Fest examines the problem of communicating the constantly increasing amount of scientific-technical information. In addition, Fest explores complex consequent social adjustments growing out of this explosion. In "How to Develop a Communication System" George T. Vardaman discusses organizational communication concepts; he then gives a procedure for communication system analysis and control. Melvin S. Day's "NASA's Developmental Program for Selective Dissemination of Information," is concerned with the why and the what of the National Aeronautics and Space Administration's Selective Dissemination of Information program. In "Information Systems and Evidential Meaning" Carroll C. Halterman sets forth basic models of communication, followed by a discussion on models of communication in administered organizations.

13

EMPLOYEE COMMUNICATION: ALL DRESSED UP AND NO PLACE TO GO? *

James Menzies Black

In a world beset with sociologists, psychologists, publicists, and utopian economists, there is one product we do not lack—communications. Never before in history have so many had so much to say on such a multitude of topics to anybody who will listen.

Today everybody is communicating. We have developed the machinery to deluge the country in a turgid flow of words—written or oral—on any subject whatsoever, and to do it almost instantaneously. We possess the technology to give the people the facts, the background on the facts, and our interpretation of both the facts and their background, on any question that may arise. And we do this on a somewhat nonselective basis, regardless of whether or not the people are interested in the particular facts we are telling them about.

How much of this communication is effective is another question. Perhaps in communications, as in other things, our technology for saying things has outstripped what we have to say. Perhaps the public, accustomed to the monotonous plop, plop of bromides on its galvanized mental roof, has developed a resistance to organized communications of any kind. But if this is true, the last to discover the fact will be the communicators themselves. So absorbed are they in documenting their theories and interpreting statistics on the results of their activities that they seldom stop to think that the opinions people hold are due as much to circumstances or individual self-interest as they are to tireless efforts to advance a point of view.

* Reprinted from *Management Review,* July, 1959, pp. 4–8ff.

This is no argument against communications. Indeed, intelligent communications is vitally needed. Nor is it intended as a case against propaganda. Obviously, a nation, a company, a union, or any other organization not only has a right but a duty to tell its story in such a way that its actions and objectives are put in a favorable light.

The intelligent communicator gives the people the facts, he interprets those facts according to the case he is presenting, he points out the answer that he wants people to come up with, and he demonstrates why it is to their advantage to do so. Furthermore, he depends on timing as much as facts to make his argument persuasive.

It may be wise to take a hard look at some of our ideas about communications. It is well worth while for any management to evaluate its communications constantly to be sure that it is saying neither too much nor too little, that it is using judgment in selecting the topics it wants to talk about, that it never communicates simply because everybody else is doing it, and that it has a precise idea of the attainable goals in every aspect of its communications program.

COMMUNICATIONS AND RESPONSIBILITY

The communications of management is effective when it is realistic and objective. To retain this clearsightedness in communications, it is necessary to have a precise understanding of the motives, objectives, and techniques of other groups that seek to influence public opinion. Furthermore, management must have the courage to avoid irresponsible or unethical techniques—even though they may appear overwhelmingly successful. After all, the investiture of responsibility itself denies to industry methods available to groups concerned only with their special objectives.

Management seeks to create the image of its own responsibility. It desires the public to respect its integrity. It wants the reputation for courage, honesty, competence, intelligence, and impartial fair dealing. These are virtues that cannot be pushed by "hard sell"; they must be demonstrated by example. But for the long term, they outweigh the immediate benefits of partisanship.

Sometimes industry must champion an unpopular point of view simply because it is the right one. This may be occasionally a short-term handicap, but in the final analysis it has its advantages. After all, truth is eventually accepted, not because people have reasoned it out, but because it cannot be avoided. The consequences of denying it are disastrous.

A LONG-RANGE PROGRAM

These facts sometimes put management in a difficult position so far as communication is concerned. Except defensively, it cannot appeal to emotional self-interest to win a point. The communications of a company is designed to make people think for themselves. It relies on reason and logic to persuade. Its goal is to talk to people, not to impose on them a system of thought. People are tiring of high-pitched emotionalism and demagoguery. They know the idealistic phrase has become a false front for too many self-serving objectives.

The company that expects to accomplish lasting results from its communications program must work at it consistently and not be discouraged by temporary set-backs. It must be far more concerned with the substance of what it has to say than the techniques it uses for saying it. It must avoid the easy generalism and the presentation of stereotyped, "acceptable" points of view. Finally, it must look penetratingly at the philosophy of false humanism that has poured a sweet syrup of sentimentality on the country and clogged, or at least soothed, the thinking processes of far too many people.

THE RIGIDITY OF THE DOCTRINAIRE

The communications machinery of any organization is no more effective than the thought that is put in it. The communications approach of the doctrinaire, although it has the initial advantage of systematic efficiency, soon palls because it is boring even to the people it has originally convinced. The doctrinaire communicates from a fixed position; he cannot maneuver strategically, only tactically. To sell his philosophy he depends on technicians of propaganda who can hollow out the inside of complicated ideas and leave only a gleaming, chromium-plated shell, highly adaptable for quick sale on a mass market.

The communications effort of organized labor, for example, frightens the people who believe that unions have gained too much power. Yet, all you have to do is read a typical union newspaper to understand why even labor leaders privately complain that their publications don't hold the attention of their intended readers. So much of what is said is so palpably partisan and surcharged with class emotionalism that the middle-income blue-collar employees who receive them no longer identify themselves with the audience these papers are striving to reach.

This does not mean that labor does not influence its constituents; it does. But the reason lies in the fact that unions have identified themselves with a political philosophy that many persons in an industrial society accept as necessary to their economic security, rather than to their direct communications with the rank and file.

SOME QUESTIONS FOR MANAGEMENT

What does this mean to management? It offers a tremendous opportunity for leadership, particularly if industry continues to avoid the entrapment of prefabricated thinking and knows exactly what it expects its communications program to accomplish. To keep its objectivity about communications, a company should ask itself these pointed questions about its program. Frank answers to them will enable the company to keep proper balance, even when it is under pressure.

1. *Do you know exactly what you expect your communications program to accomplish?* Some companies have prepared communications creeds to describe their communications principles. These statements range anywhere from pompous rewrites of the Declaration of Independence to such simple brevities as "It is our objective to tell the employee what he wants to know, what he needs to know, or what he ought to know"—which could mean everything, or nothing.

There is nothing wrong with creeds in themselves. Certainly, it is highly desirable to spell out objectives in order to establish the means to accomplish them. But it is also a good idea to analyze such creeds in the light of actual practice, to see that they are closely related to actual practice and that they are implemented with workable machinery to translate them into reality.

2. *Do you communicate too much?* In the desire to develop communications channels fully, there is always the danger of talking too much on subjects that hold only casual interest to the employee. How often have you heard the remark, "We send our letters to the employee's home. That way, mother and all the children will see them too. When the family is gathered around the dinner table, father may even read the letter to the group as a matter of general interest." This happy picture of domestic bliss may be a trifle exaggerated. Just ask yourself: How often have I read such a letter to my own family? Of course, if a letter concerns a matter of vital interest to the family, it may be reviewed in this manner. But if it is on a topic as broadly general as the free enterprise system, the danger of communism, or the importance of individual liberty, it is likely to get the same kind of attention that is usually paid to the editorial page of the average newspaper.

3. *Are you realistic in what you expect your communications to accomplish?* On matters of mutual interest, company communications can accomplish dramatic results, particularly if the subject is something that employees can do something about. It is even possible through communications to dissuade people from embarking on a course of action that may lead to a work stoppage. But it is wise to remember that simply because an objective has been achieved, a point of view has not necessarily been sold. The logical arguments used in support of a perfectly proper position may have been accompanied by implied force to support that position. When this is true, it is fear, not "friendly persuasion," that has won the day.

4. *Are you disappointed when employees refuse to face unpleasant facts despite the cogency of your arguments?* When a company has unpleasant facts to relate to employees—and it is obviously true that these occasions occur from time to time—it has the obligation to do so. But it cannot expect the employees to like what they hear or to analyze the facts objectively. Nor can it suppose a union will not seize on the situation as an opportunity for extremely emotional propaganda. This propaganda may not even convince the members of the union, but it may be temporarily accepted by them because it relieves their frustrations and simulates dramatic action in their behalf. When situations like this occur, don't be discouraged about your communications program. Time is probably on your side. Just keep your head and your sense of responsibility.

5. *Are you too concerned with measuring the results of your communications program?* Surveys of employee opinion are valuable as a guide, but they can also be misleading. The fact that employees read the company publications, admit their accuracy, and can play back specific facts discussed in particular stories may not be as meaningful as would appear on the surface. As long as there are no difficulties between employees and management, the communications effort of a company may be extremely effective. When there are conflicts of interest, it may appear that the reservoir of good will built up through long years of solid communications work vanishes overnight. Actually, the communications program may have been most worth while. When the crisis has passed, it is much easier to re-establish sound working relations when you have had a good communications program.

6. *Do you impose too many communications responsibilities on your line supervisors?* A foreman should certainly be informed, in advance whenever possible, of all matters affecting his company and his job. He is entitled to that knowledge by his position in management. But aside from job-related matters that affect him and the people who work for him, are you not asking too much if you insist that he discuss with his subordinates topics that require a highly specialized knowledge? If he does, it may lead

to distortions in communications or improper interpretations of company policy. In delegating communications duties to the various levels of management, a company should be entirely realistic in taking into account the experience, education, interest, and capabilities of each level of its management team.

7. *Have you established the various media of written communications that exist in your company to fill a particular requirement, or because other companies have adopted them?* Company magazines, newspapers, and management and employee letters can make a vital contribution to a corporation's communications program—but only if they exist with a purpose and have something worthwhile to say. To be effective, written communications must reflect your philosophy of management. Furthermore, readership is not necessarily a trustworthy criterion of a publication's success. Obviously, if you print interesting feature stories, gossip columns, and the like, your magazine may be read. But from the viewpoint of effective communications, little is accomplished. A company is not in business to publish trivia.

Nor can you go to the other extreme. If your publications become simply propaganda sheets to promote a particular point of view, they will soon lose their readers. Obvious propaganda converts only the converted.

A CHECK LIST FOR MANAGEMENT COMMUNICATIONS

After these questions have been answered clearly and frankly, management is in a position to appraise its communications program realistically. Management is concerned with developing its communications, not preoccupied with the creation of new communications methods. Technique, no matter how well thought out, may become the shadow that camouflages lack of substance. An elaborate communications system is not the point; no system is any more effective than the information put into it.

Communications is a full-time responsibility of every company. Its ability to present its point of view to the public, to government, and to its own employees plays a tremendous part in its progress. There are certain principles that responsible industry must never forget in maintaining a successful communications program. The following check list includes some of the most important.

1. *Avoid the bathos of the bromide.* When you see trite phrases popping up in company copy, strike them out. High-sounding generalities and tag-end idealisms like "The battle to win men's minds," "The right of all to share in our abundant economy," "The faith of all Americans working together to provide a better tomorrow for generations yet unborn, without

regard to race, creed, or color," have been repeated so much that they are becoming as meaningless as a witch's incantation.

Furthermore, if you want to perk up the readability of your communications, you might keep a sharp blue pencil handy to scratch many of those adjectival labels that have become so much a part of our stylized public address language that they seem coupled to the nouns they parade before with bands of steel. Descriptions like "freedom-loving democracies," "right-thinking Americans," and "forward-looking leader" have served their time and deserve the retirement their many years of over-work entitle them to.

2. *Duck the danger of slogans and generalities.* Among the greatest of our difficulties today is that we are inclined to seize on great generalities that have no real bearing on the situation at hand. Writing in the *Harvard Business Review,* Paul Cifrino has pointed out one prime example of this approach: "A brochure currently supplied by one of our large trade associations seeks to motivate the newly hired teen-ager by stressing how essential the food business is, how many products come from mysterious lands overseas, how many fortunes have been made. This is supposed to inspire him to place the eggs on the top of the sack instead of on the bottom! Why isn't it both simpler and more effective just to tell him to pack the eggs this way so they don't get broken?"

Careless use of generalities can also border on the dishonest. How often have you read in company periodicals, for example, that automation will create more jobs. Undoubtedly, it will—but not necessarily for the people who have been displaced by more efficient methods or better machinery. If you run a general article on this subject in the plant newspaper just before you introduce improved equipment that will enable you to reduce your need for manpower, you undermine the integrity of your communications by holding out glowing promises of what automation will do for people who will soon be looking elsewhere for work. That is why it is so important for management to interpret facts exactly as they will apply to the particular group they affect, not to take refuge in generalities.

3. *Stay clear of excessive do-unto-otherism.* Too often are we basing our communications approach on a kind of "do-unto-otherism" in which the "doing" is entirely one-sided. This has led to the development of an elite group, thoroughly trained in the dialectics of the social scientists, who predetermine what should be done unto others by using their own theories of social progress as the criteria. This attitude of "outer directed" good will and institutionalized paternalism has even caused some well-intentioned managements to make unwarranted intrusions into the private lives of employees in the misguided attempt to help them find "life adjustment." Certainly no one can criticize a company for having a deep interest in the welfare of its people. But perhaps the best way to promote their social welfare

and social maturity is to provide an atmosphere in which grown-up people are expected to behave like grown-up people, not treated as though they were a crowd of jittery, self-indulgent neurotics.

4. *Never assume that you have to sell the free enterprise system to employees.* The vast majority are already sold. The only time the average person questions it is when, due to business fluctuations, he suffers economically. Even then, he doesn't necessarily wish to change the system; he simply wants somebody to do something to fix it so he can benefit from its advantages. Undoubtedly, unemployed people in depressed areas are highly susceptible to what might be termed radical propaganda. They may not necessarily believe it, but it may be in their self-interest to go along with it temporarily. If you want people to buy free enterprise, remember, they must have the money to make the purchase.

5. *Make sure that each medium of communications that you use carries its full payload.* If you establish a company magazine, don't let it go at that. Hire an editor who knows his job, and give him access to company news and to you. Don't sit on his stories when he submits them to you. And judge the story from the point of view of content, facts, and interpretation of facts, not style. Remember, if you blue-pencil every important business item in an article on the grounds that its release may be dangerous, you will quickly reduce your magazine to a journal of inconsequential trivia that is a waste of money to publish.

6. *Be sincere in all you say.* If you want acceptance for your facts, present them in a straightforward way. If you discuss that news that affects the employee and his job—pleasant or unpleasant—in a candidly open manner, you may not always please him, but you will at least gain credibility for your statements—good or bad.

7. *Don't over-communicate.* If you deluge employees with company communications, you probably defeat your purposes. The saturation method of communications is not only expensive, it is also monotonous, and it won't work unless you can control all communications facilities—and that is impossible in a democracy.

8. *Don't be falsely folksy, over-intimate, or self-righteous.* Write directly to employees, and keep your approach simple. Remember that management is responsible for running a business. This calls for sound organization, high morale, teamwork. All members of an organization are bound together by mutual interests and self-interests, not by pseudo goodfellowship. Folksiness and the pretension of an intimacy that doesn't exist is communicating "down" in the worst sense of the word. And self-righteous outrage at the absurd opinions of others can destroy your case, even when it is a good one and the opinions of others are just as absurd as you think they are.

9. *Don't be general.* Employees are basically interested in specifics. If you can show how increased costs because of increased wages will have a direct effect on their job security, you may sell your argument on inflation. But a general article on the evils of inflation, although it wins readership and even acceptance, may not have any effect on an employee's opinion when it comes to a question of his own self-interest.

10. *Don't be afraid to use emotionalism.* But be subtle in your use of it. If you are faced with a labor crisis or some other problem that affects your business, naturally you have to appeal to the employee's hopes, interests, fears, and selfishness. But you must do this in a responsible way. Although emotionalism may underlie what you say, your approach must be calmly objective.

11. *Be certain that what you say is accurate.* Even a minor discrepancy in fact can hurt you very much if it is spotted. "Unions make factual mistakes," you say. "It doesn't hurt them." That may be true, but unions don't have to be as careful. Employees often don't mind if a union plays fast and loose with figures or facts if, by doing so, they achieve an objective they want. But employees expect you to be able to prove anything you say. You provide jobs; unions only bargain about them.

12. *Make sure your communications are interesting.* What interests you may not interest an employee at all. What you think he ought to know may not be what he wants to know. Unless you can make him want to know what you want to tell him, he won't get the message, no matter how important it is. It takes communications imagination to communicate effectively. Keep in mind what motivates people. Pride, group identity, recognition, and other motivational factors can be used in your appeal. If you relate them to self-interest, it is surprising how far they will go to insure the effectiveness of your employee communications program.

14

AN EXAMINATION OF THE NOTION OF COMMUNICATION IN INDUSTRY *

P. H. Cook

CURRENT TRENDS

A survey of standard works in the closely related fields of personnel management and industrial psychology suggests that it is only in quite recent years that the importance of communication in industry has been recognized. Indeed, communication is not even mentioned in some of the textbooks still in general use and regarded as authoritative. That communication has become a matter of considerable interest, however, to industrial managements is evident by the amount of space given to it in the personnel and other management journals. Thus, Pigors in *Effective Communication in Industry* (National Association of Manufacturers, New York, 1949), the first attempt to give a comprehensive account of the principles of industrial communication, is able to include a bibliography of 103 titles, only two of which are dated earlier than 1940. Why has there been this increase of interest in communication?

(a) Since the end of World War I there has been a marked increase in the size of industrial and commerical undertakings and a trend towards the development of multiple organizations. Where this has led to the extending of the lines of management and supervision it has created special communication problems. Too much stress should not, however, be put on this matter of size. As has been recently pointed out in a Princeton report, large organizations have been in existence for a long time, and, moreover, "blocks to the effective exchange of information may be more frequent and as serious in the small organization".[1]

* Reprinted from *Occupational Psychology*, January, 1951, pp. 1–14.

(b) The growth of trade unionism, in U.S.A. particularly during the nineteen-thirties, and the political and economic power of the unions at national and local levels, have created demands from employees for more information about all matters affecting their work and terms of employment. Even if they would like to continue the policy of "tell them nothing," employers feel that this is no longer a safe policy.

(c) During the last fifty years, particularly during the last decade or so, there has been a profound change in the nature of the management-employee relationship. The old relationship—employer and his "hands," master and servant—maintained by the incentives provided by the "big stick" and sometimes by a small "carrot," is giving way to a new relationship. This emerging relationship, in that it seeks to cultivate mutual understanding and co-operation, inevitably focuses attention on the means of communication.

(d) As a result of improved educational opportunities and the exposure of all members of the community to a whole host of media of mass communication—the Press, news magazines, radio, films, etc.—both management and employees have been led to consider the possible uses of some of these media within industry.

(e) The dispersal and decentralization of industries formerly confined to specific localities, technological changes, the widening of the individual's range of job opportunities due to high levels of employment, have all made for greater mobility of labour. No longer can an employer assume that his employees have been born and brought up in the district, following their parents into the same industry, perhaps the same firm, and that, therefore, they will have a common background of essential information. Means must be developed to put each new employee "in the picture." Hence much of the interest in induction and training procedures, employee handbooks, news-sheets, and so on.

(f) One factor, referred to in the Princeton report, may perhaps apply in the U.S.A. more than in some other countries still maintaining the private enterprise system. "The present world political situation, along with the collectivist challenge to the enterprise system, has convinced many industrial leaders that industry must demonstrate to its own members the benefits of capitalism if that system is to survive." [2] Presumably this is what Pigors is referring to when he says: "If mutual understanding and two-way communication in industry measure up to present opportunities, management and labour can do much to meet a vital challenge of our time. Can democracy (in the Anglo-Saxon meaning of the word) survive?" [3]

Considering the factors that have led to increasing awareness of the importance of communication in industry, it is clear that there is little likelihood that it will become less important in the future; the reverse is much more probable. What, then, are the significant trends revealed in contemporary writing on communication? This question can be answered by examining the 103 publications given by Pigors in his annotated bibliography,[4] and on the basis of this material an attempt will be made to indicate the general pattern of thinking about communication. (In doing this, it must be admitted that the writer cannot avoid being influenced by his own point of view; others may draw different conclusions to those that follow.)

1. With the exception of Pigors' own work and a small number of less ambitious statements, there has been little attempt to present a coherent theory of industrial communication. Without coherent theory it has not been possible to present a comprehensive account of communication practice. The emphasis, therefore, has been on certain techniques of communicating—employee publications, notice-boards, broadcasts, films, committees, propaganda campaigns, and so on—which have been developed very largely as communication "gadgets."

2. In adopting a technique-centred approach to communication, the stress has been on the use of formal techniques. Although the place of informal means (not ordinarily regarded as "techniques") of communicating is freely acknowledged, in view of the part played by these means in any human society, it is surprising that they have not received more attention. Two reasons can be suggested for this neglect.

(a) Faulty communication is often due, in part at least, to a deterioration in inter-personal relations as a result of an institutionalization which is not firmly rooted in the needs of the organization regarded as a social unit. As Daniel Katz has pointed out in another connection, management often makes the mistake of trying to meet this situation simply by increasing the amount of institutionalization,[5] for to deal directly with problems of communication would bring management face to face with the basic problems of inter-personal relations in which management itself is personally involved. This might be painful and anxiety-provoking. Hence the interest in formal institutional techniques, seen in isolation from the total communication process, formal and informal.

(b) As formal techniques are developed and assume institutional status those responsible tend to acquire a vested interest in them and the techniques, as institutions, become ends in themselves. The interested parties are then likely to seek to extend the scope and influence of their particular institution by the elaboration of further techniques (e.g. employee polls), by promotional activities (e.g. journal articles), and through combined action with other similarly interested parties (e.g. associations of house magazine editors). These further activities, each with its own problems, help to reinforce management's evasion of the basic inter-personal and inter-group problems which are reflected in problems of communication.

3. In general, communication appears to be regarded primarily, often exclusively, merely as a matter of passing on information. Thus much of the discussion hinges around the question: "How much should management tell?" This approach involves two assumptions which are not commonly recognized.

(a) It is often assumed that all information will be perceived simply as further facts and will be accepted as such. There may be, however, a marked difference between the reaction of employees to some interesting facts about the early history of the company and their reaction to information about the operation of an incentive bonus scheme. The critical point is whether or not what is communicated is interpreted as requiring a change in attitudes, beliefs, or behaviour.

(b) It is also assumed that passing on information will lead, of itself, to better industrial relations, and indirectly to better public relations. If workers are dissatisfied, "feed them more facts" and then they will be happy! In challenging this second assumption it is not being denied that passing on information *can* contribute to better industrial relations; although when this happens it is probably due not to the facts that are communicated, but to the attitudes behind the act of communicating which are also communicated. The fact that management is willing to give information is most important.

4. Communication tends to be regarded as the process of getting information across from one group, the management, to another group, the employees. There is even a tendency to concentrate on one employee group, the manual workers, with little attention being given to other employee groups—office workers, sales staff, etc. It is true that increasing attention is being given to communicating to supervisory groups, but sometimes this is due not to a recognition of the need of this for its own sake, but to the realization that those in supervisory positions are important links in the chain of communication from top management to employees.

Two observations can be made on this aspect of the current approach to communication.

(a) The emphasis on communication from management to employees might be interpreted as an acceptance by management of the two-party split, management and the employees. Thus the development of communications *on this basis* could contribute to intensifying one of the problems that, in principle, it is intended that better communication should help minimize.

(b) It is assumed that there are no problems of communication within the management group, or that if there are, they are somehow different. This would seem to be most unlikely. The hierarchical management structure, the specialization of functions, line and staff relationships, and other features of the management group are apt to create more acute communication problems than might be expected in the more simply organized employee group. Moreover, it is not uncommon to find . . . acute communication problems within management. It may be . . . that preoccupation with the problems of management-employee communication represents, to some extent, a displacement of the anxiety that management feels about its own interpersonal relationships. If this be so, then management will be unable to deal objectively with the problems arising from its relations with employees . . . communication right down the line and between those at the same levels down the line is not likely to be effective if there are difficulties, particularly unrecognized difficulties, at or near the top.

5. In much of the literature communication between management and employees is conceived essentially as a one-way process. Those down the line are regarded as the passive recipients of what is passed down to them. In this the literature is merely reflecting practice in the field. The communication techniques which are most commonly found in industry and are most popular with management are those that ensure that communication will be one-way or predominantly so; for example, noticeboards, plant broadcast systems, meetings addressed by senior executives, handbooks, house magazines, etc. Even where techniques are adopted that provide an opportunity for two-way communication, for example, joint-consultative committees, very often restrictions are introduced by management and sometimes by the employees too, consciously or unconsciously, which set definite limits to the nature and amount of two-way communication. A common restrictive device, for example, is the banning of the discussion by a Works Council of certain matters, usually those most closely related to major problems. While there can be two-way communication about the maintenance of lavatories, this must not apply to the review of promotions policy or of the wage structure.

As communication is conceived in terms of techniques for the one-way traffic of information to employees, it is not surprising that this leads to the adoption of further techniques—employee polls, attitude surveys, and so on—which are needed as a check on the effectiveness of the regular communication techniques. In their application these additional techniques restrict communication to a one-way process also; this time information of a specified kind passes from employees to management.

A THEORY OF COMMUNICATION

The evident limitations of much communication practice point to the need for a theory of industrial communication which can serve as a basis for the development of appropriate and effective techniques. As a starting point let us take a definition of communication, the sense of which, if not the actual formulation, would probably be accepted by most social scientists who have been concerned with communication in one field or another. The definition is Lundberg's:

"We shall use the word communication, then, to designate interaction by means of signs and symbols. The symbols may be gestural, pictorial, plastic, verbal or any other which operate as stimuli to behaviour which would not be evoked by the symbol itself in the absence of the special conditionings of the person who responds." [6]

For some purposes this definition could be regarded as unnecessarily abstract for the discussion of a particular set of phenomena; for other purposes it may not be at a high enough level of abstraction. However, three propositions follow from it that are relevant to the subject of this paper:

(a) All communication involves the interaction of two or more organisms, in our context individuals or groups.

(b) Communication takes place through the medium of symbolic behavior.

(c) Propositions (a) and (b) lead to a third, namely that communication is a social process.

COMMUNICATION AS AN INTERACTION PROCESS

Whenever one individual is in contact with another, or one group with another, that is, these individuals or groups have a connectedness or relatedness, there is an interaction process. The behaviour of A in making or maintaining contact with B evokes a response from B; both A's action and B's response to it make a difference to A; similarly, B's response and the subsequent reaction of A make a difference to B. This interaction process is either direct, $A \rightleftharpoons B$, or indirect, that is the connectness between A and B is mediated by a third party, $A \rightleftharpoons X \rightleftharpoons B$. For example, the managing director may establish direct contact with an operative by calling him into his office, or the contact may be mediated by one or more persons down the line of management and supervisory personnel.

Whether direct or indirect, the means for setting up a state of interaction may also be formal or informal. Thus a grievance may be communicated from employees to management by formal means created for this, and perhaps for other purposes, a joint management-employee consultative committee, or it may be communicated by informal means such as the "grapevine." The interaction process, therefore, may be brought about by one or more of four means: direct contact, formal and informal; indirect contact, formal and informal.

The choice of means is determined by two factors, their availability and how they are perceived in relation to the objectives of the person or persons wishing to communicate. Thus while it may be possible for the managing director to communicate directly with an employee, it may be impossible because of geographic and psychological barriers for an employee to communicate directly with the managing director. As direct means are not available to the employee he is obliged to use indirect means. If he has a suggestion to make to management he may be able to use indirect formal means, for example, the suggestion scheme; but, if no such scheme exists, he may be forced to use indirect informal means, for example, in the course of his work he may mention the matter to his foreman.

The notion of availability requires further comment. For a means to be available it is not sufficient that it exists, it must also be socially approved and accepted by the group or community concerned. Thus our managing director may establish as a matter of policy an "open door" to all employees, and this relatively informal means of communication may even acquire some formal or institutional status; but for certain groups within the organization or for the communication of certain matters this means may neither be approved nor accepted. Whatever the managing director might think, his "open door" may not, in fact, be available as a means of communication.

As mentioned earlier, the choice of means is also determined by how the various means that are available are perceived in relation to the objectives of those wishing to communicate. Thus, faced with a choice between direct, personal contact, the use of consultative committee machinery, and the "grapevine," the last may be adopted as likely to be most effective for a particular purpose, or it might be decided to use more than one means. (It could be argued that here we are dealing with simply another aspect of availability—some means are rejected because they are perceived as not being available as a means of communication for a particular purpose.

But whatever the means, all communicating behaviour involves an interaction process, however it may be regarded by those who are part of the process. The autocrat may regard communication as episodic and one-way; he may be indifferent as to the full effects of his communicating behaviour on the other party who may be treated as if he were completely passive in the process; but this does not alter the fact that the other party is reacting to the communicating behaviour of the autocrat, and the autocrat—however much he may try to insulate himself in this dynamic process—is being affected by it. As Pigors points out, it is quite unrealistic to assume that communicating can be a one-way act like sawing off a board.[7] (Even this analogy is not an exact one, if the situation is considered dynamically.)

In discussing communication use is often made of such phrases as "effective communication," "true communication," "the quality of communication," "degrees of communication." It may be that the experience behind such expressions represents the extent to which the interaction process is reciprocal and takes place in mutually desired directions. This experience might be called optimum interaction. Everyday experience and some experimental evidence point to the conditions necessary for this optimum interaction. These conditions can be summed up in the notion of a high degree of mutuality between the interacting individuals or groups. Lewin refers to this as the degree of dynamical dependence between the two regions.[8] Pigors, in discussing the conditions necessary for "success" in communication, refers to relationships that are "characterized by shared purpose, community of feeling and mutual respect." [9] Martin Buber is getting at the same sort of thing when, in another connection, he insists that for communications to take place there must exist an inter-personal relationship based on genuine mutual respect. He calls this an "I-thou" relationship, as distinct from an "I-it" relationship.[10] When we treat the other person as an "it," he ceases to be "there for us," and we fail to communicate.

To sum up the argument so far. Whenever individuals or groups are in contact with one another, that is they are in a state of connectedness, communication as an interaction process takes place. Whether or not this communicating achieves the objectives desired by both parties depends on the nature of their inter-personal relationships. Two conclusions which are of practical importance for industry follow from those two propositions. First, much more communication takes place in industry than management (or employees for that matter) ordinarily recognizes. Secondly, what is usually referred to as "effective," "successful," or "true" communication is not a means of creating harmonious industrial relations, for these relations are a *condition* of such communication. In other words, the level of morale determines the effectiveness of communication.

COMMUNICATION THROUGH SYMBOLIC BEHAVIOUR

According to our working definition communication involves interaction by means of signs and symbols. First, it must be recognized that there is no one form of symbolic expression. In industry most attention has been given to communication through the use of verbal symbols—spoken and written —with some attention to pictorial symbols—the use of charts, photographs and films, displays, etc. Little attention, if any, has been given to what can be grouped together as behavioural symbols, for example, gesture, bodily movement, action and inaction, situations. It may be that whereas verbal communication tends to be regarded as something relatively impersonal, and hence open to study and criticism, behavioural communication is regarded as being much more ego-involved, hence the study of it would represent too much of a personal threat to those involved. A managing director may welcome the research worker who wishes to study the firm's house magazine as a means of communication, but may be much less enthusiastic about a study of his behaviour.

No one symbol can be employed in communicating in isolation from others. Even the simplest spoken word in a face-to-face situation has an emotional toning, involves facial expression, is accompanied by either the presence or absence of bodily movement and action, and has its situational context. The various symbols employed in the act of communicating, however, are not perceived as a number of unrelated elements, they are perceived as a gestalt, as a single piece of behaviour, however complex it may prove to be on analysis. Indeed, the individual elements may not appear "to add up" on analysis; for example, what was said may conflict with what was implied by gesture or action. Thus management may seek to communicate by verbal symbols its belief, sincerely held at the conscious level, that its foremen are the "key" people in achieving increased production, but these symbols may be at variance with other symbols—the authority management gives to the foremen, salary differentials, attitudes displayed in day-to-day contacts. Rightly or wrongly the foremen may react by thinking: "Management doesn't really believe we are of much account, but for its own ulterior purposes would like us to think that we are: they are trying to put something over on us."

The totality of symbolic behaviour in the communication process has important implications for industry. If communication is to achieve the particular objectives desired, then all the behaviour operative in the interaction process should convey the same meaning or at least should be reasonably consistent. Similarly, in communication between groups there is need for consistency in the interaction behaviour of the members of the group wishing to communicate. (This is one of the major problems of recently nationalized industries. Because of differences in understanding and in deeply-rooted attitudes, management, as represented by the Government, the controlling boards, and higher and lower executives, is apt to speak with many voices in the totality of its interaction with employees.) Consistency in interaction behaviour requires personal insight and integrity on the part of the individual and mutual understanding and harmonious relations amongst individuals as members of an interacting group.

The elements which are perceived in the totality of the interaction process are determined by three factors:

(a) The sensory equipment of the individual sets limits to what can be perceived in general and in a particular situation.

(b) Perpetual discrimination is affected by the individual's past experience, training and knowledge.

(c) Motivation acts as a highly selective agent in the act of perception. Within the given perceptual field elements tend to be perceived that are positively motivationally related, that is, we tend to perceive what we want to perceive, and those elements which evoke pain or discomfort, that are negatively motivationally related, tend to be directly repressed or distorted.

Thus if management or any other group in industry intends that another group with which it is in the communication relationship should attend to certain aspects or elements of its interaction behaviour, within the limits of control made possible by its degree of insight, it should adopt a pattern of behaviour that is in accord with the perceptual capacities (biological and acquired) and motivational states of those comprising the other group.

From the point of view of communication, however, it is not simply a question of what is attended to or perceived in the interaction process; it is also a question of *how* this behaviour is perceived, that is, what does it signify, how are the symbols interpreted? For our purposes three aspects can be distinguished in the interpretation of symbols, whether the symbols be those of language or behaviour, and to a greater or lesser extent each of these aspects are present in the interpretation—conscious and unconscious—of all symbols used in communication.

(a) Each symbol, as a symbol, has a referent. The logical positivists have done a valuable service in stressing the need for symbols to be closely tied to the facts or operations for which they stand. The more removed symbols become from their referents, the greater the possibility for their misinterpretation. It would seem that much of the misunderstanding in industry arises just at this point. Symbols are used which do not have an unequivocal relationship to their referents, for example, management's use of such verbal symbols as "efficiency," "morale," "co-operation" and employee's use of such symbols as "the rights of employees," "victimization."

(b) A symbol never represents to the percipient simply a physical object or an operation, for in addition it carries a culturally-determined content. Thus the behavioural symbol of shaking hands not only signifies that the parties carry no lethal weapons, it may also signify intentions of friendship, goodwill or something of the sort, but not necessarily so. In some groups within a hand-shaking society this simple act may signify an expression of superiority, affectation, hypocrisy or something quite different from its more generally held meaning.

(c) A symbol has its personal, idiosyncratic aspect, the result of the personality and experience of the individual. In a well-integrated, homogeneous group these individual differences in the meaning of symbols may ordinarily not have very much practical significance, except in the case of the deviant individual (with a psychotic person the idiosyncratic may heavily over-lay the other aspects of the symbols employed and responded to) and in circumstances of special—and not infrequently crucial—significance for the individual. An employee who once lost his job as the result of management action involving the use of a stopwatch is likely to react to the use of a stopwatch on another occasion differently from those who have not had this particular experience.

From this discussion of the nature of symbols in the interaction process involved in communication, it can be deduced that communication is not likely to convey intended meanings unless the symbols used have the same referents for each of the parties, and unless each party has an adequate understanding of the cultural and idiosyncratic factors operating in the process.

Communication as a Social Process

According to the point of view adopted in this paper communication can best be understood as a social process. All communication requires a community of at least two groups. How an individual or a group perceives and interprets the behaviour of another and the nature of the individual or group response in this interaction process can only be understood if the total social context of this behaviour is taken into account. Pigors makes this point in terms of an individual, but his observation applies also to a group. He suggests that there are three variables affecting the behaviour of the individual-in-the-social-context which are important for an understanding of communication:

(a) *What* he is. That is, his function in the total scheme of things—staff officer in cost control, line supervisor, unskilled operative, and so on. This affects his *angle of view*.

(b) *Where* he is. That is, where he comes in the social hierarchy of the particular community—at the top, in the middle, at the bottom. This affects his *scope of view*.

(c) *Who* he is. This refers to his pattern of abilities, interests, motivations, personality traits, as a person and as a member of a particular interest group. This affects his *point of view*.[11]

These considerations are of more than theoretical interest. It follows that an individual or a group is never simply the passive recipient of instructions, information, or the content of whatever it is intended to communicate. What is communicated is restructured according to the angle, scope, and point of view of the recipient as an active agent in a process. He is not a bin into which facts are poured.

Thus the same manifest content of a communication will not mean the same thing to, and hence elicit the same response from, different individuals or groups. To take a simple example, a managerial announcement that overtime is to be worked. To the cost control officer this may mean that certain adjustments will need to be made to his calculations of labour costs. He may also decide that the extra costs will need to be offset by savings in other directions, for example, by more stringent interpretation of regulations covering allowances of various kinds. This reaction may come into conflict with the response of others in the situation, for example, the personnel manager. To the works manager the decision to work overtime may mean that he must set in motion a whole series of technical operations relating to the supply of materials, the planning of production procedures, and so on. He may welcome the decision, in the expectation of overtime enabling him to meet his production target. To the individual worker overtime may appear as a means of adding to his pay envelope (a different response to that of the cost control officer), but may also be resented as an interference with his leisure and as an added physical strain, the resentment being expressed in a determination to do as little work as possible (a response which conflicts with the expectation of the works manager). Thus one simple announcement may evoke a complex pattern of reactions, give rise to misunderstanding based on different interpretations of the same "sign," and may even result in open conflict.

Moreover, the extent to which a communication is responded to in accordance with the *what, where* and *who* variables is not a constant, another source of misunderstanding. Thus on one occasion foremen may interpret a communication in the fullest sense intended by management, that is in accordance with the *what,* their supervisory responsibilities as part of management. Next time, however, they may adopt what to management is a very limited, inadequate interpretation. In accordance with the *where,* their position in the hierarchy, they may respond by saying in effect, "we don't regard this as our business, let top management do its own dirty work." Yet again, they may respond in terms of the *who,* as members of the union, they may decide to resist actively a managerial decision.

There is a further aspect of communication as a social process. In the industrial setting communication is not restricted to the two individuals or two groups, *A* and *B,* in direct contact at any given moment. Neither *A* nor

B operates in a social vacuum, each is connected not only with the other, but is also connected directly with other groups and indirectly with all the groups which comprise the particular industrial community. (The pattern of relatedness extends, of course, outside that community into the wider society of which it is an organic part.) Thus the communication involving interaction between A and B is accompanied by other interactions, between A and A', B and B', and so on. This does not mean that the interactions between A and B, A and A', B and B', are similarly interpreted, that is, convey the same meanings to A, A' B and B'. The reverse is usually the case, with the resulting misunderstanding which is such a common experience in industry.

Because of the connectedness of all those in a given community, for example a factory, it is not possible, strictly speaking, for one group to by-pass another in the communication process. It is unrealistic to think of communication as something that takes place between management as one group and the employees as another, or similarly between top management and foremen. Top management may decide to communicate with employees through their representatives on a Works Council and in so doing ignore those in the intervening supervisory hierarchy. But this interacting behaviour means something to the supervisors. They may interpret management's communication to *them* to mean that management doesn't believe that the opinions of supervisors are worth having, or that management is seeking to weaken their authority and prestige by discussing matters that concern them with employees.

It can be seen, therefore, that attempts to improve understanding between any two groups in a factory, say top management and employees, by particular techniques of communication designed to this end, even if successful, can quite easily create misunderstanding between either of these groups and other groups in the factory community. Unless what are usually referred to as "problems of communication" are approached with an understanding of the implications of communication as a social process, attempts to solve these problems will inevitably lead to further, perhaps more serious, problems. The position may be made more difficult by the fact that the new problems may not be immediately apparent and may not present themselves as communication problems.

MANAGEMENT OBJECTIVES

In conclusion, let us look briefly at communication in relation to the objectives of management. The management of any enterprise can be regarded as seeking to attain, with varying degrees of emphasis, three objectives. First, management is concerned with running an efficient enterprise, whether efficiency is conceived in terms of the maximizing of profit, the attaining of production targets, or the providing of goods or services of a particular standard. The relevance of communication to this objective is evident. The fact that a factory or any other enterprise consists of interrelated groups of people means that interaction between individuals and between groups is taking place all the time. This interaction must be such that intended, essential meanings are conveyed; information and explanations of company policy and practices, rules and instructions, managerial and supervisory attitudes must reach and be understood by employees; the reactions of employees, their attitudes, opinions and ideas must reach and be understood by management. There is a certain minimum of meanings which must be communicated if a plant is to operate at all, let alone operate with maximum efficiency.

Communities based on dominance-submission relationships have demonstrated that a high degree of efficiency can be attained, at least in certain directions, for relatively limited periods, even though the structure of the community sets rigid limits to the amount and nature of the interaction between some, if not all, groups in the community, and even if there is very limited understanding of what is communicated through this interaction. There is sufficient experimental evidence, however, to justify the rejection of a dominance-submission basis for social organization and to show that the highest efficiency will be achieved and sustained when the structure of the community allows for the optimum of interaction between individuals and groups, with the optimum of mutual understanding. In this sense, effective communication can contribute much to efficiency.

Secondly, management has a human relations objective, what Pigors refers to as "helping employees to meet central human needs" by providing "work relationships that are humanly satisfying." In the heyday of unfettered capitalism this objective was neither generally recognized nor accepted. This is no longer the case. While there are those who regard the human relations objective simply either as a by-product of, or a contributor to, the efficiency objective, it is being increasingly accepted as an objective in its own right. Much of the current writing on communication in industry presents communication in relation to this objective. It is commonly claimed that the passing on of information, giving employees facts, streamlining and extending the means of communication, and a whole host of techniques can, of themselves, contribute to improving morale, management-employee relations, employee goodwill, and so on.

Now according to argument developed in this paper, much of this is wishful thinking. Communication may take place in a face-to-face situation, where it is direct, personal, and two-way. The meaning it is intended to communicate may appear to be precise, unequivocal, and appropriate. But what in fact is communicated, the interpretation of the interaction behaviour, is dependent on the quality of the relationships already operating between the parties to the communication process. What is usually meant by effective communication is not the means for achieving harmonious human relations, rather is it the natural consequence of such relations. Moreover, in some situations it is possible that an increase in the effectiveness of communication will lead to the realization by the parties that they are seeking mutually incompatible goals. The alternatives will then be to terminate their working relationship and pursue their goals independently or, if this is not possible, to adopt a compromise, with the distinct possibility of open conflict whenever either party appears to be threatening the goal-seeking of the other. While it could be claimed that either of these alternatives would be preferable to a working relationship sustained by the ignorance of the parties of each other's objectives, this is not the sort of outcome management is looking for from its communication policy.

Thirdly, there is the objective of meeting the needs of the community—local, national, international—for goods or services. In the past there was a tendency to subsume a debased version of this third objective under the first objective or one form of it, that of profit. Accordingly, the objective was to create or stimulate consumer wants, even to the point where this conflicted with the meeting of basic needs. To-day, however, the community, of which management is part, demands—and these demands may be backed by legal sanctions—that industry should serve the community by meeting its needs, although the nature of these needs may be variously interpreted.

In the achievement of this third objective communication is of paramount importance. Unless management is in close contact with the community so that the interaction between those producing goods and services and those consuming them is effective as a two-way communication process, it is a matter of hit-or-miss whether community needs are fully met. It is at this point that much advertising and consumer research of various kinds go so sadly astray. But this is as yet relatively unexplored territory.

NOTES

[1] Baker, Helen and others. *Transmitting Information Through Management and Union Channels.* Princeton: The University Press, 1949, p. 11.
[2] *Ibid.,* p. 12.
[3] Pigors, Paul. *Effective Communication in Industry.* New York: National Association of Manufacturers, 1949, p. 77.
[4] *Ibid.,* pp. 78–85.

5 Katz, Daniel. Morale and Motivation in Industry, in *Current Trends in Industrial Psychology*. Pittsburgh: The University Press, 1949, p. 149.

6 Lundberg, G. A. *Foundations of Sociology*. New York: Macmillan, 1939, p. 253.

7 Pigors, *op. cit.*, p. 2.

8 Lewin, Kurt. *Principles of Topological Psychology*. London: McGraw-Hill, 1936, p. 217.

9 Pigors, *op. cit.*, p. 6.

10 Buber, Martin. *I and Thou*. New York: Scribner, 1937; *Between Man and Man*. New York: Macmillan, 1947.

11 Pigors, *op. cit.*, p. 17.

15

MANAGEMENT INFORMATION CRISIS *

D. Ronald Daniel

In late 1960 a large defense contractor became concerned over a major project that was slipping badly. After 15 months costs were running far above the estimate and the job was behind schedule. A top-level executive, assigned as program manager to salvage the project, found he had no way of pinpointing what parts of the system were causing the trouble, why costs were so high, and which subcontractors were not performing.

Recently an American electronics company revamped its organization structure. To compete more aggressively in international markets, management appointed "area managers" with operating responsibility—e.g., in Latin America, Western Europe, and the Far East. After nine months it was apparent that the new plan was not coming up to expectations. On checking with three newly created area managers, the company president heard each say, in effect:

"In half of the countries in my area the political situation is in flux, and I can't anticipate what's going to happen next."

"I'm still trying to find out whether our operating costs in Austria are reasonable."

"I don't know where in South America we're making a profit."

A small but highly successful consumer products company recently followed the lead of its larger competitors by establishing product-manager positions. Although outstanding men were placed in the new jobs, an air of general confusion soon developed, and the product managers began to show signs of frustration. After much study it became apparent that an important cause of the trouble was that no one had determined what kind of

* Reprinted from *Harvard Business Review*, September–October, 1961, pp. 111–121.

information the product managers would need in order to perform their new functions.

In retrospect it is obvious that these three companies were plagued by a common problem: inadequate management information. The data were inadequate, not in the sense of there not being enough, but in terms of relevancy for setting objectives, for shaping alternative strategies, for making decisions, and for measuring results against planned goals.

ASSESSING THE GAP

In each company the origin of the problem lay in the gap between a static information system and a changing organization structure. This difficulty is not new or uncommon. There is hardly a major company in the United States whose plan of organization has not been changed and rechanged since World War II. And with revised structures have come new jobs, new responsibilities, new decision-making authorities, and reshaped reporting relationships. All of these factors combine to create new demands for information—information that is usually missing in existing systems. As a result, many leading companies are suffering a major information crisis—often without fully realizing it.

Far-Reaching Trends

Some of the scope of this problem can be gained by reviewing the intensity of the three major causes of recent organization changes in American business:

Growth. Since 1945 the Gross National Product has risen 135%. In specific industries the growth rate has been even greater. Plastic production, for example, tripled between 1948 and 1958; electronics sales nearly quadrupled in the decade from 1950 to 1960. Many individual companies have shown even more startling growth. This growth, in turn, has fostered organizational change:

Divisions have been created and decentralization has been encouraged.

Greater precision in defining line-staff relationships has been necessitated.

Organization structures that were once adequate for $50-million businesses have proved unworkable for $500-million enterprises.

Diversification. Merger and acquisition have accounted for the growth of many large organizations. For these companies, the task of finding, evaluating, and consummating diversification deals—and assimilating newly acquired products and businesses—has required continuous organizational adjustment. Some corporations have diversified by developing new product lines to satisfy shifting market requirements; some have used other means. But always the effect has been the same: different organization structures for parts of or perhaps for the entire enterprise.

International Operations. There has been a threefold increase in the value of United States investments abroad since World War II. Major companies that once regarded foreign markets as minor sources of incremental profits, or as markets for surplus production, now look overseas for the bulk of their future profits and growth. They are setting up manufacturing and research as well as marketing organizations in foreign countries. Consequently, we are growing used to seeing a company's "export department" evolve into the "international division," and national companies grow into world-wide enterprises.[1] All this calls for extensive modifications of organization structure.

The impact of any one of the above factors alone would be sufficient to create great change in an enterprise, but consider that in many cases at least two, and sometimes all three, have been at work. It is easy to see why so many company organization structures do become unstable and how this creates a management information problem large enough to hamper some firms and nearly paralyze others.

Linking Systems & Needs

Organization structure and information requirements are inextricably linked. In order to translate a statement of his duties into action, an executive must receive and use information. Information in this case is not just the accounting system and the forms and reports it produces. It includes *all* the data and intelligence—financial and nonfinancial—that are really needed to plan, operate, and control a particular enterprise. This embraces external information such as economic and political factors and data on competitive activity.

When viewed in this light, the impact of organization structure on needs for management information becomes apparent. The trouble is that in most companies it is virtually taken for granted that the information necessary for performance of a manager's duties flows naturally to the job. To a certain extent this is so. For example, internally generated information—expecially accounting information—does tend to flow easily to the job or can be made to do so. Also, in companies doing business in only one industry and having a small, closely knit management group much vital interdepartmental and general information is conveyed by frequent face-to-face contact and coordination among executives. Economic and competitive information from outside is similarly transmitted, the bulk of it coming into the concern informally. Further, through trade contacts, general reading, and occasional special studies, executives toss bits of information into the common pool and draw from it as well.

The point is, however, that while such an informal system can work well for small and medium-size companies in simple and relatively static industries, it becomes inadequate when companies grow larger and especially when they spread over several industries, areas, and countries. At this point, most large companies have found that information has to be conveyed in a formal manner and less and less through direct observation.

Unfortunately, management often loses sight of the seemingly obvious and simple relationship between organization structure and information needs. Companies very seldom follow up on reorganizations with penetrating reappraisals of their information systems, and managers given new responsibilities and decision-making authority often do not receive all the information they require.

CAUSES OF CONFUSION

The cornerstone for building a compact, useful management information system is the determination of each executive's information needs. This requires a clear grasp of the individual's role in the organization—his responsibilities, his authorities, and his relationships with other executives. The task is then to—

Design a network of procedures that will process raw data in such a way as to generate the information required for management use.
Implement such procedures in actual practice.

Such action steps, while demanding and time-consuming, have proved to be far less difficult than the creative and conceptual first step of defining information requirements. Seldom is the open approach of asking an executive what information he requires successful. For one thing, he may find it difficult to be articulate because the organization structure of his company is not clearly defined.

Further, and more important, there is a widespread tendency among operating executives to think of information exclusively in terms of their companies' accounting systems and the reports thus generated. This way of thinking can be a serious deterrent because:

1. Many conventional accounting reports cause confusion in the minds of nonfinancially trained executives. Take, for example, the profit-and-loss

statement, with its arbitrary treatment of inventories, depreciation, allocated overhead expenses, and the like, or the statistical sales report, which is often a 40-page, untitled, machine-prepared tabulation of sales to individual customers. Such reports have made an indelible impression on managers' thinking, coloring their understanding and expectations of reports in general.

2. By its very nature traditional accounting fails to highlight many important aspects of business operations. Accounting systems often are designed primarily to meet SEC, Internal Revenue, and other statutory requirements—requirements that, more often than not, fail to correspond to management's information needs. Accounting describes the past in dollars, usually without discriminating between the critical and noncritical elements of a business—the elements that control competitive success in a particular industry and the elements that do not.

3. Accounting reports generally describe what has happened inside a company. Just consider what this approach omits:

Information about the future.

Data expressed in nonfinancial terms—e.g., share of market, productivity, quality levels, adequacy of customer service, and so on.

Information dealing with external conditions as they might bear on a particular company's operations.

Yet all of these items are essential to the intelligent managing of a business.

PLANNING NEEDS DEFINED

The key to the development of a dynamic and usable system of management information is to move beyond the limits of classical accounting reports and to conceive of information as it relates to two vital elements of the management process—planning and control. In the pages to follow I shall focus largely on the planning aspect.

We hear more and more these days about new techniques for inventory, cost, and other types of control, but information systems for business planning still represent a relatively unexplored horizon.

Planning, as used in this article, means: setting objectives, formulating strategy, and deciding among alternative investments or courses of action. This definition can be applied to an entire company, an integrated division, or a single operating department.

. . . The information required to do planning of this kind is of three basic types:

1. *Environmental Information.* Describes the social, political, and economic aspects of the climate in which a business operates or may operate in the future.

2. *Competitive Information.* Explains the past performance, programs, and plans of competing companies.

3. *Internal Information.* Indicates a company's own strengths and weaknesses. Now let us consider each of these categories in some detail.

Environmental Information

The environmental data category is one of the least formalized and hence least used parts of a management information system in most companies. Specific examples of the data included in this category are:

Population—current levels, growth trends, age distribution, geographical distribution, effect on unemployment.
Price levels—retail, wholesale, commodities, government regulation.
Transportation—availability, costs, competition, regulation.
Foreign trade—balance of payments, exchange rates, convertibility.
Labor force—skills, availability, wages, turnover, unions.

To this list a company operating internationally would add another item—systematic collection and interpretation, on a country-by-country basis, of information on political and economic conditions in the foreign areas where business is being done. Here is an example of what can be accomplished:

A well-established international corporation with a highly sophisticated management makes a three-pronged effort to get data on local political and economic conditions. (*a*) There is a small but highly competent and well-paid four-man staff at corporate headquarters which travels extensively and publishes, using its own observations plus a variety of other sources, a weekly commentary on world events as they relate to the company. (*b*) This corporation has trained all its country managers to be keen observers of their local scene and to report their interpretive comments to headquarters regularly. (*c*) There is a little-talked-about group of "intelligence agents" who are not on the company's official payroll but are nevertheless paid for the information they pass along.

Certainly, not every organization has to go to these ends to keep itself informed of the situation in which it operates. However, those organizations that ignore environmental data or that leave its collection to the informal devices of individual executives are inviting trouble. Those companies that are knowledgeable concerning their environment are almost always in tune with the times and ahead of their competition. To illustrate:

1. Good intelligence on the sociological changes taking place in the United States led several heavy manufacturing companies to enter the "leisure time" field with a great deal of success.

2. Insight into the possible impact of foreign labor costs on parts of the electronics industry caused some U.S. corporations to acquire their own manufacturing facilities abroad. As a result, the firms were able not only to protect their domestic markets but also to open up profitable operations overseas.

3. Knowledge of trends in age distribution in the United States added to an awareness of the rate of change of scientific learning provides ample proof for some firms of the desirability of being in the educational publishing field for the next decade.

To be of real use, environmental data must indicate trends; population figures, balance-of-payment data, or political shifts are of little significance when shown for one period because they don't help management make *analytical* interpretations.

The collection and transmission of good environmental data are often problematical. Even in the United States some kinds of information are not readily available and must be pieced together from several sources or acquired *sub rosa* from officially inaccessible sources. Transmitting environmental data, particularly political information, is so awkward that sometimes the data collector must sit down personally with those who need to know the information.

In sum, environmental data are an aspect of planning information that requires more attention and warrants formalization, especially in large geographically dispersed companies. The emergence of the corporate economics department [2] is one development that could lead to better results in this area, but it is my impression that so far the progress of these units has been uneven.

Competitive Information

Data on competition comprise the second category of planning information. There are three important types to consider:

1. *Past Performance.* This includes information on the profitability, return on investment, share of market, and so forth of competing companies. Such information is primarily useful in identifying one's competitors. It also is one benchmark when setting company objectives.

2. *Present Activity.* This category covers new product introductions, management changes, price strategy, and so on—all current developments. Good intelligence on such matters can materially influence a company's

planning; for example, it may lead to accelerating research programs, modifying advertising strategy, or switching distribution channels. The implication here is not that a company's plans should always be defensive and prompted by a competitor's moves but simply that anything important a competitor does should be recognized and factored into the planning process.

3. *Future Plans.* This includes information on acquisition intentions, facility plans, and research and development efforts.

Competitive information, like environmental data, is an infrequently formalized part of a company's total information system. And so there seldom is a concerted effort to collect this kind of material, to process it, and to report it to management regularly. But some interesting exceptions to this general lack of concern exist:

Oil companies have long employed "scouts" in their land departments. These men report on acreage purchases, drilling results, and other competitive activity that may be pertinent to the future actions of their own company.

Business machine companies have "competitive equipment evaluation personnel" who continually assess the technical features of competitors' hardware.

Retail organizations employ "comparison shoppers" who appraise the prices and quality of merchandise in competitive stores.

Commercial intelligence departments are appearing more and more on corporate organization charts. An excerpt from the charter of one such group states its basic responsibility thus:

"To seek out, collect, evaluate, and report information covering the past performance and future plans of competitors in such a manner that the information will have potential utility in strategic and operational planning of the corporation. This means that in addition to reporting factual information, emphasis should be on determining the implications of such information for the corporation."

Internal Information

The third and final basic category of planning information is made up of internal data. As it relates to the total planning process, internal data are aimed at identifying a company's strengths and weaknesses—the characteristics that, when viewed in the perspective of the general business environment and in the light of competitive activity, should help management to shape its future plans. It is useful to think of internal data as being of three types:

1. *Quantitative-financial*—e.g., sales, costs, and cost behavior relative to volume changes.
2. *Quantitative-physical*—e.g., share of market, productivity, delivery performance, and manpower resources.
3. *Nonquantitative*—e.g., community standing and labor relations.

In reporting internal data, a company's information system must be discriminating and selective. It should focus on "success factors." In most industries there are usually three to six factors that determine success; these key jobs must be done exceedingly well for a company to be successful. Here are some examples from several major industries:

In the automobile industry, styling, an efficient dealer organization, and tight control of manufacturing costs are paramount.

In food processing, new product development, good distribution, and effective advertising are the major success factors.

In life insurance, the development of agency management personnel, effective control of clerical personnel, and innovation in creating new types of policies spell the difference.

The companies which have achieved the greatest advances in information analysis have consistently been those which have developed systems that have (a) been selective and (b) focused on the company's strengths and weaknesses with respect to its acknowledged success factors. By doing this, the managements have generated the kind of information that is most useful in capitalizing on strengths and correcting weaknesses. To illustrate:

An oil company devised a system of regularly reporting its "finding" costs—those costs incurred in exploring for new reserves of oil divided by the number barrels of oil found. When this ratio trended upward beyond an established point, it was a signal to the company's management to consider the acquisition of other oil companies (together with their proved reserves) as a less expensive alternative to finding oil through its own exploratory efforts.

In the minds of most executives the accounting system exists primarily to meet the company's internal data needs; yet this is often an unreasonable and unfulfilled expectation. Accounting reports rarely focus on success factors that are nonfinancial in nature. Moreover, accounting practices with respect to allocation of expenses, transfer prices, and the like, often tend to obscure rather than clarify the underlying strengths and weaknesses of a company. This inadequacy should not be surprising since the *raison d'être* of many accounting systems is not to facilitate planning but rather to ensure the fulfillment of management's responsibility to the stockholders, the government, and other groups.

TAILORING THE REQUIREMENTS

If a company is to have a comprehensive, integrated system of information to support its planning process, it will need a set of management reports that regularly covers the three basic categories of planning data—i.e., environmental, competitive, and internal. The amount of data required in each area will naturally vary from company to company and will depend on such factors as the nature of the industry, the size and operating territory of the company, and the acceptance by management of planning as an essential function. However, it is important in every case for management to *formalize* and *regularize* the collection, transmission, processing, and presentation of planning information; the data are too vital to be ignored or taken care of by occasional "special studies." It is no accident that many of the most successful companies in this country are characterized by well-developed planning information systems.

. . .

Many companies have found that the most effective approach to determining requirements for planning information, whether it be for one executive or an entire company, is to relate the three types of planning data described earlier to the steps in the planning process—i.e., setting objectives, developing strategy, and deciding among alternative investments. Thus, one asks himself questions like these:

What political data are needed to set reasonable objectives for this company?

What sociological and economic data about the areas in which this company operates are needed to formulate new product strategy?

What competitive intelligence is necessary to develop share-of-market objectives?

What internal cost information is needed to choose beween alternative facility locations?

. . .

FUTURE DEVELOPMENTS

The heightened interest of management in its information crisis is already unmistakable. Dean Stanley F. Teele of the Harvard Business School, writing on the process of change in the years ahead, states, "I think the capacity to manage knowledge will be still more important to the manager. . . . The manager will need to increase his skill in deciding what knowledge he needs." [3]

Ralph Cordiner of General Electric Company in his book, *New Frontiers for Professional Managers,* writes:

"It is an immense problem to organize and communicate the information required to operate a large, decentralized organization. . . .

"What is required . . . is a . . . penetrating and orderly study of the business in its entirety to discover what specific information is needed at each particular position in view of the decisions to be made there. . . ." [4]

Invariably, increasing attention of leaders in education and industry precedes and prepares the way for frontal attacks on business problems. In many organizations the initial reaction to the management information problem is first evidenced by a concern over "the flood of paper work." Eventually, the problem itself is recognized—i.e., the need to define concisely the information required for intelligent planning and control of a business.

Following this awakening interest in business information problems, we are likely to see the acceleration of two developments already in view: (*a*) improved techniques relating to the creation and operation of total information systems, and (*b*) new organizational approaches to resolving information problems.

IMPROVED TECHNIQUES

While the crisis in management information has been growing, tools that may be useful in its solution have been under development. For example, the evolution of electronic data-processing systems, the development of supporting communications networks, and the formulation of rigorous mathematical solutions to business problems have provided potentially valuable tools to help management attack its information problems. Specifically, progress on three fronts is an encouraging indication that this kind of approach will prove increasingly fruitful:

1. Managements of most companies are far more conversant with both the capabilities and the limitations of computer systems than they were five years ago. This growing understanding has done much to separate fact from fancy. One key result should be the increasing application of electronic data-processing concepts to the more critical, less routine problems of business.

2. Computer manufacturers and communications companies are learning the worth of their products. They show signs of recognizing that it is not

hardware but an information system which is extremely valuable in helping to solve management's problems.

3. Significant improvements have been made in the techniques of harnessing computers. Advances in automatic programming and developments in creating a common business language are gratifying evidence that the gap is being narrowed between the technical potential of the hardware and management's ability to exploit it.

Organizational Moves

The development of new organizational approaches is less obvious. Earlier in this article I noted that: (*a*) progress in the systematic collection and reporting of information dealing with a company's environment or with its competitive situation has been slow, and (*b*) traditional accounting reports are often inadequate in providing the data needed for business planning. These conditions may result from a very basic cause; namely, that most organization structures do not pin down the responsibility for management information systems and tie it to specific executive positions. Controllers and other financial officers usually have been assigned responsibility for *accounting* information—but this, of course, does not meet the total need.

Nowhere has the absence of one person having specific and *total* responsibility for management information systems had a more telling effect than in defense contractor companies. In such organizations the usual information problems have been compounded by the rapid rate of technological advance and its attendant effect upon product obsolescence, and also by the requirement for "concurrency," which means that a single product or product complex is developed, tested, produced, and installed simultaneously. Under these conditions, some companies have been nearly paralyzed by too much of the wrong information.

Having recognized this problem, several corporations have attacked it by creating full-time management information departments. These groups are responsible for:

1. Identifying the information needs for all levels of management for both planning and control purposes. As prerequisites to this responsibility it is necessary to (*a*) define the authority and duties of each manager and (*b*) determine the factors that really contribute to competitive success in the particular business in question.

2. Developing the necessary systems to fulfill these information needs.

3. Operating the data-processing equipment necessary to generate the information which is required.

To some extent these departments, reporting high in the corporate structure, have impinged on responsibilities traditionally assigned to the accounting organization since they are concerned with financial as well as nonfinancial information. But to me this overlapping is inevitable, particularly in companies where the financial function operates under a narrow perspective and a preoccupation with accountancy. The age of the information specialist is nearing, and its arrival is inextricably tied in with the emergence of some of the newer tools of our management sciences. This notion is not far removed from the concept of Harold J. Leavitt and Thomas L. Whisler, who foresee the evolution of information technology and the creation of a "programing elite." [5]

CONCLUSION

The day when management information departments are as common as controller's departments is still years away. But this should not rule out concerted effects to improve a company's information system. In fact, I would expect many broad-gauged controller's organizations to assume the initiative in their companies for such programs.

. . .

The impact of the information crisis on the executive will be significant. To an increasing extent, a manager's effectiveness will hinge on the quality and completeness of the facts that flow to him and on his skill in using them. With technology changing at a rapid rate, with the time dimension becoming increasingly critical, and with organizations becoming larger, more diversified in product lines, and more dispersed geographically, it is inevitable that executives will rely more and more on formally presented information in managing their businesses.

What is more, some organizations are concluding that the easiest and most effective way to influence executive action is to control the flow of information into managerial positions. This notion holds that the discipline of information can be a potent factor in determining just what an executive can and cannot do—what decisions he can make, what plans he can draw up, what corrective steps he can take.

To the extent that this is true, information systems may be increasingly used to mold and shape executive behavior. Better data handling might well become a substitute for much of the laborious shuffling and reshuffling of positions and lines of authority that now goes on. Most reorganizations seek to alter the way certain managers or groups of managers operate. But simply drawing new organization charts and rewriting job descriptions seldom ensure the implementation of new concepts and relationships. The timing, content, and format of the information provided to management, however, *can* be a strong influence in bringing about such purposeful change.

Thus, developments in management information systems will affect the executive in two ways. Not only will the new concepts influence what he is able to do, but they will to a great extent control how well he is able to do it.

NOTES

[1] See Gilbert H. Clee and Alfred di Scipio, "Creating a *World* Enterprise," *HBR* November–December 1959, p. 77.

[2] Clark S. Teitsworth, "Growing Role of the Company Economist," HBR January–February 1959, p. 97; and the article by Henry B. Arthur in this issue, p. 80.

[3] "Your Job and Mine," *The Harvard Business School Bulletin,* August 1960, p. 8.

[4] New York, McGraw-Hill Book Company, Inc., 1956, p. 102.

[5] "Management in the 1980's," *HBR* November–December 1958, p. 41.

16

THE ORGANIZATION AND ITS
COMMUNICATIONS PROBLEM *

Jay M. Jackson

Business executives, I am told, are very similar to other people: they have communication problems, too. They are concerned, of course, about better understanding among all persons. They are interested in overcoming barriers to communication between members of the public and their own particular industry. They are especially concerned, or should be, about problems of communication within an organization, since business administration by its very nature is a collective enterprise, and people in this profession must spend their days in organized groups, or organizations.

First, I want to discuss some characteristics of all organizations that create communication problems. Second, I shall present some conclusions based on recent research findings regarding the forces which determine the flow of communication in an organization. Next I shall consider the consequences of communication in a number of conditions that often exist within an organization. Finally, I shall attempt to indicate that what we call problems of communication are often merely symptomatic of other difficulties between people.

CHARACTERISTICS OF ORGANIZATIONS

What is it about organizations that seems to make communication especially difficult? An organization may be considered a system of overlapping and interdependent groups. These groups can be departments located on the same floor of a building, or they can be divisions scattered over the

* Reprinted from *Advanced Management*, February, 1959, pp. 17–20.

face of the earth. Other things being equal, people will communicate most frequently to those geographically closest to them, even within a relatively small organization. Spatial distance itself can thus be a barrier to communication.

Each one of the subgroups within an organization demands allegiance from its members. It has its own immediate goals and means for achieving them. It distributes tangible or intangible rewards to members of the group, based on their contribution to these objectives. When any particular communication is sent to a number of subgroups in an organization, each group may extract a different meaning from the message, depending upon its significance for the things the group values and is striving to accomplish.

The groups in an organization often represent different subcultures—as different, for example, as those inhabited by engineers, accountants, and salesmen. Each occupational or professional group has its own value system and idealized image, based on its traditions. These are guarded jealously, since to a considerable degree they give the members of that group their feelings of identity. Other groups in an organization, based on experience, age, sex, and marital status, have to varying degrees similar tendencies. Each develops along with its peculiar value system a somewhat specialized system of meanings. What is required to communicate effectively to members of different groups is a system of simultaneous translation, like that employed by the United Nations. This simultaneous translation must be taking place both within the sender and the receivers of a communication.

It is also characteristic of organizations that persons are structured into different systems of relationships. A work structure exists: certain persons are expected to perform certain tasks together with other persons. An authority structure exists: some people have responsibility for directing the activities of others. The status structure determines which persons have what rights and privileges. The prestige structure permits certain persons to expect deferential behavior from others. The friendship structure is based on feelings of interpersonal trust.

These systems of relationships overlap but are not identical. Each has an important effect upon communication in an organization, by influencing the expectations people have regarding who should communicate to whom about what in what manner. Now, how often do people openly and freely discuss these matters and come to agreement? Since these areas involve ranking of persons and invidious distinctions, they are commonly avoided. Yet disagreements and distorted perceptions about questions of relationship in an organization are the source of many communication difficulties.

What intensifies these communication problems is the fact that relationships among persons in an organization are in a continual state of flux.

Personnel losses, transfers, promotions and replacements are occurring. Decisions about new policies and procedures are being made, and often modify people's relationships. Some people are informed about changed relationships before others; some are not informed at all. Although it is common practice to communicate decisions to all the persons who are affected by them, the problem is often to determine who are the relevant persons. Unless we are extremely sensitive to the social structure of our organization, it is likely that we shall restrict communication too narrowly. The restrictive communication of decisions about change, however, can be extremely disruptive to any consensus people have about their relationships to one another, and thus can create for them problems of communication.

THE FLOW OF COMMUNICATION

Any solution of a communication problem must be based on analysis of the particular situation in which the problem occurs, and an application of general principles about communication. It is possible, on the basis of findings from research, to formulate a number of principles about the forces in an organization which direct the flow of communication.

You may have heard at one time or another that communication flows downward all right in an organization; the problem is to get communication from below. This is only partially true. In fact, any generalization that communication flows down, up, or across, is equally false. Communication is like a piece of driftwood on a sea of conflicting currents. Sometimes the shore will be littered with debris, sometimes it will be bare. The amount and direction of movement is not aimless, nor uni-directional, but a response to all the forces—winds, tides and currents—which come into play.

What forces direct communication in an organization? They are, on the whole, motivational forces. People communicate or fail to communicate in order to achieve some goal, to satisfy some personal need, or to improve their immediate situation. Let us examine briefly some of the evidence from research which supports this statement.

A study was made of the communication patterns among the personnel of a medium-sized government agency.[1] Everyone was included in the research, from the director to the janitor. It was found that people communicated far more to members of their own subgroups than to any other persons. They also preferred to be communicating to someone of higher status than themselves, and tried to avoid having communication with those lower in status than themselves. The only exception to this tendency was when a person had supervisory responsibilities, which removed his restraints against communicating with particular lower status persons. When people did communicate with others of the same status level in the organization, there was a strong tendency for them to select highly valued persons, and to avoid those they thought were making little contribution.

Let us see if we can find a principle which explains these results. The formal subgroupings in an organization are usually based upon joint work responsibilities. There are strong forces, therefore, to communicate with those whose work goals are the same as one's own. A supervisor can accomplish his work objectives only by having relatively frequent contact with his subordinates: and he probably would like to have more contact than he has. The people in an organization who are most valued for their ability to contribute are those who can give the best information and advice. People seek them out. These findings all seem to point to the same conclusion:

1. *In the pursuit of their work goals, people have forces acting upon them to communicate with those who will help them achieve their aims, and forces against communicating with those who will not assist, or may retard their accomplishment.*

In the midst of one study of a housing settlement,[2] a rumor swept through the community and threatened to disrupt the research. The investigators turned their attention to this rumor and were able to trace its path from person to person. They were trying to understand the forces which led people to communicate. Later on they tested their understanding by deliberately planting a rumor in an organization and again tracing its path by the use of informants.[3] They concluded that people will initiate and spread rumors in two types of situation: when they are confused and unclear about what is happening, and when they feel powerless to affect their own destinies. Passing on a rumor is a means of expressing and alleviating anxiety about the subject of the rumor.[4]

Let us consider one more fact before we draw a general conclusion from these findings. Studies in industry, in a hospital, and in a government agency all yield the same result: people want to speak to higher status rather than lower status persons.[5] Why are there these strong forces on people to direct their communications upwards? Higher status persons have the power to create for subordinates either gratifying or depriving experiences. These may take the form of tangible decisions and rewards, or perhaps merely expressions of approval and confidence. Lower status persons need reassurance about their superiors' attitudes, evaluations, and intentions toward them. We can conclude that:

2. *People have powerful forces acting upon them to direct their communication toward those who can make them feel more secure and gratify their*

needs, and away from those who threaten them, make them feel anxious, and generally provide unrewarding experiences.

People's needs largely determine content of their communication to others of different status. There is evidence that subordinates will often be reluctant to ask supervisors for help when they need it, because this might be seen as a threatening admission of their inadequacy.[6] And superiors tend to delete from their communications to subordinates any reference to their own mistakes or errors of judgment.[7] I am sure that these findings are in accord with the experiences that many of us have had in organizations.

A third principle which helps us understand the flow of communication is this:

3. *Persons in an organization are always communicating as if they were trying to improve their position.*

They may or may not be aware of their own behavior in this respect. But the evidence indicates that they want to increase their status, to belong to a more prestigeful group, to obtain more power to influence decisions, and to expand their authority.

It has been said that talking upwards is a gratifying substitute for moving upwards. Persons in an organization who are attracted to membership in a particular department or group will feel inclined to direct much more communication in that direction than will those who do not want to belong to it. If they are excluded or barred from membership and their desire to belong persists, they will increase their communication even further, as if this represented a substitute for actually moving into the desirable group.[8]

In a study of the role relationships of three types of professionals who work together in the mental health field [9]—psychiatrists, clinical psychologists, and psychiatric social workers—it was found that the direction, amount, and content of their communication to one another could be predicted largely from two factors. These were: their perception of the other professions' power relative to their own; and how satisfied they were with their own power position compared to that of the other groups. The general principle that forces act on persons to communicate so as to improve their relative position in the organization seems to be supported by all these findings.

THE CONSEQUENCES OF COMMUNICATION

Recent research also has something to tell us about the consequences that communication will have when various conditions exist within an organization. Again we find that it is not possible to state that a particular type of communication will always have the same effect, without specifying the conditions in which the generalization will hold true. At the present time, however, the evidence from research appears to warrant four general conclusions.

1. *The effect of any particular communication will depend largely upon the prior feelings and attitudes that the parties concerned have towards one another.*

Findings from a number of different studies support this statement. During World War II, hostile attitudes and negative stereotypes existed between the inhabitants of a housing project for industrial workers and members of the surrounding community. An action research project was undertaken to increase contact between these two groups of people.[10] It was found, however, that after increased contact the attitudes and feelings of these people had become polarized: those that were initially positive became more positive, and those that began by being negative became even more negative. The effect of stimulating greater contact could have been predicted only from a knowledge of the pre-existing attitudes and feelings.

In another study of the communication patterns in a large organization, it was found that increased communication did make people more accurate about others' opinions, but only when they initially trusted one another and already were in considerable agreement.[11] When people are in disagreement or do not trust one another, an increase in communication will not necessarily lead to greater understanding.

It was found in another study that frequent communication among personnel made working for the organization either more or less attractive for them. The mediating factor was whether or not the persons who were in constant communication valued each others' contribution to the work of the organization.[12]

2. *The effect of any particular communication will depend upon the pre-existing expectations and motives of the communicating persons.*

Executives of a large organization were asked to indicate on a check-list how much time they spent with each other, and the subject of their interaction.[13] In one-third of the answers they were in disagreement about the subject of their communication. For example, one reported that he had been discussing personnel matters with another; the latter thought they had been discussing questions of production. When these executives differed, each assumed that the problem with which he was personally most concerned was what they had really been talking about.

The subjects of this study were men with an engineering background. They consistently overestimated the amount of time executives spent on production matters and underestimated the amount of time spent on personnel problems. The impressions their communication made upon them had been shaped by their own goals and motives.

From this and other studies it seems clear that the consequences of communication are limited by people's interest in achieving certain effects, and lack of concern about achieving others. They will be inclined to remember and feel committed to those decisions which are consistent with their own expectations and motives.

3. *The effect of a superior's communication with a subordinate will depend upon the relationship between them, and how adequately this relationship satisfies the subordinate's needs.*

Communication between superior and subordinate often has consequences which neither of them anticipates nor welcomes. It is especially difficult to avoid problems of misinterpretations or ineffectiveness in this area.

In one organization it was found that some employees who received frequent communication from their supervisor became more accurately informed about their supervisor's real attitudes; but this was not true for other employees who also had constant contact with their supervisor.[14] The difference was traced to whether or not a supervisor said he trusted his subordinates. When he did not trust them, he was more guarded in what he said to them, revealing less of his true feelings. A lack of trust between superior and subordinate can thus act as a barrier to the creation of mutual understanding.

We have discussed how people's need for security directs their communication toward higher status persons in an organization. A study was conducted in a public utility company,[15] where it was possible to vary experimentally the kind of communication supervisors gave their subordinates. People became anxious and threatened in response to two different conditions: when communication from their supervisor was unclear, and when the supervisor was inconsistent in what he said from one time to another.

We have also pointed out that the persons in an organization tend to communicate as if they were constantly attempting to improve their positions. This is consistent with the finding that the experienced employees in an organization resent close supervision,[16] since it implies that their power and prestige are less than they want them to be.

The study of the senior staff members in a British engineering plant, referred to earlier, led to the discovery of a process of "status protection." When these men received instructions from their superiors, they often treated them as merely information or advice. In this manner they in effect achieved a relative improvement in their own position in the authority structure, by acting as if no one had the right to direct their activity.

Thus the findings from laboratory and field research point unequivocally to the supervisor-subordinate relationship as one of the crucial factors determining the effect of a supervisor's communication to subordinates. Another major factor is whether or not the subordinate stands alone in his relationship to the supervisor, or belongs to a group of peers in the organization.

4. *The effect of a superior's communication with a subordinate will depend upon the amount of support the subordinate receives from membership in a group of peers.*

An experimental study has demonstrated the remarkable effect of belonging to a group of equals on a subordinate confronted by a powerful and directive superior.[17] Being a member of a group decreased a person's feelings of threat and freed him to disagree with his supervisor and make counterproposals. The person who had the moral support of membership in a group reacted to his supervisor's communication with less defensive and more problem-oriented behavior.

There is a considerable body of evidence, too, that a group acts as a source of "social reality" for its members, providing them an opportunity to validate their ideas and opinions.[18] When communication from a superior is directed to a group as a whole rather than to isolated individuals, it is likely that more accurate transmission of information will be achieved.

PROBLEMS OF COMMUNICATION ARE OFTEN SYMPTOMATIC

From our discussion thus far, I think it should be clear that what we call communication problems are often only symptomatic of other difficulties which exist among persons and groups in an organization. To summarize what has been said or implied, I should like to point to four problems which people in organizations must solve in order to overcome barriers to communication.

1. *The problem of trust or lack of trust.* Communication flows along friendship channels. When trust exists, content is more freely communicated, and the recipient is more accurate in perceiving the sender's opinion.

2. *The problem of creating interdependence among persons: common goals and agreement about means for achieving them.* When persons have different goals and value systems, then it is especially important to create mutual understanding about needs and motives.

3. *The problem of distributing rewards fairly,* so that people's needs are being met, and so that they are motivated to contribute to the overall objectives of the organization. Nothing can be so restrictive of the free flow of ideas and information, for example, as the feeling that you may not obtain credit for your contribution.

4. The exceedingly important problem of *understanding and coming to common agreement about the social structure of the organization.* I can think of nothing which would facilitate more the free and accurate flow of communication in an organization than consensus about questions of work, authority, prestige and status relationships.

NOTES

[1] Jay M. Jackson, *Analysis of Interpersonal Relations in a Formal Organization,* Ph.D. Thesis, University of Michigan, 1953.

[2] Leon Festinger, Dorwin Cartwright, et al., "A Study of a Rumor: Its Origin and Spread," *Human Relations,* 1948, 1, pp. 464–486.

[3] Kurt Back, Leon Festinger, et al., "The Methodology of Studying Rumor Transmission," *Human Relations,* 1950, 3, pp. 307–312.

[4] For an illustration of this in a hospital setting, see: Jay Jackson, Gale Jensen, and Floyd Mann, "Building a Hospital Organization for Training Administrators," *Hospital Management,* September, 1956, p. 54.

[5] See Elliot Mishler and Asher Tropp, "Status and Interaction in a Psychiatric Hospital," *Human Relations,* 1956, 9, pp. 187–206; Jay Jackson, *Analysis of Interpersonal Relations in a Formal Organization,* Ph.D. Thesis, University of Michigan, 1953; Tom Burns, "The Directions of Activity and Communication in a Departmental Executive Group," *Human Relations,* 1954, 7, pp. 73–79.

[6] Ian Ross, *Role Specialization in Supervision,* Ph.D. Thesis, Columbia University, 1957.

[7] This finding is from an unpublished study of a public utility company by Alvin Zander.

[8] Experimental evidence exists for this statement in: Jay Jackson and Herbert Saltzstein, *Group Membership and Conformity Processes* (Ann Arbor: Research Center for Group Dynamics, University of Michigan, 1956), p. 89; see also: Harold Kelley, "Communication in Experimentally Created Hierarchies," *Human Relations,* 1950, 4, pp. 39–56.

[9] Zander, A., A. R. Cohen, and E. Stotland, *Role Relations in the Mental Health Professions* (Ann Arbor: Institute for Social Research, University of Michigan, 1957).

[10] Leon Festinger and Harold Kelley, *Changing Attitudes Through Social Contact* (Ann Arbor: Research Center for Group Dynamics, University of Michigan, 1951).

[11] Glen Mellinger, "Interpersonal Trust as a Factor in Communication," *Journal of Abnormal and Social Psychology,* 1956, 52, pp. 304–309.

[12] Jay Jackson, *op. cit.*

[13] Tom Burns, *op. cit.*

[14] Glen Mellinger, *op. cit.*

[15] Arthur Cohen, "Situational Structure, Self-Esteem, and Threat-Oriented Reactions

to Power." A chapter in Dorwin Cartwright, et al., *Studies in Social Power* (Ann Arbor: Research Center for Group Dynamics, University of Michigan, 1959).

[16] This finding is from an unpublished study by Jay Jackson, Jean Butman, and Philip Runkel of the communication patterns and attitudes of employees in two business offices.

[17] Ezra Stotland, "Peer Groups and Reaction to Power Figures." A chapter in Dorwin Cartwright, et al., *Studies in Social Power* (Ann Arbor: Research Center for Group Dynamics, University of Michigan, 1959).

[18] See, for example, Jay M. Jackson and Herbert D. Saltzstein, "The Effect of Person-Group Relationships on Conformity Processes," *The Journal of Abnormal and Social Psychology* (in press).

17

INFORMATION TECHNOLOGY AND DECENTRALIZATION *

John F. Burlingame

Are the middle manager and the decentralized organization doomed to extinction as the result of advances in information technology—or destined to take an even greater role in business?

What kinds of management problems are most likely to lend themselves to solution by the new data-handling techniques?

In what ways can data technology be used to simplify business complexities and distribute decision-making responsibility more widely?

What must the manager do to ensure that the new techniques are used to further the ends of the company and society?

Recent progress in information technology has been so rapid that various observers have predicted the elimination of middle managers and the reversal of the trend of the last decade toward decentralization in business.[1] Computers and the associated technologies, the argument runs, will make better decisions of the type now made by middle managers and will make them faster. Companies will find it possible to process and structure relevant information in such a comprehensive fashion and so quickly that decentralized responsibilities will be withdrawn and noncomputer decision making limited to a top-level elite in the organization. Apparently the manager's work in the future will be depersonalized and personal satisfaction will have to be found in activities pursued outside working hours.

If so, technological progress will have resolved some of business's most vexing problems. No longer will there be any need to sort out and evaluate the many human, social, and economic considerations hitherto important

* Reprinted from *Harvard Business Review*, November–December, 1961, pp. 121–126.

321

in operating and organizing a business. Rather, all there will be left to do is to climb on and ride the one band wagon harmonious with previously determined future events.

I believe it can be shown, however, that these conclusions are both dubious in themselves and unreliable as a basis for organizational action. Indeed, if we couple our experience in decentralized organizations with a realistic evaluation of the nature and extent of the future impact of information technology in such organizations, we can establish a very reasonable basis for concluding that decentralization and the middle manager are much more likely to *grow* and *flourish* than to wither and die in the decades ahead.

TYPES OF DECISIONS

For the purposes of our discussion, the concept of decentralization can be simply stated. Decision-making responsibility is assigned at the lowest point in the organization where the needed skills and competence, on the one hand, and the needed information, on the other hand, can reasonably be brought together. A great improvement is believed to result in any firm when the creative talents of responsible individuals are encouraged to develop in a climate of individual responsibility, authority, and dignity—a climate that is made possible by the decentralization of decision making.

This view of decentralization is fundamentally different from the mere application of traditional centralized managerial control concepts to smaller and more dispersed units of people. Confusion over this difference may well be a fundamental factor responsible for the earlier mentioned viewpoints predicting future trends away from decentralized organizations.

In assessing the future impact of information technology on decentralized business, some attention must be paid to the subject of decision making. The philosophy within which decisions are made distinguishes the organization which is centralized from the one which is not. The aspects of decision making that are important are (*a*) the way decisions are classified and (*b*) the way responsibility for them is assigned:

In any decision system we can identify two classes of decisions—those which can be predetermined by a rigorously defined selection process and those which cannot. The former are generally decisions concerning measurable and objective physical phenomena. The latter involve human beings and intangible, subjective human values; the balancing of social, moral, and economic values; and the assessment of situations in which information needs cannot be adequately anticipated or adequately filled.

In a centralized organization, the attempt is made to retain in as small a group as possible the responsibility for the latter type decisions and to delegate only the former. But in a decentralized organization, no attempt is made to separate the types of decisions in assigning responsibility; instead, the attempt is to relate all decisions to work purpose. Responsibility is assigned where the skills and competences, on the one hand, and the needed information, on the other, can reasonably be brought together.

Thus, in a centralized organization, the decision structure tends to be one where the decisions at the top are original and sensitive to human and social considerations; decisions at the bottom are more likely to be routine and insensitive to such considerations. By contrast, in a decentralized organization, no such division exists. Rather, all types of decisions are made throughout the organization at all levels. Only the breadth and complexity of impact tends to decrease from top to lower echelons in the organization.

Sources of Confusion

It should be noted that the use of the word decision to describe both of these classes of action is unfortunate and has caused much confusion in assessing the contribution of information technology to decision making. Trouble has also been caused by the term *computer decision making,* which has been applied in a glamorizing fashion to describe the application of computers to the more routine tasks. Although the terminology is new, the concept and its application substantially predate the high-speed electronic computer. For instance, the clock thermostat which turns on the furnace at 6:30 A.M. because the house temperature is below that preset for daytime operations is a mechanical "decision maker" in the same sense as the computer is when it computes and prints a bill for a customer. So is the regulating system for traffic lights which modifies the signal sequencing depending on volume of traffic, time of day, and day of week (and sometimes it factors in holidays, as well).

We now have many mechanical devices that carry out predetermined processes and actions. The additional advantage the high-speed electronic computer brings is its ability to handle a large number of variables in a complex process at high speed. Calling the action *computer decision making,* however, implies that a computer decides a man's salary because it prints out his monthly check. Such a description is, at the very least, misleading.

POTENTIAL AND LIMITATIONS

Information technology embraces the various techniques and disciplines (applied mathematics, simulation, electronic data processing, and so on) which can be and have been applied to the development of data in business. This technology has mushroomed in the past ten years with most of the practical application confined thus far to electronic data processing. However, enough theoretical and first-stage application work has been done in such areas as business simulation and computer duplication of human logical processes to envision that, ultimately, information technology will have a major impact on business. Yet, while the future impact will be great, there are factors in the growth of the technology and the evolution of business which will limit the nature and extent of the impact.

Effect of Industry Changes

One such factor is the expected increase in the complexity of business in the next few decades. When information technology was in its early development stage, a $1 billion sales volume point was a commonly accepted dividing line between the really large business and the "all-other" category. But when the technology eventually reaches a point of reasonable maturity, $10 billion or more in sales should represent such a dividing line.

In association with such a growth in sales we can expect an increase in complexity arising from such factors as increased product variety, additional manufacturing locations, foreign expansions, and the need for additional and diversified labor, which usually attend a significant volume increase. Simultaneously, the complexities arising from the changing role of industry in society—its relations with government, labor, and other segments of the economy—will undoubtedly also increase as they have during the past decade, and will require a host of new, different, difficult decisions.

When we view the impact of the advancing information technology on business, therefore, it would be naive to predict the outcome without taking into account the increased size and more diverse nature of the industrial world. Will the simplifications possible from applications of the new science outpace, keep abreast of, or fall behind trends making business more complicated? At the same time we need to be specific about the impact of data technology. To what extent do the kinds of situations to which it is amenable represent the total range of situations that must be handled in industry?

Most Likely Applications

The status of some current work in the computer application field might help in making an assessment. The prediction has been made, on the basis of this work, that a computer will be the world's chess champion within the next decade. What is significant here, as far as impact on business is concerned, is that it will take roughly a decade for enough progress to be made to handle a problem which has no unknowns—even where the rules of play are completely defined, where the scope of action is limited, where the relationships between the elements are explicit, where there is but a single, defined objective, where the value system is determined and unambiguous, and where the problem is precisely the same now as it was 100 years ago and as it will be 100 years from now.

Suppose that we look at chess as a complicated variation of ticktacktoe —the complication arising from increases in the number and kinds of relationships, but with no reduction in definition. Then we have a reasonable basis for speculating that, during the next two decades, data technology will have the greatest impact on those facets of business where the complication is due primarily to the number and kinds of explicitly known relationships. It is highly likely, for example, that an electronic computer program will be the basis for scheduling production, ordering material, and allocating output in the case of some products which historically have had highly predictable patterns of demand.

The Human Element

Such programs, however, will contain as one of their elements the limits within which scheduling, ordering, and allocating are to be computer-determined. When these limits are exceeded, as happens when the data inputs indicate environmental changes, the expansion of established patterns, or factors requiring human value consideration, then the program will shut the computer down awaiting human instruction. For example:

A large industrial company is developing an automated information system designed to permit its salesmen (located throughout the United States) to determine immediately the availability of thousands of products and, if an order is placed, when and from where an item will be shipped. This system, using the latest techniques and equipment, will keep continuous records of all products and update them each time an order is placed, a shipment made, or product manufactured. When an order is placed, the system—in accordance with the rules of its design—will automatically process it, selecting the warehouses best able to fill it.

The first step in the automatic processing of an order in this system is to check the credit status of the customer. If the order, together with the unpaid balance, is less than the customer's credit limit, the complete order process is carried out and the proper warehouse is automatically instructed when and how to make the shipment. But if the credit limit is exceeded, this information is printed out and the system holds up processing of the order until it receives further instruction.

This company considers the decision involved in selecting a course of action when a customer's order exceeds his credit limit to have enough important intangible considerations so that human judgment should be exercised in each case and so that the disposition should be made humanly, not mechanically.

Similarly, when the business situation is one where the market is being developed, the product is new, and the distribution channels include perhaps a variety of foreign markets (all with volatile characteristics), then the information-handling techniques, while providing a factual base, will still fall very short of the requirements for taking action. The final assessment of the risk and the decision to act must be made by a manager integrating the factual information with the less well-defined elements in the situation.

Since in a great number of businesses this last kind of situation predominates, and since the number of such situations increases with the growth in complexity, we can anticipate that the major long-term impact of the new technology will be to improve the basis of human decision making rather than to make decision making routine and mechanical.

Now let us proceed to the next part of our problem. If we couple experience with decentralization and the application of information technology with likely trends in business and data technology, what conclusions can be drawn about the probable results of their interaction over the next few decades?

GREATER DECENTRALIZATION

Counter to many arguments, the anticipated advances in information technology, in my opinion, can *strengthen* decentralization in those businesses that have adopted it and will encourage *more* managements to experiment and to operate in accordance with the decentralization philosophy.

A great many businessmen are repelled by the idea that most people in industry can be used only to execute, within narrowly defined limits, the orders of an elite group who alone can exercise judgment, imagination, creativity, and intuition. They feel that this concept shuts the door on a major resource—the creative and imaginative talents and the growth potential of large numbers of people. On the other hand, these same businessmen recognize the need to guide the use of creativity and imagination so that the sum total will not be dissipated inefficiently, but will be applied in a disciplined fashion to achieve the selected goals of the organization.

This is where information becomes vital. Employees have to have the pertinent facts if they are to see clearly the interrelationships between their contribution and the contribution of others, and to act, on their own initiative, in a manner which will serve the best interests of all. The advancing data technology can make remarkable contributions to meeting this need. *This, in fact, may be its most significant feature.*

But to succeed in this way, information technology needs constantly to be guided away from its Babel-like preoccupation with designing superhuman intellects to make superhuman decisions, and brought back to its primary business purpose: contributing to the simplification of business complexities. Because this is a more difficult purpose to achieve and because it means more focus on steady, day-by-day accomplishment and less on intoxicating expectations, shifting the emphasis to simplification will not be an easy task.

Pattern Identification

Today advanced techniques and large computers are coupled in a great assault on complex systems. Systems are analyzed microscopically and synthesized; over-all performance is predicted by considering the behavior of each element. This approach is fine as far as it goes, but often just does not go far enough.[2]

What is needed, and what information technology *can* produce, if properly guided by the businessman, is the next step: simplification through pattern identification. This step can provide the kind of information which permits individuals to act responsibly on their own initiative. It also can make it possible to sort out those things which can best be done humanly from those best done mechanically, in order to obtain most effective use of both human and machine resources. Thus:

One of the products of a manufacturing business was an instrument device. Some 85,000 units of 400 different models were manufactured annually with no apparent stable patterns of market preference for any particular model. Each model was manufactured to order, and shipment averaged about six weeks from the date the order was placed. All of the paper work involved in processing the order was originally handled manually, but, with the advent of electronic computing equipment, it was no trick to convert to machines.

However, those responsible for the conversion in this instance were not satisfied simply to mechanize an existing complex human routine. They felt that before a major investment was made in mechanizing the paper flow, an effort should be made to determine whether or not there were fundamental patterns in this operation which ought to be taken into account.

Although there was no apparent stable pattern of demand on a model basis, they found from an analysis of the major components (which, when assembled, made up the models) that there were significantly greater requirements for some components than for others, and that a high degree of stability existed in this pattern. They determined, by a process of regrouping and redefining components, that of the 1,800,000 components of 280 different varieties required annually, some 99% could be classed under only 84 types.

With this new understanding, they were able to change the basic concept of the business from one where each model was fabricated to order to one where 84 types of components were manufactured in more or less continuous production, 196 being stocked in inventory. Final assembly alone was accomplished subsequent to the receipt of an order. The average delivery cycle went from six weeks to four days. More important, from the point of view of this discussion, an information structure was developed showing how families of models were related through the identical components in their composition. The resulting simplification made possible better and faster decisions and permitted further delegation of decision making to lower organizational echelons.

Prior to the work described, realistic forecasting on a model-by-model basis was just about impossible with or without a computer. Decisions on advance ordering were difficult to make and, because of the lack of pertinent information, were made relatively high in the organization. Subsequent to the simplification work, and with the business process organized around component types rather than end-product models, forecasts by family were all that were needed. Not only were these forecasts much easier to make and inherently much more accurate, but they permitted the responsibility for advance ordering to be placed at a lower organizational echelon, one nearer the level of actual manufacture since the information could now be made available for decisions at this level.

The contribution of information technology was increased manifold in this case by a recognition of the responsibility, not only to find a way to carry out complex operations more quickly, but also to find a way to simplify an operation so that a more efficient total system could be developed, one in which both the human and the machine resources could be most effectively utilized.

Dispelling Illusions

Insisting on simplification as the desirable end result is a task which must fall to businessmen. The danger of a parochial viewpoint is great, and one detects a strong tendency on the part of some to consider the complicated model as itself the "goal" and a kind of monument to their technical skills. In some instances the lack of widespread knowledge about the technology and its associated jargon is even used as a sort of witch doctor's cloak behind which to hide a growing empire, supposedly capable, ultimately, of making many of the businessman's decisions.

Businessmen, along with the technical experts, have a responsibility to ensure the technology's being used in a manner to further the ends of the company. Defining the business purposes to which the technology should be applied is essential to discharging this responsibility and cannot be left to the technologist alone.

Help for Middle Managers

How will information technology fortify the role of the middle manager in a decentralized business? As stated earlier, a characteristic of such a firm is a decision structure where the breadth of impact of the decision, rather than the judgment content, varies in the organization. Both upper-level managers and managers at the first level are deeply involved in problems where judgment and human values are the important elements. They are concerned with situations where the decisions cannot be anticipated, the information needs predicted, or the decision elements quantified. And this is equally true of many functional specialists reporting to these managers.[3]

The stock in trade of these managers is their ability, as leaders, to obtain balanced results through the work of other people. To perform adequately here requires the ability to synthesize information, intuition, judgment, and values into courses of action and decisions which will produce the balanced results. It is reasonable to anticipate that the new technology will, over the next few decades, make a major contribution by providing such men with powerful tools to accomplish their work better. Their ability to exercise initiative and judgment responsibly should be strengthened. This effect should far outweigh in importance any tendency of computers to eliminate jobs where the nature of decisions is mechanical, especially when it is remembered that the growth in the complexity of business is increasing the need for effective managers.

IMPACT IN CENTRALIZED FIRM

I have been discussing the situation of the company with a philosophy of decentralization. But what about the firm with the opposite concept of operations?

There are two paths along which centralized businesses are likely to move as a result of the impact of information technology. Thus:

If the managers are committed to their philosophy and if the purpose for which the technology is employed is limited to the mechanization and improved efficiency of the operation as it exists, then the likely evolution will be along those lines predicted by a number of writers. Under these conditions, organizational reconsolidations will be encouraged and the ability of the few who have nonroutine, decision-making responsibility to make better decisions will be enhanced. Many currently in middle management will be replaced. Because men in this group were needed for their knowledge of complex but now obsolete routines, relocation will be difficult for them.

On the other hand, some businesses have adopted the centralized decision-making philosophy because of the difficulties involved in achieving a harmonious unifying of individual creativity and initiative. Here the technology can be used as a tool for simplification rather than simply mechanization, and will provide a basis for the adoption of a decentralized approach as a more desirable and more effective way.

CONCLUSION

It seems hardly conceivable that the social forces which are present today and which will be important in the future could permit the separation of society into two classes—one, an elite corps of thinkers (top managers, technologists, or some combination of the two), and the second, all other human beings.

It is a simple matter to conclude, as some writers have, that information technology has the potential to force the entire organization—from the middle manager on down—to satisfy personal needs and aspirations off the job. However, with a rapidly increasing percentage of our population acquiring advanced education, it is difficult to believe that the members of this group who go into business will be satisfied with spending their daily working hours, comprising a great part of their lifetime, in pursuits devoid of intellectual satisfaction. It is more than likely that they will attempt to curtail the freedom to act of businessmen or any other group that tries to force such a condition on them.

Since at least one sound, well-conceived concept—decentralization— provides an economically and socially acceptable alternative, it appears that the nub of the situation is not in the technology but in the wisdom with which managers apply it. Businessmen should have had enough experience with the Technocrats, on the one hand, and the self-seeking, public-be-damned Robber Barons, on the other, to realize that continued progress and growth lie in the best match of economic efficiency and social responsibility. This need is met by decentralization, coupled with an advancing information technology.

If, during the next decade or two, we do not see a continued trend in the direction of business decentralization, we must look for the failure, not in any unalterable laws of technological advance, but in the decisions of businessmen.

NOTES

[1] See Ida Russakoff Hoos, "When the Computer Takes Over the Office," *HBR* July–August 1960, p. 102; and Herbert A. Simon, *The New Science of Management Decision* (New York, Harper and Brothers, 1960.)

[2] See W. Ross Ashby, *An Introduction to Cybernetics* (New York, John Wiley and Sons, Inc., 1956).

[3] Melvin Anshen, "The Manager and the Black Box," *HBR* November–December 1960, p. 85.

18

CLOSING THE COMMUNICATIONS GAP *

Thorrel B. Fest

Man is the victim of his own curiosity, and in a dynamic universe he must always expect to be stretched and pushed as he seeks to respond to what the universe offers. Unless or until science comes to an end because all that there is to know has been discovered—which seems too improbable to consider—we face an unlimited procession of discoveries and consequent adjustments. It is about the communication of those discoveries and the understanding of the needs for adjustment that you people are concerned. I should like to consider with you some aspects and implications of this process as they bear upon our society and perhaps upon the unique relationship between scientists themselves and between scientist and layman. If you interpret my message in one way, it will have overtones of pessimism. If you place it in a larger framework, I believe it can only be optimistic.

I can think of no better way to launch this discussion than the observation of Walter Orr Roberts when he pointed out: ". . . the aim of science after all is simply to know, to understand, to appreciate . . . . (we) must bridge the gap between scientist and layman, between these two parts of society which, at a time when the need for understanding has become so great, understand each other so little. Until the gap is bridged, democratic societies will scarcely be able to understand the uses of sciences, or to protect themselves from the danger that arises from the assumption of too much power by those that wrap themselves in the cloak of scientific wisdom . . ." [1]

It seems paradoxical that a major contributor to human understanding has a major problem in communicating that understanding. C. P. Snow describes the difficulty well in his book, *The Two Cultures and the Scientific*

* Reprinted from *Proceedings of the 1962 Institute in Technical and Industrial Communications,* Colorado State University, pp. 93–99.

Revolution: "Constantly, in my everyday life," he writes, "I felt I was moving among two groups—comparable in intelligence, identical in race, not grossly different in social origins, earning about the same income, who have almost ceased to communicate at 'all—who in intellectual, moral, and psychological climate have so little in common that instead of going from Burlington House to South Kensington, Chelsea, one might have crossed the ocean. In fact, one had travelled much farther than across the ocean —because after a few thousand Atlantic miles, one found Greenwich Village talking precisely the same language as Chelsea, and both having as much communication with MIT as though the scientists spoke nothing but Tibetan . . ." [2]

The ramifications of this paradox are clear, but I should like to invite you to consider several aspects of this problem from a slightly different point of view than might at first seem germane to your immediate pressures. In so doing, I am considering the reluctance of some scientists to communicate at all, and will offer suggestions as to how scientists might become better communicators as well as how communicators might become better scientists. (With your permission and for brevity, I should like to use the terms "science" and "scientist" to embrace the entire area and all persons that it would appropriately include and shall use this terminology in the discussion which follows.)

The problem of communication of scentific-technical information includes three aspects. First is the *generation* of the information which depends, of course, upon the goals of the work or types of information to be sought and the conditions under which such research efforts are carried out. Obviously, these will significantly affect both the quantity and the quality of the product.

Once generated, the information must be managed and *organized*. This, then, becomes the second problem.

The third aspect concerns the wise *use* of the information once it has become available. Clearly, its existence and dissemination may be stimuli to further investigation and relationships on the professional level. Its dissemination to and intelligent interpretation by the non-scientific public are major problems which must be solved if our scientific and technological developments are to continue and be socially productive. Certainly the wise use of such information is the basis for social, economic, and political decisions having both national and international implications.

These three aspects of the communication problem—generation, organization and use—are functionally related and should not be considered in isolation. I will also attempt to deal with three structural and personal factors that affect the scientist, the engineer, the technicians, the administrator or the scientific communications experts as they work within this broad area. These are: (1) Communication among scientific colleagues; (2) communication between scientists and non-scientific public; and (3) why it is imperative that the scientist accept responsibility to become a better communicator.

In considering these questions or problems, it may be helpful to examine the nature of communication and of the individual most intimately related to the information—the scientist. What helpful concepts should be noted about the process and the person?

If communication is anything, it is a social event. This truism may require no elaboration, but it does plead for recognition. Our civilization and its technology are predicated on a social structure that has been and must continue to be held together and sustained by millions and millions of messages of all sorts. The basic purpose of such messages or communications has been the pointing out of relationships among two or more things, events, or concepts. It is thus that understanding is approached. When we are concerned about relating entities our communication is relevant. When we lose sight of this concern, for whatever reason, our communication is inappropriate. Thus, even in the most pure, independent and isolated efforts of the scientist, there always exists the potential of communicating with others and the potential resulting effect which his discoveries have upon the other members of the society of which he is a part.

The true scientist has been in the forefront of the struggle for the freest possible exchange of information among and between all peoples. He deeply desires that the channels be numerous, be open, be free. But the process is not a thing apart from the man, and in our modern world the scientist and his discipline have attained a special role or status. This entire matter of status or role is not one of the scientist's choice, but results from circumstances. Yet it cannot be ignored.

". . . The caricature of the absent-minded scientist in his white smock is vanishing from our modern folklore . . . Scientists in general probably have achieved a higher level of respect in society than at any time in history . . ." In fact and in hope, our society looks to the scientist as a semi-superman. He makes a fundamental and critical contribution to our material well-being. His research maintains and improves our standard of living. The scientist has helped extend human life, done much to free it from disease and pain and has played a major part in helping us to understand the nature of man in the universe.

In addition, the scientist has become the backbone of our national security. His discoveries and applications not only modernize the fighting equipment for the individual G.I., but from his theorizing and his laboratories evolve the radar screens, the missiles, the analysis of weapons systems and the predictions or speculations as to the outcome of potential military actions.

Without belaboring the cause and effect relationships, it seems clear that the scientist has become a powerful and pervasive force in our society, and this position obviously affects him and his communication. He is a high status individual. He earns more money than many of his peers. He often works in special or more desirable surroundings. He may be engaged in mysterious or even classified projects. His activities and his utterances may carry a halo effect entirely disproportionate to his desires, his intent or the intrinsic worth of the utterance. If he does not exercise great restraint and apply to his self-evaluation the same objectivity which he uses in his laboratories, his communication either about his work or himself may become unrealistic.

Against this background, let us turn first to the conditions under which the scientist communicates with his colleagues in professional working relationships. In modern society the explosion of scientific-technical information is to a large extent the product of a highly organized and dynamically directed effort. The contemporary scientist has become a part of a semi-impersonal organization that affects his life, his work and his attitudes—and consequently, his communication. The physical resources which his work requires are seldom available to the single individual. Instead, they come from the corporation, the university, the government or the foundation.

The human resources—the brains and bodies required—are so numerous and of such special development that the concept of team research has replaced the individual worker. Only a few of the exceptionally fortunate (or perhaps unfortunate) are able to become directors or administrators.

Communication must take place with those who affect the achievement of goals or work. But this is not easy because the organized complex laboratory or development division is often beset by the same problem that faces the educational or business organization; and that is that communication must proceed through layers. Inevitably there are both inaccuracy and inefficiency as the number of layers or filters through which this information must pass increases. The resulting frustrations and conditioning occur wherever the individual may be in the hierarchy. They bear with brutal force upon the director and the new team member alike. They cannot help but have a stultifying influence upon certain types of communication.

With increasing frequency the problems, projects and goals are those of the organization and are evaluated by the leader. At certain stages in his career, the individual scientist may discriminate between organizations or laboratories on the basis of his particular interests and desires, but his frame of reference will of necessity be molded by the organization of which he becomes a part. His attitudes and beliefs about his work in general and his projects in particular are inevitably influenced by his environment. These forces bear upon him by hour, day, week and year.

Within any organizations are independent and overlapping sub-groups —divisions, committees, teams. Like all of us, the scientist tends to communicate with those closest to him in a spatial or geographical sense and with those closest to him in a substantive sense. Thus, he may create an increasing amount of isolation not only from the lay public but even from specialists in other scientific or technical areas. This produces what the sociologist or psychologist term "in-groups" where communication among individuals of a highly specialized nature using a particular and often unique vocabulary may result in the extension of working relationships to social relationships. The stimulus of interaction with able and dynamic colleagues in a special area may have serious limitations, for the stimulus of interaction with other personalities may not only be lessened, it may eventually be avoided. We may in some instances reach a stage comparable to the old man who said to his wife, "All the world is queer except thee and me. And sometimes I think thou are a little queer!"

Each of these sub-groups will have its own image and value system. Thus, there intrudes the problem of relationships among and between scientist and administrator, technical writer, or other competing scientist. Communication between these persons and groups may not have the same meaning because orientations will differ.

Within the organization, each sub-group will have its demand for loyalty and allegiance. As the organization increases in size, takes on special responsibilities, becomes committed to particular goals or in other ways defines its character, these groups become more numerous and powerful and it becomes increasingly difficult and perhaps impossible for each scientist member to understand and relate appropriately to those policies, programs and individuals that affect him and his work. There are well-known instances where the scientist must undertake work without knowing its ultimate potential for use even if his special efforts are successful. It may be difficult to explain to him the reordering of priorities and personnel. The intricacies of the total project and the factors to be considered in evaluating the parts may have to be accepted as matters of faith.

Without proper management, these complex conditions may tend to stifle communication that has creative potential. They may tend to channel effort and communication, they may tend to dictate an adjustment that is less than desirable and perhaps, worst of all, they may tend to result in the solidification of the in-group communication both within the field and within the particular sub-area or sub-activity. A major danger may lie in the auto-persuasion on the part of the scientist that the particular and specific thing he is doing is both good and necessary, and that he should do more of it. Thus, he may become so engaged in building his own house that both his personal and social potential are not fully developed.

And we should not leave the problem without mentioning in passing the effect of the mountain of paperwork—the paper blizzard—that seems to become a part of our contemporary society and which certainly produces some unique and often violent reactions on the part of scientists. I refer here not to the substantive reports but to the requisitions, justifications, interim progress reports, personnel surveys and all the other matters that the organization may feel to be necessary but which the scientist may regard as an abomination.

Lastly, scientists and others in the organization have many structural relations which are always in flux. These may relate to work or task, prestige, power, friendship, etc. Some areas such as prestige may not be discussed openly but the impact is felt. Dr. Jacob L. Halberstam told a national health forum audience "One professional is this high on the ladder because he gets paid X number of dollars. Another has such and such civil service status or social status." The problem is accentuated by the position which professions claim for themselves. It has been alleged that there is a professional pecking order among the associations. For example, in areas where responsibility may overlap, Dr. Halberstam makes the point that ". . . Frequently, jealousies become so intense that professionals don't speak to each other. There have even been instances of professionals deliberately withholding information until a case conference, when one professional suddenly reveals his information to display his knowledge, to show off his know-how, and to put his colleagues at a disadvantage." [3] Clearly, such relationships between individuals and groups determine who gets what information and how this information is accepted.

These are all practical considerations that affect the scientist. He may adjust by insulating himself from those irritating, frustrating or insoluble imponderables. For some individuals there may come the tendency, conscious or otherwise, to restrain, safeguard or in other ways control certain areas or types of information because in simple terms, such control (whether it be held by the scientist, the educator, the administrator, or the witch doctor) provides the individual with a sense of power and security not readily available through other means.

In contrast, some individuals are unable to either accept the information available or to place it in proper relationship. An interesting account is reported by a senior military officer responsible for the maintenance of jet planes when he described the inability of a fellow officer to accommodate himself to the conditions under which technical information was available. Having crawled into a jet engine to inspect turbine buckets on the rotors, the senior officer was attempting to point out where failures might occur and how their beginnings might be detected. Naturally, this was a dirty, dark, confining space, with sharp and burning fumes making it thoroughly unpleasant. The second officer gave verbal evidences of understanding, but something prompted the senior officer to turn, even with some difficulty, to look at him, only to discover with considerable shock that the other man's eyes were tightly closed!

Another illustration is drawn from the personal experience of working with a military officer who was summoned by his commanding general to report on the status of a problem related to the operation of a certain type of aircraft involved in flying regular patrols. A significant number of major failures had occurred, endangering not only the lives of crew members but also threatening to force the temporary cancellation of this important operation. It is undoubtedly true that the officer summoned to report knew more about the particular patrol operation and its problems than any other man in the command. He had been involved in the conception of the idea and had been active in all phases including planning, training, flying, maintaining and evaluating its work. He had, in fact, already determined the cause of the difficulty, had taken the necessary corrective steps to maintain the patrol and had even instituted long range action to further eliminate problems of this type. In short, he had nothing but success to report. Yet psychologically, he was so involved in what had happened and so fearful of communicating to a superior officer that he lost sight of his important message of success and recounted in great detail all of the background and difficulties leading up to his solution. His major problem was perception—of himself, his accomplishments and his commanding officer. The motives of communicators are important factors here. For instance, the private and public goals of the administrator and the expressed goals of his company, laboratory or group sometimes require major accommodation. When the scientist's duties are changed from those of research worker or designer to those of executive or administrator, does he continue to see himself in his old position, in his new position, or does he suffer from ambivalence?

Communication between superior and subordinate is another internal problem area. We generally tend to communicate with the people who are most likely to help us satisfy our needs. This may mean that a superior communicates with subordinates in order to get work done or otherwise meet demands placed upon him. The subordinate, in turn, may communicate with the superior about markedly different things such as the modifications or even reduction of his work, the providing of special arrangements, the granting of favors, or requests for favorable evaluation. Certainly he communicates about the achievement of his accepted work goals, but this may be only a part of his need. For example, a study of communication direction in three different organizations [4]—industrial, military and academic—indicated that most individuals, regardless of their level or status in the organization, reported that their communications were mostly with those at a higher level. It would be interesting to know how those at any given lower level ever received any information! Obviously, communication does not always go up, but these people perceived it as being up. Another special instance concerns the attitude which engineering executives demonstrate when receiving orders from superiors. A significant number treated these not as directions but as suggestions, and some disregarded them entirely. This may be a reflection of the high status in which such persons regard themselves. Whatever it may be, it suggests a high element of ego protection.

Next, let us examine the nature and importance of the communication between scientists and our society.

Clearly, it is not enough that scientists communicate among themselves. With respect to certain types of knowledge, there must be the widest possible diffusion and understanding. *This can only be achieved when effective two-way communication has been established between the scientist and the non-scientific public.* The communication specialist has special opportunities and responsibilities in this area.

The general justification for such exchange will probably arouse little argument, but the implications of the ever-widening gap between the specialist and the layman merit exploration. To the degree that the scientist, the engineer and the technician become separated not only from their counterparts in the humanities, the arts and the social studies, but from the great mass of the public as well, integration of these critical areas and hence our sense of purpose and direction are weakened.

Robert Oppenheimer expressed this well when he wrote in *Harpers* for October 1958: "Scientific knowledge has become the property of specialized communities . . . who by and large pursue their own way with growing intensity further and further from their roots in ordinary life." [5] Thus, it is that many of our most able people may be inarticulate, timid and ineffectual in contributing to our democratic society.

It seems imperative that people *must know more about the concepts and fact structures of the physical and natural sciences* for it is within the laws and applications of these that man must make one of his major adjustments. It seems equally clear that such communication will not be effective at the level of high abstractions. People at every level would profit from the concepts, principles and analogies derived from science and applied to human problems. Doctor Oppenheimer further underscored this point when he said:

". . . generally the new things we have learned in science and specifically in atomic physics do provide us with valid and relevant and greatly needed analogies to human problems lying outside the present domain of science or its present borderlands. . . . Analogy, often of great depth and scope in which views have been created or substantiated in some scientific enterprise are similar to those which might be held with regard to metaphysical, political and ethical problems." [6]

He goes on in a later article to which reference has been made:

". . . For example, in my opinion, it is almost impossible to explain what the fundamental principle of relativity is about, and this is even more true of the quantum theory. It is only possible to use analogies to evoke some sense of understanding. . . . Scientific knowledge today is mostly new; it has not been digested." [7]

There is a further practical problem of the serious lag between the diffusion of scientific information that exists and the translation of this information into appropriate action. Not all the responsibility for the personal and public persuasion should fall on the scientist, but the question may well be raised as to whether he should assume more responsibility than at present.

Communication about the nature and implication of scientific advances has generally been left to the public relations consultant, and the social worker. Admitting and recognizing the notable exceptions, there is no one in such a unique position as the scientist to communicate with authority and clarity in this important area. We know much about preventive medicine. Yet the transmission of information about these implications has often been relegated to those on the periphery of medical science. There have at times been important developments in mechanical and electrical machines, appliances and related items, but the organization scientist has often had to remain mute in the face of an economy geared to planned obsolescence.

Whatever the program or project in which the scientist works, he must ultimately draw his support from the people. Currently, the belief in and support for science is relatively strong. This is appropriate, but I suggest the support derives from *faith, fear* and *economic materialism*. These are powerful forces and will undoubtedly continue to be operative, but as the scientist is dedicated to objectivity and reason, so it seems that his ultimate support and achievement might be enhanced if the public trust were based upon deeper and broader understanding of his work.

Perhaps one example will illustrate the point. We are all familiar in principle, if not in detail, with the various electronic screens that ring our continent to provide warning against either air breathing or ballistic missile attack. Those with technical knowledge and/or professional judgment understand the limitations of such devices. It would be interesting to compare by some type of attitude study the relative degrees of faith which electrical engineers and the lay public place in this system. If the electronic screen should fail in any significant degree, who would the public blame?

One of the major revolutions, of which even some of the participants are not aware, is that of agricultural technology. Some people have suggested this is more significant in its impact than the industrial revolution was in former times. Those specialists concerned with generating new methods, species and equipment are living and working in one atmosphere—that of the agricultural college or the large industrial organization. Those concerned with communicating this information to the mass of farm folk have not only the problem of what to communicate, but also choosing the personnel and the media to employ. In spite of all the channels available—extension workers, television, pamphlets, newspapers, etc.—the diffusion of information still remains painfully slow with respect to large segments of the population, and one of the most effective means yet discovered is still the neighboring farmer across the fence. The acceptance of such information and its implications is a problem for still another group—namely those who must provide increasing quantities of agricultural credit for the farm operator. What this means to the average consumer as he shops in the supermarket or reads about the costs of government farm programs is even less well understood.

What then can be said about the orientation, attitudes and opportunities of the scientist in this difficult communication situation? He, too, has his problems and many of the forces affecting his communication within the organization operate here. To be sure, he faces the very difficult task of translating special and complex ideas and materials into more simple and meaningful terms. It is equally true that such efforts may tear him from his laboratory or library, but we have notable examples of scientific leaders who have been able to communicate with the public effectively and profitably. Their names are numerous and any listing here would be unjust by the omissions it would necessitate. This crisis—an external one—may be more significant than the internal one.

The antiseptic and detached attitude of some individuals in the scientific and technical areas is illustrated by one person's experience while screening prospective faculty for a school being set up for American troops following the end of World War II hostilities. It was necessary to recruit some teachers from the native Germans and in interviewing them, it was important to determine their political affiliation or association. My friend tells of interviewing a man in the physical sciences, who when asked about his relation to the Nazi party, his sympathies with it, his knowledge of its program and his sense of responsibility and desire to oppose its practices, merely shrugged his shoulders and replied: "It could be no concern of mine. I do not deal with politics. I am a scientist."

Lest we judge the scientist too harshly, it is well to consider how he thinks, reacts, and relates. Again Dr. Roberts provides helpful insight when he points out that: ". . . The scientist can never fully understand what he sees, and therefore he must settle for partial understanding, incompleteness and tentativeness. . . . This makes the scientist's communication with the rest of society frustrating and difficult; the layman, who is often less aware of the tentativeness of perception, expects more from science than science is prepared to give him, and therefore he fails to see why the scientist insists on such constant, careful qualification. On the other hand, if scientists did not qualify their statements carefully, they would then deserve the criticism of Anthony Standen, who said in his book, *Science is a Sacred Cow,* that 'the world is divided into scientists who practice the art of infallibility and nonscientists who are taken in by it.' . . ." [8]

We are again reminded of C. P. Snow's dual worlds and the unrealistic expectations of the inhabitants of each.

Now let us briefly treat the last point which deals with the scientist's responsibilities to understand the nature of communication and develop his own personal proficiency in this fundamental process.

There is ample evidence to indicate that he regards communication as important but generally prefers to leave this to someone else. He will often propose that specialists be hired to relieve him of this responsibility. In some cases he is suspicious of the individual who is highly verbal and may actually feel that to initiate discussion of his work and its significance outside his professional skill is political, unscientific and perhaps even base.

But whatever may be the contribution of the specialist in communication, there still remains the fundamental need for the scientist to develop his communicative skills to appropriate levels for it is thus that his ideas and his contributions may be known. It is thus that his needs as a scientist and an individual may be expressed. It is thus that he must interact not only with his professional colleagues, but with the organization of which he is a part and the society to which he belongs. It is thus that his individual self-realization may be most fully developed and as a receiver of communications, he must be able to contribute through understanding of the process and the problems faced by the individual who is generating messages. Only from such a background of understanding and experience can he secure to himself the necessary knowledge, insights, and attitudes.

Communication truly is a social event and the isomorphisms for the scientist cannot be created for him by the communication specialist, by his group leader or by any other individual. In fact, they cannot be created by him alone. They can only be created by the skillful inter-action of two or more communicators.

What then can be said about the structural and personal factors in the crisis of communication of scientific-technical information? What action can be taken to minimize the difficulties?

First, *there must be heightened concern for the human and organizational elements as well as the great necessity to systemize and handling of information.* Secondly, *there must be an acceptance of responsibility by each individual for understanding and improving his own effectiveness in communication.*

Thirdly, there is critical need to support *basic research concerning communication in all of its significant forms.* It is truly surprising that we take for granted the nature and use of this most fundamental of all activities upon which our social organization is built. Such research is, in every sense, truly a part of the field of science and its exploration will require far more generous support than is now available.

Finally, scientists might *draw upon research and resources outside the immediate area of their activity for analogies and improvement of their communication.* Conferences such as this are significant beginnings. I sincerely hope that additional meetings may be held at the national and regional levels. Seminars studying the communication process and its applications for the scientist might well be a part of every laboratory development program or industrial organization. I sincerely believe that it is in such approaches that the communication specialist as well as individuals from related areas can make contributions of more far reaching effect than would be possible if the scientist were to delegate increasingly long segments of his communication activity to someone else.

If the gap, not only between scientists, but between scientists and laymen, is to be closed, we must commit ourselves to this task. Without specifically planning for such closure, the job will not be done. Our plan must include both the scientist and the layman, for important as are the specialists in scientific-technical communication, it is neither possible nor socially desirable that the burden rest solely on their shoulders.

The consequences of not closing this gap are intolerable. One of the prime facts of life today is the explosive impact of science. Through it, man has acquired power of incredible potential. He constructs mechanisms and machines of bewildering complexity that help him overcome problems on the one hand, while creating additional problems on the other. Accompanying social change is accelerated, and our power to control that change is so immense that we have no alternative but to direct our every resource to the fullest possible understanding and the democratic determination of our destiny.

NOTES

[1] Roberts, W. O.; *Scientists and Society;* Adult Leadership; 10: No. 4, 96–7 ff., October 1961.

[2] Snow, Charles P.; *The Two Cultures and the Scientific Revolution;* Cambridge University Press, New York, 1959, p. 51.

[3] Neal, Helen; *Better Communications for Better Health;* Columbia University Press, New York, 1962, pp. 223 and XIII.

[4] Goetzinger, C. and Valentine, Milton A.; "Communication Patterns, Interactions and Attitude of Top-Level Personnel"; unpublished study—University of Colorado, 1961.

[5] Oppenheimer, Robert A.; *The Tree of Knowledge;* Harpers 217:55–60, October 1958 (p. 57).

[6] Oppenheimer, Robert A.; *Science and the Common Understanding;* Simon & Schuster, New York, 1954, p. 120 (pp. 8–9).

[7] Oppenheimer, Robert A.; *The Tree of Knowledge; op. cit.*

[8] Roberts, W. O.; *op. cit.*

19

HOW TO DEVELOP A
COMMUNICATION SYSTEM *

George T. Vardaman

What is meant by a communication system? More specifically, what is meant by an organizational communication system? I want to address this article to answering these questions, as well as to discussing a general method of setting up a workable one.

Our first step is the clarification of some key terms, the first of which is a *communication purpose* or *objective*. This term refers to operational goals, or those ends toward which communication is directed. Consider an illustration: As a transmitter, there are about five different general objectives or ends towards which I could work. For one thing, I could attempt *to inform* you. This is the act of giving out certain kinds of data, certain kinds of information—a purpose, in fact, which is basic to everything else.

Another purpose is *to convince*. By convincing, I mean getting belief, getting intellectual or mental assent to some idea. That the University of Denver has more than 6,000 students is a matter of information. That the University of Denver is a great academic institution is a matter of conviction.

A third possible purpose is *to impress*. The word impress comes from two Latin terms, "in," meaning *in* and "premere" which means *to press*. Literally, then, it means to press into, that is, a reinforcement of existing attitudes, ideas and feelings. Obviously, it is an important and completely legitimate communication goal.

Yet another purpose is termed *leading to action*. Obviously it grows out of any or all of the preceding ones. In leading to action, I may give information, or I may convince, and I may impress, but, as an end, it obviously transcends all of these.

* Reprinted from *ICIE Reporting,* January, 1964, pp. 10–11.

A final objective is *to entertain,* which in certain circumstances is certainly a legitimate communication purpose. However, I question that it is a final, defensible purpose in industrial communication. Entertainment can be used as a means, or as a supplement to achieve one of the other four ends, but as editors we need to be very clear that we are not primarily in the business of entertaining.

As a matter of interest, two of our graduate students recently finished one survey of a major business firm in the Rocky Mountain region in which they found that there was absolutely no correlation between the purposes that were set forth by the writers of company reports and the responses of the readers of those same reports. In this instance, no real communication appears to have taken place. Rather, an almost complete by-passing was going on. For if transmitters do not know their own purposes, or exactly what ends they are after, how can they expect their receivers to respond in the desired way?

Let us now consider another key term, *communication standards.* A standard in the sense that I am using it refers to a yardstick, a measuring unit, a criterion. We should remember also that a standard refers to what should be, not what is.

Let us consider an application of communication standards in organizational communication. Using appropriate standards, an organization can specify required levels of communication proficiency for every position within the firm. The communication standard then becomes the unit of measurement against which all communication performance can be assessed.

The next term is *communication operations.* This refers to fundamental communication ingredients. For example, basic writing skills are essential to the several kinds of written communication. Again, fundamental speaking skills are essential in public speaking, in conference leadership, or in person-to-person discourse. In an organization, one must assess clearly what important communication operations are required in each position and at what level of proficiency.

We are now ready to consider *communication tasks.* If the communication operation is the ingredient, the communication task is the recipe. The task is a blending of appropriate operations to carry out a specific communication job. Giving a speech, conducting a conference, writing a memo or reading a report—all these are examples of communication tasks. We should remember, however, that a communications task is limited in terms of time and function. It is finite, because once accomplished, it is set aside. In this it differs fundamentally from the next object of our concern.

The *communication system* is the universe within which communication purposes, communication standards and communication tasks function. It is the total pattern of an organization's communication. This, as I see it, is the great need in industrial, professional, educational, governmental institutions.

In order to better understand the nature of a communication system, let us examine in highlighted form how the foregoing ingredients can be blended so as to control organizational communication. I call this a "Procedure for Communication System Analysis and Control," consisting of six basic steps as follows:

PROCEDURE FOR COMMUNICATION SYSTEM ANALYSIS AND CONTROL

Step I. Identification and/or establishment of communication objectives and standards.

This includes the consideration of such questions as:

A. What communication purposes (overt and covert) should be pursued?

B. What communication tasks should be accomplished?

C. Into what basic communication operations do the communication tasks fall?

D. What standards of proficiency should be required in each task and operation?

Step II. Identification of the existing communication situation.

Using the criteria in Step I, a systematic analysis is made of the communication as it actually exists. This may require extensive time and intensive effort. Direct observation, interviews and other forms of research may be necessary to do a genuine assessment.

Step III. Identification of Communication Problems.

This step comes only after proper treatment of Steps I and II. Essentially the communication problems are the *differences* found between I and II. Problems, in addition to being identified, must be ranked in terms of importance, temporality and type.

Step IV. Overcoming the Communication Problems.

Growing directly out of Step III, the solutions here focus on such factors as:

A. Making organizational adjustment and revision

B. Effecting personnel changes.

C. Setting up training programs.

Step V. Establishing Evaluational Procedures.

Evaluation goes back to Step I for standards, applying them to the procedures emerging from Step IV.

Step VI. Establishing a Continuing Communication Program.

Here the focus is on keeping the communication gain as well as effecting continuing improvement, including (*a*) needed revision of communication standards and objectives and (*b*) needed revision of Steps III, IV, and V. Obviously this step goes back to Step I, completing the circuit so that the system becomes modifiable and self-correcting.

It seems to me that a genuine practical system along the above lines is one way to the kind of communication which demonstrably contributes to organizational improvement. With it, random, haphazard grinding out of gimmick-centered house organs, speeches and memos ceases; the focus becomes a coherent, consistent pattern within which all communication is programmed to accomplish efficiently and effectively the most important functions of the organization.

20

NASA'S DEVELOPMENTAL PROGRAM
FOR SELECTIVE DISSEMINATION
OF INFORMATION *

Melvin S. Day

Rather than to assume that you know all about NASA's scientific and technical information program and jump right in to describe our Selective Dissemination of Information program—which we call NASA-SDI—I should like to start with a brief overview of our total information program and the philosophy behind it.

The Space Act of 1958, Public Law 85-568, which created the National Aeronautics and Space Administration, laid out our job in very broad terms: To publish and disseminate widely the results of NASA research activities and findings. This we do through our technical publications program in which the primary activity is large scale publication and distribution of NASA (and NASA contractor) formal research and development reports. This series includes Technical Reports, Technical Notes, Technical Memorandums, Technical Translations, Technical Reprints, and NASA Contractor Reports. A second major activity of our technical publications program is the "repackaging" of scientific and technical information. This includes the compacting and translation, in a sense, of highly specialized technical information for broader, interdisciplinary audiences, or for lay audiences; the quick collection and publication of papers presented at scientific meetings and symposia that are of interest to aerospace audiences; and the issuance of data compilations, handbooks, sourcebooks, technical reviews, and state-of-the-art surveys.

Our publications, however, are only the most visible products and ser-

* Reprinted from *Proceedings of the 1964 Institute in Technical and Industrial Communications,* Colorado State University, pp. 35–39.

vices of NASA's Scientific and Technical Information Division. For our job is not only to disseminate the results of NASA's work to the scientific community, but to provide to NASA scientists and engineers, and those of its contractors, worldwide research results of interest and significance to our own aerospace programs. We therefore conduct an aggressive program to: (1) acquire the world's literature on aerospace results and findings; (2) to organize this literature and bring it rapidly under bibliographic control; and (3) to both announce and disseminate this literature to those who need it in the shortest possible time.

To carry out this program we have contracted with Documentation Incorporated, Bethesda, Maryland, to acquire, process, and announce the world's technical aerospace *report literature*—that body of information which in the traditional sense has been considered informal or unpublished. Similarly, by cooperative arrangement with NASA, the American Institute of Aeronautics and Astronautics, New York City, acquires, announces, and processes the world's *formerly published* aerospace literature, i.e., learned journal articles, scientific meeting papers, monographs, books, etc. The output of the joint effort is published in the abstract journals, *Scientific and Technical Aerospace Reports* (*STAR*) and *International Aerospace Abstracts* (*IAA*). *IAA* which covers the world's aerospace published literature appears on the 1st and 15th of each month; *STAR* which covers the world's aerospace report literature appears on the 8th and 23rd. The journals are identical in categories of information covered, in their subject, author, corporate source, and accession number indexes, and both provide quarterly, semi-annual, and annual indexes. These two journals complement each other and provide comprehensive coverage of the world's aerospace literature—both published and report. During calendar year 1964, it is anticipated that the two journals will abstract and announce in excess of 40,000 items. In line with the concept of speed of abstracting and announcement, every item received appears in an issue of the appropriate abstract journal within four to six weeks of receipt. While incoming new material is being processed for announcement, it is simultaneously microfilmed, reproduced on single film sheets 105 mm x 148 mm (approximately 4 x 6 inches), which carry 60 pages of images and distributed to our Research Centers and major contractors six to ten days in advance of the mailing dates of the abstract journals. Thus a scientist or engineer who scans a current issue of the abstract journal and finds an abstract of an article or report of specific interest knows with certainty that the entire report in microfiche *is already available* for his use within his own organization.

To complement and enhance the printed indexes in the abstract journals, the Scientific and Technical Information Division produces multiple copies of indexes on magnetic tapes, on which are stored index entries in much greater depth than is feasible on a printed page. These tapes are provided to NASA Research Centers and contractors.

WHY AN SDI SYSTEM?

Even though we have what is regarded as an effective on-going operation, we ourselves are by no means satisfied that we have achieved the optimum program. And this brings me to why we are moving into selective dissemination and how we are approaching it.

Ever since World War II, we have heard at scientific and technical meetings, and at meetings of information and communication people, of the "information explosion." In our boredom with this expression and the companion one—"that 90% of the scientists who have lived since the beginning of time are alive today"—we should not forget that they point up a very real problem. A number of solutions are being tried or have been proposed.

Certain thoughtful individuals have called for "compacting the information stockpile." In general, they have expressed this compacting process in terms of critical reviews, state-of-the-art summaries, data compilations, handbooks, monographs, and books. We all realize the importance and value of these approaches in separating the wheat from the chaff. At the same time, we are too painfully aware of the agonizing slowness with which such efforts reach fruition. Even when such efforts are successful, they do not solve the problem for getting to the scientist or engineer today's information coming "hot off the press."

What we in NASA are doing, therefore, through the initial assistance of the Advanced Systems Development Division of International Business Machines Corporation, Yorktown Heights, New York, is pushing the development of a system, utilizing computers, that brings to man's attention only current awareness information pertinent to his working needs or interests and, hopefully, obviates the necessity of his wading through masses of newly published material in order to find the relatively small amount of information he really requires. The heart of this system, as I shall detail a bit later, is the ability to operate it on a highly decentralized basis—a concept on which all our other information services, products, and tools are designed.

The basic tool we have created for the announcement of new scientific and technical report literature is our abstract journal *STAR* (*Scientific and Technical Aerospace Reports*), which I mentioned earlier, along with the companion journal, *International Aerospace Abstracts*. Although *STAR* was established in January 1963, it is increasing in size at a very rapid rate.

While the abstracts are grouped into 34 fairly broad subject categories to facilitate scanning, we believe that very shortly the large number of abstracts carried may make even the scanning process a laborious one for scientists and engineers.

Moreover, the mission orientation of Government research and development agencies, such as NASA, results in information requirements that span a number of conventional scientific and engineering disciplines. Thus announcement media and abstracting tools to meet such needs must cut across disciplinary boundaries and attempt to cover newly created interfaces between scientific disciplines. As a result, they may tend to become amorphous in their announcement capabilities. I wish to make clear, however, that we shall continue to regard *STAR* as our basic announcement tool for the overall aerospace community of users. The Selective Dissemination of Information program which we have under development is regarded as a significant adjunct to, and not a replacement for, *STAR*.

WHAT'S NEW: COMPUTER TECHNOLOGY

What do we mean by a program for Selective Dissemination of Information? What is new or different about such a program? Any librarian worth his salt has been conducting just this sort of program almost from his first day on the job. Why then the sudden resurgence of interest? And why the feeling that it is an exciting breakthrough? Quite simply, it is because experiments conducted over the past three or four years have demonstrated the feasibility of using computers to compare words and phrases that describe an individual's range of subject interest with words and phrases that describe the contents of newly received documents, select documents which are pertinent to the man's interest, and reject the remainder. This is not to say that all of the bugs have been eliminated, or that all problems have been solved to create an effective mechanized system for selecting on a mass matching basis only that information which is needed or wanted by particular scientists and engineers.

Selective dissemination may be described as the inverse of information retrieval: Characterizations of the users, rather than of documents, are initially stored; and, instead of an information retrieval system being stirred into operation by a request for a literature search, the SDI system is stimulated into action by the arrival of a new document. The impetus for flow of information rests with the system, rather than with the user. The flow of information consists of notification to each user of applicable new documents, automatically and promptly.

The underlying concept of mechanized selective dissemination of information is a simple one—the machine matches the profile of the incoming document against the profile of the potential user. Very real problems are encountered, however, in actual practice. For example, there are great complexities of interests among the thousands of scientists and engineers who will ultimately participate in the program. These interests range from detailed specificity in some fields to quite general in others; from information requirements on hundreds of topics to a need for information on a single topic; from a desire to have the system provide a review function only, which will highlight major areas to the demand for very specific technical data. There also may be the problem of ability of the operator of the system to keep the interest profiles of the users accurately updated.

The effectiveness of any selective dissemination system also depends, naturally, on the quality of the document indexing. In the NASA program the indexing is done, not by machine, but by professional indexers, and we feel that the resultant document profiles are of sufficiently high quality to provide for satisfactory selection and discrimination in actual practice. It is worth noting here that this indexing is not done primarily for the SDI program, but for the magnetic-tape indexes that we provide to our Research Centers and major contractors for retrospective literature searching. This dual use of our tape indexes makes our SDI much less expensive than it would be if not a part of our overall information program.

Two other complications in the SDI concept may be considered jointly. These are the growing volume of the literature and the potential size of the participating audience. Our abstract journal, *STAR,* and its companion journals, *IAA,* are approaching 50,000 announcements annually, and the volume continues to grow. At the same time, it is entirely conceivable that the NASA-SDI system may be asked to serve as many as 20,000 individual customers.

Satisfactorily meeting these problems to come up with an effective SDI system involves selecting significant items from a great bulk of material, using not the original information per se, but a representation of it in index terms, and dispatching these items to the appropriate individual, among thousands, who in turn is represented by a description or index of his interests. Inherent in a successful solution is the firm premise that the user must not be sent too much of that which is of no interest to him nor too little of that which *is* of interest to him. Stated somewhat differently, the system must register a high percentage of hits, and an exceedingly low percentage of misses, of pertinent documents.

NASA-SDI IN ACTION

This is how our system works: it uses the basic NASA scientific and technical information facilities, which are built around a modern high-speed computer. In essence, SDI describes to the computer the interests of individual scientists and engineers. The computer then compares individual interests with profiles of newly acquired reports. When individual interest and document match, the computer sends two cards to the scientist or engineer. One card contains an abstract of the document along with other pertinent information to help him decide whether or not he wants a copy. He may, if he wishes, file the abstract card as a permanent reference.

The second card is a response card pre-addressed to the individual's local library. The response card carries five die-cut windows, so that the user, by merely punching out the appropriate hole, can indicate: (*a*) that the document is of interest, and a copy is desired; (*b*) that the document is of interest, but a copy is not needed; (*c*) that the document is of interest, but that he has already seen it; (*d*) that the document is of no interest; and (*e*) that, in addition to the punched response, the user has a written comment or question in a special area provided on the card for this purpose. Should the user punch out the hole requesting the document and drop it in the mail, he will automatically receive from his library either a full-size copy or a miniature film transparency, called a microfiche, which can be read on a special reading device. The actual form of the report depends on local library practice.

Regardless of whether the individual wants the report, the response card is returned in all cases to the operator of the SDI program for his use in measuring the effectiveness of the system.

If machines and men were perfect, if the English language were non-redundant and semantically accurate, the SDI system might work with the kind of perfection achieved only in Utopia. But this is an imperfect world, and the system takes thought and effort to achieve a useful order of accuracy without ever hoping for overall perfection.

In an ideal system, the individual would receive announcement cards for every available report within his field of interest—and would not receive notices of reports outside of his interests or of only marginal interest. This ideal can be achieved, theoretically, where the field of interest is narrow and sharply defined and has a non-ambiguous terminology. Unfortunately, from this viewpoint solely, scientists and engineers have broad interests, and the language is imprecise and full of synonymous words and phrases. Nevertheless, a high batting average can result from care in using the system.

Each time an individual orders a report, or punches out the window meaning "of interest but not wanted," it is called *hit*. Each time the machine fails to send an announcement card on a report of interest, it is a *miss*. The *hits* are easy enough to check. Running the returned cards through the machine produces a statistic on how many cards were sent and how many of those were hits.

Checking on *misses* is more difficult. The best way, although somewhat time-consuming, is for each individual to check the announcement cards he receives against the current issue of *STAR*. If a report of interest is listed but no card was received, it's a clear miss. Examination of the report usually shows how the individual's profile should be amended to eliminate misses of that particular kind. This procedure is, of course, for use primarily during the developmental phase of SDI. It should *not* be necessary when the program becomes operational—although an occasional check of cards against *STAR, IAA,* or other journals covered by the operational program would be useful.

SDI hedges its bets by an ingenious machine technique, in case not all users are meticulous or faithful about checking for themselves. During each run some reports are selected at random and notices of them are sent to a random selection of individuals. If the individual returns a random card with a positive indication of interest, it means that the customer either failed to include pertinent terms in his profile, or, if his profile has the terms, that the accuracy of the match is not as good as it should be. If the report contains terms not in the user profile, he is then invited to revise his profile accordingly.

TECHNIQUES OF MATCHING

The simplest way of describing the matching process is that the man "tells" the machine what his interests are. Such man-to-machine communication requires a common language. In this case, the language is composed of terms taken from common and technical English, called *index terms* because the people who catalog the contents of reports and articles use the terms as an index to the contents of the report. It is this subject index that is fed into the computer's memory. A simple hypothetical example is shown in Fig. 1. If one is accustomed to the conventional type of indexing

Typical terms stored in computer	
N64 00001 (Accession number for a document)	
Liquid	Weightlessness
Propellant	Zero gravity
Cryogenic	Expulsion
Transfer (noun)	Fuel (noun)
Pressurization	

Figure 1. Typical terms stored in computer.

by major headings and sub-headings, this pattern of indexing with a list of terms may seem strange. It is called "coordinate indexing," and it makes information storage and retrieval by computer much easier and more efficient than trying to use a formal classification scheme.

The next step in man-to-machine communication is to apply coordinate indexing to the man's needs and interests. Naturally, terms from the same vocabulary must be used. If we tell the machine that Dr. Smith's interests are *transfer* of *cryogenic propellants* at *zero-gravity,* the machine will let him know that report N64-00001 is available (Fig. 2), and in addition it

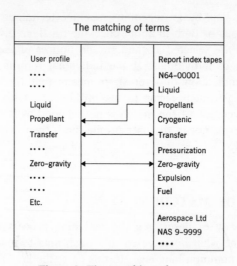

Figure 2. The matching of terms.

will send him cards containing abstracts of all other reports in which those terms are indexed, in whatever context. Thus he might well get a number of documents that he didn't want at all. For instance, all new reports on the study, manufacture, processing, hazards, chemistry, physics, availability, and cost of all cryogenic liquids.

Fortunately, the computer can handle phrases. If the scientist's interest is stated solely as "transfer of cryogenic liquids at zero-gravity" that is all the computer will identify for him. (Fig. 3)

If a profile is made too general, the individual may receive notices of too many reports that are of no interest to him, for the more general the profile, the greater the number of mismatches the machine will make.

A profile that is too specific, on the other hand, will result in the man *not* being notified of some reports that may be of critical interest; that is, the narrower the profile, the greater the number of losses. The optimum profile, therefore, is the one that will produce the least amount of unneeded

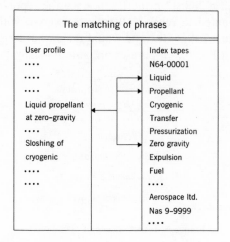

Figure 3. The matching of phrases.

information while not missing anything of real importance. This optimum profile is a combination of words and phrases. The phrases can be made up of two, three, or four words or terms.

Redundancy is essential to communication, and in creating a profile it means including synonyms and related expressions. In our example, it means including phrases like those shown in Fig. 4.

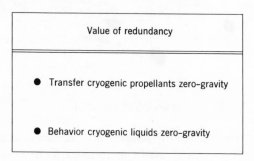

Figure 4. Value of redundancy.

Note also that the specificity of the phrase increases as qualifying words are added (Fig. 5), thus reducing the number of reports the computer announces to the scientist. Some day we may be able to add more phrases, like "transfer cryogenic liquids zero-gravity cisplutonian space prodsponder valves." But not yet—our machine would have a nervous breakdown!

Another important element in a profile is the "must" term. When the machine finds such a "must" it must announce the report to the customer. If our scientist wanted to receive all reports indexed with the term *cryogenic,* no matter in what context, he would make that term a "must" in his profile as shown in Fig. 6. All phrases are automatically "musts."

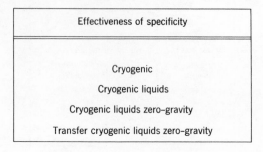

Figure 5. Effectiveness of specificity.

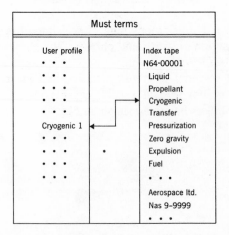

Figure 6. Must terms.

Exclusion of reports not of interest can be accomplished by writing "Negative" or "Neg." before one or more index terms in one's profile. Assume one is interested in all types of loads on spacecraft, launch vehicles, satellites, etc., but not on aircraft. Since there is interest in all types of loads the term *loads* has been "musted." Ordinarily, an announcement of the report shown in Fig. 7 would have been sent; but the negative indication has properly barred such an announcement, which would not have been of interest to our man. The negative indication overrides all other instructions. Contract numbers, as well as subject terms, can be indicated as "musts" or "negs."

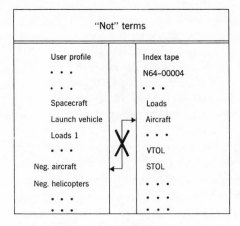

Figure 7. "Not" terms.

The computer is able to match a series of interest profiles with a series of report indexes using all of the above types of matching techniques simultaneously. Widely different profiles, containing one, two, or all these types of entries, and ranging from a few terms and phrases to many hundreds, are accommodated. Thus it can be seen that a profile is a highly individual affair, and that the user profile is really the key to an effective Selective Dissemination of Information system.

KEYS TO PROFILE MAKING

Perhaps it would be of value, therefore, to discuss in some detail the creation of a user profile. A number of specific points are emphasized in our advice to participants in the NASA-SDI:

The profile may be changed as often as one wishes.

Any number of terms and phrases may be used, including any number of "must" terms.

No phrase can exceed four words or terms.

Since the machine's language is that of the indexer, it can recognize only those terms used in the reports. The user's librarian is usually in a position to supply the index vocabulary guide.

The language is growing. If one becomes aware of terms in his own specialty that will be used in future indexing—such as upcoming project names, codes or terminology—these should certainly be used.

Terms and phrases that define a field of interest, including "near-synonyms," should be incorporated in the profile.

It must be remembered that the computer can only match terms. If there is no term, there is no match.

Remember, though, that every term which is included broadens the field of interest and so increases the probablity of false matches. This means announcement of more reports of no interest.

"Must" terms should be used with restraint. Unless they are quite specific, the "idiot" machine will flood the user with announcements, one for each time the term occurs in the indexing of any report regardless of its general content.

If one's interests are broad, a broad profile will be wanted, naturally.

It should be borne in mind that the increase in numbers of reports is exponential. The profile must not be so broad that one is buried under mailbags each time the postman arrives.

As in all things, moderation is the key to happiness.

With a good profile, comprehensive in coverage of the field of interest but not too general, the number of reports missed can be reduced to an insignificant number. In our agency, we shall continue attempts to improve our indexing and refine the system as our users go about the job of refining their profiles. We believe that *this* sort of goal is attainable: that three out of every four announcements sent to our participants will be directly pertinent to their work and interests.

Profile development as the key to successful SDI operation is shown in the program statistics. During the first month of SDI, with slightly over 400 NASA scientists and engineers participating, a hit average of nearly 40 percent resulted. That is, of each 100 notification cards received by an individual, about 40 were of interest. Immediate refinement of the system began, first by changing the matching statistics of the computer's program, then by profile refinement. Within three months, the hit average went up to 65 percent. With further refinement based on longer experience with more individual participants, a hit percentage of 75 percent is predicted.

So far, the statistics of success are encouraging, but they represent the average of hits over a sample of 500 participants. Interviews with the participants and examination of individual results showed an actual spread from highly satisfied to grossly disappointed. Some individuals had developed such confidence in the system that they stopped checking the abstract journals, depending entirely on NASA-SDI to call new reports to their attention. At the other extreme were a small number of individuals with a high percentage of misses, and a heavy flow of non-pertinent announcement cards. The key in every case was profile adequacy. The happy clients had good profiles; the unhappy ones did not. These poor profiles were promptly corrected and most of our unhappy customers became happy customers also.

LOOKING AHEAD

The operational phase of NASA-SDI is already in sight. The exact timing will vary from place to place, because NASA's approach to efficient scientific and technical information dissemination is decentralization. The basic work of accession, indexing, and tape punching is performed centrally; but copy tapes and reproducible report microfiche are sent to our Research Centers in the field so that each can service its people locally. Similarly, each Center will operate its own SDI program, using materials supplied from our central Scientific and Technical Information Facility. Each center will decide for itself when it is ready to move from the centralized developmental phase to the local operational phase with its greatly expanded number of participants.

I am sure that some of you have been thinking in terms of the dollar costs of establishing an SDI program in your organizations or institutions. In this regard, I cannot at this time give you precise information. In NASA's development of SDI, as noted earlier, we are using as *by-product information* the report index-data already produced for other aspects of our information system. The indexing which is done in depth on our magnetic tapes is accomplished primarily to establish our own bibliographic control over all materials entering our system and to enable our information people in the field to perform their own literature searches *locally,* since they automatically receive copies of these tapes. *At no additional cost,* therefore, we have the basic data in the form of report indexes on the tape which the computer matches against human profiles. Thus, in our case, the only real cost element of the system is putting human interest profiles on tapes, machine matching, and distributing announcements.

How does one measure the success of the system? The answer obviously lies with *satisfied* customers. Our SDI program has just started and it is still much too early to have accumulated solid convincing statistics. I do have one statistic which is interesting. The volume of requests from *users* of SDI for reports has *tripled* since implementation of the system. Here again we don't claim that this is an accurate measurement of the effectiveness of the system, but it does indicate that SDI is calling to the attention of one group of technical people reports which apparently were unknown to these technical people.

21

INFORMATION SYSTEMS AND
EVIDENTIAL MEANING *

Carroll C. Halterman

(*Some Effects of Subsystem Orientations on Communication Capability*)
This examination of communication (and information) systems is restricted to human or "man-machine" organizations. The author admits a
preoccupation with "large" organizations, and, in that group, with administered organizations.[1] His selection of large, administered, organizations is
not meant to suggest that the same functional and dysfunctional aspects are
not present in other smaller types; it is simply a convenience since the
characteristics described are more prominent throughout units at that
level. The use of this approach, and the fact that certain business terminology is employed, in no way implies that the theoretical elements are restricted to large, profit-making institutions.

An organization cannot be understood except through analysis of its
communication patterns and interaction networks. This is the avenue followed below.

COMMUNICATION IN GENERAL

People communicate in order to influence the behavior of themselves
and others. If the communication does not accomplish this end, it is ineffective even though the message may seem to have been clearly received.
Effectiveness is intimately related to the needs of the recipient. At the same
time perception and processes of selectivity throughout the network reflect
the influences of the varied needs and objectives of other persons involved.
This aspect of communication is of great importance.

* Reprinted by permission of the author.

What is Communication? Communication has been described (*a*) as an exchange of facts, ideas, opinions, or emotions by two or more persons; [2] (*b*) as primarily to influence behavior; [3] (*c*) as a transmission and reception (including comprehension) of thought, instruction, or information, [4] and (*d*) as passing on ideas, information, orders, or instructions in such a way that the recipient understands exactly what is meant. [5] Since mere words have limitations in describing such a concept, a schematic model of communications can most efficiently introduce it.

A Basic Model of Communication. A communication model is usually described as having the following parts: (1) a selector and encoder embodied in the sender, (2) a system of communication links forming the network called the channel, which actually carries the material, and (3) the steps of decoding and selecting for use which occurs in the receiver. Movement of signals through a system is influenced by two principal factors: (*a*) capacity and (*b*) noise. If the capacity of the system is not exceeded, the accuracy of the transmission is a function of the noise, which in turn can be combatted by redundancy, which uses up available channel capacity. Coding can improve accuracy. It permits more material to be communicated but at a cost of reducing the independence of choice of those involved, and of bringing about delay. Figure 1 is a basic model of a communication system.

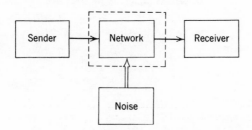

Figure 1. A basic model of a communication system.

Claude Shannon originally developed this classic model while working on problems of telephone communications. His ideas have been the foundation for many new concepts, a large number of them under the title of "Information Theory." Shannon's model is a general model of communications useful wherever there is a flow of information. [6]

Elements of the Model. The basic elements in the simplest kind of model are shown in Fig. 2. The block labeled Sender identifies the place, person, or equipment, which produces the message and sends it out. For the message to move between Sender and Receiver requires some way of its being

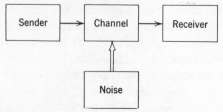

Figure 2. A simple model of communications.

conveyed, a Channel. Channels can be telephone wires, radio waves, light waves, sound waves, or pieces of paper. Channels are subject to disturbances, which distort, confuse, block and interfere with the transmission of communications. This interference is called *noise* and is comprised of anything moving in the channel apart from the actual signals or messages wanted by the sender, or, importantly, *needed by the receiver.*

PROCESSES IN COMMUNICATION

The Coding Process. Since all communication is carried on in some form of language, there must exist some process of *encoding,* that is, of reshaping information into the specific form in which it is going to be transmitted. Converting an idea into words during conversation is an encoding process. Obviously, if the information is in code form, there must also be a decoding process in the receiver that extracts the meaning the code contains. Figure 3 represents a model showing the Selection and Coding processes in relationship.

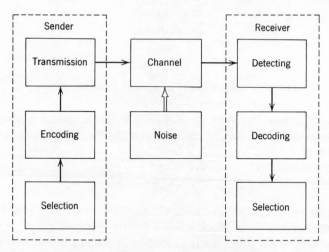

Figure 3. Selecting and encoding processes.

The Selection Process in Communications

Much selectivity is found in communications systems. It reflects the feelings of different people about what is important.

Rational Selection. Rational selectivity is of a formal or conscious nature. System analysis and improvement, queue discipline, organizational planning and message priority assignment are examples of rational selection in operation. One purpose of these activities is to keep the amount of information going through a system at a level below that which would cause overload. Another is to control noise by preventing non-relevant messages from entering the system. Rational selection is logical in nature. It is normally *functional* to the administered organization.

Non-Rational Selection. Non-rational selectivity is largely the result of perceptual bias or conceptual slant. For example selectivity occurs when information wanted by some members of an organization is kept out of the communications system or *when information important to one individual is introduced into the system by him even though it may not really be what others in the system need.* The operation of this selection process is usually subtle and unrecognized. It is not logical, not rational, *it is not according to management plan.* Being normally dysfunctional to the administered organization, this aspect of selectivity forms the center of concern in much of the following material.

The Conceptual Process in Communications

Generally, the greater the importance a particular aspect of reality has to the individual, the more elaborate will be his conceptual scheme, and the greater will be the attention to inference relating to it. The individual network member's conceptual system serves the critical cognitive function of providing a method of ordering. By means of this the environment is broken down and organized, is differentiated and integrated, into its many psychologically relevant components. Hence it performs as an intervening medium or program through which impinging stimuli are selected, coded and evaluated.

Meaning Depends on the Conceptual Process. The term *meaning* is related to concept. The entire process of conceptualization can usefully be thought of in terms of (1) apprehending, (2) abstracting, (3) inferring, and (4) processing.

Apprehending is, briefly, the focusing on particular stimulus or stimuli from the total stimuli field; *Abstracting* governs the organization of sensory impressions in a fashion congruent with one's psychological make-up. It is "a way of thinking about something," wherein the cognitive instrument is the concept; *Inferring* is simply extending from the concept, and testing the accuracy and sufficiency of it against some standard; and, finally, *Processing* means the manipulating of concepts (sorting and recombining), out of which function new concepts are evolved. (Colloquially this can be called reasoning.)

The individual's interpretation of stimuli (their meaning to him) is thus seen to depend upon his conceptual framework. It can also be inferred that an individual's conceptual framework is dependent upon the particular organization system of which he is a member.

System Membership Affects the Conceptual Process. Sherif and others have adequately demonstrated that one's thought and actions are governed by the norms and expectations of his reference groups.[7,8,9] Shull [10] has produced a paradigm demonstrating how norms affect an individual's conceptual process (see Fig. 4).

NORMS FUNCTIONING RELATIVE TO THE INDIVIDUAL IN TERMS OF:

I. Conceptual Processes:	*Norms present (sub) cultural prescriptions as to:*
Conceptual Operations	*Normative Focus*
1. Apprehending	1. Stimuli that should be attended.
2. Abstracting	2. Appropriate concepts and conceptual schemes.
3. Inferring	3. Acceptable methods of testing the reality (validity and reliability) and sufficiency (number of dimensions) of the conceptual scheme
4. Processing	4. Appropriate reasoning process
II. Value System:	Norms offer prescriptions as to the value (worth) of particular concepts
III. Sentiments:	Norms present the group's prescription as to the appropriate
1. Direction and 2. Intensity	of emotional response centering around a concept or object
IV. Response or Behavior:	Norms present prescriptions for appropriate behavioral reactions to stimuli

Figure 4. A scheme from Shull and Del Beque.

As Shull observes:

"Considerable evidence indicates the propensity of the individual to bring his own perceptions into line with those of the group in order to avoid the discomfort of conceptual incongruency, sometimes achieving a readjustment of the conceptual system even at the price of conscious perceptual distortion." [11]

And as Sherif points out, interaction itself adds to the differentiation of identifiable sets of individuals.

"When individuals interact with one another, the interaction process and its process produce differential effects upon their experience and behavior. "Differential effect" means changes in perception, discrimination, emotions, thinking, personality features, and action which result from becoming a functioning part or member of social interaction." [12]

Since there is no reason to exclude any specific kind of "communication" from the scope of interaction, it is reasonable to assume that the membership and role-set of each different organizational subsystem creates its own unique constellation of demands, normative ideas, actual or perceived sanctions, and resultant emergent activities.

Communication Processes Affect Evidential Meaning

Sherif's observations were made on the basis of "group" and "near-group" experimentations (that is to say, not restricted to bona fide *groups* in the sociological sense), and the author of this paper extends their applicability to other organizational entities (for example, social cliques; task-oriented units; project-oriented teams and role-systems (however defined) in enduring situations; and managerial sets. The author posits: (1) that communications systems within organizations can be identified by their communication networks; [13] (2) that the unique orientation of each of these systems affects its members' perception—through processes analogous to those described by Shull, Sherif, and others; and (3) that the resultant incongruities and incompatibilities among the joint set of systems results in lowered total performance as a result of both information variability and communications systems hysteresis.

COMMUNICATIONS SUMMARIZED

Since communication involves transactions between people, its interpersonal nature makes it fundamental to the study of organizations. Communications are basic to an organization. Analysts have previously suggested that if we could (1) identify all the channels conveying material and (2) describe the means by which this communication influences the behavior of the organization, we could (3) then get very close to understanding the organization itself.[14] Groups are characterized by a relatively easy flow of communications, which property is a basis for their very coherence. By giving a person ideas and impressions a group helps him form his perception of the world. Through communication people receive stimuli which evoke sets of alternative actions and induce them to behave. Groups can be differentiated in larger organizations by identifying the unique nature of their communications. Conversely, it can be reasoned that each separate communication network defines members somehow different from those who belong to other systems. This paper directs attention to one missing step: recognizing how membership of the organization's systems affects the information content.

INFORMATION SYSTEMS ARE PROBLEM-CENTERED NETWORKS

One sector of communication, *semantics,* concerns itself with the meaning of symbols and words. Another sector, *syntax,* is concerned with the systematic properties of communication, that is the relations between the symbols used. A third part of communication is concerned with *pragmatics* and focuses *on the relationship between communication and purposeful action.* It is toward this third part that the author's concern is now directed. It centers on *informational* communication, and how it moves through an organization. What then is *information,* or more importantly, what is an *information-system?*

Information Systems Defined

It is important not only to understand the *similarities* between the terms *information* and *communication,* but also to be able to distinguish between them. While both depend upon a degree of conceptual congruity (or at least compatibility) between the emitter and the receiver, the former—*information*—implies a perceived relevance to need. Since a need can be viewed as a "want" or "gap" in one's satisfaction scheme, a need legitimately can be classified as a problem. Information is problem-oriented in both a broad and a specific sense. Any communication system, then, where a problem is involved, is an information system (if one admits minor and trivial "problems," hardly any communication system can be excluded).[15]

An Information System Model

Immediately that the network member becomes problem-obsessed, his communication network is transformed into an information system, even though in its naive state it may be notoriously inefficient. Some additional elements are immediately evident in the model: (1) problem-related criteria are linked in, and (2) intervention channels are installed through which the member may request action, issue advice, or install correctives. Figure 5 displays one form of such an information system. Note that for the sake of simplicity these new elements are shown only in one segment.[16]

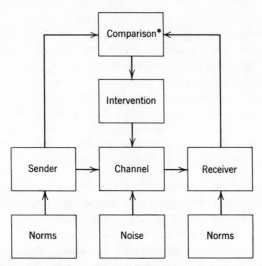

Figure 5. A naive model of an information system. * Locus of problem orientation or need awareness.

INFORMATION SYSTEMS IN ADMINISTERED ORGANIZATIONS

Information systems in administered organizations can be classified into four different types: *socially-oriented, functionally-oriented, bureaucratically-oriented,* and *managerially-oriented.*

Socially-oriented. Socially-oriented information systems grow up around socializing needs, and include coffee-cliques, card-playing groups, proximity-based conversational teams and the like. Also included are luncheon-gatherers, gossip-networks, associations based on such characteristics as sex, age, church, membership, hobbies and athletics. Memberships can be inter-organizational in nature. Crescive and informal, they are characteristically amorphous and unplanned.

Functionally-oriented. Functionally-oriented information systems center around skills, or are geared to professional standing or to membership in a particular type of organizational activity. Technical associations, craft membership, assignment as part of production line might qualify under this category. Where divisionalism is on the basis of operation (such as production, sales, etc.) division membership could be an appropriate basis. Importantly, the affinity stems from the commonalities and propinquity attaching to the skill areas of concern. These are usually departmentally contained.

Bureaucratically-oriented. Members of this system category derive their relationships from their legal status in the organization. Authority patterns strongly orient the nature of activity and of information flow. Supervisors, managers, subordinates and staff members form the network nodes. Problems of this system are *role*-centered. Incumbency of a particular position is a prime qualification for membership and although this seems to be a shared basis for some of those in functionally-oriented systems, the difference here is incumbency *in a prescribed position* (not a skill). Rigid and formal, these are characteristically structured and planned.

Managerially-oriented. Members of managerially-oriented systems are without clear definition. The system centers around organizational problem situations, and around the "manager" (who exists solely as a problem-solver). The "manager" may be a project leader, a staff section head, or chairman of the board. Highest in this hierarchy of information system types, it can be likened in form to a sunburst, with the problem-solver at the center. Project-and-problem-centered in nature, this system is the most demanding of (but also the most dependent on) the rest of the organization for information. This system is volatile, but planned. It is both the most precious and the most precarious of the lot.

A Problem Distance Model

In terms of social distance, problem-orientation, and managerial relevance, the dense shell of socially-oriented information is probably farthest away from the organizational epicenter. One model, similar in construction to the layers of an onion, is shown in cross-section below (Fig. 6). In order, approaching the center, are the Social and Functional layers. At the center is the managerial core.

A Traditional Model

It may be instructive to show an organization model of a similar, but slightly different kind. Assume first that the organization if viewed traditionally would be represented by the chart in Fig. 7. This is the simplest kind

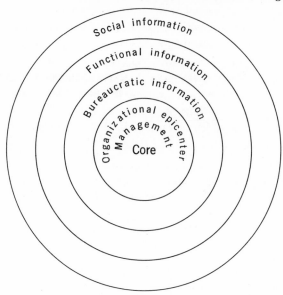

Figure 6. Information related to managerial need.

of structure, where there are subordinate units having different properties (based on, for example, process, output, location or skill requirement). A further breakdown in each of these units is depicted (departments 1, 2, and 3), each having a manpower force of persons. Taken together, the persons assigned are P_n in number. Several persons from departments 2 and 3 are shown as being members of a "friendship" or *social* group, S.

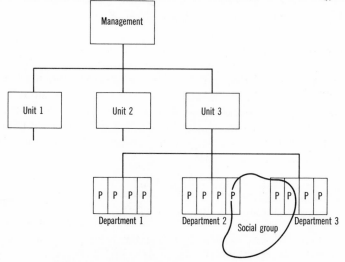

Figure 7. Traditional model of an organization.

An Interaction Model

Alternately it is possible to show these relationships more meaningfully in a different way. Figure 8, similar to a Venn diagram, has limitations due to its two-dimensional nature. However, if thought of as an arbitrary arrangement of the cross-sections of coalescent spheres, it conveys more import. Figure 8 has the added advantage in that it shows areas of interface among organizational parts, in the areas I_1, I_2, I_3, as well as the area of interlock, M.

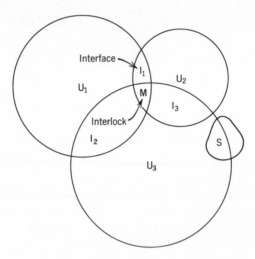

Figure 8. An interaction model of an organization.

It is possible, through variation of the *size* of the circles, the degree of overlap, etc., to depict to an extent the amounts of communication between the parts much better than can the traditional organizational chart. In the illustration here the parts are simplified, since further complications—for example, to show all friendship groups, and perhaps, to show several more operating divisions with their many tiers of organizational level—would seriously mitigate the heuristic value of the model.

A Management Information System Model

At this point attention is invited to the communication networks which overlay Fig. 8. See Fig. 9.

The Total (Management Information) System. Primary (formal) channels are shown in bold, solid lines. Secondary (informal and/or ephem-

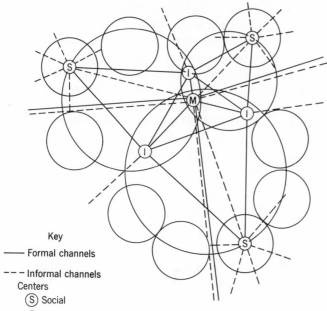

Key

—— Formal channels

--- Informal channels

Centers

Ⓢ Social

Ⓘ Functional

Ⓜ Management

Figure 9. A Communication network model of an organization.

eral) channels are shown in dotted lines. Arrows can be added to show the direction in which information flows. Note that the dotted lines depict links in the *social* system, as well as certain channels in the centralized or *managerial* system. The solid and dotted lines radiating from and terminating into the interlock center form the *Management Information System*. Some connect with the interface centers, some with the social centers, and some with the environment.

Hierarchy of Systems Defined. Thus we can roughly define the hierarchy of information systems by inspecting our network patterns. (*A*) There are a large number of socially-oriented networks to which individuals belong. The bulk of these are peripherally located. A number of small vacant circles are shown to imply their multiplicity. (*B*) There are relatively fewer functionally-oriented networks, in comparison, all of which in a practical, viable, organization are interconnected. The center of each of these information nets is shown as the interface center. Note that these centers, too, have intercourse with the outside world—as they see it—as well as with each other and the individuals in their own unit. (*C*) The entire network of solid lines is known as the bureaucratically-oriented network system. This roughly corresponds to what would be the connecting lines on a traditional organizational chart. (*D*) The interlock center, with its multiplicity of radiating lines, is the managerially-oriented information system. Note that its sources terminate into (1) the bureaucratic net; (2) each functional net; and (3) certain individuals which are part of social nets. Thus the managerial information system has inputs from all possible sources, has outputs to a great number of places, and must ingest and manipulate data that sometimes travels through each of the other networks in turn. It should not be overlooked that every terminal of the managerial net is into a human being. This is always so, if only in the sense that the processes and programs for certain automatic inputs have been humanly determined.

Communications Mass in the Organization

Due to the tremendously large number of transactions on the social level, communications mass is greatest there. A plot of *socially-oriented* communications where density is a function of the distance from the "executive suite" might look something like Fig. 10.

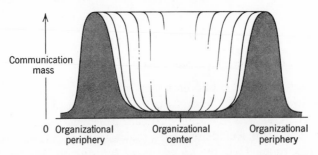

Figure 10. Cross section of solid representing a hypothetical *socially oriented* communications density function.

A plot of *functionally-oriented* communications might have a shape something on the order of Fig. 11. And a plot of *Bureaucratically-oriented* communications density probably has a shape something like Fig. 12. The *Managerially-oriented* density plot is some combination containing all three, and although the function will vary from organization to organization, a typical plot would probably resemble Fig. 13.

Relation of Communication Mass to Information Content. The problem-oriented manager is interested in the information-content of what he receives through his network—that is to say, he is concerned with estimating problem-related real-world *parameters,* from the "statistics" he receives as communications.[17] Although we do not allege to deal with normally-distributed populations of communications items, it is intuitive that any variability present in one system is going to be added to by the variability

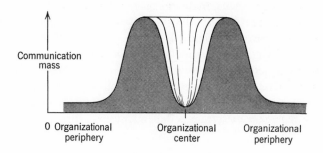

Figure 11. Cross section of solid representing a hypothetical *functionally oriented* communications density function.

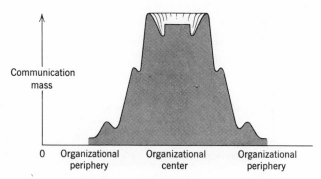

Figure 12. Cross section of solid representing a hypothetical *bureaucratically oriented* communications density function.

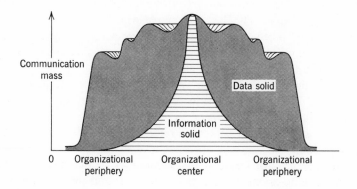

Figure 13. Cross section of solid representing a hypothetical *managerially oriented* communications density function.

in another. This is related to "noise" or perhaps "entropy" in the system.

It is not uncommon to represent the *information content* of a process by the letter I. The letter I is usually equated to the inverse of the variance, or $1/\Sigma 2$.[18] In any chain of processes, the variance of their joint outcomes can be roughly equated to the sum of the process variances. For example, where communication must travel through (first) the *social system* then (secondly) the *functional system* and (finally) the *bureaucratic system*, before it reaches or becomes active in the *managerial system*, then the total variance becomes greater than in any one involved, approaching as a limit the sum of all the variability combined. *Information content*, therefore, is lowered, wherever a management system is dependent upon disparate or differentiable subsystems.

CONCLUSION

Communication systems which are problem-centered are called information systems. Since strictly speaking, every communicator has a problem in the trivial sense, communication/information systems are usefully differentiable only on the basis of "whose problems are they structured around?"

In those large, administered organizations like those typified by big business, the military, and public enterprises, there is a hierarchy of socially-oriented, functionally-oriented, bureaucratically-oriented, and managerially-oriented problems. Information systems based on these problems are similarly named.

The first can be thought of as serving the social needs of members; the second as being related to skill, departmental, and professional requirements; the third as dependent upon role demands and structural survival in the formal organization. The last, or managerial, system is oriented to those organizational problems which the executive perceives, and for which he must tap existing data sources as well as new ones. The latter system is most critical to total organization viability.

Material flowing in each of these systems differs by virtue of membership, problem (or conceptual) orientation, and perceptual differences. Since compatibility among the several different systems is always imperfect the proportion of information content is reduced, and efficiency of the total system is impaired.

Related to the problem above is the situation of communications mass. The prolific socially-oriented systems generate a tremendous amount of socially-oriented communications, located largely at the periphery of total organizational need. Functionally-oriented systems have yet a different

profile, with their communications mass most dense in nature at the interface regions, the locale where their types of problems are of most concern.
The managerial net, which must carry material input from all the others as
well as that from its own informal channels experiences an immense build-
up in the area near the problem core. In general, the resultant tax on channel capacity constrains the managerial system to suboptimal performance.

Summary of Deleterious Aspects. Thus some characteristically deleterious aspects of information systems in large organizations are italicized:
(1) *Evidential meaning differs* at various locations in the organization.[19]
This is a function of the perceptual biases and conceptual differences related to differences in the memberships of the different schemes. (2) *Density imbalance* (unequal mass) creates capacity problems. (3) *Organizational myopia* means that material introduced into the total system by the
various precincts is problem-related in a strictly parochial sense (that is, it
is primarily useful to the individual who solicits or introduces it). To others,
it is *noise.* (4) *Information content (ratio of relevant to other data) suffers*
whenever separate systems are serially combined. The above four problems
are interrelated, and are stated separately only for the conceptual convenience of the reader.

Some Approaches to Problems. Organization analysis and formal redesign can improve the *Managerial information system* significantly. Unfortunately, the improvement of any one system is usually at the expense of
others. See Table 1.

Table 1 is far from inclusive. It contains only a few examples out of an
endless universe of dilemmas.

This paper has presented a broad band of perspectives from which large
organizations can be viewed. In particular, it presented the implicit thesis
that dysfunctions in informational nets are inherent in large, administered
organizations. The astute reader will recognize that a business is never
again "the same" after information system analysis and redesign. Deciding
whether it is better or worse is an arbitrary normative judgement. To an
extent, then the manager must choose between two evils: (1) should he
mutilate or destroy the ongoing system, so that the "new" organization can
better survive? or (2) should he wait for the old unit to strangle itself, or
worse—for it to vegetate and decay? Whatever he chooses, you may be
certain that the unit's successor will soon develop peculiar problems of its
own which can be discussed under the heading of "Information Systems
and Evidential Meaning." [22]

TABLE 1. FUNCTIONAL AND DYSFUNCTIONAL ASPECTS OF PROBLEM SOLVING

Problem	Corrective Activity	Improvement in Management Net	Side-Effects
1. Evidential meaning differs at various locations in the organization.	Solicit data from only selected groups (perhaps on the basis of experienced success.)	Greater precision in parameter estimates, and higher percentage of (problem-related) information context.	Data which are indicative of internal failure (for example) may be screened out. New problems may be allowed to build up unnoticed.
	Eliminate non-problem-related nets.	This would reduce communication density significantly and eliminate "noise" in the managerial system.	It would also destroy the perceived usefulness of the organization to many of its members, and may create a feeling of *anomie*.
2. Density imbalance creates capacity problems.	Reduce or eliminate rigidity of purely "role" requirements (for example).	Much merely "maintenance" communications would be eliminated.	Loss of anchorages among members would create apprehensions. Recruiting and training problems should increase.
	Increase velocity of communications.	To the extent this drives problem-oriented data nearer to real-time, it is salutary.[20]	If this is merely done by overlaying an "automated" system over the existing ones, it will be generally disrupting (as are all intrusions).

3. Organizational myopia on the part of members causes them to contribute "noise."	Discourage local problems from being fed into the system.	Creates a fools paradise for management who are unaware of developing crises. Alienates workers and subordinates.
4. Information value of data is reduced because various networks are serially combined.	Use only the relevant network.	Higher efficiency in problem-solving. Percentage of information in communications is increased.	Actual effectiveness may be reduced. *Total* information flow imperiled. Wrong network may be fortuitously selected.
	Coordinate the various systems by analysis and redesign.	At best, this may allow the most favorable features of each to be exploited.[21]	At worst, this may impair the unique contributions the individual systems make to the members. If so, viability of the entire organization is threatened.

NOTES

[1] "Collectivities which exhibit sustained activity; are part of a larger system; have specialized purposes; and are dependent upon interchange with the larger system." James D. Thompson, et al., *Comparative Studies in Administration* (Pittsburgh: University of Pittsburgh Press, 1959) p. 6.

[2] W. H. Newman and C. E. Summer, *The Process of Management* (Englewood Cliffs, N. J.: Prentice-Hall, Inc., 1961), p. 179.

[3] T. J. Williams, *Executive Control* (New York: John Wiley and Sons, Inc., 1961), p. 133.

[4] R. C. Anderson, *Management Practices* (New York: McGraw-Hill Book Company 1960), p. 124.

[5] Ernest Dale, *Management: Theory and Practice* (New York: McGraw-Hill Book Company, 1965), p. 717.

[6] See Claude E. Shannon and Warren Weaver, *The Mathematical Theory of Communications,* (Urbana: University of Illinois Press, 1963).

[7] Muzafer Sherif and Carolyn W. Sherif. *An Outline of Social Psychology* (New York: Harper and Brothers, 1956).

[8] Solomon E. Asch, "Opinions and Social Pressure," *Scientific American* **193** #5, November, 1955, pp. 31–35. Also in Haberstroh, *Some Theories of Organization.* (Homewood, Illinois: Richard D. Irwin, Inc., and the Dorsey Press, Inc., Homewood, Ill., 1960) pp. 242–249.

[9] Alvar O. Elbing, "A Model for Viewing Decision Making in Interaction Situations from an Historical Perspective," *University of Washington Business Review* (June, 1961), pp. 38–49.

[10] Fremont Shull and Andre Del Beque, "Norms, A Feature of Symbolic Culture: A Major Linkage Between the Individual, Small Group, and Administrative Organization," in William Gore and J. W. Dyson (eds.) *The Making of Decisions.* (New York: Free Press of Glencoe, 1964). pp. 248–275.

[11] *Ibid.* This supports the findings of Asch, *op. cit.*

[12] Sherif, *op. cit.* p. 156.

[13] This is also an allegation of Deutsch. See Karl W. Deutsch, "On Communication Models in the Social Sciences," *The Public Opinion Quarterly,* **16**, 1952, p. 367.

[14] Deutsch, *op. cit.*

[15] Probably the most trivial "problem" is that of determining if what one says is heard. In this case, the *criterion* is the sender's idea of what he said. His feedback channel samples the receiver's actions, or perhaps simply asks for the material to be "read back." Intervention may well be nothing more than correctly repeating the message, or it may consist of corrections to it.

[16] Compare with Fig. 2.

[17] Savage points to two inadequacies of "decision theory" (equated by many with *organization theory*), which he defines as (1) the vagueness difficulties associated with unsure probabilities; and (2) the special problems arising from more than one person participating in a decision. In fact he alleges that *statistics proper* can perhaps be defined as the art of dealing with vagueness and with interpersonal difference in decision situations. He speaks of "multipersonal problems," such as those which arise "out of differences of taste and judgement . . ." and he observes:
. . . it may well happen that different people are faced with partition problems that

are the same in that the same variable is to be observed by each person, but differ in that each person has his own a priori probabilities B and his own set of Available acts F." See Leonard J. Savage, *The Foundations of Statistics*. (New York: John Wiley and Sons, 1954) Chapter 8.

[18] See Harold Bierman, Jr., Charles P. Bonini, Lawrence E. Fouraker and Robert K. Jaedicke, *Quantitative Analysis for Business Decisions* (Homewood, Illinois: Richard D. Irwin, 1965) p. 110. They state: "Assume the prior distribution of a population mean is normal and has a mean of $\bar{u}_o$ and a standard deviation of σ_o. A sample is taken: the sample mean is $\bar{X}$, and the standard deviation of the sample is σ_s (σ_s is an estimate of σ_p, the standard deviation of the population).

To simplify the formulas which we shall use, we introduce the symbol I to represent the amount of information contained in a distribution, and define I as being equal to the reciprocal of the variance, i.e.:

$$I_o = \frac{1}{\sigma_o{}^2}$$

$$I_{\bar{x}} = \frac{1}{\sigma_{\bar{x}}{}^2} = \frac{r}{\sigma_p{}^2}$$

$$I_t = \frac{1}{\sigma_1{}^2}. \quad "$$

It is readily grasped that such a concept is useful in only a trivial way, and particularly, has limited application. In the case above the distribution not only must be known, but also normality is assumed.

[19] Birnbaum, in an insightful article on *informative inference* stresses the universality of the likelihood ratio in that it embodies the characterization and interpretation of statistical evidence. However, he is careful to constrain its "unlimited applicability" to those cases where the adequacy of a complete mathematical model can be assumed. His implied caveat, in other words, suggests that *evidential meaning* (in a mathematical as well as a social sense) is related as much to the denominator of the fraction (analogous to that part which is evident or observed). Allan Birnbaum, "Another View on the Foundations of Statistics," *The American Statistician*, February, 1962.

[20] Adrian M. McDonough. *Information Economics and Management Systems* (San Francisco: McGraw-Hill Book Company, 1963) "One other aspect adds mass to a data-processing system, and that is the notion of spatial considerations over which and through which the data must be assembled. This can set up what in a physical model might be called inertia and entropy, factors that reflect resistance and diffusion in the channels of the system. Mass in this sense can be made more effective as advances are obtained in high-speed equipments for data transmission." p. 245.

[21] *Ibid.* p. 246. "An organization may have a large number of low-mass systems; i.e., they operate with little or no interconnections, each achieving its autonomous purpose. If and when such an organization decides to bring now separated systems into a larger, more coordinated systems structure, it has the challenges of a mass data system."

[22] One sees things strung on the latticework of his personal conceptual scheme; they have meaning for him if they conform to a perceived pattern. One pattern for

examining titles such as these is "definitional." Hence, it may be of interest to examine the various words according to their origins, meanings, and roots.

Information: To give form or character to. *Form:* (Latin, *forma,* a shape, figure, image.)

System: A set or arrangement of things so related or connected as to form a unity or organized whole. (Greek, *systema,* from *synistanai* which is from syn- plus *histanai.*)

Evidential: Of, serving as, or based on evidence. *Evidence:* (Latin, *e-* plus *videns,* ppr. of *videre.*) Something which can be seen.

Meaning: What is meant; what is intended to be, or in fact is, signified, indicated, or understood: signification, purport, import, sense, or significance. *Mean:* probably akin to German *meinen,* to have in mind; perhaps from Indo-European *main,* to be of opinion.)

RELATED READINGS

SECTION 4: MODELS OF ORGANIZATION

Section 4 is concerned with theories and constructs of organization. Some of the selections are philosophical and abstract; others are related to more specific organizational dimensions.

In "An Analytic System Model for Organizational Theory" Gwen Andrew identifies a set of logical properties in theories of organizations. These properties are discussed and their interrelationship is explained. "General Systems Theory—The Skeleton of Science," by Kenneth E. Boulding, sets forth the nature of general systems theory. Boulding admonishes management science that, although it has advanced beyond simple models of organizations and control, there is still much distance to go in order to arrive at adequate models of human behavior and organization dynamics. In "A Mathematical Model for Integrated Business Systems" George Kozmetsky and Irving J. Lieberman discuss how integrated business systems are developed for managerial planning and control. In addition, they offer a mathematical model of integrated business systems. Alfred G. Smith's article, "The Organization Man and the Research Man," discusses research concerning the analysis of the organization man contrasted to the research man. In "Technology and Some Aspects of Industrial Supervision: A Model Building Approach" Elmer H. Burack looks at the influence of process technology and level of process technology on supervisory direction. He develops both general and detailed models of industrial organization units. "Communication Networks in Intermediate Markets" by F. E. Balderston considers some properties of communication networks in intermediate markets, setting forth an optimal structure. This article is a good example of the use of some of the components of the personnel networks and the output systems discussed in this book. In "Basic Concepts for a Theory of Organization" Ralph M. Stogdill proposes a different model of organization, one that he asserts reconciles classical and behavioral theories.

22

AN ANALYTIC SYSTEM MODEL FOR ORGANIZATION THEORY *

Gwen Andrew

This paper represents an effort to synthesize the work of philosophers of science with regard to teleological or adaptive systems. Methodological in focus, the intent is to identify a set of logical properties inherent in theories pertaining to organizations. This set of properties is referred to as a *general analytic model* for teleological systems and is construed to have heuristic value for the analysis of bureaucratic organizations as well as for development of a general theory appropriate to these organizations. The concepts of goal directedness, plasticity, interdependence of parts, system persistence and system change are examined and an explication of their relevance and interrelationship is attempted.

ESSENTIAL DEFINITIONS

The problem of defining a system is that of determining which characteristics of systems are relevant for a model applicable to a theory of bureaucracy. Such a theory will have to refer to a bureaucratically arranged social group with at least one specifiable goal. A bureaucratically arranged group is one whose members have differentiated functions relative to some goal of the organization.

Definition of System

A system will be taken to be a conventionally selected set of variables which putatively interact. This set of interacting variables may be (and

* Reprinted from *Journal of Academy of Management*, September, 1965, pp. 190–198.

doubtless will be) a sub-set of a larger set of variables; in other words, the system chosen for study may be a part of a larger system. While this is the case, the sub-system can nevertheless be viewed as a delimitable unit constituting a separate system, i.e., an organization. Whether the variables conventionally selected do indeed interact and whether their interactions are the significant relationships for the organization in question is a matter of empirical test. But some common sense selection must precede analysis. The interactions or interrelationships are the variable's "behavior" which tie the system together. In brief, they constitute the processes of the system.[1]

System Components

Elements and variables of a system may be distinguished as follows. Elements or entities of the system reflect its substantive content. Variables are the conditions of relevant properties of these elements at given times and carry the implication of change or variation regardless of the precision with which this change can be quantified or indeed measured. For example, the planets are elements of the solar system. Their location and momentum are variables. In a bureaucracy specific roles may be the important elements and power a relevant variable.

Each system, if it is to be a system, must have certain variables which are closely interrelated. Adjustment of their interrelationships accounts for the survival of the system in some specified state. These variables may be called the essential variables of the system after Ashby.[2] The values of these essential variables, and of any other variables which the investigator has included in the system, define the state of the system at any given time. All that is implied by the "value of a variable" at the moment is that the variable can be measured, whether in precise terms or in such terms as "more" or "less" or "present" or "absent."

A system operates in an environment which may be viewed in at least two ways: (1) Using a given organization as a system, one way of considering it is to determine those variables which are outside the formal system (but which interact with it) and to hold these as the *environment* of the organization. (2) Another way is to accept these outside variables as environment of the organization but to hold that the organization variables and the environmental variables together make up an absolute system. In this sense the set of variables are taken to exist without relation to any other thing or as self-sufficing entities disengaged from interrupting causes.

In the former method, which appears preferable, the system is specified on the basis of the variables considered as part of the organization. Variables outside the organization but acting upon it are considered as the *parameters* of the system.

All variables in an organizational analysis can then be divided into two classes; those which are within the system and are labeled variables and those which are outside the system but interact with it and are labeled parameters. Parameters have varying extents of relationship to the system. The task is to determine those which are significant for the system. This again, beyond an initial common sense selection, is based on empirical test. For example, industrial bureaucracies appear to interact with the political environment, here defined as parameters of the system. Whether or to what extent such parameters do in fact influence a given industry is open to test.

Open Systems and Determinism

As a part of the background for developing this *general analytic model,* it is important to consider the concept of closed and open systems since this distinction is fundamental to the use of a model which takes system parameters into account.

Closed systems, the systems of conventional physics, are isolated from their environment. There is no import or export of material from them and *their final state is unequivocally determined by their initial conditions.*[3] Bergman defines a closed system as one in which what happens inside the limited piece of space which is a system is not affected in any way by any factor outside of it.[4]

An open system, on the other hand, exchanges materials with the environment *and has the basic characteristics of self-regulation.* Social systems are open systems since they have this exchange with environment and, therefore, interrelationships of variables within open systems are influenced from outside the system, that is, by the system's parameters.

Is it possible then, to predict the state of an open system at one time from a description of its state at another? Can the probability of achievement of a governmental health agency program be predicted when the agency's operating funds, provided by legislative appropriation, are earmarked for different purposes? To reach a decision it is necessary to consider briefly the basic concept involved in determinism.

A deterministic theory has a particular logical structure such that the laws of the theory combined with a particular description of the system to which the theory is applied at one time enables deduction of one and only one description of the system at some other time. Thus, the laws of celestial mechanics guarantee that the state of the solar system at any time can be predicted from its state at any other time.

The predictive statements of a deterministic theory are of an "if . . .

then" form which indicated that *if* a certain condition prevails there will be certain consequences for the system.

In this regard there is sometimes confusion about the significance of statistical theories, i.e., it is thought that a theory which predicts events on a probability basis cannot be deterministic. Two concepts of probability are to be recognized in this context. The first is that probability which might be called the extent or degree of confirmation of a description of a phenomenon. This probability is applicable to all theories in science. The second kind of probability refers to the relative frequency of an event in the long run. This is the probability of statistical theories. A theory may be deterministic and statistical just as it may be deterministic and involve probability only in the sense of degree of confirmation.[5]

Social theories probably are most commonly of a statistical form although the probability functions are rarely stated precisely. It would appear that, by the nature of the variables involved in social systems and perhaps because of the influence of system parameters, the "if . . . then" statements will usually include a statistical factor becoming "if . . . then with a probability of *P*." This does not rule them out as deterministic theories. A theory of organizations which is a system theory will be deterministic and will deal with open systems. In principle, the probability that a government health agency will achieve a given program can be predicted from a system theory. Whether the prediction is accurate will not rest on the logical structure of the system theory but on the adequacy of the theory as an empirical description of the phenomena involved.

TELEOLOGICAL EXPLANATIONS

Although the goal reference is not always explicit and is not always set into a system framework, theories of organizations characteristically refer to system goals, that is, they are teleological in nature.[6] Teleological explanations are causal statements referring to systems which display a tendency toward certain sub-sets of all possible end states the system might achieve.[7] These systems are often said to be purposive or goal directed or directively organized systems because of this tendency.

Braithwaite has labeled the distinctive criterion of teleological explanation *plasticity* which is defined as a property of the system which eventuates in the attainment of a certain goal under different circumstances by alternative forms of activity. The essential feature of plasticity is that the goal can be achieved under a variety of circumstances not that it can be obtained by a variety of means.[8] To say that a system will attain a goal is to say its variables can alter enough to compensate for every set of circumstances likely to occur, i.e., the system can adapt.

The range of circumstances under which a system can arrive at a goal state will be referred to as the *variancy* of the system.[9] Knowledge of the variancy can be obtained for bureaucracies by inferences from knowledge of the circumstances or conditions under which the system, or systems like it, have achieved a goal in the past. That is, variance may be inferred from knowledge of conditions where similar teleological behavior has occurred rather than controlled by an experimenter or a manager of the organization.[10]

This knowledge of variance, embedded in a teleological explanation, makes prediction for a system possible when it is known that the set of circumstances which will, in fact, occur in the future will fall within that variance. For social organizations this is, of course, not a simple task but neither is it impossible. City planning agencies must make inferences as to the range of circumstances which could influence achievement of their goals and must make at least intuitive probability estimates of the likelihood of the occurrence of each of these. This knowledge is then used to arrange adaptations of a wide enough range to permit handling the alternative circumstances while moving to the goal. If the circumstances force adaptations beyond the capacity of the organization this goal will not be reached.

Determining a System Goal State

There have been a number of references in this discussion to system goals and goal states. It is now necessary to come to grips with the problem of determining what system state is a goal state.[11] A goal state has been said to be that state toward which a system tends to move. It is also that state which a system will adjust to maintain once it has been achieved. It has also been suggested that an adaptive (teleological) system will move to a goal state from a variety of initial states and that prediction of adaptation toward a state to be identified as a goal state will necessarily be statistical in character, i.e., predictions will be probabilistic.

The degree to which a system is directed toward *attaining* a goal state is a probability statement such as follows. Taking a system in which the values of the variables at time t do not equal the goal state, and given that one of the variables takes on a certain value, there is the probability P that the other variables will take on such values that they, with the first variable value, will determine the occurrence of the goal state at time t_1.

The tendency of a system to *maintain* a goal state by compensating alterations in its interdependent variables is stated in terms of the probability for occurrence of such compensating action. That is, a change in one variable from time t to time t_1 will be accompanied by probability P that the other variables will take on new values so that at time t_1 the sum of all variables will equal their sum at time t.

The significance of teleological explanations in social science is probably most clearly seen in the frequency with which functional explanations are encompassed in its theories. Functional explanations are a sub-class of teleological explanations. In the functional system, there is a chain of states which occur in order to arrive at or to maintain a goal state. The laws of the theory relevant to the system specify that a property of some element of the system is either a sufficient condition or a correlated condition with the occurrence of a state which is, in turn, a necessary or correlated condition for the occurrence of the goal state of the system.

For example, take the gift funds so common in office organizations. When a gift is sent to an absent employee during an illness the gift serves as a symbol of group membership reaffirming the absentee's integration in the group (end state) which serves the system need for social cohesion (goal state). The means, the giving of gifts, is not the important element. Rather there is some means taken to arrive at an end state which is prior and relevant to the goal state. This is the import of the chain of states arrived at through variety of possible means, ending in a goal state, all of which are characteristics of systems with plasticity.

In recent years it has become common to talk of adaptive systems, or plastic systems rather than teleological systems, doubtless in reaction to certain philosophical problems with the concept of teleology. Teleological systems as they have been discussed here are synonymous with adaptive systems and the latter expression will be more useful in the remaining comments which are concerned with system persistence and change.

System Persistence and Change

The logical properties of adaptive system models seem to have important possibilities for administrative science confronted, as it is, with the problem of change in social systems at the same time as their stability must be recognized. In short, social systems persist and only if this is the case does it make sense to talk about a given system except in an historical sense. But they do not persist in an absolute static arrangement. They experience change.

An adaptive system, which by definition is a system with a goal state, will adapt to shifts in parameter values by changes in system variables. In stable systems, the variables alter together. For a change in one there is a change in other(s) which maintains the sum of all of them at a certain level called a goal or which shifts the total system toward the goal state. In this sense, change in a system is a part of the process of adaptation in order to persist—to be stable. System change, then, is adaptive behavior and it follows that the more stable a system the more likely it is to adapt successfully, i.e., maintain or achieve its goal state.

Sub-Systems, Independence and Dependence

The analysis thus far has considered organizations as "wholes" with interdependent parts. But administrative science usually is concerned with systems made up of sub-systems which have some degree of independence. Sub-systems are sets of variables which interact and have the characteristics of systems as they have been discussed. Their distinguishing characteristic is that they happen to be significant sets of variables within a supra-system. A bureaucracy with its many departments is an obvious example of supra- and sub-systems.

The problem is to determine the way in which a system encompasses subsystems with partial, fluctuating and possibly temporary independencies without losing its essential wholeness.

Sub-systems may react to stimuli from their environment by adaptive behavior in the course of seeking or attaining a goal without affecting the remaining sub-systems in the whole. It is to be noted that this lack of effect on other sub-systems is not equivalent to saying there is no relationship to the goal state of the supra-system. It is crucial to recognize that while there may be *independent* adjustment or goal-seeking behavior on the part of individual sub-systems there remains *interaction* of these sub-systems within the supra-system. A sub-system is independent if it is not affected by action of any other sub-system in the whole even though its own action may affect other sub-systems. If there are two sub-systems A and B and an action of A is followed by an action of B but an action of B is not followed by an action of A, then A is independent of B but B is not independent of A. It is also the case that if B is dependent on A and A is dependent on C then B is dependent on C. In this case a change in C will be followed by a change in B.[12]

Interdependent sub-systems adapt to each other in the process of achieving or maintaining goal states whether this be in a one-to-one relationship or through a chain of dependency. Sub-systems which are independent need not adapt but those sub-systems dependent upon them will change if they change. The net result for the supra-system will be coordination among sub-systems which tends to keep the whole within the range of variation appropriate to *its* goal state.

The coordination of sub-systems in the movement of the supra-system to its goal state, or in striving to maintain it, depends in part on the principle that for any stimulus the response may be any of several different possible combinations of the values of variables of the sub-systems. There may be a trial and error action and that trial which results in success will end the adaptation or change period. The next time a like stimulus occurs it will initiate system behavior based on the prior successful combination of sub-system interactions. But, especially with systems exposed to the variety of conditions characteristic of social organizations, there is likely to be some change in the environment of the system and the formerly successful method may not work. A new combination of sub-system interactions is likely to eventuate.

For this reason, attention to the action of the sub-systems with an attempt to *predict* their exact interrelations may be fruitless. It is the range of circumstances under which adaptive systems are able to achieve or maintain a goal state which is the focus of attention. The range of variation which is permissible for sub-system variables and the probability that these ranges will not be exceeded determine the persistence of the system.

Using a simplified example, an auto manufacturing industry may have as its primary goal a certain margin of profit. Sales, as a sub-system, must sell enough cars to meet this profit which it does through its goal of selling the greatest possible number of cars. Engineering has a goal of designing the finest automobile possible within the constraints placed upon it by sales and accounting, other sub-systems. Each of these sub-systems adapts to the behavior of the other sub-systems. Under conditions of economic recession the goal state of sales will be changed; accounting may have to change its requirements on maximum cost permitted relative to selling price; and, the supra-system may have to change its accepted profit margin. The actual means for these adaptations may be to sell fewer cars of superior design to a limited population at a higher price or it may be to produce lower quality cars at a cheap cost but at a greater sales volume equaling the same margin of profit. Whichever method is used may be altered if it doesn't lead to the desired supra-system goal state of at least some margin of profit.

Compatibility of Goal States of Sub-Systems

The notion of essential wholeness of the system is obviously important but the concept of sets of sub-systems with goal states leads to the question of the compatibility of these goal states among sub-systems as well as with the goal of the supra-system. This problem may be handled through resort to a set of patterns for variable action.[13]

Variables may be classified into three types according to the extent of constancy or persistence in the same state which they display. The full-function variable has no finite interval of constancy, it is in constant flux.

The part-function variable has finite intervals of change and finite intervals of constancy. The step-function represents the variable with finite intervals of constancy separated by instantaneous jumps. It could be portrayed as a set of stair steps changing directions. The full-function shows no change at all in its value.

This classification permits extension of the model of teleological or adaptive systems into two important areas. First it permits logical understanding of the way in which variables change and a way of looking at the range of variation which variables may show within the system. For example, change in a full-function variable which happens to be a variable upon which a step-function variable is dependent will, if the change is great enough, cause an instantaneous jump in the value of the step-function variable. If this jump is of such great magnitude that it falls outside the permissible range of the variable, i.e., is greater than adjustments of variables related to it can accomplish in accommodation, the system (or sub-system) will lose its goal state.

Conversely, if a step-function change is caused by outside stimulus, any variable dependent on that particular step-function variable will also change in order that their values can equal, in sum, the initial sum of their values prior to the step-function change.

This possibility of accommodation is inherent in the understanding of the relationship of a set of sub-systems to the goal of a supra-system. Limitations of space preclude elaboration of the explanation but the significant point is that a set of variables with the characteristics of step-, part- and full-functions makes it possible to conceptualize a set of sub-systems which have incompatible goals and which may appear contrary to the goal state of the supra-system. In such instances the variables in a given sub-system may remain in a period of constancy outside the goal state of that sub-system due to its dependence on a second sub-system which is in its goal or moving toward it and which is incompatible with the goal state of the first sub-system.

The supra-system made up of independent and dependent sub-systems, some of which have incompatible goals, will be in a continuous process of adaptation resulting in system persistence up to the point that the stimulus is so disruptive that some sub-system variable(s) is pushed beyond the range of variation the sub-system (or the supra-system) can tolerate. The supra-system in its goal state and with a set of sub-systems all in their goal states is a system in perfect equilibrium, not likely to be found in bureaucratic organizations.

This very point is an explanation for the competitive relationships often observed among the sub-parts of a given organization. The sub-system which is successful in staying in its goal state at the expense of other sub-systems or of the supra-system may be extruded from the supra-system. In such instances the extruded sub-system has failed to adapt. In bureaucracies this extrusion phenomenon is usually expressed through a "shake-up" in the management. The system model makes it possible to predict the likelihood of such "shake-ups" and the actual purpose they serve in a given instance.

SUMMARY

The foregoing analysis of teleological or adaptive systems has attempted to provide a general analytic model for such systems which will be helpful to the scientist working toward a theory of bureaucratic organizations. It is also believed that this formulation will be useful to the observer of a particular organization. There is no question that it deals with a complicated set of interrelated concepts but the systems with which students of organizations deal are, in fact, complex. The details of their complexity may be better understood through a general logical framework in which to set them.

The *general analytic model* presents an organization as an adaptive system (i.e., goal directed) with a set of interdependent variables, adjusting to each other upon stimulation of one or more of them from system parameters. The plastic nature of adaptive systems is characterized essentially as the ability of these systems to arrive at goals under a variety of different conditions. The concept of an adaptive system, thus defined, permits explanation of the nature of both persistence and change in an organization and further of the nature of interrelationships between sub-parts of the total organization.

Finally the model should be fruitful in finding solutions to conceptual problems regarding organizations such as whether and, if so, what distinctions must be made between public and private bureaucracies in explanatory theories.

NOTES

[1] This definition of *system* conforms to that provided by most commentators. See for example, Bergman and Ashby in the citations that follow.

[2] W. Ross Ashby, *Design for a Brain* (New York: John Wiley and Sons, Inc., 1952), p. 14.

[3] L. Von Bertalanffy, "General System Theory," *General Systems, Yearbook of the Society for the Advancement of General System Theory,* Vol. 1 (1956), p. 3.

[4] G. Bergman, *Philosophy of Science* (Madison, Wisconsin: University of Wisconsin Press, 1957).

5 R. Carnap, "The Two Concepts of Probability," *Readings in the Philosophy of of Science,* ed. H. Feigl and May Brodbeck (New York: Appleton-Century-Crofts, Inc., 1953), p. 442.

6 See for example Etzioni who distinguishes goal models and system models. Gouldner refers to the rational model and the natural system model. A. Etzioni, "Two Approaches to Organizational Analysis: A Critique and a Suggestion," *Administrative Science Quarterly,* Vol. 5, No. 2 (September, 1960). A. Gouldner, "Organizational Analysis," *Sociology Today,* ed. M. Merton, L. Broom and L. Cottrell (New York: Basic Books, 1959).

7 Ernest Nagel, "Teleological Explanation and Teleological Systems," *Vision and Action: Essays in Honor of Horace Kallen on His Seventieth Birthday,* ed. S. Ratner (New Brunswick, N.J.: Rutgers University Press, 1953).

8 R. B. Braithwaite, *Scientific Explanation* (New York: Harper and Brothers, 1960), p. 328.

9 *Ibid.*

10 Managers can control variance in some situations as they do in designing an automobile which is built to adapt to a wide range of conditions.

11 For this discussion I am indebted to R. Rudner for a manuscript, "The Problem of Functionalism," Second Research Conference, Michigan Department of Mental Health, 1959.

12 The environment of a sub-system includes the supra-system itself and, therefore, variables of other sub-systems are parameters of the first sub-system as defined here.

13 Based on W. Ross Ashby, *op. cit.,* p. 80 ff.

23

GENERAL SYSTEMS THEORY—THE SKELETON OF SCIENCE *

Kenneth E. Boulding

General Systems Theory [1] is a name which has come into use to describe a level of theoretical model-building which lies somewhere between the highly generalized constructions of pure mathematics and the specific theories of the specialized disciplines. Mathematics attempts to organize highly general relationships into a coherent system, a system however which does not have any necessary connections with the "real" world around us. It studies all thinkable relationships abstracted from any concrete situation or body of empirical knowledge. It is not even confined to "quantitative" relationships narrowly defined—indeed, the developments of a mathematics of quality and structure is already on the way, even though it is not as far advanced as the "classical" mathematics of quantity and number. Nevertheless because in a sense mathematics contains all theories it contains none; it is the language of theory, but it does not give us the content. At the other extreme we have the separate disciplines and sciences, with their separate bodies of theory. Each Discipline corresponds to a certain segment of the empirical world, and each develops theories which have particular applicability to its own empirical segment. Physics, Chemistry, Biology, Psychology, Sociology, Economics and so on all carve out for themselves certain elements of the experience of man and develop theories and patterns of activity (research) which yield satisfaction in understanding, and which are appropriate to their special segments.

In recent years increasing need has been felt for a body of systematic theoretical constructs which will discuss the general relationships of the empirical world. This is the quest of General Systems Theory. It does not

* Reprinted from *Management Science*, April, 1956, pp. 197–208.

395

seek, of course, to establish a single, self-contained "general theory of practically everything" which will replace all the special theories of particular
disciplines. Such a theory would be almost without content, for we always
pay for generality by sacrificing content, and all we can say about practically everything is almost nothing. Somewhere however between the specific that has no meaning and the general that has no content there must be,
for each purpose and at each level of abstraction, an optimum degree of
generality. It is the contention of the General Systems Theorists that this
optimum degree of generality in theory is not always reached by the particular sciences. The objectives of General Systems Theory then can be set
out with varying degrees of ambition and confidence. At a low level of ambition but with a high degree of confidence it aims to point out similarities
in the theoretical constructions of different disciplines, where these exist,
and to develop theoretical models having applicability to at least two
different fields of study. At a higher level of ambition, but with perhaps a
lower degree of confidence it hopes to develop something like a "spectrum"
of theories—a system of systems which may perform the function of a
"gestalt" in theoretical construction. Such "gestalts" in special fields have
been of great value in directing research towards the gaps which they reveal. Thus the periodic table of elements in chemistry directed research for
many decades towards the discovery of unknown elements to fill gaps in
the table until the table was completely filled. Similarly a "system of systems" might be of value in directing the attention of theorists towards gaps
in theoretical models, and might even be of value in pointing towards
methods of filling them.

The need for general systems theory is accentuated by the present sociological situation in science. Knowledge is not something which exists and
grows in the abstract. It is a function of human organisms and of social
organization. Knowledge, that is to say, is always what somebody knows:
the most perfect transcript of knowledge in writing is not knowledge if nobody knows it. Knowledge however grows by the receipt of meaningful information—that is, by the intake of messages by a knower which are capable of reorganizing his knowledge. We will quietly duck the question as to
what reorganizations constitute "growth" of knowledge by defining "semantic growth" of knowledge as those reorganizations which can profitably
be talked about, in writing or speech, by the Right People. Science, that is
to say, is what can be talked about profitably by scientists in their role as
scientists. The crisis of science today arises because of the increasing difficulty of such profitable talk among scientists as a whole. Specialization has
outrun Trade, communication between the disciplines becomes increasingly
difficult, and the Republic of Learning is breaking up into isolated subcultures with only tenuous lines of communication between them—a situation

which threatens intellectual civil war. The reason for this breakup in the body of knowledge is that in the course of specialization the receptors of information themselves become specialized. Hence physicists only talk to physicists, economists to economists—worse still, nuclear physicists only talk to nuclear physicists and econometricians to econometricians. One wonders sometimes if science will not grind to a stop in an assemblage of walled-in hermits, each mumbling to himself words in a private language that only he can understand. In these days the arts may have beaten the sciences to this desert of mutual unintelligibility, but that may be merely because the swift intuitions of art reach the future faster than the plodding leg work of the scientist. The more science breaks into sub-groups, and the less communication is possible among the disciplines, however, the greater chance there is that the total growth of knowledge is being slowed down by the loss of relevant communications. The spread of specialized deafness means that someone who ought to know something that someone else knows isn't able to find it out for lack of generalized ears.

It is one of the main objectives of General Systems Theory to develop these generalized ears, and by developing a framework of general theory to enable one specialist to catch relevant communications from others. Thus the economist who realizes the strong formal similarity between utility theory in economics and field theory in physics [2] is probably in a better position to learn from the physicists than one who does not. Similarly a specialist who works with the growth concept—whether the crystallographer, the virologist, the cytologist, the physiologist, the psychologist, the sociologist or the economist—will be more sensitive to the contributions of other fields if he is aware of the many similarities of the growth process in widely different empirical fields.

There is not much doubt about the demand for general systems theory under one brand name or another. It is a little more embarrassing to inquire into the supply. Does any of it exist, and if so where? What is the chance of getting more of it, and if so, how? The situation might be described as promising and in ferment, though it is not wholly clear what is being promised or brewed. Something which might be called an "interdisciplinary movement" has been abroad for some time. The first signs of this are usually the development of hybrid disciplines. Thus physical chemistry emerged in the third quarter of the nineteenth century, social psychology in the second quarter of the twentieth. In the physical and biological sciences the list of hybrid disciplines is now quite long—biophysics, biochemistry, astrophysics are all well established. In the social sciences social anthropology is fairly well established, economic psychology and economic sociology are just beginning. There are signs, even, that Political Economy, which died in infancy some hundred years ago, may have a re-birth.

In recent years there has been an additional development of great interest in the form of "multisexual" interdisciplines. The hybrid disciplines, as their hyphenated names indicate, come from two respectable and honest academic parents. The newer interdisciplines have a much more varied and occasionally even obscure ancestry, and result from the reorganization of material from many different fields of study. Cybernetics, for instance, comes out of electrical engineering, neurophysiology, physics, biology, with even a dash of economics. Information theory, which originated in communications engineering, has important applications in many fields stretching from biology to the social sciences. Organization theory comes out of economics, sociology, engineering, physiology, and Management Science itself is an equally multidisciplinary product.

On the more empirical and practical side the interdisciplinary movement is reflected in the development of interdepartmental institutes of many kinds. Some of these find their basis of unity in the empirical field which they study, such as institutes of industrial relations, of public administration, of international affairs, and so on. Others are organized around the application of a common methodology to many different fields and problems, such as the Survey Research Center and the Group Dynamics Center at the University of Michigan. Even more important than these visible developments, perhaps, though harder to perceive and identify, is a growing dissatisfaction in many departments, especially at the level of graduate study, with the existing traditional theoretical backgrounds for the empirical studies which form the major part of the output of Ph. D. theses. To take but a single example from the field with which I am most familiar, it is traditional for studies of labor relations, money and banking, and foreign investment to come out of departments of economics. Many of the needed theoretical models and frameworks in these fields, however, do not come out of "economic theory" as this is usually taught, but from sociology, social psychology, and cultural anthropology. Students in the department of economics however rarely get a chance to become acquainted with these theoretical models, which may be relevant to their studies, and they become impatient with economic theory, much of which may not be relevant.

It is clear that there is a good deal of interdisciplinary excitement abroad. If this excitement is to be productive, however, it must operate within a certain framework of coherence. It is all too easy for the interdisciplinary to degenerate into the undisciplined. If the interdisciplinary movement, therefore, is not to lose that sense of form and structure which is the "discipline" involved in the various separate disciplines, it should develop a structure of its own. This I conceive to be the great task of general systems theory. For the rest of this paper, therefore, I propose to look at some possible ways in which general systems theory might be structured.

Two possible approaches to the organization of general systems theory suggest themselves, which are to be thought of as complementary rather than competitive, or at least as two roads each of which is worth exploring. The first approach is to look over the empirical universe and to pick out certain general *phenomena* which are found in many different disciplines, and to seek to build up general theoretical models relevant to these phenomena. The second approach is to arrange the empirical fields in a hierarchy of complexity of organization of their basic "individual" or unit of behavior, and to try to develop a level of abstraction appropriate to each.

Some examples of the first approach will serve to clarify it, without pretending to be exhaustive. In almost all disciplines, for instance, we find examples of populations—aggregates of individuals conforming to a common definition, to which individuals are added (born) and subtracted (die) and in which the age of the individual is a relevant and identifiable variable. These populations exhibit dynamic movements of their own, which can frequently be described by fairly simple systems of difference equations. The populations of different species also exhibit dynamic interactions among themselves, as in the theory of Volterra. Models of population change and interaction cut across a great many different fields—ecological systems in biology, capital theory in economics which deals with populations of "goods," social ecology, and even certain problems of statistical mechanics. In all these fields population change, both in absolute numbers and in structure, can be discussed in terms of birth and survival functions relating numbers of births and of deaths in specific age groups to various aspects of the system. In all these fields the interaction of population can be discussed in terms of competitive, complementary, or parasitic relationships among populations of different species, whether the species consist of animals, commodities, social classes or molecules.

Another phenomenon of almost universal significance for all disciplines is that of the interaction of an "individual" of some kind with its environment. Every discipline studies some kind of "individual"—electron, atom, molecule, crystal, virus, cell, plant, animal, man, family, tribe, state, church, firm, corporation, university, and so on. Each of these individuals exhibits "behavior," action, or change, and this behavior is considered to be related in some way to the environment of the individual—that is, with other individuals with which it comes into contact or into some relationship. Each individual is thought of as consisting of a structure or complex of indivividuals of the order immediately below it—atoms are an arrangement of protons and electrons, molecules of atoms, cells of molecules, plants, animals and men of cells, social organizations of men. The "behavior" of each individual is "explained" by the structure and arrangement of the lower individuals of which it is composed, or by certain principles of equilibrium or homeostasis according to which certain "states" of the individual are "preferred." Behavior is discribed in terms of the restoration of these preferred states when they are disturbed by changes in the environment.

Another phenomenon of universal significance is growth. Growth theory is in a sense a subdivision of the theory of individual "behavior," growth being one important aspect of behavior. Nevertheless there are important differences between equilibrium theory and growth theory, which perhaps warrant giving growth theory a special category. There is hardly a science in which the growth phenomenon does not have some importance, and though there is a great difference in complexity between the growth of crystals, embryos, and societies, many of the principles and concepts which are important at the lower levels are also illuminating at higher levels. Some growth phenomena can be dealt with in terms of relatively simple population models, the solution of which yields growth curves of single variables. At the more complex levels structural problems become dominant and the complex interrelationships between growth and form are the focus of interest. All growth phenomena are sufficiently alike however to suggest that a general theory of growth is by no means an impossibility.[3]

Another aspect of the theory of the individual and also of interrelationships among individuals which might be singled out for special treatment is the theory of information and communication. The information concept as developed by Shannon has had interesting applications outside its original field of electrical engineering. It is not adequate, of course, to deal with problems involving the semantic level of communication. At the biological level however the information concept may serve to develop general notions of structuredness and abstract measures of organization which give us, as it were, a third basic dimension beyond mass and energy. Communication and information processes are found in a wide variety of empirical situations, and are unquestionably essential in the development of organization, both in the biological and the social world.

These various approaches to general systems through various aspects of the empirical world may lead ultimately to something like a general field theory of the dynamics of action and interaction. This, however, is a long way ahead.

A second possible approach to general systems theory is through the arrangement of theoretical systems and constructs in a hierarchy of complexity, roughly corresponding to the complexity of the "individuals" of the various empirical fields. This approach is more systematic than the first, leading towards a "system of systems." It may not replace the first entirely, however, as there may always be important theoretical concepts and constructs lying outside the systematic framework. I suggest below a possible arrangement of "levels" of theoretical discourse.

1. The first level is that of the static structure. It might be called the level of *frameworks.* This is the geography and anatomy of the universe— the patterns of electrons around a nucleus, the pattern of atoms in a molecular formula, the arrangement of atoms in a crystal, the anatomy of the gene, the cell, the plant, the animal, the mapping of the earth, the solar system, the astronomical universe. The accurate description of these frameworks is the beginning of organized theoretical knowledge in almost any field, for without accuracy in this description of static relationships no accurate functional or dynamic theory is possible. Thus the Copernican revolution was really the discovery of a new static framework for the solar system which permitted a simpler description of its dynamics.

2. The next level of systematic analysis is that of the simple dynamic system with predetermined, necessary motions. This might be called the level of *clockworks*. The solar system itself is of course the great clock of the universe from man's point of view, and the deliciously exact predictions of the astronomers are a testimony to the excellence of the clock which they study. Simple machines such as the lever and the pulley, even quite complicated machines like steam engines and dynamos fall mostly under this category. The greatest part of the theoretical structure of physics, chemistry, and even of economics falls into this category. Two special cases might be noted. Simple equilibrium systems really fall into the dynamic category, as every equilibrium system must be considered as a limiting case of a dynamic system, and its stability cannot be determined except from the properties of its parent dynamic system. Stochastic dynamic systems leading to equilibria, for all their complexity, also fall into this group of systems; such is the modern view of the atom and even of the molecule, each position or part of the system being given with a certain degree of probability, the whole nevertheless exhibiting a determinate structure. Two types of analytical method are important here, which we may call, with the usage of the economists, comparative statics and true dynamics. In comparative statics we compare two equilibrium positions of the system under different values for the basic parameters. These equilibrium positions are usually expressed as the solution of a set of simultaneous equations. The method of comparative statics is to compare the solutions when the parameters of the equations are changed. Most simple mechanical problems are solved in this way. In true dynamics on the other hand we exhibit the system as a set of difference or differential equations, which are then solved in the form of an explicit function of each variable with time. Such a system may reach a position of stationary equilibrium, or it may not—there are

plenty of examples of explosive dynamic systems, a very simple one being the growth of a sum at compound interest! Most physical and chemical reactions and most social systems do in fact exhibit a tendency to equilibrium—otherwise the world would have exploded or imploded long ago.

3. The next level is that of the control mechanism or cybernetic system, which might be nicknamed the level of the *thermostat*. This differs from the simple stable equilibrium system mainly in the fact that the transmission and interpretation of information is an essential part of the system. As a result of this the equilibrium position is not merely determined by the equations of the system, but the system will move to the maintenance of any *given* equilibrium, within limits. Thus the thermostat will maintain *any* temperature at which it can be set; the equilibrium temperature of the system is not determined solely by its equations. The trick here of course is that the essential variable of the dynamic system is the *difference* between an "observed" or "recorded" value of the maintained variable and its "ideal" value. If this difference is not zero the system moves so as to diminish it; thus the furnace sends up heat when the temperature is recorded as "too cold" and is turned off when the recorded temperature is "too hot." The homeostasis model, which is of such importance in physiology, is an example of a cybernetic mechanism, and such mechanisms exist through the whole empirical world of the biologist and the social scientist.

4. The fourth level is that of the "open system," or self-maintaining structure. This is the level at which life begins to differentiate itself from not-life: it might be called the level of the *cell*. Something like an open system exists, of course, even in physico-chemical equilibrium systems; atomic structures maintain themselves in the midst of a throughput of electrons, molecular structures maintain themselves in the midst of a throughput of atoms. Flames and rivers likewise are essentially open systems of a very simple kind. As we pass up the scale of complexity of organization towards living systems, however, the property of self-maintenance of structure in the midst of a throughput of material becomes of dominant importance. An atom or a molecule can presumably exist without throughput: the existence of even the simplest living organism is inconceivable without ingestion, excretion and metabolic exchange. Closely connected with the property of self-maintenance is the property of self-reproduction. It may be, indeed, that self-reproduction is a more primitive or "lower level" system than the open system, and that the gene and the virus, for instance, may be able to reproduce themselves without being open systems. It is not perhaps an important question at what point in the scale of increasing complexity "life" begins. What is clear, however, is that by the time we have got to systems which both reproduce themselves and maintain themselves in the midst of a throughput of material and energy, we have something to which it would be hard to deny the title of "life."

5. The fifth level might be called the genetic societal level; it is typified by the *plant,* and it dominates the empirical world of the botanist. The outstanding characteristics of these systems are first, a division of labor among cells to form a cell-society with differentiated and mutually dependent parts (roots, leaves, seeds, etc.), and second a sharp differentiation between the genotype and the phenotype, associated with the phenomenon of equifinal or "blueprinted" growth. At this level there are no highly specialized sense organs and information receptors are diffuse and incapable of much throughput of information—it is doubtful whether a tree can distinguish much more than light from dark, long days from short days, cold from hot.

6. As we move upward from the plant world towards the animal kingdom we gradually pass over into a new level, the "animal" level, characterized by increased mobility, teleological behavior, and self-awareness. Here we have the development of specialized information-receptors (eyes, ears, etc.) leading to an enormous increase in the intake of information; we have also a great development of nervous systems, leading ultimately to the brain, as an organizer of the information intake into a knowledge structure or "image." Increasingly as we ascend the scale of animal life, behavior is response not to a specific stimulus but to an "image" or knowledge structure or view of the environment as a whole. This image is of course determined ultimately by information received into the organism; the relation between the receipt of information and the building up of an image however is exceedingly complex. It is not a simple piling up or accumulation of information received, although this frequently happens, but a structuring of information into something essentially different from the information itself. After the image structure is well established most information received produces very little change in the image—it goes through the loose structure, as it were, without hitting it, much as a sub-atomic particle might go through an atom without hitting anything. Sometimes however the information is "captured" by the image and added to it, and sometimes the information hits some kind of a "nucleus" of the image and a reorganization takes place, with far reaching and radical changes in behavior in apparent response to what seems like a very small stimulus. The difficulties in the prediction of the behavior of these systems arise largely because of this intervention of the image between the stimulus and the response.

7. The next level is the "human" level, that is of the individual human being considered as a system. In addition to all, or nearly all, of the characteristics of animal systems man possesses self consciousness, which is something different from mere awareness. His image, besides being much more complex than that even of the higher animals, has a self-reflexive quality—he not only knows, but knows that he knows. This property is probably bound up with the phenomenon of language and symbolism. It is

the capacity for speech—the ability to produce, absorb, and interpret *symbols,* as opposed to mere signs like the warning cry of an animal—which most clearly marks man off from his humbler brethren. Man is distinguished from the animals also by a much more elaborate image of time and relationship; man is probably the only organization that knows that it dies, that contemplates in its behavior a whole life span, and more than a life span. Man exists not only in time and space but in history, and his behavior is profoundly affected by his view of the time process in which he stands.

8. Because of the vital importance for the individual man of symbolic images and behavior based on them it is not easy to separate clearly the level of the individual human organism from the next level, that of social organizations. In spite of the occasional stories of feral children raised by animals, man isolated from his fellows is practically unknown. So essential is the symbolic image in human behavior that one suspects that a truly isolated man would not be "human" in the usually accepted sense, though he would be potentially human. Nevertheless it is convenient for some purposes to distinguish the individual human as a system from the social systems which surround him, and in this sense social organizations may be said to constitute another level of organization. The unit of such systems is not perhaps the person—the individual human as such—but the "role" —that part of the person which is concerned with the organization or situation in question, and it is tempting to define social organizations, or almost any social system, as a set of roles tied together with channels of communication. The interrelations of the role and the person however can never be completely neglected—a square person in a round role may become a little rounder, but he also makes the role squarer, and the perception of a role is affected by the personalities of those who have occupied it in the past. At this level we must concern ourselves with the content and meaning of messages, the nature and dimensions of value systems, the transcription of images into a historical record, the subtle symbolizations of art, music, and poetry, and the complex gamut of human emotion. The empirical universe here is human life and society in all its complexity and richness.

9. To complete the structure of systems we should add a final turret for transcendental systems, even if we may be accused at this point of having built Babel to the clouds. There are however the ultimates and absolutes and the inescapable unknowables, and they also exhibit systematic structure and relationship. It will be a sad day for man when nobody is allowed to ask questions that do not have any answers.

One advantage of exhibiting a hierarchy of systems in this way is that it gives us some idea of the present gaps in both theoretical and empirical knowledge. Adequate theoretical models extend up to about the fourth level, and not much beyond. Empirical knowledge is deficient at practically all levels. Thus at the level of the static structure, fairly adequate descriptive models are available for geography, chemistry, geology, anatomy, and descriptive social science. Even at this simplest level, however, the problem of the adequate description of complex structures is still far from solved. The theory of indexing and cataloguing for instance, is only in its infancy. Librarians are fairly good at cataloguing books, chemists have begun to catalogue structural formulae, and anthropologists have begun to catalogue culture trails. The cataloguing of events, ideas, theories, statistics, and empirical data has hardly begun. The very multiplication of records however as time goes on will force us into much more adequate cataloguing and reference systems than we now have. This is perhaps the major unsolved theoretical problem at the level of the static structure. In the empirical field there are still great areas where static structures are very imperfectly known, although knowledge is advancing rapidly, thanks to new probing devices such as the electron microscope. The anatomy of that part of the empirical world which lies between the large molecule and the cell however, is still obscure at many points. It is precisely this area however—which includes, for instance, the gene and the virus—that holds the secret of life, and until its anatomy is made clear the nature of the functional systems which are involved will inevitably be obscure.

The level of the "clockwork" is the level of "classical" natural science, especially physics and astronomy, and is probably the most completely developed level in the present state of knowledge, especially if we extend the concept to include the field theory and stochastic models of modern physics. Even here however there are important gaps, especially at the higher empirical levels. There is much yet to be known about the sheer mechanics of cells and nervous systems, of brains and of societies.

Beyond the second level adequate theoretical models get scarcer. The last few years have seen great developments at the third and fourth levels. The theory of control mechanisms ("thermostats") has established itself as the new discipline of cybernetics, and the theory of self-maintaining systems or "open systems" likewise has made rapid strides. We could hardly maintain however that much more than a beginning had been made in these fields. We know very little about the cybernetics of genes and genetic systems, for instance, and still less about the control mechanisms involved in the mental and social world. Similarly the processes of self-maintenance remain essentially mysterious at many points, and although the theoretical possibility of constructing a self-maintaining machine which would be a true open system has been suggested, we seem to be a long way from the actual construction of such a mechanical similitude of life.

Beyond the fourth level it may be doubted whether we have as yet even the rudiments of theoretical systems. The intricate machinery of growth by which the genetic complex organizes the matter around it is almost a complete mystery. Up to now, whatever the future may hold, only God can make a tree. In the face of living systems we are almost helpless; we can occasionally cooperate with systems which we do not understand: we cannot even begin to reproduce them. The ambiguous status of medicine, hovering as it does uneasily between magic and science, is a testimony to the state of systematic knowledge in this area. As we move up the scale the absence of the appropriate theoretical systems becomes ever more noticeable. We can hardly conceive ourselves constructing a system which would be in any recognizable sense "aware," much less self conscious. Nevertheless as we move towards the human and societal level a curious thing happens: the fact that we have, as it were, an inside track, and that we ourselves *are* the systems which we are studying, enables us to utilize systems which we do not really understand. It is almost inconceivable that we should make a machine that would make a poem: nevertheless, poems *are* made by fools like us by processes which are largely hidden from us. The kind of knowledge and skill that we have at the symbolic level is very different from that which we have at lower levels—it is like, shall we say, the "knowhow" of the gene as compared with the knowhow of the biologist. Nevertheless it is a real kind of knowledge and it is the source of the creative achievements of man as artist, writer, architect, and composer.

Perhaps one of the most valuable uses of the above scheme is to prevent us from accepting as final a level of theoretical analysis which is below the level of the empirical world which we are investigating. Because, in a sense, each level incorporates all those below it, much valuable information and insights can be obtained by applying low-level systems to high-level subject matter. Thus most of the theoretical schemes of the social sciences are still at level (2), just rising now to (3), although the subject matter clearly involves level (8). Economics, for instance, is still largely a "mechanics of utility and self interest," in Jevons' masterly phrase. Its theoretical and mathematical base is drawn largely from the level of simple equilibrium theory and dynamic mechanisms. It has hardly begun to use concepts such as information which are appropriate at level (3), and makes no use of higher level systems. Furthermore, with this crude apparatus it has achieved a modicum of success, in the sense that anybody trying to manipulate an economic system is almost certain to be better off if he knows some economics than if he doesn't. Nevertheless at some point progress in economics is going to depend on its ability to break out of these low-level systems, useful as they are as first approximations, and utilize systems which are more directly appropriate to its universe—when, of course, these systems are discovered. Many other examples could be given—the wholly inappropriate use in psychoanalytic theory, for instance, of the concept of energy, and the long inability of psychology to break loose from a sterile stimulus-response model.

Finally, the above scheme might serve as a mild word of warning even to Management Science. This new discipline represents an important breakaway from overly simple mechanical models in the theory of organization and control. Its emphasis on communication systems and organizational structure, on principles of homeostasis and growth, on decision processes under uncertainty, is carrying us far beyond the simple models of maximizing behavior of even ten years ago. This advance in the level of theoretical analysis is bound to lead to more powerful and fruitful systems. Nevertheless we must never quite forget that even these advances do not carry us much beyond the third and fourth levels, and that in dealing with human personalities and organizations we are dealing with systems in the empirical world far beyond our ability to formulate. We should not be wholly surprised, therefore, if our simpler systems, for all their importance and validity, occasionally let us down.

I chose the subtitle of my paper with some eye to its possible overtones of meaning. General Systems Theory is the skeleton of science in the sense that it aims to provide a framework or structure of systems on which to hang the flesh and blood of particular disciplines and particular subject matters in an orderly and coherent corpus of knowledge. It is also, however, something of a skeleton in a cupboard—the cupboard in this case being the unwillingness of science to admit the very low level of its successes in systematization, and its tendency to shut the door on problems and subject matters which do not fit easily into simple mechanical schemes. Science, for all its successes, still has a very long way to go. General Systems Theory may at times be an embarrassment in pointing out how very far we still have to go, and in deflating excessive philosophical claims for overly simple systems. It also may be helpful however in pointing out to some extent *where* we have to go. The skeleton must come out of the cupboard before its dry bones can live.

NOTES

[1] The name and many of the ideas are to be credited to L. von Bertalanffy, who is not, however, to be held accountable for the ideas of the present author! For a general discussion of Bertalanffy's ideas see *General Systems Theory: A New Approach to Unity of Science, Human Biology*, Dec., 1951, Vol. 23, p. 303–361.

[2] See A. G. Pikler, Utility Theories in Field Physics and Mathematical Economics, *British Journal for the Philosophy of Science*, 1955, Vol. 5, pp. 47 and 303.

[3] See "Towards a General Theory of Growth" by K. E. Boulding, *Canadian Journal of Economics and Political Science,* 19 Aug. 1953, 326–340.

24

A MATHEMATICAL MODEL FOR
INTEGRATED BUSINESS SYSTEMS *

George Kozmetsky and Irving J. Lieberman

To indicate clearly the requirements for management planning and control, the terms "programming," "scheduling," and "feedback" are first introduced (Exhibit 1).

Programming, in this context, is a scientific approach to planning. The specific policies and plans are developed. We attempt to solve both the financial and operational problems. In programming, we attempt to define, measure, and analyze all the relevant factors in the business situation. Programming is undertaken in two stages: (1) determination of long-range policies, and (2) establishment of short-run goals and operational plans.

Scheduling is the detailed means of carrying out the program. Scheduling a program involves the physical details—quantities, qualities, locations, the precise times when the various business activities are to be started and completed, and by whom. Today this is accomplished by middle management decisions—aided by established company policies, the systems and procedure manuals, and the budgeting process. The *feedback* concept is the method of determining which data are relevant, how they should be obtained, and how they should be presented in order to accomplish the purposes of programming and scheduling. An integrated business system can be viewed as a communication process (Exhibit 2). Transactions occur, are recorded, and the record communicated or stored. The flow of transactions can be called the formal communications channel. Information can be communicated through informal channels as well—for example, by word of mouth or personal observation. Both the formal and informal communicating systems are used for management action.

* Reprinted from *Organizing for Effective Systems Planning and Control,* American Management Association, 1956, pp. 173–185.

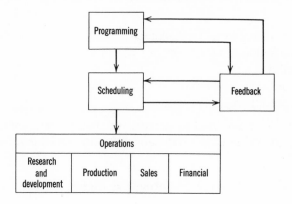

Exhibit 1.

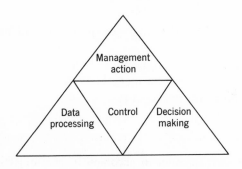

Exhibit 2.

The communication network is feedback as defined earlier, and the integrated business system is a means for implementing the feedback concept.

CASE ILLUSTRATION—"A" SHOE COMPANY

The illustration here presented describes the collection and use of figures by "A" Shoe Company. The company employs about 350 persons; its sales are $5 million to $7.5 million per year. The "A" Shoe Company has developed a fairly competent standard cost control system integrating production planning and scheduling, production control, sales control, cost and general accounting, and management reporting.

The company originates 25 source documents on which appear about 50 distinctly different categories of information. The source documents are processed to produce 38 additional reports. These reports are used as follows:

Production planning and scheduling	5
Production and inventory control	14
Sales control	5
General and cost accounting	38
Management report	2

Seventeen clerks are used to process the data for accounting purposes, and four to six are used in production planning, scheduling, and control.

Design Requirements for a Mathematical Model

Design Objectives. If we are to describe the business system employed at the "A" Shoe Company by using a mathematical model, the model must meet the following design objectives:

1. The model presents the total system in an easily comprehensible form.
2. The model presents the details of the system.
3. The model has a method for manipulation.
4. The model shows the effects of system changes.

The mathematical model must also be flexible enough to provide data for the decision model and satisfy the requirements for management action.

Aims of the Model. In order to accomplish these objectives, the mathematical model must provide for:

1. A mathematical representation of the actual data processing in all its detail.
2. Lag time in the data-processing and reporting system.
3. Frequency of information and report transmission.
4. Organization factors—formal and informal.
5. Method for determining management needs.
6. Method for manipulating a system to satisfy management needs.

Only when all these requirements are met will it be possible to have a model which fills the gaps in current mathematical techniques of operations research. No method exists to do all of this at the present time, although the directions for further research are clear.

Model Design. The model which will be constructed for the "A" Shoe Company meets all the design objectives and provides for a method of manipulating the system to satisfy management's need.

Definition of Terms

We must first systematize the information contained in the "A" Shoe Company's forms, documents, and reports. In addition, their flow through the data-processing and control system must be represented. This means we must define the symbols and terms which will be used in construction of the model. These definitions are used only to convey the concepts of the model.

Business Function (B). A business function is defined as a set of managerial activities which are assigned to a group according to types of duties.

Class of Information (C). A class of information consists of one or more pieces of information, all having common qualities. A class may have any number of members.

Identification Type of Class Information (i). These classes describe or identify a form or document.

Quantitative Type of Class of Information (q). These are the classes of information which give a quantitative measure.

Form (F). Two documents are said to be the same form if they have all the same classes of information and no other classes.

Source Data Forms (S). Source data forms are those upon which quantitative information is recorded for the first time and is not obtainable from any other form by using some operation or combination of operations.

Report Forms (R). Report forms are those which arise from performing an operation or combination of operations on source data forms.

Construction of the Mathematical Model

With these definitions and symbols in mind, we may construct a mathematical model in the form of matrices. The first step is to show the classes of information, i's and q's, which are available on each source data form, S. This has been done for the "A" Shoe Company in the Matrix M_s (Exhibit 3).

For this model, we are interested in whether the information is on the form or not on the form. This is designated by putting a 1 or 0 in the intersection of the row headed by the symbol for the information and the column headed by the symbol for the form. For example, in the matrix, the class of information *Number of Pair by Size* (q_{14}) appears in the three source

Column legend (S_1–S_{25}):

- S_1 Catalogue of Operations
- S_2 Customer Order
- S_3 Customer Make-up Order
- S_4 Back Order
- S_5 Employee Data Form
- S_6 Non-productive Labor Report
- S_7 Productive Labor Report
- S_8 Time Card
- S_9 Customer Credit Memo
- S_{10} Customer Check
- S_{11} Receiving Slip
- S_{12} Vendor Invoice
- S_{13} Purchase Order
- S_{14} Returns & Sales to Vendors
- S_{15} Cash Sales Slip
- S_{16} Findings Requisition
- S_{17} Findings Receiving Slip
- S_{18} No. Feet Returned
- S_{19} Estimate Material Cost Book
- S_{20} Production Per Machine
- S_{21} Leased Machinery Book
- S_{22} Sundry Sales Book
- S_{23} Damaged Shoe Memo
- S_{24} Substitute Material Memo
- S_{25} Salesman Quota Book

	S_1	S_2	S_3	S_4	S_5	S_6	S_7	S_8	S_9	S_{10}	S_{11}	S_{12}	S_{13}	S_{14}	S_{15}	S_{16}	S_{17}	S_{18}	S_{19}	S_{20}	S_{21}	S_{22}	S_{23}	S_{24}	S_{25}	Total
q_1 Time-In								1																		1
q_2 Time-Out								1																		1
q_3 Extra Time-In								1																		1
q_4 Extra Time-Out								1																		1
q_5 Total Time						1	1	1																		3
q_6 Unit Price		1	1						1			1	1	1	1	1						1	1			10
q_7 Rate/Hr						1	1																			2
q_8 Rate/Pr	1																									1
q_9 Quantity		1	1				1		1	1	1	1	1	1	1	1	1			1		1	1	1		16
q_{10} Total Amount		1	1						1	1		1	1	1	1	1	1					1	1			12
q_{11} Deduction, Income Tax					1																					1
q_{12} Deduction, War Bonds					1																					1
q_{13} Deduction, Insurance					1																					1
q_{14} No. Pair by Size		1	1												1											3
q_{15} Quantity Shipped														1												1
q_{16} Quantity to be Shipped		1																								1
q_{17} Commission Rate																									1	1
q_{18} Bonus Quota																									1	1
q_{19} Total Sales Quota																									1	1
q_{20} Discount Terms												1	1													2

412

Estimate Unit Cost	q_{21}																			1							1
Estimate Material Unit	q_{22}																			1							1
Insurance Value	q_{23}																					1					1
Return Charge	q_{24}																					1					1
Monthly Rental	q_{25}																					1					1
Rate of Royalty	q_{26}																					1					1
M_S No. Feet Returned	q_{27}																	1									1
Date	i_1		1	1	1		1	1	1	1	1	1	1	1	1	1	1	1			1	1	1	1	1		20
Name	i_2		1	1		1	1	1	1	1	1	1	1	1	1	1		1					1	1			16
Address	i_3		1	1		1				1	1		1	1	1	1							1	1			11
Number	i_4		1	1		1			1	1						1							1	1			8
Department	i_5							1									1				1	1					4
Operation No.	i_6	1																									1
Description of Work	i_7	1					1	1																			3
Social Security No.	i_8					1																					1
Date Received	i_9			1																							1
Date Required	i_{10}													1													1
Document No.	i_{11}		1									1					1	1									4
Product Description	i_{12}		1	1								1	1	1	1	1	1	1		1			1		1		12
Product No.	i_{13}		1	1	1					1		1	1	1	1	1	1	1		1			1	1	1		15
Case No.	i_{14}				1																			1	1		3
Salesman Name	i_{15}		1	1																						1	3
Grade of Shoe	i_{16}			1																							1
Difference between Graded & Ordered Shoe	i_{17}			1																							1
Shipping Instructions	i_{18}			1																							2
Territory	i_{19}																									1	1
Description of Damage	i_{20}																							1			1
Lease No.	i_{21}																					1					1
Royalty Base	i_{22}																					1					1
Machine Name	i_{23}																				1	1					2
Machine No.	i_{24}																				1	1					2
		3	13	15	6	7	6	8	8	8	4	6	9	10	8	11	8	6	1	4	5	10	9	10	5	5	

Exhibit 3.

documents S_2, S_3, and S_{15}, indicated by the 1's, and does not appear in any other source document, indicated by the blanks which can be considered as 0's.

This first matrix, M_8, can be analyzed to see how often information is repeated and to determine the amount of information on each form. When the numbers in each row are added, the result indicates the amount of repetition. When the numbers in the columns are added, the result indicates the amount of information on each form. At this point the systems analyst must use his judgment to evaluate the results and determine if the source documents are encumbered with extraneous information and if they are poorly designed.

The "A" Shoe Company has very little duplication of information among its 25 source documents, and the forms are well designed, since they are not encumbered with too much information. For example, S_8, the *time card,* has just eight items of information, of which five are quantitative in nature and non-repetitive in information, compared with the other source documents, and three identify the time card.

The next step is to show how the source forms are used to prepare the 38 report forms. It is evident that the "A" Shoe Company had orderly report levels in its data-processing systems. For example, *customer order* (S_2) was used to prepare the cost-figuring sheet ($R_1{}^1$), which in turn was combined with the make-up cost sheet to prepare a second-level report form coupon sheet ($R_1{}^2$). It is important to note that the report levels do not correspond to organizational levels.

The model for the first level of reporting is the matrix M_1 (Exhibit 4), which shows the source documents used to prepare the first level of reports.

In the "A" Shoe Company, we found that there were nine report levels. This meant we had to build nine matrices to clearly describe the data-processing system. Finally, we had to show what reports were sent to various business functions. This information is presented in matrix M^B (Exhibit 5).

Manipulation of the Model

A model of the formal information flow which includes the details of the system has been constructed to this point. The next step is to illustrate how this model may be manipulated—in other words, how to introduce system changes in the matrices. The manipulation permits one to show what information finally reaches each business function after going through the report levels represented by the matrices.

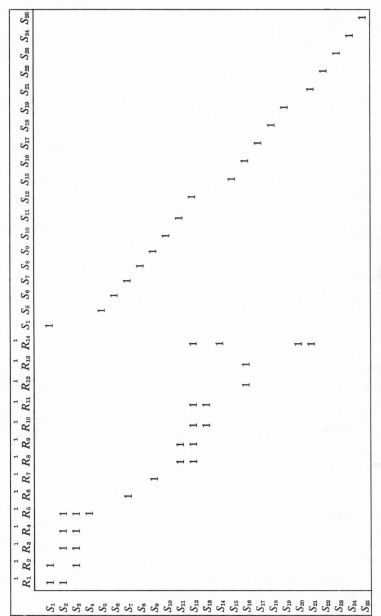

Exhibit 4. First-level reporting (M_1)

	Sales Control	Inventory Control	Production Control	Production Planning and Scheduling	Cost Accounting	General Accounting	Management Reports
	B_1	B_2	B_3	B_4	B_5	B_6	B_7
Income Statement R_1^{9}							1
Balance Sheet R_2^{9}							1
General Ledger R_1^{8}						1	
Payroll Expense R_1^{7}					1		
Salary Expense R_2^{7}					1		
Cash Book R_3^{7}	1				1		
Commission Ledger R_4^{7}	1						
Estimate Labor Cost R_2^{4}					1		
Estimate Material Cost R_3^{4}					1		
Estimate Factory Overhead Cost R_4^{4}					1		
Lining & Trim. Report R_6^{4}			1		1		
Findings Report R_7^{4}			1		1		
Upper Material Report R_8^{4}			1		1		
Upper Leather Inventory Card R_9^{4}		1					
Lining & Trim. Inventory Card R_{10}^{4}		1					
Production Tag R_2^{2}		1	1				
Est. Cost of Sales R_3^{2}					1		
Cost Figuring Sheet R_1^{1}				1			
Make-up Cost Sheet R_2^{1}				1			
Customer Order Card R_3^{1}	1			1			
Productive Labor Report R_6^{1}			1				
Findings Inventory R_2^{5}		1					

M
B

Exhibit 5. Reports used for management control.

		Sales Control B_1	Inventory Control B_2	Production Control B_3	Production Planning and Scheduling B_4	Cost Accounting B_5	General Accounting B_6	Management Reports B_7
Time-In	q_1	2				3	4	8
Time-Out	q_2	2				3	4	8
Extra Time-In	q_3	2				3	4	8
Extra Time-Out	q_4	2				3	4	8
Total Time	q_5	10		1		15	20	40
Unit Price	q_6	27	12	8	3	55	68	136
Rate/Hr.	q_7	8		1		12	16	32
Rate/Pr.	q_8	12	2	2	1	27	26	52
Quantity	q_9	38	14	10	3	67	94	188
Total Amount	q_{10}	32	12	8	3	55	77	154
Deduction, Income Tax	q_{11}	2				3	4	8
Deduction, War Bonds.	q_{12}	2				3	4	8
Deduction, Insurance	q_{13}	2				3	4	8
No. Pair By Size	q_{14}	18	8	8	3	34	42	84
Quantity Shipped	q_{15}	2	1	1		6	6	12
Quantity To Be Shipped	q_{16}	2	1	1		6	6	12
Commission Rate	q_{17}						1	2
Bonus Quota	q_{18}						1	2
Total Sales Quota	q_{19}						1	2
Discount Terms	q_{20}	5	3			8	11	22
Estimate Unit Cost	q_{21}	12	4	4		22	28	56
Estimate Material/Unit	q_{22}	12	4	4		22	28	56
Insurance Value	q_{23}	4				8	9	18
Return Charge	q_{24}	4				8	9	18
Monthly Rental	q_{25}	4				8	9	18
Rate of Royalty	q_{26}	4				8	9	18
No. Feet Returned	q_{27}	4	2	2		8	10	20

q_{15}

Date	i_1	49	14	10	3	84	116	232
Name	i_2	41	12	9	3	67	103	206
Address	i_3	30	11	8	3	55	70	140
Number	i_4	26	8	8	3	47	61	122
Department	i_5	12	1	1		20	28	56
Operation No.	i_6	12	2	2	1	27	26	52
Description of Work	i_7	20	2	3	1	39	42	84
Social Security No.	i_8	2				3	4	8
Date Received	i_9	2	1	1			6	12
Date Required	i_{10}						1	2
Document No.	i_{11}	16	9	7	3	34	41	82
Product Description	i_{12}	36	17	12	3	65	90	180
Product No.	i_{13}	42	18	13	3	77	106	212
Case No.	i_{14}	6	1	2		12	16	32
Salesman Name	i_{15}	17	8	8	3	34	42	84
Grade of Shoe	i_{16}	2	1	1			6	12
Difference Between Regular and Ordered Shoe	i_{17}	2	1	1			6	12
Shipping Instructions	i_{18}	17	8	8	3	34	41	82
Territory	i_{19}						1	2
Description of Damage	i_{20}						1	2
Lease No.	i_{21}	4				8	9	18
Royalty Base	i_{22}	4				8	9	18
Machine Name	i_{23}	8				14	17	34
Machine No.	i_{24}	8				14	17	34

Exhibit 6. Information available to business functions.

This can be done if the matrices are multiplied together. (The supplementary note illustrates this process.) By multiplying the matrices, we can show the number of times each source document or each class of information is made available to each business function. For example, in the matrix (Exhibit 6) the information q^{15}, *quantity shipped,* is available to all the business functions except production planning and scheduling. The number which is at the intersection of the row headed by the symbol for the class of information and the column headed by the business function gives a measure of the redundancy in the data-processing system.

The meaning of redundancy in data processing is illustrated when considering the use of an electronic computer for data processing. If all the information in the source documents is put on a magnetic tape, the tape would have to be run through the computer the number of times indicated by the measure of redundancy given in the matrix. In the "A" Shoe Company, there was a great deal of redundancy in the data-processing system, even though the source documents were well designed and had little redundancy, as shown in Exhibit 6.

What this matrix shows is that the systems design may be good at the start and at the end, but the processing in between is very inefficient. In addition, a quantitative measure of the redundancy is provided. It is not enough to have good source documents and good management reports; you must have a good processing system in between.

CONCLUSION

The mathematical model constructed for the "A" Shoe Company offers a number of advantages:

1. The business system is presented in a condensed form which enables the systems analyst to see the total system at a glance.

2. This condensed form presents all the details of the system.

3. Alternative ways of designing the integrated business system can be tested and evaluated scientifically.

4. A determination of what is extraneous data can be made more easily.

5. If there is a request for new information, a way to collect and report it, which minimizes the data processing, can be determined.

6. Total effects of systems changes can be determined without changing the system.

7. The systems study may be divided among a number of people and each coordinated easily, since the business system is precisely delineated.

8. A rating by the recipient of the usefulness of any information can be incorporated in the matrices, and from this the desired changes in the data processing and source documents can be determined.

There are many other advantages afforded by the use of this type of model. However, the last we shall mention here is the important opportunity which is offered the analyst to incorporate in his system the advances taking place in programming, scheduling, and feedback—both conceptually and in terms of electronic equipment.

The major problem in systems planning and control is to find a way to integrate the communication process with the information requirements for financial and operational planning and control. We have tried to show one way in which this may be accomplished. In any case, we sincerely believe that some new way of describing business systems is needed if we are going to help management overcome its difficulties in the area of planning and control.

25

THE ORGANIZATION MAN AND THE RESEARCH MAN *

Alfred G. Smith

The structure of the center and the function of the center are horns of a dilemma. They create a paradox of self-contradictions and they are personified in the organization and the research man.

The organization man serves the structure, while the research man serves the function. It takes both kinds to have a center. Each kind can serve well, and neither kind is superior to the other. They should complement one another. But, in fact, they do not communicate. They are in a sense strangers to each other. And people do not as a rule communicate with strangers.

This chapter will describe and analyze these two types of men in four successive steps. It will first present what the general characteristics are of the organization man and of the research man. It will then consider the patterns of communication of each type. Thirdly, this chapter will present who in the center belongs to which type, according to the perceptions that the members of the center have of themselves and of each other. Finally, this chapter will consider how each kind of man affects the research and the growth and development of the center.

GENERAL CHARACTERISTICS

The Organization Man

In general, the organization man is primarily concerned with the group. He thinks of belonging to a collectivity of people, of participating in a corporate enterprise. For him, there is one fact of life that is so obvious that it

* Reprinted from *Communication and Status: The Dynamics of a Research Center,* University of Oregon, 1966, pp. 29–38.

never needs to be formulated into words: the center exists. And its existence implies that it is an end that must be served.

The Research Man

The research man, on the other hand, regards the center as a means. The center is a tool for him to use. It serves him by facilitating the collection of data, aiding in the analysis of data, and helping to disseminate the results. In terms of communication, the organization man makes sure that his messages go through channels, while the research man makes sure that his messages go through. Channels, bureaucratic structures, and even the center itself, are not good things in their own right for the research man. Instead, the center is a means for achieving something beyond itself.

These general characteristics of the organization man and of the research man are generalizations that were derived from the responses. In the course of conducting these interviews, it became unmistakable that there were two different patterns of responses. At first it was not clear how the patterns of responses actually differed from one another. In the subsequent analysis of these responses, however, the specific differences between the two patterns seemed to arrange themselves under four headings: how the respondents identified people; where the respondents met people; how the respondents communicated with other people; and how they influenced people. Inductive generalizations sprung from under each heading as if self-propelled, yet clear and unmistakable.

An inductive generalization is not a verified hypothesis, but if we have faith, faith in the uniformity of nature, then an inductive generalization can be a persuasive basis for anticipating other phenomena. Moreover, these two categories of men are ideal types. Like folk societies and urban ones, or introverts and extroverts, they are categories constructed by an investigator. They help him to organize and interpret data. They permit him to reshuffle the statuses that others perceive so that he can group their perceptions. In general, these categories are perceived quite discretely. As the center grows and develops, they could become points along a continuum, but they could also become more discrete and grow further and further apart.

DISTINGUISHING CHARACTERISTICS

Identification of Others

The first characteristic that distinguishes the organization man and the research man from another is how they respond to the interview question,

"Do you know John Able?" Or, "How about Mary Baker?" The response to this question indicates how the interviewee identifies people. In general, the organization men know all the regular professional staff, at least by name, rank, field, and where their offices are located. The organization man also knows many more of the graduate assistants and identifies them as graduate assistants rather than regular professional staff or as classified personnel. All the classified personnel knew all the other classified personnel. The organization men were troubled when they were given someone's name whom they did not know. They wanted to look him up, or they asked the interviewer who that person was. The organization man feels it is his duty to know everyone in the center.

The organization man is deeply concerned with status and identifies other people in terms of their official statuses within the center. All of the classified personnel, for example, are organization men and they have little knowledge of the actual research work of the center. They are not particularly concerned about it. If a man gains prestige and a special status because of his research, the classified personnel are likely to know about it. But they will know only about the status and not the research.

There is a similar concern for status among all the organization men. They show a great concern when any one person's status is not clearly defined. There was, for example, an administrative officer for the center, and each interviewee was asked what that officer's position was. All the organization men were troubled, not by this question, but by the position and its definition.

Finally, when an organization man was asked about himself—when Mary Baker was asked, "Do you know Mary Baker?"—the response and self-identification was in terms of the official status within the center. The organization man identifies himself with one of the groups within the center.

The research men identify people quite differently. They knew fewer classified personnel, fewer graduate assistants, and they did not always know all of the regular staff. When the research man did know someone by name, he was still more likely to be unsure of the rank, field, or the location of the office. But in the interview the research men were not troubled when they discovered members of the center whom they did not know, or whose position they could not define. A research man never reached for a roster of the center in order to identify someone named by the interviewer. He did not feel it his duty to know. When the research man did identify people, he identified them more in terms of the work they were doing than in terms of the position they held.

Furthermore, the research man was much less troubled by ambiguous statuses. He was not troubled by the status of the administrative officer, for example, while the organization men were. The research man thought that this officer got his job done, and therefore his position was quite clear. Finally, in responding with their self-identifications, the research men did not speak of themselves as members of an official group, such as the regular professional staff, graduate assistants, or as one of the directors. Instead, the response had the form, "I'm working with Joe on decision-making processes." In all, there is a clear and distinct difference between research men and organization men in the way they identify people and themselves.

Use of Communicational Facilities

They also differ in where they meet and communicate. Who turns out for the seminars that are held within the center? Who uses the center's library? Who reads the center's newsletter? The organization man does and the research man does not. The organization men bemoan the fact that others do not turn out for the seminars. The librarian and the editor bemoan the fact that "some people"—whom we can identify as research men—do not take full advantage of the services offered. Seminars, libraries, and newsletters are public centers of communication. They are explicitly and formally established for this purpose. The research man is less formal and less organized. He is much more direct in his communications. If he wants to find something out, he will find it for himself and spare himself no efforts. He will go to the university library rather than the center's library. The research men do not fully utilize the formal communicational facilities established by the center. This does not mean, however, that those facilities exist in vain. They are used by the organization men who find them to be a boon and a necessity.

Methods of Communication

Memoranda. Closely related to seminars, libraries, and newsletters are memoranda. These too are formal and deliberately established units or media of communication within the center. The center is showered and bathed in a monsoon of memoranda. Like the seminars and other formal media of communication, these memoranda are produced and consumed primarily by the organization men. These memoranda also serve as a transition in this analysis from where people meet to how they communicate with one another.

In comparison with face-to-face oral communication or even telephone conversations, memoranda give rise to little feedback. They are, in fact, not very communicative. I define communication as the reciprocal exchange of signals, and memoranda do not stimulate very much reciprocity.

No matter how one writes a memorandum, the result always looks like a directive. Even when a memorandum tries to consider two sides of a problem, and tries to explore a situation as open-mindedly and fairly as possible, it still sounds like an executive decree and a bureaucratic ruling. It is Jacob's testament. The voice remains the voice of authority and power, even though the hands are made up to feel gentle and permissive. In their interviews, the research men almost always volunteered some waggish remark about these memoranda to show that they did not take them seriously or that they were irritated by them. Their quips and facetiae may also have served as a substitute for any substantive feedback. The organization men did not volunteer any comments on these memoranda.

We could classify the different ways people communicate with each other by simply noting the different types of feedback that are used in communicational systems. In the simplest system of organizing lines of communication, there is never more than one way of going from one person to another. There is just one line that connects John and Mary. If we want to go from Mary to John, we have to retrace that same line. The simplest set of lines that can connect a group of individuals to one another is the family tree or kinship chart. "There are thus no closed circuits, and the 'network' scarcely deserves the name. But as soon as the schema becomes more complicated, closed circuits (also termed 'loops' or 'meshes') make their appearance. The presence of such loops in the schema of a servo-mechanism is quite fundamental; it is from them that 'reflex' and 'reactive' structures are formed" (Kirchoff quoted in Guilbaud 1959:17). When the amount of meat that a butcher sells depends on how much the tailor can buy, which depends on how many suits the tailor has sold to the shoemaker, which in turn depends on how many shoes the shoemaker has sold to the butcher, then there is a mesh or loop. The circulation of money in the market, or the movement of impulses in a neural network is a self-regulatory system. It is a fundamental principle of cybernetics in our time that goal-directed organization requires such a closed circuit. It depends on such feedback. The research men regarded the memoranda as directives, and not as parts of a self-regulatory system within the center. The research men thought of them as legislative bills, not as self-corrective thermostats. There is perhaps a bit of an anarchist in every research man, or a bit of the little boy who would rather do it himself—and who does not want to be told how. Memoranda are the bullets and bombs of bureaucrats, the ordnance of organization men.

Advice-Seeking. The conception and use of memoranda is only the first of several ways in which organization men and research men differ from one another in how they communicate. In the interviews, I repeatedly asked who initiated each communicational exchange, and what the communication was about. In general, this permitted two kinds of responses: John could ask Mary to do something, which meant that John was able to order Mary to do something; or John could ask Mary for advice, which meant that John was showing deference. In general, the organization men do not ask for advice. This is irrespective of rank. When a secretary asks the administrative officer for a new typewriter, she is telling him. And a secretary is an organization man. When she asks a member of the executive committee whether there is a meeting of that committee today, she does not ask for advice.

The interviews indicate that only research men ever ask for advice or suggestions from graduate assistants. This is somewhat unusual because the graduate assistants working under research men are younger and have less practical experience in the field. The graduate assistants in educational administration are organization men, and are generally mature persons who have been school principals and superintendents. They were never asked for advice by the organization men who are their supervisors. As organization men themselves, these graduate assistants were very conscious of status, and being treated simply as graduate assistants was for these former principals and superintendents a traumatic let-down.

Degree of Influence

One gains the distinct impression from the interviews that the communication of the organization men is oriented around leadership, legislation, organization, and power. This is another way of saying that the organization man is concerned with status. He is often concerned with the recruitment and organization of people. The research man, however, is more concerned with the collection and organization of data.

The superior and the subordinate are dependent on one another. From an evolutionary point of view, the more two organisms are dependent on one another for meeting such functions as sex and protection, the more flexible their relationships have to be. This kind of flexibility and dependence describes what Durkheim would call an organic solidarity. This is the kind of relationship that research men seem to pursue. Among the organization men there is more a mechanical solidarity, and fewer closed circuits or loops. In a word, there is less feedback. The presence or absence of these loops is neither good nor bad. It is a matter of choice—whether the center is directed by directors, or whether the reins are left in the invisible hand of laissez faire as memorialized by Adam Smith.

CENTER PERSONNEL: ORGANIZATION MEN OR RESEARCH MEN?

Let us stop for a moment and see where we are. There are four steps in this chapter by which it analyzes the differences between the organization man and the research man. The first step presented the general characteristics of these two kinds of men. The second step showed how the patterns of communication differed between these two. This second step was subdivided into four headings. Under the first of these headings it analyzed how the respondents in the interviews identified other people and themselves. Under the second heading it analyzed where the respondents met and communicated, that is, in seminars, in memoranda, or in what other kinds of facilities. Under the third heading the chapter analyzed how the respondents communicated with one another—who initiated the communications and whether the initiation involved asking for advice or giving an order. The fourth and final heading of the second step analyzed how people influenced one another, what kind of social controls were used. This involved loops and feedbacks and either mechanical or organic social solidarity.

The third step now before us is to identify who within the center is an organization man and who is a research man. These categories cut across many of the commonly perceived statuses within the center. In particular, they cut across rank and field. All the organization men are either classified personnel or associate directors (which are ranks) or they are people in educational administration (which is a field). These two groups of people join to form a single group, one which we have called the organization man.

The classified personnel (the secretaries and the administrative assistant), and the editor are the only full-time employees of the organization. I include in educational administration everyone in the center who either has an appointment in the School of Education or is a candidate for a degree in that School. This includes the regular professional staff in educational administration and their graduate assistants who were majoring in educational administration.

Both associate directors of the center were also organization men. Their positions required them to promote and coordinate the contribution that individual members could make to the function of the center as a whole. These associate directors integrated, organized and legislated. Their administrative positions led them to respond in their interviews as organization men, although one was a social scientist and the other an educational administrator. The director of the center, however, responded like a research man. Whoever was not one of the classified personnel, and not in educational administration, and not an associate director was a research man.

There are, of course, differences between the individuals in both of these groups. And people also differed in the intensity with which they exhibited the characteristics of their particular groups. But a clear line of demarcation between the two groups is deeply etched throughout all the interviews.

THE EFFECT ON CENTER DEVELOPMENT

The fourth and final step in this analysis examines the effect that each kind of man has on the research and on the growth and development of the center. This takes us beyond the data of the interviews and even beyond the realm of knowledge. It takes us from the categorical to the hypothetical. It takes us into the realm of if-then.

William H. Whyte, Jr., in his popular, suggestive, and one-sided polemic, *The Organization Man,* has written, "The principal features of organized research—emphasis on methodology, research design, and planning by committee—are not of themselves wrong, but they have now become so venerated as to be destructive" (1956:244). Even though he does not say it himself, we can recognize in his statement that the phrase "organized research" is a kind of paradox and self-contradiction. Anything that is organized emphasizes togetherness and belongingness, and generally promotes conformity. Without conformity, any organization would fly apart. Conformity also allows us to do things and believe things without continuously examining them. This is, however, wholly contrary and repugnant to research. Research requires a perpetual examination of what we do and what we believe.

If the center were controlled by organization men, they could stifle research. But if the center were controlled by research men, there might not be a center at all. The organization man feels a need for a further clarification of the mission of the center in order to clarify his own role in the center. The research man feels that such a further clarification may constrict the mission of the center and throttle his own role in it. This impasse is a matter of the structure and the function of the center. It is not a matter of the specific personnel. That is, if the center recruited a brand new staff, the same problems would remain.

26

TECHNOLOGY AND SOME ASPECTS
OF INDUSTRIAL SUPERVISION: A
MODEL BUILDING APPROACH *

Elmer H. Burack

The dynamic factor *technology,* has received increased attention as a major variable in industrial management. Yet, its role is as yet to be more clearly defined.[1]

An increasing number of articles and books, both theoretical and empirical, have appeared in the recent past dealing either explicitly or implicitly with the role of technology. In the organizational area, many behaviorally oriented studies or discussions have assumed "the state of technology" as a constant. In empirical studies reported in the literature, there is often an implication that the findings in one production unit might bear directly on organizational problems in another.

Frequently, however, these studies cannot be directly related because of differences in the degree of technological advancement of a production unit. Furthermore, "data" reported from a study may be in a form obviating objective comparison. In some contemporary studies, evidence has been presented which indicates that the *state of technology* is an important determinant of organization behavior in technical units, affecting such factors as group formation, organization, structure, communication, and needed qualities of managerial leadership.[2]

Technology and technological change have become increasingly dynamic factors in the technical or operations organization. The impact on the organization has led to issues of major importance, some with general economic implications. Issues of national concern to industry, government and union alike have included job displacement, retraining and premature job

* Reprinted from *Journal of Academy of Management,* March, 1966, pp. 43–66.

retirement. To a great extent these national issues are a reflection of a major upheaval taking place at the company level. Modification and change in technical organization are felt no more keenly than within managerial and supervisory groups. Problems within these groups are similar to those identified at the national level as well as particularized issues such as re-definition of supervisory role resulting from modification of the task environment.

This paper considers the influence of process technology and changes in the level of process technology on one major functional activity of supervision, viz., supervisory *direction.*

The interrelationships are analyzed through a model building approach. The type of model approach employed reflects the relatively low state of knowledge that exists concerning these variables. The models are of both the propositional and schematic type and facilitate the conceptualization of seemingly unrelated data and information, an approach similar to that taken in the March and Simon book.[3] Four general and eight detailed models are developed for industrial organization units that straddle a wide range of technological attainment.

For ease in analysis, the "technological range" considers two broad categories of companies: (1) units that can be classified as "craft" to advanced "craft" type (assuming "mass production" characteristics); and, (2) units that can be classed as "mass production" to advanced "mass production" (assuming "automation" characteristics). The supervisory activity considered is *direction* or "closeness of supervision," that is, directive authority exercised by the first line operations supervisor in direct interaction with his subordinates in order to check, instruct and in general, regulate worker discretion in job-performance.

ANTECEDENTS TO CONTEMPORARY, EMPIRICAL ANALYSES

The United States has been transformed into a highly complex industrial society in the relatively short time interval following the first Industrial Revolution. In almost step-wise fashion, America's productive facilities have moved successively through the technical organizational phases of "craft," early factory operations, through "mass production" into an era of so-called "automation." This technical-organizational evolution has been brought about through the interaction of a number of factors—social, economic, political and ideological. Technological development, the application of the industrial arts and sciences, has been a part of this dynamic system, acting as an agent of change as well as being the target of change by other factors.

Historically, supervisory *direction* of subordinates has been a keynote of the supervisor's functional responsibilities. Historically, supervisory directive activities such as subordinate guidance, aid, training and reprimand have been a major part of job responsibilities. From the early days of the overseers and supervisors of our first major industry—textiles—down through industries of the scientific management era, these responsibilities have been important. Over time some differences have arisen in supervisory practices due to such factors as owner philosophy, management capability, market and product differences.[4] Considering these phenomena, an implicit assumption underlying this paper is that *technology and technological change* have assumed an *increasingly dominant* position in their effect on authority based supervisory functions.

A CONCEPT OF TECHNOLOGY FOR ANALYSIS

The identification of common factors or dimensions associated with process technology provides a basis for comparing production units otherwise differing in technical details. Just as technical processes have progressed *over* time ("craft" through "mass production" to "automation"), production units exist in varying stages of technological refinement as a point *in time*. This line of reasoning introduces two notions:

1. An ordinal array of industry production units spanning the range from the outmoded (low level) to the most advanced (high level). Here, relative position is influenced by the state of knowledge.

2. A method by which process improvements typically take place, viz., both intrastage and interstage.

If, for convenience, we term the industry stages existing at some point in time as "craft," "mass production," and "automation," these stages in turn can be incorporated into a *technological continuum* as follows: [5]

Craft	Mass Production	Automation
Low		High

State of technology continuum (relative state of technology)

This concept of a *technological continuum* temporarily sets aside customary industry boundaries and sets forth a broad view of operational units and attendant change to facilitate comparative analyses. In addition, dimensions of technology such as the "degree of mechanization" or "interdependence" suggest a basis for classification irrespective of industry—company specifics. Some of the complexities associated with the analysis of these variables are more readily appreciated when the wide range of definitions and concepts of these terms are viewed.

USAGE AND DEFINITIONS

The word technology, often used interchangeably with the term *process* technology, has been employed in the literature in a number of different ways. At the macro-economic or society level in Sociology and Social Anthropology the concept of technology involves such traits and activity levels as "Basketry," "Mining" and Patrilocal Residence.[6] Technology has also been used in a more narrow sense reflecting such things as manufacturing processes, scientific know-how and *new* product and process innovations.[7]

Process Technology (T)

Some rather general, descriptive terms have been employed to describe "process technology." These terms have included characterizations such as "craft processes," "technology," "mass production" and automation." These terms in turn have been used in a number of different ways to indicate techniques, processes, worker skills, information systems, and a basis for differentiating intermittent and continuous manufacturing procedures.[8]

For the purposes of this study, the terms "craft," "mass production" and "automation" have been used *only as descriptive terms* to reflect the relative technical state achieved by particular industries or companies. The terms are employed in the indicated manner with "craft" corresponding to low or elementary states of technology and "automation" associated with advanced states of technology; "mass production" occupies the middleground. The many different meanings of technology, even in the case of a relatively narrow manufacturing focus, suggest reference to a more basic source of definition—the dictionary. Here it is suggested that technology represents a "branch of knowledge that deals with industrial arts" [9] or "industrial and applied science as contrasted with pure science." [10]

Our use of technology reflects science as it is applied to the industrial arts. We are concerned with the practical uses of technology as they are embodied in processes for the transformation of tangible material and products to semi-finished or finished states. By "process" we mean a "systematic series of activities directed to some end." [11]

"The variable, process technology, is considered as a systematic series of actions transforming materials into semi-finished or finished products based on scientific concepts as applied to the industrial arts."

Viewing process technology as a composite of common system features provides a conceptual framework to facilitate comparison and evaluation of empirical studies reported in the literature. Five major dimensions of technology are considered as a basis for depicting increased rationalization of operations and interstage movement.[12] These dimensions include:

1. *The degree of mechanization*: Given a state of knowledge or information, this dimension reflects the extent to which semiautomatic process and service equipment are employed relative to the total potentially employable. By semi-automatic, we infer that some portion of an operation or cycle has been assumed by powered equipment.

2. *The degree of time interdependence.* This factor reflects the extent to which the *inputs* of one operation are dependent on the output of a prior operation in the technical unit. If one were to consider only a single production unit, for example, a mechanized belt conveyor with multiple operations and no in-process storage, a high degree of time interdependence would exist.

3. *The degree of control instrumentation and computerized process control.* This dimension reflects the relative system capabilities to "contain" process variables and to adhere to predetermined programs utilizing system components of detection, comparison, correction and feedback.[13] This category would include the use of tape controlled instruments and computers where they are employed for *direct process control.* Conventional process control equipment would include such types as "on-off," "cycle and sequence" and "proportioning."

4. *The degree of subdivision of labor.* Here, the motion is employed of the relative length of task time. This concept is most useful as applied to mechanically based industries. The shorter the task time, the greater the subdivision of labor. This dimension of "process technology" would approach "zero" as a limiting case in a highly rationalized technical system. In highly advanced states of technology, there would be no direct human intervention in the process.

5. *The degree of technical engineering organization of the process.* In this concept, we consider the expertise with which the various individual technological components are related to each other to form an efficient production system.

This concept of "process technology" is as of a point in time and relative to some state of scientific knowledge. Over time, man is constantly adding to the understanding of his environment. To avoid further complication in the analysis, we assume some point in time or a relatively short time span so that the "state of knowledge" [14] is considered a constant.

Closeness of Supervision (CS)

Our primary interest in supervisory authority is centered in the activities of the foreman or first line supervisor in the discharge of his responsibility. Total supervisory activity is considered as a composite of three principal parts as follows:

1. Supervisory *direction* of his subordinates ("Closeness").
2. Non subordinate control activities by the supervisor in conjunction with staff specialists and work related colleagues.
3. Administration, training and other foreman activities relating to such things as the personal needs of his men and paper routines of the company.

For the purposes of this study, we consider only the foregoing authority component (1) in relation to process technology. Although our primary focus is on authority at the foreman level, it is recognized that various environmental factors would tend to reinforce (or reduce) his ability to influence subordinates. The presence of such factors as budgets, procedures and fixed work stations have provided a discreet complement to supervisory authority. Peter M. Blau and W. Richard Scott have termed these supportive factors "impersonal control." [15] Although our primary focus is on Closeness of Supervision, it appears that "impersonal control" is an important adjunct to rationalizing possible associations or relationships. On these grounds, the concept of "impersonal control" is retained and employed in the model building.

Concepts of Authority (Including Closeness of Supervision)

The definitions and concepts of authority in the organizational literature encompass a staggering array of ideas involving such factors as legitimacy, source, direction, acceptancy and relation to power. Formally assigned or informally assumed, they are to be found in a broad span of organizational literature from empirical studies to "wisdom" reflection.[16]

Kahn and Katz suggest that authority encompasses *formally* delegated responsibilities and duties as well as *informal* ones assumed by first line supervision.[17] Another concept of authority assumes a superior-subordinate relationship that is "to inspect with authority" or "to oversee for direction." [18] Other concepts of authority relate directly to responsibility. Stogdill suggests that authority is the "degree of freedom that the occupant of a position is expected to occupy in initiating performance and interaction within a formally acknowledged structure" and responsibility is the ". . . . range of performance that a member is expected to exhibit by virtue of the operational demands in a formally acknowledged structure." [19]

For the purpose of this study, the Kahn and Katz type of approach is employed. Within authority, formally delegated responsibilities as well as informal ones assumed by first line supervision are considered. The notion of overseeing or initiating activity in response to operational demands is employed.

For the purpose of this investigation, the major authority component direction or "closeness of supervision" is defined as follows:

> This category of foreman activities includes interaction of the supervisor with his subordinates in order to check or direct his personnel and generally to limit worker discretion in job performance.

Unquestionably, in a company situation the actual "closeness" observed may reflect confounding influences such as pressure from higher administrative levels and personality characteristics.[20] In the development of the propositional models, these confounding variables have been considered as sources of variation at particular levels of technology, distinguishing individual situations—not primarily causal factors in interunit comparisons. Furthermore, we deal with a *group* phenomenon which would tend to "level out" some of the individual factors. Finally, "closeness of supervision" is affected by such added factors as:

1. The ratio of supervisors to workers.
2. Worker ability relative to job needs.
3. Variation in the frequency of occurrence of process problems in different parts of a production unit reflecting:
    (a) Modification or variations in the technologies.
    (b) Work crew differences.

In addition, the major organization variable of impersonal control is conceived of as follows:

> *The degree of impersonal control* as we use it, reflects the extent to which subordinates of first line supervision (workers-operators) are constrained or regulated in their activities by non-human mechanisms, devices, procedures, schedules and progress. These in turn might include such things as operating procedures, fixed stations along a production line and largely machine controlled cycles.

"Impersonal control" is not one of the "dependent" variables studied, but we have chosen to identify and define this concept to facilitate discussion and analysis.

INITIAL STUDY HYPOTHESES

Blau and Scott [21] have carried out an insightful series of comparative analyses dealing with technology and some authority components of supervision. We infer from their discussion that with an increasingly advanced state of technology, e.g., from "craft" toward "mass production" (our representation $T_{C \to MP}$):

1. Production procedures should become more rationalized;
2. Product and task are increasingly standardized;
3. Maintaining *rate* of *output* becomes increasingly important as breakdown cost increases; and,
4. First line supervision is increasingly involved with staff units and with process problems.

Considering these factors, technological transitions from "craft" to "mass production" operations (represented as $LIM \ T_{C \to MP}$) would tend to decrease "closeness of supervision." [22] This trend should be reinforced by increasing "impersonal control," constraining worker and to some degree, foreman activity.

As higher states of technology are realized, e.g., from "mass production" toward "automation," Blau and Scott anticipated an increase in "closeness of supervision." Their inference was apparently based more on a few isolated studies of automation situations than on more general theoretical grounds. Our review of the Blau and Scott analysis, one of the very few in the literature relating these variables, has suggested the following, *possible* translations in graphical and analytical terms in Exhibit 1.[23]

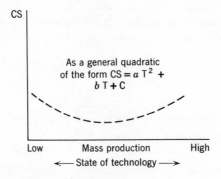

Exhibit 1. Conceptual model of the possible relation of the state of technology to one component of first line supervisory authority.

The representations in Exhibit 1 are based on a translation of our preliminary notion of the indicated relationships. For lack of any other initial information, the relationship between closeness of supervision (CS) and the state of technology (T) might assume the character of a general quadratic: the quadratic initially decreases as the stage of "mass production" is approximated and then starts to increase as process units become more interdependent. Cost of breakdown increases at the more advanced states and supervisors must spend an increasingly *greater* amount of time with their men. The highly complex processes of automation require specialized knowledge for the remedy of breakdown. The supervisor's repertoire of experience doesn't encompass many of the problems he is encountering.[24] He is faced with a conflict between individual capabilities and job needs.

Perhaps an additional reason for the increase in supervisory "closeness" at advanced technological states might be his attempting to maintain a facade of one commanding a greater amount of relevant information than his subordinates. Whereas Blau and Scott visualized a transference of control from "supervision" to the "process," that is, increasing "impersonal control," we visualize at least two organizational groups that would relate to the transference of control. Higher levels of supervision as well as staff units would be the recipients of at least a portion of the transferred control plus possibly new authorities not previously possessed.

If the prediction of the direction of relations is correct, it is obvious that the same general direction of relation could be represented by a large number of *different* functions. For example, "closeness of supervision" (CS) could also be of the following functional forms and still meet direction requirements. (See Exhibit 2.)

In concluding this section on the initial hypotheses, it appears obvious that additional considerations could cloud an analysis of the Technology-"closeness" relationship. Factors such as the ecological conditions,[25] organization of internal communications,[26] personality variations and leadership qualities [27] represent added complicating variables. The need for added data is obvious.

MODEL DEVELOPMENT BASED ON CONTEMPORARY EMPIRICAL STUDIES

Classification of the reported studies into broad technological classes provides the first step in interrelating the reported work. The reported studies are largely based on analyses of technological transitions. Conse-

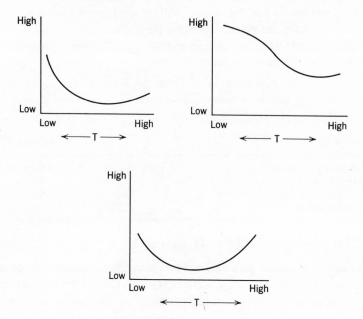

Exhibit 2. Possible relations of technology and closeness of supervision.

quently, the assignment of studies to technological categories deals largely with studies relating transitions from:

(a) "Craft" toward "mass production" operations.

(b) "Mass Production" toward "automated" operations.

Again, the terms employed are purely for descriptive purposes. The classification of literature studies is rather arbitrary. Since the studies involve a diversity of procedures and process such as oil refining, assembly, power generation and T.V. manufacture, our criteria are necessarily broad. The class categories employ the following criteria:

1. Craft—when previously existing operations involved:

(a) Largely manual procedures.

(b) Extensive manual, material transport.

(c) Production operations largely influenced by an operator.

2. Mass Production—when the previously existing or newly developed operations involved:

(a) Relatively small operator participation or some amount of operator control of procedure or operations.

(b) Semi-continuous operations.

(c) The use of production lines.

3. Automation—when the newly realized operations involved:
   (*a*) Virtually no direct, operator participation.
   (*b*) The extensive use of mechanical and electronic controls.
   (*c*) Near continuous operation.

To facilitate the development of these models, we employ a propositional numbering system similar to that used in March and Simon.[28] The designations are as follows: [29]

Variable	Designation	Numbers
Relating to Technology (T)	Independent	1.00–1.09
Impersonal Control and Coordination	Supporting	1.80
Closeness of Supervision (CS)	Dependent	1.90–1.91
Intermediate	Linking	1.10–1.79

Model (1) (Conceptual scheme in Exhibit 3.)

The series of mass production and automation studies reported by Walker, or by Walker and his associates (Guest: Guest and Turner) appear to share a common feature, standardization of procedure as operations

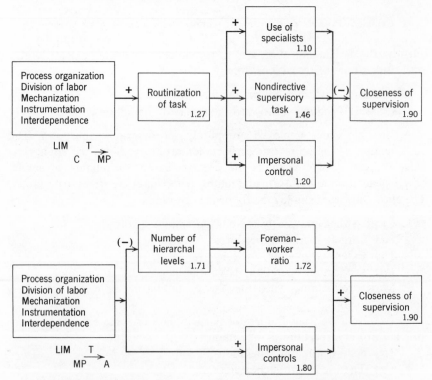

Exhibit 3. Models relating the state of technology to closeness of supervision.

are technologically improved. Operator or supervisor leeway is neither wanted nor desired by the operating managements. The increasing interdependence of operations requires forward planning for efficient, continuous operation. In a sense, the mechanical system could be anticipated more fully than the human components. The decrease in personal supervisory control is paralleled by the expansion of built-in process mechanisms for control and the extension of staff responsibility.[30] In the mass production situation, "closeness of supervision" decreased as the foreman acquired a variety of new tasks.[31] On the other hand, in the automation "area," supervisory layers are actually eliminated so that the net residual of foreman directive authority seems to point to an increase in "closeness of supervision." In a refinery studied by Bright, he suggested that, "Another big advantage (of "Automation") is that of having all the men in one area that you can control. The supervisor and the foreman's job are much easier." [32]

1–1. The greater the advancement of the technological state (from craft toward mass production) 1.00–1.04, the greater the routinization of task 1.27, the greater the initiation of requests for staff services by front line supervision 1.10, and the greater the delegation of control authority to the process 1.86 and the greater the supervisory assumption of non-directive tasks 1.46, the less the foreman-worker contacts leading to a decreased "closeness of supervision" 1.90. 1–1   190:(1.00–1.04), 1.27, 1.10 and 1.86, and 1.46   LIM   T
$C \rightarrow MP$

1–2. The greater the advancement of the technological state (from mass production toward automation) 1.00–1.04, the less the number of hierarchical levels. 1.71, the greater the foreman worker ratio 1.72, the greater the use of impersonal controls 1.86, the greater the "closeness of supervision" 1.90. 1–2   1.90: 1.00–1.04, 1.71 and 1.86, 1.72, 1.90
LIM   T
$MP \rightarrow A$

Model (2) (Conceptual scheme in Exhibit 4.)

In a mass production type study on an engine block line, another possible dimension of "closeness of supervision" is introduced.[33] Closeness of supervision may be viewed both objectively and subjectively. In the case of the former, objective criteria such as sociometric contact and the foreman-worker ratio can provide guides for evaluating a particular situation. However, subjective increases in "closeness" may have been involved in worker declarations that "supervision *felt* closer" after a technological transition. This subjective feeling might have been the result of a modification of physical or spatial relationships in the work environment and not necessarily

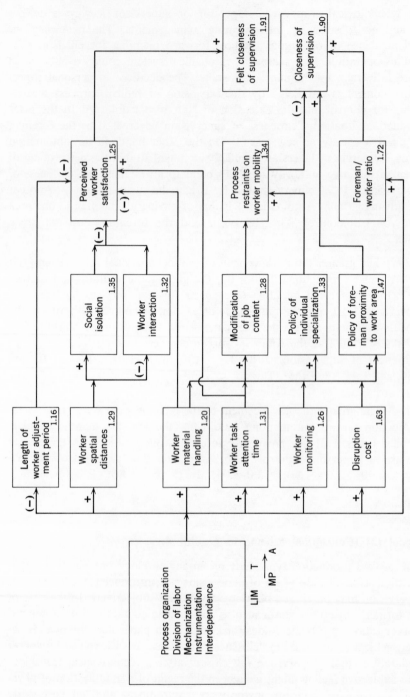

Exhibit 4. Models relating the state of technology to closeness of supervision.

the consequence of an objective increase of supervisor-subordinate interaction.

In the studies thus far cited, the consolidation of process controls and higher costs of disruption [34] modifies both work and social relationships. Process disruptability encourages a company policy of: (1) keeping supervision closer to the manufacturing lines; and, (2) extending worker specialization. Inter-job transfers are discouraged. The development of automatic production and transfer equipment changes job content, decreases material handling and greatly reduces the number and size of work groups previously associated with this type of work. Worker interaction decreases with the increasing social isolation. The worker's expressed feelings of greater dissatisfactions and yet, still preferred the new jobs to their previous jobs. In a study made by Walker the relative levels of worker satisfaction appear importantly dependent on the length of time that has passed at the time a particular response is elicited.[35] Worker response appears to be cyclical in nature.

2–1. The more advanced the state of technology (from mass production toward automation) 1.00–1.04, the greater the disruption cost 1.63, policy of individual specialization 1.33 and foremen proximity to work area 1.47, and increase in the foreman-worker ratio (1.72), the greater the "closeness of supervision" 1.90. 2–1 1.90: 1.00–1.04, 1.63 (1.33 and 1.47) and 1.72, 1.90
LIM   T
MP → A

2–2. The more advanced the state of technology (from mass production toward automation) 1.00–1.04, the greater the worker monitoring 1.26 and task attention time 1.31 and the less the worker material handling 1.30, the greater the modification of job content 1.28, the greater the process restraints on worker mobility, the less the "closeness of supervision." (1.90). 2–2   1.90: 1.00–1.04, 1.30 and 1.31 and 1.26, 1.28, 1.34
LIM   T
MP → A

2–3. The more advanced the state of technology (from mass production toward automation) 1.00–1.04, the greater the spatial work distances 1.29, the greater the social isolation 1.35 and the less the worker interaction 1.32, the less the perceived worker satisfaction 1.25, and the shorter the adjustment period 1.36, the greater the *felt* "closeness of supervision." (1.91). 2–3   1.91: 1.00–1.04, 1.29, 1.35 and 1.32, 1.25 and 1.36, 1.91
LIM   T
MP → A

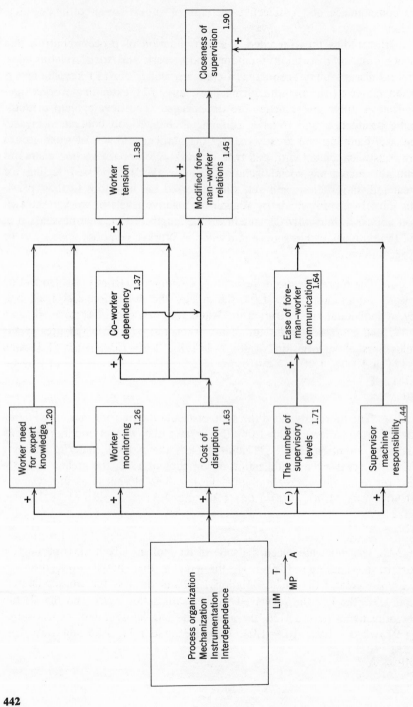

Exhibit 5. Models relating the state of technology to closeness of supervision.

Model (3) (Conceptual Scheme in Exhibit 5.)

The Mann and Hoffman study of power plants undergoing modification and updating suggests some further considerations for our organizational models.[36] Workers appear more uncertain of their job permanence and their abilities relative to their job assignments when caught in this major technological change. Hierarchical levels of authority are reduced. As suggested previously in the government studies in an oil refinery and in the Bright studies, the worker task increasingly becomes one of patrolling and monitoring operations. In the highly interdependent operations, minor breakdowns could readily compound into a major disruption of operations. A depth of knowledge and experience is required to understand the nature of a potential breakdown and the appropriate corrective measures. Worker background and training often appear to barely meet initial job needs. Workers come increasingly to rely on each other as well as supervision for counsel. The relative level of skill required of operators for adequate performance in the new jobs does not appear to be completely fulfilled in this instance. Where the worker isn't provided with enough additional training, feelings of uncertainty are probably reinforced.[37]

In some of the studies reported in the literature, including those of the Department of Labor, problems of definition and classification cast some doubt on the extent of reported changes. The indicated skill level is often the consequence of job evaluation procedures involving different factor definitions or reflects union influence in the bargained rate. To some extent worker confidence appear to be bolstered by working in a facility that represents a high point in technical knowledge where the job threat of further technical improvement is (apparently) removed. They are now the "in" group, whereas workers in older plants are the "outs."

3–1. The more advanced the state of technology (from mass production toward automation) 1.00–1.04, the greater the disruption cost 1.63 and the worker monitoring 1.26; the greater the disruption cost, the greater the felt co-worker dependency 1.37 and the greater the worker need for expert knowledge 1.20 where training falls short, the greater the worker tension 1.38, the greater the interdependency of workers and supervision and modification of foreman-worker relations 1.45, the greater the "closeness of supervision" 1.90. 3–1 1.90; 1.00–1.04, 1.63 (1.37 and 1.20, 1.38, 1.45) and 1.26   LIM   T
MP → A

3–2. The more advanced the state of technology (from mass production toward automation) 1.00–1.04, the fewer the number of supervisory

levels 1.71, the greater the use of supervisor-worker communication 1.64, the more more advanced the state of technology, the greater the supervisory machine responsibility 1.44, the greater the "closeness of supervision" 1.90. 3–2   1.90; 1.00–1.04, 1.71, 1.64; 1.44   LIM   T
$$MP \rightarrow A$$

Model (4) (Conceptual Scheme in Exhibit 6.)

A number of the reports and discussions on technology have pointed up the concurrent changes in worker role and process rationalization. Under the pressure of increasing mechanization and process interdependence, old trades deteriorate, employee job involvement is discouraged and the concept of a "satisfactory worker" changes.[38]

The more desirable worker is now one who can adhere to schedules. Even such things as worker pay are increasingly dependent on machine performance; in the event of breakdowns, workers are often sent home.[39] In the plants studied, machine operations increase and manual operations decrease.[40] In the case of rationalization in a pulp procedure, the supervisor assumes added equipment responsibilities, decreased directive responsibilities, and appears to be able to supervise and control somewhat larger work crews.[41] The response of the workers to the process changes differs. The *sex* of the workers involved appears to be one of the factors underlying the reported worker perception of the changes. In a TV plant with a large number of female workers on rather tedious operations, it is suggested that the workers seem relatively more satisfied after the changes.[42]

4–1. The greater the mechanization 1.02 and the interdependence of operations 1.04, the less the worker task involvement 1.21, and the increased worker dependence on machines 1.23 and adherence to schedules 1.22, and increased supervisory machine responsibilities 1.44, the less the "closeness of supervision." 1.90. 4–1 1.90: 1.02 and 1.04 (1.21 and 1.22 and 1.23, 1.25); 1.22 and 1.23 and 1.44   LIM T
$$C \rightarrow MP$$

ANALYSIS AND SUMMARY

The major and intervening variables have been jointly analyzed in relation to their indicated direction of influence. This analysis is facilitated by setting the variables down in a tabular array. (See Exhibit 7.)

It should again be noted that a loose classification scheme is employed in keeping with the type of "data" available. It has already been indicated

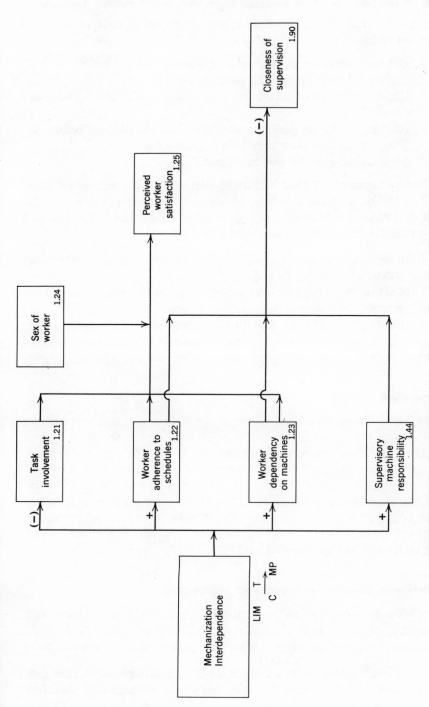

Exhibit 6. Models relating the state of technology to closeness of supervision.

that these "data" resulted from an extensive amount of interpretation (on our part) because of the:

1. Different bases for measurement employed in the studies;
2. Number of studies largely descriptive in nature;
3. Use of perceptual data (reporting on situations amenable to more objective procedures);
4. Number of studies dealing with transitional situations ("before and after") but which themselves were only "expost"; and,
5. Biases reflected in our own interpretations.

It may be seen in Exhibit 7 that the intervening variables are set down and related to the basic interstage transitions suggested by the studies (*a*) "Craft"-"Mass Production" and (*b*) "Mass Production"-"Automation." From this transitional model it may be seen that:

1. In general, "closeness of supervision" (1.90) is a decreasing functional activity in transition from C→MP.
2. In transitions from MP→A, results are generally mixed with "closeness" increasing in some and decreasing in others.
3. "Coordination and control" (1.80) identified with the general phenomenon "Impersonal Control" is a monotonically increasing function with the state of technology through both C→MP and MP→A.

Impersonal Control

In the preliminary analyses, it was suggested that increased coordination and control ("Impersonal Control") might be vested in the process, procedures, specialists and/or higher supervisory levels. The indicated increase of coordination and control (1.80) appears to bear out this idea. The need for and use of specialists (1.10 and 1.11) measurably increased due to increased communication needs (1.61), and the inadequacy of supervisory background (1.41, 1.42 and 1.43). The increase of impersonal controls is further reinforced by decreased involvement of worker in the task (1.21) and increasing task routinization (1.27).

Supervisory Direction (Closeness of Supervision)

"Closeness of supervision" is a monotonically decreasing function with technology within a technological range bounded by "craft" and "mass production" operations (LIM T). The routinization of worker tasks
$$C→MP$$
(1.27), forced adherence to schedules (1.22) and decreased worker task involvement (1.21) reduced the supervisor's need for personally directing

Intervening Variables	C → MP			MP → A		
	1.80	1.90	1.91	1.80	1.90	1.91
1.10 Use of Specialists	+++	(+)		+		
1.11 New Specialist Requirements						
1.20 Need for Expert Worker Knowledge	+				+	
1.21 Worker Task Involvement	(−)	−		(−)		
1.22 Worker Adherence to Schedule		+				
1.23 Worker Dependency on Machines		+				
1.24 Sex of Worker						
1.25 Perceived Worker Satisfaction						(−)
1.26 Worker Monitoring				+	(+)+	
1.27 Worker Routinization of Task	+	(+)				
1.28 Modification of Worker Job Content					+	
1.29 Work Spatial Distances						+
1.30 Work Material Handling						(+)
1.31 Task Attention Time					(+)	+
1.32 Worker Interaction						(−)
1.33 Policy of Individual Specialization					(+)	
1.34 Process Restraint on Worker Mobility					(+)	
1.35 Social Isolation						+
1.36 Worker Adjustment Period						(−)
1.37 Felt Co-Worker Dependency					+	
1.38 Worker Tension					+	
1.40 Need for Expert Knowledge						
1.41 Adequacy of Sup'r Background						
1.42 Hiring of Highly Trained Sup'r	+					
1.43 Supervisor Retraining						
1.44 Supervisor Machine Responsibility		(+)			+	
1.45 Modification of Sup'r-Worker Rel.				+	+	
1.46 Supervisory Nondirective Tasks						
1.47 Policy of Sup'r Proximity to Work					+	
1.50 Supervisory Conflict						
1.60 Variability and Contingency						
1.61 Need for Direct Communication	+					
1.62 Communication Parallel-Work Flow	+					
1.63 Disruption Cost				−	(+)	
1.64 Ease of Communication					+	
1.70 Cutting of Hierarchical Lines						
1.71 No. of Hierarchical Levels					(+)	
1.72 Foreman-Worker Ratio					(+)+	

Exhibit 7. A tabular model for analysis of the propositions. $+$ = Increase $-$ = decrease ( ) = change differs from 1.80, 1.90 or 1.91.

his men. To some extent, new supervisory responsibilities are created or old ones become relatively more important, for example, foreman machine responsibilities (1.44) increase.

"Closeness of Supervision" in Transitions towards "Automation"

The relationship between "closeness of supervision" and technology (LIM   T) is not clearly indicated from the reported studies
  MP → A
Some of the studies reported information that appeared perceptual in nature which we classified as *felt* "closeness of supervision" (1.91) as compared with a more or less objective change in "closeness" 1.90.

As the rationalization of operations increases, worker routines (1.28) and social relations are modified with increased monitoring (1.26), less worker mobility (1.34), smaller work groups and in some cases, increased social isolation (1.35). Interpersonal relations appear to be modified with some increased co-worker dependency (1.37) and modifications of relationships with the supervisor (1.45).

With a reduction of the number of hierarchial levels (1.71), involving increased supervisory responsibility for equipment (1.44) and process requirements relative to worker background (1.20), "closeness of supervision" (1.90) increases. In situations where workers are increasingly confined to immediate work areas (1.34) and where tasks become increasingly specialized (1.27) or simplified, "closeness of supervision" (1.90) is reduced.

These changes in "closeness" appear to take place regardless of increases or decreases in the foreman-worker ration (1.72), disruption costs (1.63) or worker monitoring (1.26) or operations.

The divergence of results concerning "closeness of supervision" (LIM   T) might be related to the relative employee skill levels involved
  MP → A
in the change. One study of a steel company suggests moderately higher worker skill requirements as a consequence of a transformation to an automation type facility. In the power plant studies and in the automated block plant certain jobs assume new importance and older, more traditional jobs are threatened. In the absence of retraining or upgrading, these older jobs would then have assumed more of a secondary position in job status. The Bright studies suggest that worker skill requirements decrease in advancing technological situations as opposed to the Walker findings in the steel mill.

Considering these apparently diverse aspects of employee skill level, two mechanisms might more readily provide a basis for rationalizing the direction of change in "closeness of supervision" in technical transitions toward "automated" operations:

(a) *Conversions to automation involving substantially different equipment and controls from that previously existing.* In this type of situation, extensive retraining and/or updating of workers might be expected. In situations involving workers with higher skill levels, the past trend of decreasing "closeness of supervision," from "craft" toward "mass production," might be expected to continue through the range from "mass production" to "automation." Perhaps the supervisor does not find it necessary to spend as much time in direct supervision of his men due to: (1) the increased worker skill levels; and, (2) the increased constraints provided by the automated process.

(b) *Conversions involving more complicated equipment and control instrumentation with men relegated to increasingly simplified tasks.* In these task situations, workers assume such jobs as light and dial watching. Dial indications in these situations represent complex relationships among the process variables, requiring advanced education or experience for complete understanding. New specialists such as instrument engineers and maintenance people assume responsibilities for equipment performance. The worker in this situation supports the equipment rather the equipment serving as an adjunct to the man. Perhaps supervision has to keep the worker under increased surveillance as the costs of breakdown become very large. The supervisor lacks confidence in his workers' ability to cope with operational problems due to their lack of skill and training relative to the complex and process variables.

CONCLUSION

Our appraisal of the propositional models and some of the possible mechanisms relating to our authority variable, indicates that:

1. Problems of control and coordination become increasingly greater as higher levels of technology are achieved.

2. The organization's response to greater control requirements may result in the following possibilities:

(a) Greater use of specialists;

(b) More "built in" process and regulatory controls which we term "impersonal control";

(c) More control assumed by higher management levels; and/or,

(d) Various combinations of the above.

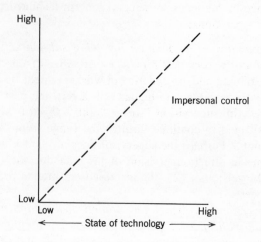

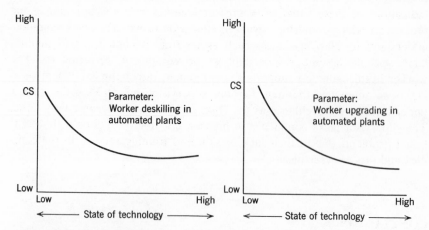

Exhibit 8. Refined models of our working hypotheses based on analysis of the empirical studies. CS = closeness of supervision.

3. The results reported in the literature study seem to largely *reinforce* increased control by:

(*a*) The process and procedures, that is, "impersonal control"; and,

(*b*) The increased use of staff specialists.

4. "Closeness of supervision" appears to decrease in the technological progression from *"craft" towards "mass production"* operations as the supervisor assumes new responsibilities for jobs which: (*a*) perhaps did not exist heretofore; or, (*b*) were only of minor importance. In the technological progression from *mass production to automation* two possibilities seem realistically attainable:

(*a*) A leveling out or slight increase in "closeness of supervision" as a consequence of job deskilling and major worker readjustments; and, (*b*) A possible decrease in "closeness of supervision" resulting from an upgrading of worker jobs and further corresponding decreases in the amount of time the supervisor spends with his men.

These tentative summary conclusions are depicted as conceptual models in Exhibit 8.

NOTES

[1] The writer would like to acknowledge the counsel of Professors Harold Guetzkow, Albert H. Rubenstein, and Arthur R. Tebbutt of Northwestern University in the original development of this topic. This paper draws on a portion of the final development which was incorporated in the author's doctoral dissertation, Northwstern University, 1964.

[2] Systematic changes in the organization and activities of industrial supervision are suggested in Joan Woodward, *Management and Technology* (London: Her Majesty's Stationery Service, 1958) and further reinforced (with added detail) in the more recent K. E. Thurley and A. C. Hamblin, *The Supervisor and His Job* (London: Her Majesty's Stationery Office, 1963).

[3] James G. March and Herbert A. Simon with the collaboration of Harold Guetzkow, *Organizations* (New York: John Wiley and Sons, Inc., 1958).

[4] Some evidence is provided on this point in a historical organization analysis of two major U. S. industries—oil refining and textiles; see Elmer H. Burack and Fred D. Sturdevant, "Technology and the Management of Industrial Enterprise." (Forthcoming.)

[5] A stage-like approach has often been used as a conceptual device. The overall, historical approach is similar to that of: W. W. Rostow, *The Stages of Economic Growth* (New York: Cambridge University Press, 1960), pp. 4–16 and Alaine Touraine, "A Historical Theory in the Evolution of Industrial Skills, *Modern Technology and Civilization: An Introduction to Human Problems in the Machine Age,* ed. Charles Walker (New York: McGraw-Hill, 1962); A more detailed approach is taken to inter-firm technical comparisons in James R. Bright, *Automation and Management* (Cambridge: Research Division, Harvard Graduate School of Business, 1958).

[6] For example, see Alvin W. Gouldner and Richard A. Peterson, *Technology and the Moral Order* (Indianapolis: Bobbs-Merrill, 1962), p. 25.

[7] Some indication of this broad usage is given by: Ward C. Low, "Identifying and Evaluating the Barrier Problem in Technology," *Technological Planning on the Corporate Level,* ed. James R. Bright (Boston: Harvard University Press, 1962); Touraine, *op. cit.,* pp. 429–437; Charles R. Walker, *Steeltown: An Industrial Case History of the Conflict Between Progress and Security* (New York: Harper and Bros., 1950); William Foote Whyte, "An Interaction Approach to the Theory of Organization," *Modern Organization Theory,* ed. Mason Haire (New York: John Wiley and Sons, 1959), p. 159.

[8] Some idea may be gained of the varied usage of these terms in the following references: George B. Baldwin and George Schultz, "Automating: a New Dimension to Old Problems," *Proceeding of the Sixth Annual Meeting Industrial Relations*

Association, 1959, p. 11; Charles C. Kellingsworth, "Forward," *Annals of the American Academy of Political and Social Science,* CCCXL (March, 1962); Charles R. Walker, Robert H. Guest and Arthur N. Turner, *The Foreman on the Assembly Line* (Cambridge: Harvard University Press, 1956). The term "automation" itself has been used in a variety of ways reflecting such things as a system of thought, feedback, integrated operation and electronic data processing. A few examples of this outpouring of concepts may be found in Lee D. DuBridge, "Educational and Social Consequences," *Automation and Technological Change,* ed. John T. Dunlop (New Haven: Yale University Press, 1962), p. 30; Robert A. Brady, *Organization, Automation and Society* (Los Angeles: University of California Press, 1961), p. 237; Walter Buckingham, *Automation* (New York: Harper and Bros., 1961), p. 6.

9 *The New Century Dictionary* (New York: D. Appleton-Century Co., 1948).

10 *Webster's New International Dictionary,* Second Edition, Unabridged (Springfield: G. and C. Merriam Company, 1961).

11 *The New Century Dictionary, op. cit.,* p. 1398.

12 These dimensions are based on our historical analysis and several industrial studies including: Robert Dubin, *The World of Work* (Englewood Cliffs: Prentice-Hall, 1958), pp. 179 and 182; Floyd C. Mann and L. Richard Hoffman, *Automation and the Worker* (New York: Holt, Rinehart, 1960), pp. 7–17; Charles R. Walker and Robert H. Guest, *The Man on the Assembly Line* (Cambridge: Harvard University Press, 1952), pp. 9–14.

13 Mann and Hoffman, *op. cit.,* pp. 7–10.

14 Dubin, *op. cit.,* pp. 179 and 182.

15 Peter M. Blau and W. Richard Scott, *Formal Organizations: A Comparative Approach* (San Francisco: Chandler Publishing Company, 1962), pp. 160–192.

16 This diverse range of concepts is suggested by the following references: Dubin, *op. cit.,* p. 33; Robert L. Kahn and Daniel Katz, "Leadership Practices in Relation to Productivity and Morale," *Group Dynamics: Research and Theory,* eds. Dorwin Cartwright and Alvin Zander (Evanston: Row Peterson, 1960), p. 559; Michael Argyl, Godfrey Gardner and Frank Cioffi, "The Management of Supervisory Methods," *Human Relations,* X (Fall, 1957) No. 4, 125: Talcott Parsons et al., *Working Papers in the Theory of Action* (Glencoe: Free Press, 1953, p. 39; March and Simon, *op. cit.,* p. 167; George Strauss and Leonard R. Sayles, *Personnel: The Human Problems of Management* (Englewood Cliffs: Prentice-Hall, 1960), pp. 124 and 184.

17 Kahn and Katz, *op. cit.,* pp. 554–569.

18 Webster's, *op. cit.,* p. 2533.

19 Ralph M. Stogdill and E. L. Scott, "Responsibility and Authority Relationship" in R. M. Stogdill, *Leadership and Structure of Personal Interaction,* Monograph No. 54, (Columbus: Ohio State University, 1957), Bureau of Business Research, pp. 129–133.

20 Some recent studies made of supervisory interaction with subordinates would tend somewhat to discount the importance of personality as a confounding factor in "closeness of supervision." For example, see Floyd C. Mann, "Toward an Understanding of the Leadership Role in Formal Organizations," A paper, Survey Research Center, University of Michigan, 1963, p. 6, and later incorporated in Robert Dubin, et al., *Leadership and Productivity* (San Francisco: Chandler Publishing Co., 1965), for a discussion of some general considerations.

21 Blau and Scott, *op. cit.,* pp. 176–194.

22 We employed a shorthand, symbolic type nomenclature to represent relations in a more compact form. Specifically, we have used the following:

LIM = LIMIT (A suggestion that the relation only applies over a limited range.)
C = Craft
MP = Mass Production
A = Automation
T = State of Technology
$\rightarrow$ = Toward

23 It should be understood that the Blau and Scott analysis is a completely verbal discussion so that the responsibility for the graphical and analytical interpretation are those of the writer and not necessarily those of the authors.

24 Strauss and Sayles, *op. cit.,* pp. 347–351.

25 Blau and Scott, *op. cit.,* p. 171.

26 Harold Guetzkow, "Differentiation of Roles in Task Oriented Groups," eds. Cartwright and Zander, *op. cit.,* pp. 683–704.

27 Argyl, et al., *op. cit.,* pp. 295–304; R. Lippitt, *An Experimental Study of Authoritarian and Democratic Group Atmospheres* (J. of Iowa Studies in Child-Welfare, 1940); Daniel Katz, N. Macoby, Nancy C. Morse, *Productivity, Supervision and Morale in the Office Situation* (Ann Arbor, U. of Michigan, 1950); Kahn and Katz, *op. cit.,* pp. 554–569.

28 March and Simon, *op. cit.,* "Introduction." This form is equivalent to stating that the dependent variable is influenced (increased) by the independent variable via some intervening variable.

29 If, in a particular propositional relation, we designate a so-called independent *or* dependent variable, the relation is indicated as follows:

1.80, 1.81, . . . , 1.90, . . . : Number of dependent variable (Closeness or Control Variable)	(1.01, 1.02, . . .) Number of independent variable (Technology Variable)	1.17, 1.18, . . . Number of intermediate variable

Many of the propositional mechanisms are interrelated and consequently an intermediate "dependent" variable in one relation is designated as an intermediate "independent" variable in the next successive relationship. In order to put the propositions in a compact form and avoid redundancy in the statement of direction of influence or consequence, the initial proposition is stated as a complete functional relation. Successive, related propositions reflect the transposition of result to cause unless otherwise indicated. We adhere as closely as possible to the line of reasoning of the original researcher in model construction. In many cases certain results are not explicitly stated by the researcher. We employ words such as "seemed" and "approach" to convey the idea of our interpretation of results. In general, the interpretation of the findings of the studies are ours. The term coordination," that is, ordering or regulating, is used in conjunction with control recognizing common industrial use.

30 Charles R. Walker, *Towards the Automatic Factory* (New Haven: Yale University Press, 1967), pp. 27–29; Walker and Guest, *op. cit.,* pp. 9–14; Walker, Guest, and Turner, *op. cit.,* pp. 34–36.

31 Georges Friedmann, *Industrial Society: The Emergence of the Human Problems of Automation* (Glencoe: Free Press, 1955), pp. 200–210 indicate the need for new foreman aptitudes in knowledge and skill.

32 Frank J. Jasinski, "Adapting Organizations to New Technology," *Harvard Business Review,* XXXVII, (Jan., Feb., 1959) No. 1, pp. 79–86; March and Simon, *op. cit.,*

p. 159; Robert Dubin, *The World of Work* (Englewood Cliffs: Prentice-Hall, 1958), p. 347; Richard L. Simpson, "Vertical and Horizontal Communication in Formal Organizations," *Administrative Science Quarterly,* IV (1959), pp. 188–196; Bright, *Automation and Management, op. cit.,* p. 142.

33 William A. Faunce, *op. cit.,* pp. 401–407; William A. Faunce, "The Automobile Industry: A Case Study in Automation," *Organization, Automation, and Society,* ed. Robert A. Brady (Los Angeles: University of California Press, 1961), pp. 44–51; Simpson, *op. cit.,* pp. 186–196.

34 Greater commitment to high cost capital equipment and greater interdependencies between units.

35 Walker, *Automatic Factory, op. cit.*

36 Mann and Hoffman, *op. cit.;* Floyd C. Mann and L. Richard Hoffman, "Individual and Organizational Correlates of Automation," *The Journal of Social Issues,* VII. (1956) No. 2; Floyd C. Mann. "Psychological and Organizational Impacts," *Automation and Technological Change,* ed. John T. Dunlop (New York: American Assembly, Columbia University Press, 1962), pp. 51–52.

37 Skill levels are reportedly decreased in an automation situation according to James R. Bright, ed., *Technological Planning on the Corporate Level* (Boston: Harvard University, 1962), p. 97 whereas Walker, *Automatic Factory, op. cit.,* p. 211, indicated slightly higher skill levels. Certain jobs such as maintenance assumed new importance, further threatening the status of senior employees. In a study aboard a naval vessel, status changes were also noted as a consequence of technological change. James F. Downs, "Environment, Communication and Status Change Aboard an American Aircraft Carrier," *Human Organizations,* XVII (Fall, 1959), No. 3.

38 Friedman, *op. cit.,* pp. 200–218.

39 Howard Boone Jacobson and Joseph S. Roucek, *Automation and Society* (New York: Philosophical Library, 1959), pp. 466–498.

40 U.S. Dept. of Labor, Bureau of Labor Statistics, "Impact of Technological Change and Automation in the Pulp and Paper Industry," *Bulletin No. 1347* (Washington: U.S. Printing Office, 1962), pp. 35–40.

41 *Ibid.,* pp. 1–38. These inferences are based on a reported study that paralleled our concept of transition from C→MP. Some of the other studies in this industry appeared to reflect MP→A.

42 J. M. Hund, "Automated Manufacture of Machines of Communication," *Automation and Society,* eds. Howard Boone Jacobson and Joseph S. Roucek, *op. cit.,* pp. 82–93.

27

COMMUNICATION NETWORKS IN
INTERMEDIATE MARKETS *

F. E. Balderston

I. INTRODUCTION

Most commodities move from points of production through successive stages of processing or manufacture and further stages of intermediate distribution before reaching points of final purchase. The final value of a commodity, in fact, is often analyzed by observing the amounts of labor and capital services that are added to it at each of these stages by the firm which owns it at each stage. The concept of value added has gained great currency in national income computations and other applications to cost and price theory. If there is pure competition and reasonably full information in all markets, it is assumed that the number of stages of ownership and of provision of services will be consistent with the costs and benefits of organizing the commodity flow in an optimal manner. Presumably, each operating enterprise or each potential entrant into a particular stage of the market can gauge the desirability of adding services to the commodity—and charging a margin which it is hoped will cover the costs of such services—on marginal considerations. The number of successive owners of a commodity, and the allocation of various functional types of effort among them, are not of much interest in the domain of purely competitive behavior. This unconcern extends, in fact, to problems of vertical integration of business enterprises, since it is possible to generalize from the marginal analysis that the performance of a particular set of activities by one firm as against two separated firms will not make any effective difference in the accumulation of value in a commodity under pure competition in all markets.

* Reprinted from *Management Science,* January, 1958, pp. 154–171.

Where economies of scale and potential monopolization of critical stages in the commodity flow are involved, the situation is somewhat less clear. If uncertainty and less than full information are also admitted as possibilities, the presumptions arising out of the theory of pure competition are still less adequate. However, insufficient attention has been paid to the development of explanatory hypotheses regarding vertical commodity flows. The present paper is devoted to some contributions toward this end.

The setting of the problem is this. Successive stages of dealing in a commodity are in general required on account of any of the following considerations: (a) an activity may need to be undertaken at a different scale—i.e., plant size—than that at which a preceding or a succeeding activity needs to be conducted; (b) changes in the *combinations* of commodities may be required from one stage to another; or (c) information and contacts need to be mobilized in order to connect disparate groups of actors in the complex of activities.

Students of marketing have developed the concept of the marketing channel, defined as the set of entities that are brought into relation with one another in respect to a particular commodity flow. They have also pointed out that the set of activities required for effective commodity distribution can be broken down into functional classes. Some of the most important of these types of funtional effort have to do with the establishment of contacts, the negotiation of transactions, or—more generally—the generating of information leading to transactions decisions. We will consider here some properties of communication networks in intermediate markets, with a view toward determining under simplifying assumptions what might be the optimal structure for such intermediate markets. Optimal structure is defined here as the proper adjustment of the number and types of intermediary agency to the numbers and types of supplier, to the numbers and types of customer, and to the type of marketing task which is called for by the characteristics of the commodity.

II. COMMUNICATION NETWORKS IN INTERMEDIATE MARKETS

A. The Continuous-Linkage, One-Commodity Model

The simplest model of communication in an intermediate market restricts consideration to one commodity in which every supplier and every customer deals exclusively. The total commodity flow through the market is assumed to be given, in accordance with the basic cost conditions in the supplying industry and conditions of final demand facing the retail level or the ultimate transaction level in the market. As we shall concentrate on the communication network problem, we will also assume a standard order size and a single standardized method of shipment. Finally, wholesalers will be assumed not to carry any intermediate inventories. Their activities will be confined to the maintenance of contacts in the communication framework, and the actual commodity shipments will be presumed to go from the supplying points to the customer points. The chief function of the wholesaler then will be to serve as a switchboard of a communication network between the suppliers and the customers. The suppliers will be taken as the group of producers of the commodity and the customers will be taken as a group retail enterprises (if the commodity is a consumer good) or as a group of enterprises which make final sales of a raw material or other intermediate product to users of that product in production processes.

The heading of this section has indicated that this would be called a continuous-linkage model. The communication link between any two actors in the market will be assumed to be like a pipe line which is set up to connect any two points. Once built, it can carry variable flows of information (up to some maximum limit) but its current operating costs per time period will be assumed independent of the amount of information carried or the number of messages. To characterize a communication system in this way is to make a substantial abstraction from reality, as it is often true that each message between any two actors in a communication system has a separable variable cost of its own; thus, the total costs of an information flow depend on the magnitude of that flow, and there will be a problem of determining the optimal amount of information in respect to cost. We will, for the moment, neglect this problem.

The set of suppliers is assumed to be some given number S. Each of these suppliers has a certain amount of the commodity to sell in each time period and must be in touch with one or more of the members of the customer group in order to market this supply. The number of customers, also assumed given, will be called C. The number of intermediary agencies—i.e., wholesalers—will be W. In accordance with our assumption that the costs of a communication link are constant regardless of the amounts of information transmitted through it, we can assume that these costs are constant per time period. This constant cost per communication link is defined as q.

Although the continuous link is broadly enough defined to permit any two actors in the market who are so connected to exchange any type and amount of information, it is nevertheless true that the adequacy of the information in the hands of each actor depends on the number of other actors with whom he is connected.

1. *"Ideal" and "Adequate-Bargaining" Networks.* An *ideal* structure for the provision of full information would require that every actor in the market be connected with every other. For S suppliers and C customers, with no intermediary firms, the resulting network would be:

each supplier connected to every customer: S-C links

each supplier connected to every other supplier: $S\dfrac{(S-1)}{2}$ links

each customer connected to every other customer: $C\dfrac{(C-1)}{2}$ links

The sum of these links, multiplied by q, the constant cost per link, gives the total cost of the ideal network:

$$TC_1 = qSC + \frac{qS(S-1)}{2} + \frac{qC(C-1)}{2}$$

which reduces algebraically to

$$TC_1 = \tfrac{1}{2}q\,[(S+C)^2 - (S+C)] \qquad (1)$$

This is the communication network which exists, by assumption, in the pure theory of the perfectly competitive market.

Each actor may, however, be content to insist only that the communication network permit him to make a complete canvass of all actors on the opposite side of the market, for bargaining purposes. We are assuming that the actors operate in an atomistic manner in their bargaining relations. The linkages critical to any actor would then be those which could result in the completion of transactions—and these would necessarily be linkages with those on the opposite side of the market. The chief purpose of links with others on the same side of the market—in the absence of collusion—would be to verify the claims of those on the opposite side concerning bids or offers from one's competitors. Adequate protection in bargaining still might be afforded by a network connecting each actor with every actor on the opposite side. The total cost of such an adequate bargaining network, with no intermediaries, would be

$$T_2 = qSC \qquad (2)$$

This "adequate-bargaining network" will be taken as a referent against which to compare the operation of the market when intermediaries are present. This network is less than "ideal," but it is clearly more elaborate, and more satisfactory in terms of information flow, than many networks involving *segmentation* of the market. In a segmented market, each supplier is connected only with a part of the customer group, and each customer is connected with part of the supplier group. Such partial segmentation of the market will be considered at a later point.

2. *Network Costs with Wholesale Intermediaries.* If a single wholesale intermediary connects all of the actors in the market, he will require S links to the suppliers and C links to the customers. The total costs of the system will then be.

$$T_3 = q(S + C) \tag{3}$$

Every wholesale intermediary who enters the market will be assumed, for simplicity, to replicate this network, so that for any number of wholesalers, W the total costs of the system will be:

$$T_4 = qW(S + C) \tag{4}$$

3. *The "Indifference Number" of Wholesalers.* Given S and C, there is a number of wholesalers at which the costs of the indirect system would just equal the costs of the "adequate-bargaining" direct network. Setting $T_2 = T_4$, we find that this "indifference number" of wholesalers is:

$$W^* = \frac{SC}{S + C} \tag{5}$$

When the number of wholesalers is less than W^*, the indirect system is less costly than the direct; if there are more wholesalers than W^*, the indirect system is more costly. From the standpoint of the market as a whole, no indirect system would be set up whose costs exceeded T_2 and whose number of wholesalers exceeded W^*.

Note that the q's have no effect on the network, because in this model total costs are strictly proportional to the number of communication links, and this number is determined solely by sums and products of the numbers of suppliers and customers.

Some statements can now be made about the maximum number of wholesale intermediaries that can be supported in terms of total communication network costs. For very simple market structures involving low values of either S or C, no wholesale intermediary can be justified, as is shown by the following table:

S	C	W^*
1	1	½
1	C^*	$C^*/(1 + C^*)$
S^*	1	$S^*/(1 + S^*)$
2	2	1

In the above table, S^* and C^* are any non-negative values. A minimum of two suppliers and two customers is required before one wholesaler can be introduced.

4. *A Condition of Symmetry.* More generally, defining the ratio of suppliers to customers as $r = S/C$ and substituting this ratio into equation (5), we have

$$W^* = \frac{SC}{S+C} = \frac{C^2 r}{rC + C} = C\left(\frac{r}{r+1}\right). \tag{6}$$

The term $r/r + 1$ has a maximum value of ½; this occurs where $r = 1$, that is, where the numbers of suppliers and customers are equal. Thus, for any given number of customers, W^* is largest where the market structure is *symmetrical,* and at this point the indifference number of wholesalers is one half of the number of customers.

5. *The Problem of Wholesaler Monopoly Power.* It is clear that the greatest improvement as compared with a system of direct links is secured by the operation of a single wholesale intermediary as a "switchboard" in the communication network, for the amount of saving from the installation of an indirect system is $qS \times C - q (S + C)W$.

If there were only one wholesaler, the opportunity for economic profits would be greatest. The maximum gain that the single wholesaler could secure would be

$$M = q [SC - (S + C)]. \tag{7}$$

Thus, a single wholesaler could set his margin so as to make his total costs plus his profits equal to the total costs of the system of direct links.

As the number of wholesale intermediaries increases, competition between them forces the potential monopoly profit toward zero. At some point, the number of wholesalers would be great enough so that this factor alone would enforce purely competitive conditions on each of them in setting his wholesale margin, and each wholesaler would set a margin which, at the volume he would secure, would just cover his long-run costs of operation.

In addition to this, there is an absolute upper bound on the total costs of the wholesale intermediaries, inclusive of economic profit. Relations between the total costs of the network and the number of wholesalers are portrayed in Fig. 1. The ceiling on costs of the network involving wholesalers is seen to be T_2, the cost of the network of direct links between suppliers and customers. The costs of the network of "indirect" links, T_4, is a linear function of the member of wholesalers. The line $\hat{M}$ is a locus of amounts of greatest possible long-run profits (over and above linkage costs) to the wholesaler group, as the number of wholesalers increases. $\hat{M}$ is seen to be equal to zero when $W = W^*$. For a number of wholesalers, $Wk,$ the cost of linkages is DF, total economic profit is DE, and the total charges imposed

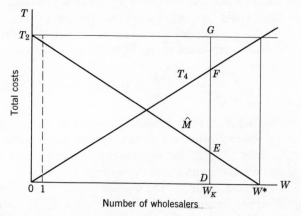

Figure 1. Total Network costs and the Number of Wholesalers. T_2 = total cost of system of direct links; T_4 = total cost of indirect links; W^* = "indifference number" of wholesalers; $\hat{M}$ = maximum values of profits to wholesaler group for each number of wholesalers, in the long run.

on suppliers and customers (equal to the costs of the direct-link network) are DG.

6. *The Profits of Wholesalers and the Total Costs of the Network.* From the stand-point of total network costs to the suppliers and customers, gains from the existence of wholesale intermediaries are conferred whenever the total economic profits of the wholesalers, as a group, are less than $\hat{M}$. While it is clear that the profits can be at most equal to M [as in equation (7)] for one wholesaler and that total wholesale profits fall to zero as the number of wholesalers approaches W^*, it is not obvious what the shape of the relation between total wholesaler profits and the number of wholesalers will be between these points.

The total costs of the network involving wholesalers, augmented by the total economic profits of the wholesaler group, are

$$T_5 = M + qW(S + C) \tag{8}$$

where

$$M = f(W). \tag{9}$$

A necessary condition for a minimum of this function is

$$\frac{d}{dW}(T_5) = f'(W) + q(S + C) = 0 \tag{10}$$
$$f'(W) = -q(S + C).$$

It is already clear, from the discussion of boundary conditions on total profits, that $M = f(W)$ has negative slope. But the profit-function must also be *concave from above* for some part of its length in order that the total costs may have a minimum value. That is,

$$\frac{d^2M}{dW^2} < 0.$$

Furthermore, the number of wholesalers for which T_5 is minimized *will be less than* W^* if the profit-function passes through the two end points (for $W = 0$, total "profit" $= qSC$; for $W = W^*$, total profit $= 0$) and is negatively sloped and concave from above throughout its length.

This is demonstrated in Fig. 2. The equilibrium number of wholesalers is W_E. But under these circumstances, the total costs of the network *rise* if new wholesalers, in addition to the W_E wholesalers already operating, attempt to enter the market. A curious fact about this equilibrium, however, is that it occurs when the economic profits of the wholesaler group are positive. A cost-minimizing solution, from the standpoint of the suppliers and customers, nevertheless permits the wholesalers to obtain positive long-run profits!

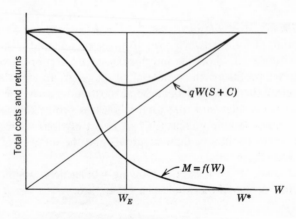

Figure 2.

The gain function may, of course, not meet the severe conditions that are specified above. Instead of attaining zero only when $W = W^*$, the profit-function may reach zero at some smaller number of wholesalers. Nevertheless, provided that M is concave from above, our conclusion that W_E occurs at a level of positive profits remains true. Only when the profit function is *convex* from above [$f''(W) > 0$] will the equilibrium number of wholesalers be at the point of zero profit, wherever M cuts the horizontal axis.

7. *Wholesaler Entry and Equilibrium Structure.* Total network costs (inclusive of economic profits to the wholesaler group) are seen to be a minimum at some number of wholesalers, W_E, which is less than the "indifference number," W^*. The commodity flow, G, is defined in units of one dollar's worth of the commodity evaluated at (identical) f.o.b. prices at the supplying points. The wholesale margin per unit of commodity flow is therefore

$$h = \frac{qW(S+C) + f(W)}{G}. \tag{11}$$

As G has been assumed to be given and constant, h is minimized where the numerator of equation (11) is a minimum—that is, where $W = W_E$. The supplier and customer groups are best served if the number of wholesalers stabilizes at W_E. Will this happen?

We may define the profits of the entering wholesaler as

$$B = hg - q(S+C). \tag{12}$$

The following profit conditions for the entering wholesaler will lead to stable equilibrium in the wholesaler group at $W = W_E$:

$$\begin{array}{lll}
\text{for } W < W_E, & B > 0, \\
\text{for } W = W_E, & B = 0, & (13) \\
\text{for } W > W_E, & B < 0.
\end{array}$$

Whether these conditions will be met depends on the values of h and g, in combination with each other. First, some statements can be made concerning the manner in which h will vary as the number of wholesalers increases. As is shown by equation (11), h depends solely on the number of wholesalers, under the assumption that all wholesalers receive the same margin per unit of business done. (Our lack of concern, at this moment, with the quality of information flows reinforces this assumption.) The rate of change of h with respect to W is

$$\underline{dh/dW} = \frac{1}{G}q(S+C) + f'(W). \tag{14}$$

The same general slope conditions apply to h and to T_5, the total cost equation. The function must be generally U-shaped, and it must be concave from above in the neighborhood of its minimum at $W - W_e$.

As for the new entrant's market share, g, two limiting cases can be established. The first is that in which the new entrant is economically marginal—obtaining zero profits. Setting $g = g(W)$, we find that when every new entrant is marginal, regardless of the previous number of wholesalers, the function must be generally bell-shaped—convex from above. Specifically,

$$g = \frac{Gq(S + C)}{qW\,(S + C) + f(W)},$$ (15)

and

$$\underline{dg/dW} = Gq(S + C)\left(\frac{-[q(S + C) + f'(W)]}{[qW(S + C) + f(W)^2}\right).$$ (16)

The second limiting case arises from the presumption that the entering wholesaler may be expected, at best, to obtain a market share proportional with those wholesalers already established. In this event, for any W,

$$g = \frac{G}{W}$$ (17)

On this proportionality assumption, and provided that the entering wholesaler earns the same margin per unit as his competitors, the entrant's economic profits are

$$B = \frac{f(W)}{W}.$$ (18)

These economic profits (over and above network costs), will be positive up to the point where $f(W) = 0$, which has been shown to be below or at the point where W reaches the indifference level.

The two limiting cases are shown in Fig. 3. The shaded area in Fig. 3 is the set of all points through which the function $g = g(W)$ may pass. All such functions must pass through point E, and if W_E is to be an equilibrium number of wholesalers, dg/dW must equal zero at this point.

More generally, from equation (12) we have

$$\underline{dB/dW} = h\frac{dg}{dW} + g\frac{dh}{dW},$$ (19)

and, from conditions (13),

$$\underline{dB/dW} < 0.$$ (20)

The following statements can be made:

$$h > 0, \qquad G > 0;$$
$$\underline{dh/dW} < 0, \qquad \text{for } W < W_E:$$
$$\underline{dh/dW} > 0, \qquad \text{for } W > W_E.$$

As $dB/dW < 0$, it follows that, as W increases beyond W_E,

$$\underline{dg/dW} < 0, \qquad \text{and} \quad \left|\frac{dg}{dW}\right| > \frac{dh}{dW}.$$

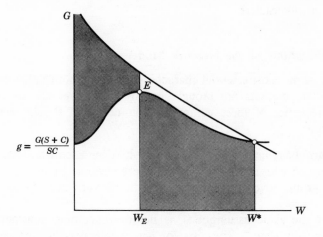

$$g = \frac{G(S + C)}{SC}$$

Figure 3.

As dh/dW rises at an increasing rate with increases of W beyond W_E, it follows that $(d^2g/dW^2) > 0$ in this interval. Thus $g = g(W)$ must be convex from above for the interval beyond $W = W_E$.

It would seem reasonable, also, that the entrant's market share should be high as the first entrants begin to compete with a monopoly intermediary, and that further entrants would win a smaller market share. That is, through the early part of the interval, $g = g(W)$ might follow generally the shape of the proportional market share curve. If this is the case, $g(W)$ must then have a flex point at $W = W_E$ in order to produce a stable equilibrium number of wholesalers at the minimum cost of the network system.

While it is possible that the actual empirical relation between the entrant's market share and the number of wholesalers could meet the severe restrictions necessary to produce a stable equilibrium at the point of minimum total cost, there is no presumption that this *must* be so. We can only conclude that an increasingly sharp rate of decline in entrant's market share would be necessary to discourage entry under conditions of rising margin per unit of business. It would be providential if this rate of decline commenced precisely at the point where the number of wholesalers reached W_E.

This model of communication networks shows, then, that an optimum structure of the market does exist for the performance of communication tasks. This optimum involves long-run positive economic profit to the wholesaler firms. The structure may or may not stabilize at the optimum point, depending on (a) the shape of the function relating the wholesaler group's economic profits to the number of wholesalers, and (b) the shape and position of the relation between the entrant's market share and the number of wholesalers.

B. Modifications of the Network Model

Some of the most essential characteristics of communication problems in intermediate markets are brought out by the model just discussed, but other properties of these communication networks should receive some comment.

1. *Partial Segmentation of the Network.* When each wholesaler need not be connected with every supplier and every customer, but only with a part of each group, several new features of the network need to be taken into account.

Under the same assumptions as before concerning constant cost per communication link, entry costs for new wholesalers are reduced. If u is the proportion of suppliers covered, and v is the proportion of customers covered, then the cost function for the entering wholesaler is of course q $(uS+vC)$. If, for simplicity, the fractions u and v are assumed equal, the indifference number of wholesalers is W^*/u.

For any given u, total network costs therefore rise less steeply than before as the number of wholesalers increases. The relation between economic profits of the wholesaler group and the number of wholesalers will also change. The first wholesaler to enter the business will be connected to only a part of the supplier and customer groups. Later entrants will presumably link themselves to suppliers and customers not previously served. Every supplier will be connected with one wholesaler when $W = S/uS = 1/u$, and every customer will be so connected when $W = C/vc = 1/v$. Until this point is reached each wholesaler can exact a high margin for his services, but thereafter, the total economic profits of the wholesaler group should begin to fall rapidly, for the possibilities for economic profit depend not only on the degree of dependence that each supplier or customer has on the (limited) number of wholesalers with whom he is connected, but also on the total size of the intermediary group. Figure 4 is a comparison between the model first described and a model involving partial segmentation of the network. It is so drawn as to show the minimum cost point in the latter case to be at a lower level of total cost than in the original model. To the extent that sheer numbers of wholesalers outweigh in importance the fewness of wholesaler connections to each supplier or customer, this cost reduction will take place.

The preceding discussion was based on the assumption that each wholesaler would set up a communication network of equal size and cost. Several factors will, however, cause wholesalers to change the size of their networks as competitive conditions change. The first few wholesalers to enter the business will have every incentive to set up as complete a communication network as possible. Suppliers and customers not served in the initial phases will seek to obtain such service, and the wholesale margin, at the

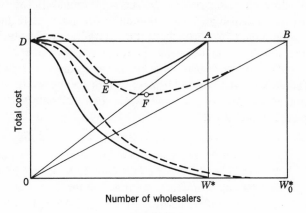

Figure 4.

volume of business passing through each wholesaler's hands, will be high enough to yield substantial economic profits to each wholesaler and to provoke expansion of coverage by the established wholesalers as well as entry by new ones. As entry does occur, each supplier may be expected to divide his output (and each customer, his purchases) among the wholesalers connected to him. As a result, the yield per communication link will fall. In the winnowing-out of the preferred contacts between any one wholesaler and his suppliers and customers, the wholesaler will profit by dropping those suppliers and customers whose business (at the declining margins secured under increasingly competitive conditions) becomes unprofitable. Each supplier and customer benefits in terms of his effort-cost in communication by being in contact with a sufficient number of wholesalers to assure adequate market information, but not a number so large as to become overly burdensome in terms of *his* effort-costs of maintaining the connection. Entrants are likely to fill the gaps in the segmented network until each supplier and customer is in contact with an adequate number of wholesalers, and, in the meantime, the size of each wholesaler's network is subject to shrinkage.

If suppliers have different output rates, the larger ones attract more wholesalers than do the smaller ones—and this larger number of wholesale contacts is needed by the supplier to assure adequate coverage of market opportunities. The same considerations hold for customers of varying size.

In the nature of the case, therefore, large suppliers and customers come into possession of more complete market information and are also better protected against monopoloid behavior by their wholesalers.

The degree of interconnection or interlocking among all parts of the segmented network depends upon the amounts of mutual overlap between the networks of different wholesalers. It seems reasonable to expect that wholesalers will so distribute their communication links as to bring about substantial interconnection throughout the market, but institutional barriers may prevent this. On occasion, in these markets, there are special groups of suppliers or customers who are not considered "eligible" by established wholesalers, and whose business cannot be easily mixed with that of the dominant supplier or customer type. Institutional barriers of this kind are discussed in Part III.

2. *Variable Costs of Communication Links.* There are several types of cost variation in communication links between actors in the intermediate markets. First, networks made up of continuous links might be subject to economies or diseconomies of scale, so that for the individual wholesale intermediary, the cost of adding further links would depend on the number he already had. The effects of scale economies would be obvious: they could reinforce the position of a few established wholesale intermediaries and prevent entry on the equal terms previously postulated.

Another source of cost variation is in the establishment of different types of informational contact between supplier or customer and the intermediary. Personal sales calls, for example, are an alternative to telephone, teletype or mail contact. The degree of reliance on these methods of course varies, but their costs differ and so does their usefulness for certain parts of the communication task.

A third source of cost variation arises in the intermittent character of information flow in marketing networks—that is, the links can be considered ephemeral, not continuous. There are differences in the types of message and in the total burden of the message flow between a supplier or customer and his wholesaler. Each message will have a cost differing with the medium of transmission and the size and complexity of the message.

Analysis of intermittent, variable-cost message-flow—in terms of types and content of messages required for different types of transaction and in terms of opportunities for consolidation of messages when the flow is large —is reserved for separate treatment in a subsequent paper.

3. *Multiple Products: Directional Changes in Communication Flow.* A few characteristics of the content of message flows will, however, be treated here. First, it is often the case that suppliers produce, and customers buy and resell, a group of closely related products rather than a single commodity. In the extractive industries, these products are often produced

under joint-cost conditions, with only partial control over the proportions of each product to total output. Wholesale intermediaries must then arrange transactions for each of the joint products. Fluctuations in relative demands or uncontrolled changes in the relative proportions of each product in the output flow lead to frequent adjustments in relative prices of the products. At any given time, prices of individual products may thus be moving in opposite directions. For the products in strong demand, *customers* will take the initiative in seeking supplies, while for those in oversupply, suppliers take initiative in seeking markets. The composition of the customer group is likely to be such that some customers absorb relatively more of one product than another, and in the supplier group, the composition of output is also likely to differ from one supplier to another.

The task of wholesale intermediaries is thus to match the differently-composed outputs of individual suppliers with the differently-composed demands of individual customers. Frequent reversals occur in the initiative taken by suppliers as against customers with respect to individual products. The result is that wholesale intermediaries benefit by being independent of either group, and therefore able to engage, simultaneously, in either market-seeking or output-seeking effort with respect to each product, and to reverse the direction of communication effort at will.

A wholesale firm that is operated as a subsidiary by a supplier or by a customer thus suffers a disadvantage as compared with independent operators. The supplier's wholesale subsidiary will find that for those products in strong demand, it cannot satisfy all customer requests from the supplier's own output but must seek elsewhere for them. Correspondingly, for products in oversupply, new customers must be sought. This difficulty may be overcome if the supplier is a very large scale, multi-plant firm, and if the wholesale subsidiary is able to embrace a wide group of customers whose local market requirements differ in product-composition. Also extreme flexibility in adding and dropping individual customers to and from the network may be helpful to such adjustment, but the *establishment* of contact is usually more difficult than the maintenance of a communication link once established.

The difficulty may also be avoided if a supplier's wholesale intermediary is empowered to buy freely from any supplier. However, wholesale representation on an integrated basis is usually arranged because the controlling firm wishes to secure special and exclusive attention to its marketing requirements. If the subsidiary must be able to buy freely from competing suppliers (when it is a wholesale subsidiary controlled by a supplier) or sell freely to competing customers (when it is a subsidiary controlled by a customer), the chief purpose of integrated wholesale representation cannot be achieved.

Frequent reversals in the direction of communication flow thus provide a rationale for autonomous operation of wholesale intermediaries. The chief exception to this is a protracted period of excess demand, or excess supply, for all parts of the product group. In this case, the direction of communication flow is the same for all of the products, and it is not subject to quick reversal. In a period of general excess demand, and rising prices, customers may thus be impelled to integrate backward, and in a period of general excess supply, suppliers may integrate forward to control wholesale outlets. Uncertainty concerning the duration of the period of excess supply or excess demand does inhibit the development of forward or backward integration.

III. INSTITUTIONAL STRESS IN COMMUNICATION NETWORKS: PERCEIVED MODELS OF THE MARKET

1. Eligible Participants in the Market

The supplier and customer groups have been considered as objectively defined in the foregoing discussion. The wholesaler's task was to establish a communication network and participate in a flow of transactions decisions by means of it. The actual definitions of his supplier and customer groups are in the wholesaler's mind, and these definitions depend, as will be shown, on his perceived model of the operation of his enterprise and of the market as a whole.

At any given time, the intermediary may catalog the actors in the market into several types:

1. Suppliers and customers who are active members of his network.
2. Suppliers and customers who are *potential* members of his network and who are presently connected to other intermediaries of the same type;
3. Other intermediaries who are "competitors"—i.e., engage in the same type of operation, and may outbid the intermediary on any transaction or may seek to connect themselves with his suppliers or customers; and
4. Suppliers, customers, and intermediaries who are "outside" the trade.

Some of the bases for exclusion will be discussed shortly, but the nature of the perceived model should first be examined.

2. The Language of Information Flow and the Perceived Model of the Market

The communication network which characterizes the market supports a flow of information—information about the inventory positions, bids and offers of individual customers and suppliers, and detailed information concerning specific transactions which the wholesaler is working out with suppliers and customers. The information-flow thus contributes both directly and indirectly to the continuing flow of transactions decisions. The content of information required for those decisions is reduced by standardization of the details of proposed transactions so that only a small number of "cues" need be received by any actor participating in a transaction decision. This reduction of information content also permits the actors to focus on the critical factor or factors—e.g., a price bargain, or delivery date. The "lore of the trade" which is known to be important in many markets is in good part a set of customs determining the language of these "cues" to transactions decisions. Use of cues, or special language, provides one contrast to the complete mapping of all aspects of every alternative choice which is one of the classic postulates of rationality in economic decision-making. But this reduction of information content does permit each actor to process a greater number of alternative choices, for given effort, than he otherwise could.

To make the system of cues work effectively, it is necessary that every actor in the network know and utilize the same special language. Each actor must be able to form stable expectations concerning the meaning of these cues when others use them. This requires that each actor have a similar perception of what the market is like: what product or products are dealt in by the actors in the market, what normal functions they assume themselves and expect other actors to perform, and what factors lead to changes in prices and the state of the market. As much bargaining is anticipatory, the last of these considerations is no less important than the first two.

3. The Perceived Model of the Wholesale Organization

In addition to this perception of the operation of the market, which must be held in common with other actors in the market in order to make the language of "cues" effective, the wholesale intermediary has a perception of the form and content of his own organization. This perceived model of his organization must be compatible with the commonly-held model of the market, but it is defined more restrictively in a number of respects. For example, it is often true that dealings in a commodity take place in a number of regional market centers. These are connected together by actual or virtual inter-regional shipment of the commodity if transfer costs are not too large. The individual wholesaler in one regional center may, however, confine himself strictly to dealings with local customers, on account of his greater familiarity with this aspect of the trade, or because his organization's supply of capital or executive talent is limited. In numerous other respects, the activities of the firm may be a subset of the activities in which it could engage without violating the general model of the market. The firm's operations may be changed to include more of these activities that are compatible with the general model, but this requires a policy decision by the executive head of the firm.

The wholesale executive's perception as to what suppliers, customers and other wholesalers are excluded from the trade is thus seen to rest on two simplifying abstractions: (*a*) his model of the operation of his own enterprise, and (*b*) his model of the operation of the market as a whole. The first of these is a much less drastic constraining factor than is the second.

4. Excluded Actors and the Perceived Model

One exclusion resting on the general model is that of suppliers of commodities other than those dealt in together by wholesale intermediaries and by the customer group. It is not unusual for members of the customer group to buy some types of product from a completely different group of wholesale intermediaries than the one under study. Also, a by-product commodity produced by supplier firms may be channelled through wholesale markets other than those utilized for the bulk of the joint product group, if the set of customers for the by-product is different from the customer group which buys the rest of the products. But if the set of commodities that is produced by the supplier group is also handled, *in toto,* by the customer group, wholesale intermediaries tend to deal in all the individual commodities unless special intermediate handling is required for certain by-products which then go through the hands of specialists.

The wholesaler does not, therefore, view his potential supplier group as being composed of all possible sellers of all possible products. The expectations of the customer group also come into play in this connection. Customers form expectations (based on the general model of the market which they hold in common with other actors) as to the possible types of source for products entering to the assortments that they wish to accumulate. Wholesale intermediaries who wish to deal in a product which customers do not ordinarily expect them to sell therefore face a considerable task of educating their customers.

Stable expectations concerning what products move together through the market, and a common language of cues for transaction-decisions, are thus made possible by the general model of the market that is held in common by its participants. Suppliers of other commodities, customers whose activities are sharply different from those of the customer group as delineated in the model of the market, are excluded from consideration.

5. Evolutionary Development of the Perceived Model

The strength, precision, and degree of rigidity of this perceptual model may, of course, vary from one market to another and may change over time in the same market.

Time is in fact a necessary element in the development of the perceived model. It is the outcome of accumulated individual and joint experience in repeated solving of decision-problems. As actors in a market are involved in a succession of transactions decisions over time, the common elements of these decisions become recognized and then are taken for granted. This gives rise to the possibility of evolving the language of cues.

In addition, experience over time leads to the development of personal ties between actors. Loyalties therefore accumulate, for actors at successive stages of the market are in frequent contact with each other and have a substantial degree of mutual interdependence: all may suffer if the flow of goods through the market falls off, or if the communication networks are destabilized. Norms of behavior resulting from this experience become expressed in moralistic terms—as, for example, the characterization of the intermediary group as "legitimate wholesalers." These norms of behavior, in turn, are inculcated into the young executives of the wholesale intermediary firm who are the main source of potential entry to the trade.

The perceived model of the market thus acquires moral status and strength. It becomes the focus of personal and group loyalties, as well as conferring efficiency benefits on those who understand and adhere to it. The result is that the perceived model can continue to be a powerful force in determining how communication networks in the market will be formed, and how they will operate, even when the objective conditions which gave rise to this model have undergone substantial change.

6. Environmental Shifts Causing Stress in Communication Networks

The objective conditions from which the market structure drew its original impetus may change in numerous ways. The active participants in the market—suppliers, customers, and wholesale intermediaries—may experience significant changes in the technology, capital requirements, or variable costs of their own operations. Changes such as these may arouse dissatisfaction with the types of arrangements for transactions which the market affords. The size distribution of the supplying industry may become more concentrated so that promotional strategy—branding, user-directed advertising, etc.—achieves new significance. There may be new entry by suppliers having a different technology and product-mix, in which some products customarily traded in the market are represented, but others are not.

The new suppliers may find it convenient to use the facilities of the established market, but they may not be familiar with the special language of the trade or with its norms of behavior and so may find these an obstacle to successful entry rather than an inducement to conform. Entry by new types of customer may, for similar reasons, give rise to demands on the market for types of service which are outside the usual range of activities forming the agreed model of behavior.

One new type of customer is particularly challenging to the prevailing model: the firm which, under earlier circumstances, bought its requirements of the commodity at retail, from the firms that are "customers" in the wholesaler's perceived model of the market, and which now desires to by-pass its former sources and buy from wholesale intermediaries. This situation can arise because the user firm has grown in response to the market conditions it faces and can now absorb shipments in the bulk amounts in which wholesalers buy and resell. Not only is this new type of customer different in credit standing and other business attributes from the established types of customer with whom the wholesale intermediary is accustomed to deal; the wholesaler will be regarded as competing with his own established customers if he by-passes them, and the stigma of illegitimate dealing will therefore attach to him.

Finally, changes in the economy at large and, particularly in consumer incomes, tastes and purchasing patterns may be an upsetting force. Sharp increases of consumer demand, for example, could give rise to the kind of transformation of a user-industry that leads to attempts at by-passing.

7. Adaptation or Destruction of the Perceived Model

The impact of these changes in environmental conditions on the market structure depends to a great extent on whether the changes are slow and sustained, or whether they are abrupt and possibly transitory. Experience with successive transactions over time gives rise to the perceived model of the market; slow, persistent changes in the basic conditions of the trade may bring about gradual adaptation. This adaptation may not occur, however, if the gradual shifts give rise to pressures that are not perceived throughout the market, but only by those firms whose survival would be most imminently threatened by the adjustments which may be necessary for the market as a whole. If the pressures for change thus accumulate, a sudden breakdown of the routine pattern of dealing may finally occur.

Also frequent is a rather abrupt change in environmental conditions that is of uncertain future duration and importance. In the face of such uncertainty, the established wholesale intermediary usually feels he has more to lose than to gain by dealing, say, with a new type of customer. The participants who benefit by it thus tend to defend their common model of the market against the incursion of the new type of customer. New entrants into wholesale trade are sometimes the vehicle of adaptation. Unlike the established firms, they have no customers whose loyalty may be impaired, or suppliers who may threaten to cut off supplies. The new entrants may, to be sure, be recruited through experience in the wholesale trade and may therefore be indoctrinated with its norms of behavior. But a new type of customer or a new type of supplier is an inviting target for the new entrant: he will not face competition from established operators in serving the new type of customer or supplier. New entrants, therefore, have a special role to play in accepting innovational opportunities that established firms avoid.

28

BASIC CONCEPTS FOR A THEORY
OF ORGANIZATION *

Ralph M. Stogdill

Classical theories of organization have been concerned with principles of departmentation and the structure of responsibility and authority relationships. Behavioral theories emphasize the effects of interpersonal relations upon member satisfaction and organizational productivity. Mathematical models have been developed for plant operations and decision processes. All of these approaches are concerned with organization, but deal with different subsets of variables. There is an obvious need for a general theory that will weld the different subsets onto a coherent system.

The accomplishment of the classical theorists in developing highly rationalized structures of departments and positions for the accomplishment of different organizational objectives is not to be minimized. However, these theories overlook the fact that their high degree of rationalization is made possible by the existence in any society of biological and psychosocial substructures that are directly transferable into formalized organization structures. A general theory should take account of, and should be based upon, these basic substructures. Allee [1] reports that all social aggregates among mammals and the social insects exhibit differentiated structures in which at least a few individuals perform specialized functions. Tuckman [14] analyzed the results of some sixty studies dealing with developmental trends in initially unstructured groups of strangers. The following stages of development were found to be common to groups engaged in therapy, role playing, sensitivity training, and problem solving.

Stage 1. *Forming*—testing and dependence; development of role structures and interpersonal dependencies.

* Reprinted from *Management Science*, Series B, June 1967, pp. B–666–B–676.

Stage 2. *Storming*—intragroup conflict and hostility; competition for position; emotional expression; group drive.

Stage 3. *Norming*—development of group cohesion, norms, and standards; pressures toward conformity.

Stage 4. *Performing*—productive task activity; stable role structure and interdependencies channel group energy into task performance.

The same sequence is not observed in all groups. The stages alternate in some groups, and occur in cycles in other groups. Some groups progress rapidly through the four stages. But if the task is difficult to face (as in therapy), if there is difference of opinion about objectives or methods, if feelings run high, or if there is competition for leadership, a group may fluctuate between the different stages over a long period of time. A group cannot engage in more than sporadic task performance until a role structure has been stabilized, drive channelized, and regulative norms and cohesiveness attained.

It is possible to draw a chart which specifies in advance the role structure of an organization. This procedure averts the necessity of developing structure out of the rigors and uncertainties of face-to-face interaction. However, it does not necessarily solve the problem of channelizing emotion and drive, or that of developing norms and cohesiveness. The subgroups of a newly formed organization must resolve these problems in much the same manner as that observed in problem solving groups. The classical theories do not address themselves to such problems. But these are the kinds of problems with which the behavioral sciences are concerned.

Davis [4] suggests that organization comes into being because of its ability to acquire, create, preserve, or distribute values. Simon [9] has developed different models for the firm (with profit as a primary objective) and the organization (with survival as a primary objective). The firm can measure profits in terms of the dollar value of inputs and outputs. But the firm represents only a small percentage of the total number of organizations that exists in a society. A theory of organization should apply to organizations in general, whether or not they deal with material or monetary values. In fact, the concept of organization can be more clearly developed if physical and monetary values are treated as specific examples of more general psychosocial values.

Since organizations differ widely in objectives and operations, a general theory must of necessity be formulated in terms of quite general concepts. Such a theory should be capable not only of describing the basic dimensions of organization structure and process; it should also account accurately for the research findings.

GENERAL STRUCTURE OF THE THEORY

An organization, in the real world, can be regarded as an input-process-output system. In order to account for such a system, a theory of organization should also be designed as an input-process-output system. The present paper will attempt merely to state a new theory in outline form. A detailed discussion of the system and experimental evidence in its support are set forth in prior publication.[10]

The theory here presented is built upon three sets of variables, (1) inputs, (2) mediators (processors), and (3) outputs, as shown in Table 1. The three sets of concepts are assumed to characterize any organization regardless of its size, and whether or not it operates upon any form of material or monetary input. The variables will be defined in the discussion that follows.

Each of the ten variables shown in Table 1 and Figure 1 is assumed to be complex in structure. Action (A), for example, represents a complex set of performances exhibited by all the members of the organization. Since the most routine performance of a single member exhibits considerable variability, the action input (A) for the total organization will be complex indeed. It is further assumed that actions, interactions, and expectations are interdependent, and are determined in part by task objectives and materials. Similarly, the processors (operation, interpersonnel, and structure) are interdependent, as are the outputs (product, drive, and cohesiveness).

**TABLE 1. INPUT, PROCESSING, AND
OUTPUT VARIABLES**

1. Inputs	2. Processors	3. Outputs
Actions (A)	Operations (O)	Product (P)
Interactions (I)	Interpersonnel (L)	Drive (D)
Expectations (E)	Structure (S)	Cohesiveness (C)
Task Materials (T)		

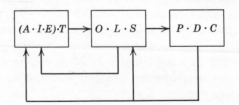

Figure 1. Direction of effects in the system.

It is assumed that the inputs are affected by feedback effects from the mediators and outputs, and that the mediators are influenced by feedback from the outputs, as shown in Figure 1. An organization also engages in exchange relationships with its environment at both the input and output ends of its operations. The theory under discussion, while recognizing the interactions between organization and environment, is concerned solely with the internal organization as a structured operational system.

THE INPUT VARIABLES

The theory requires three sets of input variables identified as member *actions* (performances), *expectations,* and *interactions.** Performance is defined as any action by an individual that identifies him as a member of the group or organization being observed. Expectation is defined as a member's readiness for reinforcement by the system of which he is a member. Interaction is defined as an action-reaction sequence in which the actions of any one member of a social system are reactions to the performances of one or more other members, and these in turn are reacted to by other members of the system. If the members do nothing but talk with each other, the inputs are numerous, varied, and complex in nature.

The *actions,* or *performances,* of the members are of primary importance in carrying out the operations of the organization. Members may work essentially alone (as in operating a lathe) or they may work in interaction with other members (as in discussing a plan). Performances are member contributions to the organization.

Member *interactions* are basic to cooperative effort. An organization, in its most elementary form, can be defined as a social interaction system in which the structuring of member expectations accounts for the differentiation of positions and roles. Such organization grows out of the interaction process itself. It is of course possible to draw an organization chart before recruiting members to fill the positions specified on the chart. But the drawing of such a chart is almost always preceded by the formation of a small group of individuals who interact, acknowledge a role structure, and agree to cooperate in the development of a larger organization. It is suggested, then, that organization is defined by the differentiation of positions and

---

* The inputs specified for this system are similar to those used by Parsons [8] to explain a societal system and by Homans [6] to explain the social group. Parsons and Homans built their theories on the basis of actions, interactions, and sentiments as input variables which are more broadly defined than are the inputs for the system presented here. Katz and Kahn [7] also regard individual actions and expectations as human inputs in any kind of organization.

roles that grows out of interaction and the mutual confirmation of inter-member expectations.

Member *expectations* are also contributions to the organization. As such, they define the role that the individual believes he and others should play on behalf of the organization. Members bring into the organization various expectations that it may or may not be able to satisfy. In general, members are able to perform their tasks more effectively when they know what they are expected to do. They tend to be better satisfied with an organization when their expectations relative to pay, advancement, hours, recognition, and treatment by supervisors are fulfilled by the organization. Many organizations thus find it advantageous to use job descriptions, policy manuals, and the like, as instruments for structuring member expectations along the lines that are capable of being satisfied.

Some sort of task material is utilized as an input in any kind of organization. Pig iron, coal, lumber, clay, leather, petroleum, and so on, are used as input materials in manufacturing organizations. In a discussion group, the input materials may be the words and sentences used in discussions. If the objective of the organization is to play a game, the input materials may be balls, bats, gloves, and the rules of the game.

Actions, expectations, and interactions are human inputs. If the group does not employ any material or financial inputs then its structure, operations, and outputs are accounted for entirely by its human inputs. Many kinds of organization, of course, utilize money, materials, and the services of other organizations, as inputs. Such inputs will influence the size, structure, operations, and outputs of the organizations that use them. An organization can exist without such inputs, but cannot exist without the inputs of human performance, expectation, and interaction. For this reason, only human inputs have been utilized in the development of the proposed theory of organization.

MEDIATING (PROCESSING) VARIABLES

Not all the inputs of an organization are transformed directly into outputs. Some portion of the inputs must be utilized in the development and maintenance of operations, structure, and interpersonnel. The mediating and processing variables that transform inputs into outputs are listed in Table 2.

The *operations* of an organization are carried out by the performances of the members individually and in interaction with others. Task performances may consist of talking, thinking, using tools, operating machines, handling materials, writing letters, selling merchandise, rendering a

TABLE 2. THE PROCESSING VARIABLES

Operations:
    Human performances
    Technical Processes
Interpersonnel:
    Interpersonal relations (superior, subordinate, peer)
    Personal—organizational exchange relations
    Reinforcement, satisfactions and dissatisfactions
    Internal—external relations (reference groups)
    Subgroup norms and pressures
    Subsystem interrelations
Structure:
    Positions (status and function)
    Roles (responsibility, authority, delegation)
    Formal and informal subsystems
    Departmentation

service, and the like. Social, educational, religious, governmental, military, financial, mercantile, and manufacturing organizations differ in the kinds of operations they perform. What is common to all of them is that operations are carried out by the task performances of their members. Even automated plants must be supplied, programmed and monitored by the performances of responsible members.

The nature of group *structure* is best understood by examining newly created groups that have no predetermined structure. Bales and Strodtbeck [2] and Heinicke and Bales [5] have shown that experimental groups assigned the task of solving problems by discussion tend to make little progress toward task accomplishment until a role structure has been differentiated and stabilized. The work of the group remains at a standstill as long as the leadership of the group remains in doubt or in contest. However, the emergence of a leader who maintains his position of leadership tends to reinforce the expectations of the group members that he will continue to act as leader, and they look to him for direction and the resolution of differences among the members. Once a structure of positions has been established, the group is free to engage in task performance. Research of the sort described above indicates that group structure facilitates operations.

The prior structuring of a group by those members who organize it and recruit new members for it tends to increase the likelihood that the structure of positions will be acknowledged and accepted by the members. The position accepted by a member defines his status and function in relation to other members and in relation to the operational tasks of the organization.

The status of a position defines the stable expectations made upon the occupant of the position in relation to his accountability to and for other members of the organization. The functions of a position define the stable expectations that are made upon the occupant of the position in relation to the tasks he is to perform on behalf of the organization. The status and functions of a position tend to remain constant regardless of the person who occupies the position.

Despite the fact that the status and functions of a position remain relatively constant over time, no two occupants of the position exhibit identical behaviors. One occupant may exercise a higher degree of authority than his predecessor, and may delegate more (or less) to his subordinates. He may assume responsibility for certain functions that his predecessor disregarded, and he may assign responsibility for other functions to his subordinates. In other words, no two occupants of the same position ever play the same role in the organization. The above considerations suggest that responsibility and authority should be regarded as characteristics of role performance. Whereas status and function are stable characteristics of position, authority and responsibility are variable aspects of role performance. Authority is highly related to status, and responsibility is highly related to function. The higher the level of a member's position, the greater his area of freedom from making decisions that affect the organization as a whole. The more clearly defined his functions, the greater the likelihood that he will assume responsibility for them.

The concept *interpersonnel* was introduced by the author [12] to account for a dimension that has not been heretofore logically integrated into a theory of organization. Interpersonnel refers to a large complex of behaviors and relationships that account for exchanges between member and member, and between member and organization. These are intraorganizational exchanges.

A member pays certain costs for belonging to any organization. For some organizations, he may invest only a small amount of money in the form of paying dues. But for others, he may make heavy investments of time, effort, skill, expectation, and endurance of interpersonal stress. All of these are costs to the individual member, and inputs into the organization. In exchange for these contributions, the individual expects certain returns in the form of rewards and satisfaction of expectations from other members and from the organization as a whole.

Members generally tend to expect that those members in status levels one or two steps above their own positions will act as mediators between themselves and the organization. They look to those persons in positions of leadership for clear definition of tasks, provision of freedom for task performance, and recognition of their contributions to, and support of, the organization. The relationships between members and their supervisors tend to affect the outputs of subgroups and of the organization as a whole.

Individual members differ markedly in their expectations, ability to interact harmoniously with other members, and ability to derive satisfaction from work, social interaction, and rewards. Their identifications with other groups and organizations in the external environment tend to condition their expectations and loyalties within the organization. On the other hand, there is a tendency for individuals to incorporate, and to be governed by, the norms of the subgroups in which they have membership in the organization. The norms of subgroups tend to regulate member performance, condition their loyalties, and affect group outputs. These factors in turn, affect the operations and outputs of the organization as a whole.

One of the most critical exchange relationships existing between a member and the organization is that involving expectations. There are numerous reasons, some having their origins in ancient customs and even in superstitions, why individuals and organizations exhibit reluctance to make their expectations clearly known. If expectations are not communicated at the beginning of a relationship, it becomes increasingly difficult as time goes on to explain respects in which a member fails to satisfy the expectations of the organization and for a member to explain his disappointments with the organization. The author has shown [13] that member satisfaction with the company and subgroup loyalty to the company are highly related to a form of supervisory behavior that lets employees know what is expected of them and what they can expect of the organization. Thus, working in return for a wage is not the only important exchange relationship that exists between a member and an organization. The personnel manager of a large organization is concerned with a wide variety of exchanges. The union-company contract specifies a variety of exchange obligations. But there remains a set of exchanges (between member and member, member and subgroup, member and organization) that is not subject to negotiation or to administration by the personnel director, and this set is the one that is most likely to affect individual and subgroup performance and organizational outputs.

The confirmation and satisfaction of member expectations, in accordance with Cyert and March,[3] should be regarded as an intermember and intraorganizational exchange process. The organization expects certain contributions and loyalties from its members. The members expect task definition, freedom for performance, and an adequate return for their contributions. Members may perform to the best of their abilities without the satisfaction of these expectations, but are likely to feel frustrated and ill at ease as a result. Extremely high degrees of satisfaction or dissatisfaction may be associated with raised or lowered norms in the subgroups. Such norms consist of mutually acknowledged expectations among the members of a subgroup, and tend to regulate the performances and loyalties of all its members even though some members may dislike the norms. When member satisfaction or dissatisfaction is translated into raised or lowered subgroups norms throughout an organization, the outputs of the organization are likely to be affected as a result. Under conditions of prevailing dissatisfaction, it is more likely that organizational cohesiveness will be seriously affected than that productivity will decline. The result may be no less costly in that the organization may find that it does not have the support of its members when it needs their loyalty in some critical situation.

In summary, the concepts *operations, structure,* and *interpersonnel* have been used to effect an integration of classical theories of organization with behavior science conceptions of organization, and to generate some new insights into the differences between positions and roles. Status and function are shown to be characteristics of positions, while authority and responsibility are shown to be characteristics of role performance. The concept *interpersonnel* accounts for a great variety of exchange relationships that exist between member and member, member and subgroup, member and organization, and subgroup organization.

THE OUTPUT VARIABLES

Inputs, in business organizations, are usually measured in terms of the dollar value of materials, man-hours, and support facilities. Output is measured as a ratio between the dollar value of the end product or service and the cost of the inputs, using a base period of time as a standard for later comparisons. The very survival of a large business organization depends upon the adequacy with which these factors are measured and controlled. But there are many kinds of organizations (religious, educational, fraternal, recreational, and the like) for which these measures have little or no relevance. Even for business organizations, we believe that there are valuable outputs other than product.

When one considers the inputs (performances, interactions, and expectations) and the mediating variables (structure, operations, and interpersonnel) used in this theoretical system, it seems reasonable to believe that they might generate a complex output. Such is found to be the case. What then is the nature of the outputs? Research in small groups indicates that groups develop cohesiveness and drive as they engage in task performance. Cohesiveness and drive may vary in degree in different groups, or in the same group over periods of time. Cohesiveness is variously defined in the literature as intermember harmony, mutual liking and acceptance, group resistance to disruptive influences, and ability to function as an integrated unit. Drive is variously defined as group freedom of action, morale, task enthusiasm, application of pressure upon an objective, member satisfaction, and spirited action. In social science literature, these two variables are considered to condition (increase or decrease) group productivity, or product. Intensive work with a great variety of models convinced the writer [10] that a logically consistent system cannot be developed when cohesiveness and morale are treated as conditioners of productivity. Nor can apparent discrepancies in experimental results be reconciled by such a model. However, if cohesiveness, morale, and productivity are all treated as outputs, a logically consistent system emerges and the previous discrepancies are reconciled.

In order to satisfy the system, the outputs must be defined in reference to the input and mediating variables. Assuming that there are no material or monetary inputs, *productivity* is then defined as the relative changes in the goal expectancy and goal achievement values of the organization. Goal expectancy sets a standard in terms of which the rate or degree of progress toward goal achievement is evaluated. Various members of organization may evaluate productivity differently, depending upon their perceptions of the goals to be achieved and of the progress made toward goal achievement. If an organization operates upon a material input, it is both convenient and legitimate to use units of product or dollar value of product in the computation of productivity indexes.

Drive is here defined as organizational morale or freedom of action. Drive thus defined, is a characteristic of organizations and of subgroups within organizations. The morale (drive) of an organization may be channeled toward task performance or toward some activity that bears little relation to the primary task of the organization. It can be diverted into competing or contradictory activities. Thus, it may not be advantageous to increase drive unless it can be utilized in strengthening the cohesiveness or productivity of the organization.

Cohesiveness is defined as the maintenance of, or capacity to maintain, structure and operations under stress. Cohesiveness characterizes the organization as a whole, as well as the subgroups within the organization. Cohesiveness in the subgroups may, or may not, add to the cohesiveness of the total organization. The latter is likely to suffer when member loyalties are to the subgroups rather than to the organization, and when the norms of the subgroups are such that they refuse to support the organization when support is needed. Cohesiveness is of importance to the survival of an organization in times of stress and emergency.

The three output variables (product, cohesiveness, and morale) are interrelated, but the correlations between them are seldom very high. A survey [10] of the research on small groups and large organizations suggested the following general trends.

1. Productivity and drive tend to be positively related.
2. Productivity and cohesiveness tend to be negatively related.
3. Drive and cohesiveness may be either positively or negatively related.

The three hypotheses stated above are based on empirical findings that were never satisfactorily explained by the assumption that cohesiveness and morale are conditioners of productivity. However, the findings appear to be logically consistent when the three variables are regarded as inter-related outputs.

The author recently completed a study in which the productivity, cohesiveness (harmony), and drive of 1267 work groups in 26 industrial and governmental organizations were rated by the superiors of the supervisors of the work groups. Correlations between the three variables are in accord with the general expectation that productivity and drive will be postively correlated, productivity and cohesiveness will be negatively correlated, and drive and cohesiveness may be either positively or negatively correlated. The number of positive and negative correlations between the three variables were as follows: volume of output and drive, 22 plus and 4 minus; volume and cohesiveness, 4 plus and 22 minus; drive and cohesiveness, 15 plus and 11 minus. Although only 17 of the 78 correlation coefficients were significantly larger than zero, the direction of correlation tended to be in the direction hypothesized by the theory.

Exceptions to the above hypotheses are found. But it seems reasonable to expect that some portion of increased group drive (morale) would be reflected in increased productivity. It also seems reasonable that as time and effort are devoted to strengthening cohesiveness, productivity would tend to decrease; and that as efforts are made to increase productivity, either the internal cohesiveness of subgroups or their support of the organization would tend to decrease. In regard to the relationship between drive and cohesiveness, the experimental literature suggests that morale (drive) tends to be expended in strengthening cohesiveness when groups are under threat. However, increased drive is associated with reduced cohesiveness when subgroups are divided into cliques or when differences in loyalties are involved. Input and mediating variables interact in complex combinations to condition the relationships between productivity, drive and cohesiveness. Extensive research will be required to determine the nature of these combinations.

The relationships hypothesized above are the ones most frequently encountered under stabilized operating conditions and with constant inputs.

Under such conditions, an increase in one output variable tends to be obtained at the cost of another. In order to increase all outputs simultaneously, it should be necessary to increase the inputs. The author [11] found support for this hypothesis in a study of six football games. Teams are able to invest intense inputs of effort, skill, and motivation during one hour of play. Such high input levels cannot be expected in organizations that require eight hours of work, day after day, throughout the year. But an intensification of inputs appears to provide one of the conditions under which all outputs can be increased at the same time.

In summary, it is suggested that any organization, regardless of its size or the nature of its material inputs or technical operations, generates three distinct outputs: product, drive, and cohesiveness. The outputs are interrelated. Material inputs and outputs were disregarded in this formulation, not because they are unimportant, but because they are present only in specific types of organizations.

DISCUSSION

The proposed theory can be said to be new in the following respects. (1) It is based on a set of newly defined input variables. (2) The mediating variables, for the first time in any theory, establish a logical differentiation between (*a*) the status and function of a position and (*b*) the responsibility and authority of a role. The concept *interpersonnel* accounts for a great complex of exchange relationships that exist within an organization, but are usually treated as separate from a theory of organization. (3) The theory generates a new set of output variables. Whereas it is generally assumed that productivity is the only output measure, the new theory requires that productivity, cohesiveness, and drive be regarded as outputs of organization. (4) The theory reconciles findings that have heretofore been regarded as contradictory. (5) The theory has provided a basis for new research designs, the results of which are in conformity with the theory and has stimulated the investigation of variables and relationships that would have gone unnoticed without the theory.

It should be noted that a theory of organization is not a theory of management. Organization theory is concerned only with what exists in organization; not with what ought to exist. Management theory, on the other hand, is concerned with decisions designed to optimize the attainment of values through the instrumentality of organization. An adequate theory of organization should provide an advantage in the understanding and management of organizations even though it generates no rules for effective management.

REFERENCES

1 Allee, W. C., *Cooperation among Animals, with Human Implications,* Henry Schuman, New York, 1951.

2 Bales, R. F. and Strodtbeck, F. L., "Phases in Group Problem-Solving," *Journal of Abnormal Social Psychology,* **46,** 1951, pp. 485–495.

3 Cyert, R. M. and March, J. G., *A Behavioral Theory of the Firm,* Prentice-Hall, Englewood Cliffs, N. J., 1963.

4 Davis, R. C., *The Fundamentals of Top Management,* Harper, New York, 1951.

5 Heinicke, C. and Bales, R. F., "Developmental Trends in the Structure of Small Groups," *Sociometry,* **16,** 1953, pp. 7–38.

6 Homans, G. C., *The Human Group,* Harcourt, Brace, New York, 1950.

7 Katz, D. and Kahn, R. L., *The Social Psychology of Organizations,* Wiley, New York, 1966.

8 Parsons, T., *The Social System,* Free Press, New York, 1951.

9 Simon, H. A., *Models of Man,* Wiley, New York, 1957.

10 Stogdill, R. M., *Individual Behavior and Group Achievement,* Oxford University Press, New York, 1959.

11 ———, *Team Achievement under High Motivation,* Ohio State University, Bureau of Business Research, Columbus, Ohio, 1963.

12 ———, "Dimensions of Organization Theory," in J. D. Thompson, *Approaches to Organizational Design,* University of Pittsburgh Press, 1965.

13 ———, *Managers, Employees, Organizations,* Ohio State University, Bureau of Business Research, Columbus, Ohio, 1965.

14 Tuckman, B. W., "Developmental Sequence in Small Groups," *Psychological Bulletin,* 63, 1965, pp. 384–399.

AUTHOR INDEX

SUBJECT INDEX

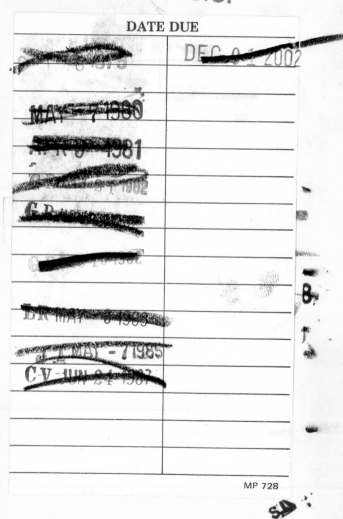

4